New Perspectives on

THE INTERNET

Brief

JAMES T. PERRY
University of San Diego

GARY P. SCHNEIDER
University of San Diego

ONE MAIN STREET, CAMBRIDGE, MA 02142

an International Thomson Publishing company I(T)P®

Cambridge • Albany • Bonn • Boston • Cincinnati • London • Madrid • Melbourne • Mexico City
New York • Paris • San Francisco • Singapore • Tokyo • Toronto • Washington

New Perspectives on the Internet—Brief is published by Course Technology.

Associate Publisher	Mac Mendelsohn
Product Managers	Rachel Crapser, Keith Mahoney
Developmental Editor	Jessica Evans
Production Editor	Seth Andrews
Text and Cover Designer	Meral Dabcovich

© 1999 by Course Technology—I(T)P®

For more information contact:

Course Technology
One Main Street
Cambridge, MA 02142

ITP Europe
Berkshire House 168-173
High Holborn
London WCIV 7AA
England

Nelson ITP, Australia
102 Dodds Street
South Melbourne, 3205
Victoria, Australia

ITP Nelson Canada
1120 Birchmount Road
Scarborough, Ontario
Canada M1K 5G4

International Thomson Editores
Seneca, 53
Colonia Polanco
11560 Mexico D.F. Mexico

ITP GmbH
Konigswinterer Strasse 418
53227 Bonn
Germany

ITP Asia
60 Albert Street, #15-01
Albert Complex
Singapore 189969

ITP Japan
Hirakawacho Kyowa Building, 3F
2-2-1 Hirakawacho
Chiyoda-ku, Tokyo 102
Japan

All rights reserved. This publication is protected by federal copyright law. No part of this publication may be reproduced, stored in a retrieval system, or transmitted in any form or by any means, electronic, mechanical, photocopying, recording, or otherwise, or be used to make a derivative work (such as translation or adaptation), without prior permission in writing from Course Technology.

Trademarks

Course Technology and the Open Book logo are registered trademarks and CourseKits is a trademark of Course Technology. Custom Edition is a registered trademark of International Thomson Publishing Inc.

I(T)P®   The ITP logo is a registered trademark of International Thomson Publishing.

Some of the product names and company names used in this book have been used for identification purposes only and may be trademarks or registered trademarks of their respective manufacturers and sellers.
Microsoft, Windows, Windows 95, Windows 98, Internet Explorer, and Outlook Express are registered trademarks of Microsoft Corporation.
Netscape, Netscape Communications, Netscape Navigator, Netscape Messenger, and Netscape's Communications logo are trademarks of Netscape Communications Corporation.
Some of the product names and company names used in this book have been used for identification purposes only and may be trademarks or registered trademarks of their respective manufacturers and sellers.

Disclaimer

Course Technology reserves the right to revise this publication and make changes from time to time in its content without notice.

ISBN 0-7600-6973-5

Printed in the United States of America

    2 3 4 5 6 7 8 9 10 BM 03 02 01 00 99

PREFACE
The New Perspectives Series

About New Perspectives
Course Technology's **New Perspectives Series** is an integrated system of instruction that combines text and technology products to teach computer concepts, the Internet, and microcomputer applications. Users consistently praise this series for innovative pedagogy, use of interactive technology, creativity, accuracy, and supportive and engaging style.

How is the New Perspectives Series different from other series?
The **New Perspectives Series** distinguishes itself by **innovative technology**, from the renowned Course Labs to the state-of-the-art multimedia that is integrated with our Concepts texts. Other distinguishing features include **sound instructional design, proven pedagogy,** and **consistent quality**. Each tutorial has students learn features in the context of solving a realistic case problem rather than simply learning a laundry list of features. With the **New Perspectives Series,** instructors report that students have a complete, integrative learning experience that stays with them. They credit this high retention and competency to the fact that this series incorporates critical thinking and problem-solving with computer skills mastery. In addition, we work hard to ensure accuracy by using a multi-step quality assurance process during all stages of development. Instructors focus on teaching and students spend more time learning.

Choose the coverage that's right for you
New Perspectives applications books are available in the following categories:
The book you are holding is a Brief book.

Brief
2-4 tutorials

Brief: approximately 150 pages long, two to four "Level I" tutorials, teaches basic application skills.

Introductory
6 or 7 tutorials, or Brief + 2 or 3 more tutorials

Introductory: approximately 300 pages long, four to seven tutorials, goes beyond the basic skills. These books often build out of the Brief book, adding two or three additional "Level II" tutorials.

Comprehensive
Introductory + 4 or 5 more tutorials. Includes Brief Windows tutorials and Additional Cases

Comprehensive: approximately 600 pages long, eight to twelve tutorials, all tutorials included in the Introductory text plus higher-level "Level III" topics. Typically includes two Windows tutorials and three or four fully developed Additional Cases.

Advanced
Quick Review of basics + in-depth, high-level coverage

Advanced: approximately 600 pages long, cover topics similar to those in the Comprehensive books, but offer the highest-level coverage in the series. Advanced books assume students already know the basics, and therefore go into more depth at a more accelerated rate than the Comprehensive titles. Advanced books are ideal for a second, more technical course.

Office
Quick Review of basics + in-depth, high-level coverage

Office: approximately 800 pages long, covers all components of the Office suite as well as integrating the individual software packages with one another and the Internet.

Custom Editions
Choose from any of the above to build your own Custom Editions or CourseKits

Custom Books The New Perspectives Series offers you two ways to customize a New Perspectives text to fit your course exactly: CourseKits™—two or more texts shrinkwrapped together. We offer significant price discounts on CourseKits™. Custom Editions® offer you flexibility in designing your concepts, Internet, and applications courses. You can build your own book by ordering a combination of topics bound together to cover only the subjects you want. There is no minimum order, and books are spiral bound. Contact your Course Technology sales representative for more information.

What course is this book appropriate for?

New Perspectives on the Internet—Brief can be used in any course in which you want students to learn all the most important topics of using the Internet, including using e-mail, browsing Web sites, searching for information, downloading data and programs, using file transfer protocol (FTP) software, and other Internet-related topics. It is particularly recommended for a short course on Web browsing using Netscape Navigator or Microsoft Internet Explorer. This book assumes that students have learned basic Windows 95 or Windows NT navigation and file management skills from Course Technology's *New Perspectives on Microsoft Windows 95—Brief*, *New Perspectives on Microsoft Windows NT Workstation 4.0—Introductory*, or an *equivalent* book.

Proven Pedagogy

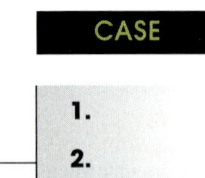

Tutorial Case   Each tutorial begins with a problem presented in a case that is meaningful to students. The case turns the task of learning how to use an application into a problem-solving process.

45-minute Sessions   Each tutorial is divided into sessions that can be completed in about 45 minutes to an hour. Sessions allow instructors to more accurately allocate time in their syllabus, and students to better manage their own study time.

Step-by-Step Methodology   We make sure students can differentiate between what they are to *do* and what they are to *read*. Through numbered steps—clearly identified by a gray shaded background—students are constantly guided in solving the case problem. In addition, the numerous screen shots with callouts direct students' attention to what they should look at on the screen.

TROUBLE? Paragraphs   These paragraphs anticipate the mistakes or problems that students may have and help them continue with the tutorial.

"Read This Before You Begin" Page   Located opposite the first tutorial's opening page for each level of the text, the "Read This Before You Begin" page helps introduce technology into the classroom. Technical considerations and assumptions about software are listed to save time and eliminate unnecessary aggravation. Notes about the Student Disks help instructors and students get the right files in the right places, so students get started on the right foot.

Quick Check Questions   Each session concludes with meaningful, conceptual Quick Check questions that test students' understanding of what they learned in the session. Answers to the Quick Check questions are provided at the end of each tutorial.

Reference Windows   Reference Windows are succinct summaries of the most important tasks covered in a tutorial and they preview actions students will perform in the steps to follow.

Task Reference   Located as a table at the end of the book, the Task Reference contains a summary of how to perform common tasks using the most efficient method, as well as references to pages where the task is discussed in more detail.

End-of-Chapter Tutorial Assignments, Case Problems, and Lab Assignments   Tutorial Assignments provide students with additional hands-on practice of the skills they learned in the tutorial using the same case presented in the tutorial. These Assignments are followed by four Case Problems that have approximately the same scope as the tutorial case but use a different scenario. In addition, some of the Tutorial Assignments or Case Problems may include Exploration Exercises that challenge students, encourage them to explore the capabilities of the program they are using, and/or further extend their knowledge. Finally, if a Course Lab accompanies a tutorial, Lab Assignments are included after the Case Problems.

New Perspectives on the Internet—Brief Instructor's Resource Kit for this title contains:

- Electronic Instructor's Manual in PDF format
- Student Files
- Solution Files
- Course Test Manager Testbank
- Course Test Manager Engine
- Figure Files
- Course Labs

These supplements come on CD-ROM. If you don't have access to a CD-ROM drive, contact your Course Technology customer service representative for more information.

The New Perspectives Supplements Package

Electronic Instructor's Manual   Our Instructor's Manuals include tutorial overviews and outlines, technical notes, lecture notes, solutions, and Extra Case Problems. Many instructors use the Extra Case Problems for performance-based exams or extra credit projects. The Instructor's Manual is available as an electronic file, which you can get from the Instructor Resource Kit (IRK) CD-ROM or download it from www.course.com.

Student Files   Student Files contain all of the data that students will use to complete the tutorials, Tutorial Assignments, and Case Problems. A Readme file includes instructions for using the files. See the "Read This Before You Begin" page for more information on Student Files.

Solution Files   Solution Files contain every file students are asked to create or modify in the tutorials, Tutorial Assignments, Case Problems, and Extra Case Problems. A Help file on the Instructor's Resource Kit includes information for using the Solution files.

Course Labs: Concepts Come to Life These highly interactive computer-based learning activities bring concepts to life with illustrations, animations, digital images, and simulations. The Labs guide students step-by-step, present them with Quick Check questions, let them explore on their own, test their comprehension, and provide printed feedback. Lab icons at the beginning of the tutorial and in the tutorial margins indicate when a topic has a corresponding Lab. Lab Assignments are included at the end of each relevant tutorial. The Labs available with this book and the tutorials in which they appear are: E-mail (Tutorial 2) and Internet: World Wide Web (Tutorial 3).

Figure Files Many figures in the text are provided on the IRK CD-ROM to help illustrate key topics or concepts. Instructors can create traditional overhead transparencies by printing the figure files. Or they can create electronic slide shows by using the figures in a presentation program such as PowerPoint.

Course Test Manager: Testing and Practice at the Computer or on Paper Course Test Manager is cutting-edge, Windows-based testing software that helps instructors design and administer practice tests and actual examinations. Course Test Manager can automatically grade the tests students take at the computer and can generate statistical information on individual as well as group performance.

Online Companions: Dedicated to Keeping You and Your Students Up-To-Date Visit our faculty sites and student sites on the World Wide Web at www.course.com. Here instructors can browse this text's password-protected Faculty Online Companion to obtain an online Instructor's Manual, Solution Files, Student Files, and more. Students can also access this text's Student Online Companion, which contains all of the links necessary to complete the steps, Tutorial Assignments, and Case Problems in the book. The Student Online Companion also contains Additional Information sections for each tutorial that provide hyperlinks to Web sites that are related to topics in the tutorial but that are not explicitly cited in the tutorial. Students and instructors may find these additional sites useful as they extend their study of a topic. Since the Web is constantly changing, the Student Online Companion will provide the reader with current updates regarding links referenced in the book.

More innovative technology

Skills Assessment Manager (SAM) This ground-breaking new assessment tool tests students' ability to perform real-world tasks live in the Microsoft Office 97 applications. You can use SAM to test students out of a course, place them into a course, or test ongoing proficiency during a course. Contact your Sales or Customer Service representative about purchasing passwords or licenses for SAM or for more information, visit our Web site at: www.course.com/products/sam.html

CyberClass CyberClass is a web-based tool designed for on-campus or distance learning. Use it to enhance how you currently run your class by posting assignments and your course syllabus or holding online office hours. Or, use it for your distance learning course, and offer mini-lectures, conduct online discussion groups, or give your mid-term exam. For more information, visit our Web site at: www.course.com/products/cyberclass/index.html

Acknowledgments

Creating a quality textbook is a collaborative effort between author and publisher. We work as a team to provide the highest quality book possible. The authors want to acknowledge the work of the seasoned professionals at Course Technology. We thank Mac Mendelsohn, Associate Publisher, for his initial interest in and continual support of our work on this book. It was Mac's vision for a book focused on the Internet, rather than on a specific software application, that motivated us to take on this project. We offer a special thank you to Martha Stansbury, our Course Technology sales representative, for introducing us to Mac. For the 19 years we have known Martha, she has always been an enthusiastic and committed professional—devoted to her business and her customers. In addition, we thank Rachel Crapser and Keith Mahoney, Product Managers; Seth Andrews, Production Editor; and Jon Greacen, Quality Assurance tester for being terrific, positive, and supportive members of a great publishing team. We also thank Seth Freeman for his work on the Student Online Companion Web pages. We cannot begin to adequately thank our Developmental Editor, Jessica Evans. She is simply the best in the business. Whether it was taking our sometimes-opaque paragraphs and making them crystal clear, or providing timely doses of encouragement when we hit the rough spots, Jessica was always there for us. We offer our heartfelt thanks to the Course Technology organization as a whole. The people at Course Technology have been, by far, the best publishing team with which we have ever worked.

We want to thank the following reviewers for their insightful comments and suggestions at various stages of the book's development: Cathy Fothergill, Kilgore College; Don Lopez, The Clovis Center; Suzanne Nordhaus, Lee College; Sorel Reisman, California State University Fullerton; T. Michael Smith, Austin Community College; and Bill Wagner, Villanova University. Margaret Beeler and Pamela Drotman provided helpful comments on early drafts of the outline for this book.

Finally, we want to express our deep appreciation for the continuous support and encouragement of our spouses, Nancy Perry and Cathy Cosby. They demonstrated remarkable patience as we worked both ends of the clock to complete this book on a very tight schedule. Without their support and cooperation, we would not have attempted to write this book. We also thank our children for tolerating our absences while we were busy writing.

James T. Perry
Gary P. Schneider

Dedication

To my oldest daughter, Jessica Perry
    Finally, you have learned to soar. Keep giving life your best. – J.T.P.

To the memory of my brother, Bruce Schneider. – G.P.S.

TABLE OF CONTENTS

Preface   iii
Read this Before you Begin   viii

The Internet—Level I Tutorials   WEB 1.1

Tutorial 1   WEB 1.3
Introduction to the Internet and the World Wide Web
History, Potential, and Getting Connected

Session 1.1	WEB 1.4
Internet and World Wide Web: Amazing Developments	WEB 1.4
Computer Networks	WEB 1.5
Client/Server Local Area Networks	WEB 1.5
Connecting Computers to a Network	WEB 1.6
Wide Area Networks	WEB 1.7
How the Internet Began	WEB 1.7
Circuit Switching vs. Packet Switching	WEB 1.7
Open Architecture Philosophy	WEB 1.8
Birth of E-Mail: A New Use for Networks	WEB 1.9
More New Uses for Networks Emerge	WEB 1.9
Interconnecting the Networks	WEB 1.10
Commercial Interest Increases	WEB 1.10
Growth of the Internet	WEB 1.11
From Research Project to Information Infrastructure	WEB 1.12
New Structure for the Internet	WEB 1.13
World Wide Web	WEB 1.14
Origins of Hypertext	WEB 1.14
Hypertext and Graphical User Interfaces Come to the Internet	WEB 1.14
The Web and Commercialization of the Internet	WEB 1.15
Quick Check	WEB 1.16
Session 1.2	WEB 1.17
Connection Options	WEB 1.17
Business of Providing Internet Access	WEB 1.17
Connection Bandwidth	WEB 1.18
Connecting Through Your School or Employer	WEB 1.19
Connecting Through Your School	WEB 1.19
Dialing in	WEB 1.20
Connecting Through Your Employer	WEB 1.20
Acceptable Use Policies	WEB 1.20
Advantages and Disadvantages	WEB 1.20
Connecting Through an Internet Service Provider	WEB 1.21
Advantages and Disadvantages	WEB 1.21
Connecting Through Your Cable Television Company	WEB 1.21
Advantages and Disadvantages	WEB 1.22
Connecting Via Satellite	WEB 1.22
Advantages and Disadvantages	WEB 1.22
Quick Check	WEB 1.22
Projects	WEB 1.23
Quick Check Answers	WEB 1.24

Tutorial 2   WEB 2.1
Basic E-Mail: Integrated Browser E-Mail Software
Evaluating E-Mail Alternatives

Session 2.1	WEB 2.2
What Is E-Mail and How Does It Work	WEB 2.2
Anatomy of an E-Mail Message	WEB 2.3
To	WEB 2.3
From	WEB 2.4
Subject	WEB 2.4
Cc and Bcc	WEB 2.4
Attachments	WEB 2.5
Message Body and Signature Files	WEB 2.5
E-Mail Addresses	WEB 2.6
E-Mail Programs	WEB 2.7
Free E-Mail Clients	WEB 2.8
Setting Up and Using Your E-Mail Client	WEB 2.9
Receiving Mail	WEB 2.9
Printing a Message	WEB 2.9
Filing a Message	WEB 2.10
Forwarding a Message	WEB 2.10
Replying to a Message	WEB 2.10
Deleting a Message	WEB 2.10
Maintaining an Address Book	WEB 2.11
Creating a Multi-Address Entry	WEB 2.11
Quick Check	WEB 2.11
Session 2.2	WEB 2.12
Netscape Messenger Client	WEB 2.12
Setting Up E-Mail	WEB 2.14
Sending a Message Using Messenger	WEB 2.17
Receiving and Reading a Message	WEB 2.19
Opening and Saving an Attached File	WEB 2.21
Replying to and Forwarding Messages	WEB 2.22
Replying to an E-Mail Message	WEB 2.22
Forwarding an E-Mail Message	WEB 2.23
Filing an E-Mail Message	WEB 2.24
Deleting an E-Mail Message	WEB 2.26
Maintaining an Address Book	WEB 2.27
Adding an Address to the Address Book	WEB 2.27
Creating a Multi-Address Entry	WEB 2.29
Quick Check	WEB 2.32
Session 2.3	WEB 2.32
Microsoft Outlook Express Client	WEB 2.32
Setting Up E-Mail	WEB 2.33
Sending a Message Using Outlook Express	WEB 2.35
Receiving and Reading a Message	WEB 2.38
Opening and Saving an Attached File	WEB 2.39
Replying to and Forwarding Messages	WEB 2.40
Replying to an E-Mail Message	WEB 2.41
Forwarding an E-Mail Message	WEB 2.42
Filing an E-Mail Message	WEB 2.43
Deleting an E-Mail Message	WEB 2.44
Maintaining an Address Book	WEB 2.46
Adding an Address to the Address Book	WEB 2.46
Creating a Multi-Address Entry	WEB 2.48
Quick Check	WEB 2.49
Tutorial Assignments	WEB 2.50
Case Problems	WEB 2.50
Lab Assignments	WEB 2.54
Quick Check Answers	WEB 2.55

Tutorial 3   WEB 3.1
Browser Basics
Introduction to Netscape Navigator and Microsoft Internet Explorer

Session 3.1	WEB 3.2
Web Browsers	WEB 3.2
Client/Server Structure of the World Wide Web	WEB 3.2
Hypertext, Links, and Hypermedia	WEB 3.3
Web Pages and Web Sites	WEB 3.5
Home Pages	WEB 3.5
Web Sites	WEB 3.5
Addresses on the Web	WEB 3.5
IP Addressing	WEB 3.6
Domain Name Addressing	WEB 3.6
Uniform Resource Locators	WEB 3.8
Main Elements of Web Browsers	WEB 3.9
Title Bar	WEB 3.10
Scroll Bars	WEB 3.10
Status Bar	WEB 3.10

Menu Bar	WEB 3.11
Home Button	WEB 3.11
Quick Access to Web Page Directories and Guides	**WEB 3.12**
Using the History List	**WEB 3.12**
Reloading a Web Page	WEB 3.12
Stopping a Web Page Transfer	WEB 3.12
Returning to a Web Page	WEB 3.13
Printing and Saving Web Pages	**WEB 3.13**
Printing a Web Page	WEB 3.13
Saving a Web Page	WEB 3.13
Reproducing Web Pages and Copyright Law	WEB 3.14
Quick Check	**WEB 3.14**
Session 3.2	**WEB 3.15**
Starting Netscape Navigator	**WEB 3.15**
Using the Navigation Toolbar and Menu Commands	**WEB 3.16**
Using the Location Toolbar Elements	**WEB 3.18**
Hiding and Showing the Location Toolbar	WEB 3.18
Entering a URL into the Location Field	WEB 3.18
Creating a Bookmark for a Web Site	WEB 3.20
Hyperlink Navigation with the Mouse	**WEB 3.24**
Using the History List	WEB 3.26
Reloading a Web Page	WEB 3.27
Going Home	WEB 3.27
Netscape's Internet Guide	WEB 3.28
Printing a Web Page	**WEB 3.29**
Changing the Settings for Printing a Web Page	WEB 3.30
Checking Web Page Security Features	**WEB 3.31**
Getting Help in Netscape Navigator	**WEB 3.32**
Using Navigator to Save a Web Page	**WEB 3.33**
Saving a Web Page	WEB 3.33
Saving Web Page Text to a File	WEB 3.34
Saving a Web Page Graphic to Disk	WEB 3.36
Quick Check	**WEB 3.38**
Session 3.3	**WEB 3.38**
Starting Microsoft Internet Explorer	**WEB 3.38**
Status Bar	WEB 3.40
Menu Bar	WEB 3.41
Hiding and Showing the Internet Explorer Toolbars	WEB 3.41
Entering a URL in the Address Bar	**WEB 3.42**
Using the Favorites Feature	**WEB 3.44**
Organizing Favorites	WEB 3.46
Hyperlink Navigation with the Mouse	**WEB 3.47**
Using the History List	WEB 3.49
Refreshing a Web Page	WEB 3.50
Returning to Your Start Page	WEB 3.50
Printing a Web Page	**WEB 3.52**
Changing the Settings for Printing a Web Page	WEB 3.52
Checking Web Page Security Features	**WEB 3.53**
Getting Help in Microsoft Internet Explorer	**WEB 3.54**
Using Internet Explorer to Save a Web Page	**WEB 3.55**
Saving a Web Page	WEB 3.55
Saving Web Page Text to a File	WEB 3.56
Saving a Web Page Graphic to Disk	WEB 3.58
Quick Check	**WEB 3.59**
Tutorial Assignments	**WEB 3.60**
Case Problems	**WEB 3.61**
Lab Assignments	**WEB 3.63**
Quick Check Answers	**WEB 3.63**

Tutorial 4   WEB 4.1
Searching the Web
Using Search Engines and Directories Effectively

Session 4.1	**WEB 4.2**
Types of Search Questions	**WEB 4.2**
Web Search Strategy	**WEB 4.4**
Web Search Tools	**WEB 4.4**
Using Search Engines	WEB 4.5
Using Directories and Hybrid Search Engine Directories	WEB 4.8
Using Meta-Search Engines	WEB 4.13
Using Other Web Resources	WEB 4.14
Quick Check	**WEB 4.17**
Session 4.2	**WEB 4.18**
Boolean Logic and Filtering Techniques	**WEB 4.18**
Boolean Operators	WEB 4.18
Other Search Expression Operators	WEB 4.19
Wildcard Characters and Search Filters	WEB 4.20
Advanced Searches	**WEB 4.20**
Advanced Search in AltaVista	WEB 4.20
Getting Help and Refining an Advanced Search in AltaVista	WEB 4.22
Advanced Search in HotBot	WEB 4.23
Complex Search in Excite	WEB 4.25
Complex Search in Northern Light	WEB 4.26
Quick Check	**WEB 4.28**
Tutorial Assignments	**WEB 4.28**
Case Problems	**WEB 4.28**
Quick Check Answers	**WEB 4.30**

Tutorial 5   WEB 5.1
Evaluating and Downloading Web Resources
Assessing Web Site Quality and Obtaining Programs and Data

Session 5.1	**WEB 5.2**
Evaluating the Quality of Web Research Resources	**WEB 5.2**
Author Identity and Objectivity	WEB 5.2
Content	WEB 5.3
Form and Appearance	WEB 5.3
Library Resources	**WEB 5.6**
Text on the Web	**WEB 5.8**
Citing Web Research Resources	**WEB 5.8**
Future of Electronic Publishing	**WEB 5.9**
Current Information	**WEB 5.9**
Getting the News	WEB 5.13
Copyright Issues	WEB 5.16
Quick Check	**WEB 5.16**
Session 5.2	**WEB 5.17**
What is FTP and Why Do You Need It?	**WEB 5.17**
Accessing an FTP Server	**WEB 5.19**
Anonymous FTP	WEB 5.19
Full-Privilege FTP	WEB 5.20
FTP Software	WEB 5.21
Locating Files and Exploring Directories	**WEB 5.23**
FTP Hyperlinks	WEB 5.23
Public Directory	WEB 5.26
Downloading Files	**WEB 5.26**
File Transfer Modes	WEB 5.27
File Types and Extensions	WEB 5.28
Decompressing Files	WEB 5.30
Checking Files for Viruses	WEB 5.30
Uploading Files	**WEB 5.31**
Compressing and Uploading Files	WEB 5.31
Freeware, Shareware, and Limited-Use Software	WEB 5.32
Quick Check	**WEB 5.33**
Session 5.3	**WEB 5.33**
Locating Software Download Sites	**WEB 5.33**
Visiting and Using Popular Download Sites	**WEB 5.35**
Downloading Programs	**WEB 5.41**
Downloading an FTP Client	WEB 5.41
Downloading Acrobat Reader	WEB 5.45
Downloading with an FTP Client	WEB 5.47
Downloading with Command-Line FTP	WEB 5.50
Quick Check	**WEB 5.54**
Tutorial Assignments	**WEB 5.55**
Case Problems	**WEB 5.56**
Quick Check Answers	**WEB 5.58**

Glossary/Index   1

Task Reference   10

Read This Before You Begin

To the Student

Student Disks

To complete the tutorials, Tutorial Assignments, and Case Problems in this book, you need four* Student Disks. Your instructor will either provide you with Student Disks or ask you to make your own.

If you are making your own Student Disks, you will need **four*** blank, formatted high-density disks. You will need to copy a set of folders from a file server or standalone computer or the Web onto your disks. Your instructor will tell you which computer, drive letter, and folders contain the files you need. You could also download the files by going to www.course.com, clicking Data Disk Files, and following the instructions on the screen.

The following table shows you which folders go on each of your disks, so that you will have enough disk space to complete all the tutorials, Tutorial Assignments, and Case Problems:

Student Disk 1

Write this on the disk label:
Student Disk 1: Tutorials 2 and 4

Put these folders on the disk:
Tutorial.02, Tutorial.04

Student Disk 2

Write this on the disk label:
Student Disk 2: Tutorial 3

Put these folders on the disk:
Tutorial.03

Student Disk 3

Write this on the disk label:
Student Disk 3: Tutorial 5

Put these folders on the disk:
Tutorial.05

Student Disk 4

Write this on the disk label:
Student Disk 4: Tutorial 5

Put these folders on the disk:
Tutorial.05

*Note: In Tutorial 5, you will download several programs and data files to your Student Disk. Depending on which Case Problem your instructor assigns, you might need two more Student Disks. If you need additional disks, write "Student Disk 5: Tutorial 5" and "Student Disk 6: Tutorial 5" on the labels, and then create a Tutorial.05 folder on each disk. Also note that over time, the sizes of the files that you download might increase, in which case more disks might be required.

When you begin each tutorial, be sure you are using the correct Student Disk. See the inside front or inside back cover of this book for more information on Student Disk files, or ask your instructor or technical support person for assistance.

Course Labs

The tutorials in this book features two interactive Course Labs to help you understand e-mail and World Wide Web concepts. There are Lab Assignments at the end of Tutorials 2 and 3 that relate to these Labs.

To start a Lab, click the **Start** button on the Windows taskbar, point to **Programs**, point to **Course Labs**, point to **New Perspectives Course Labs**, and click the name of the Lab you want to use.

Using Your Own Computer

If you are going to work through this book using your own computer, you need:

Computer System Netscape Navigator 4.0 or higher OR Microsoft Internet Explorer 4.0 or higher and Windows 95/98/NT must be installed on your computer. This book assumes a complete installation of the Web browser software and its components, and that you have an existing e-mail account and an Internet connection. Because your Web browser may be different from the ones used in the figures of this book, your screen may differ slightly at times.

Student Disks You will not be able to complete the tutorials or exercises in this book using your own computer until you have Student Disks.

Course Labs See your instructor or technical support person to obtain the Course Lab software for use on your own computer.

Visit Our World Wide Web Site

Additional materials designed especially for you are available on the World Wide Web. Go to http://www.course.com.

To the Instructor

The Student Files and Course Labs are available on the Instructor's Resource Kit for this title. Follow the instructions in the Help file on the CD-ROM to install the programs to your network or standalone computer. For information on creating Student Disks or the Course Labs, see the "To the Student" section above. To complete the tutorials in this book, students must have a Web browser, an e-mail account, and an Internet connection.

You are granted a license to copy the Student Files and Course Labs to any computer or computer network used by students who have purchased this book.

New Perspectives on

THE
INTERNET

TUTORIAL 1   WEB 1.3
Introduction to the Internet and the World Wide Web
History, Potential, and Getting Connected

TUTORIAL 2   WEB 2.1
Basic E-Mail: Integrated Browser E-Mail Software
Evaluating E-Mail Alternatives

TUTORIAL 3   WEB 3.1
Browser Basics
Introduction to Netscape Navigator and Microsoft Internet Explorer

TUTORIAL 4   WEB 4.1
Searching the Web
Using Search Engines and Directories Effectively

TUTORIAL 5   WEB 5.1
Evaluating and Downloading Web Resources
Assessing Web Site Quality and Obtaining Programs and Data

TUTORIAL 1

OBJECTIVES

In this tutorial you will:

- Learn what computer networks are and how they work
- Find out how the Internet and World Wide Web began and grew
- Obtain an overview of the tools and information that are available on the Internet
- Compare and evaluate different methods for connecting to the Internet

INTRODUCTION TO THE INTERNET AND THE WORLD WIDE WEB

History, Potential, and Getting Connected

CASE

Tropical Exotics Produce Company

Lorraine Tomassini, the owner of the Tropical Exotics Produce Company (TEPCo), is concerned about the firm's future. She started TEPCo 10 years ago to import organically grown exotic fruits and vegetables from South America, Africa, and Asia to the U.S. market. The TEPCo product line includes items such as babaco, cherimoya, feijoa, African horned melon, malanga, and tamarillo. The business has grown rapidly and thrived financially, but Lorraine is worried that TEPCo is failing to use technology effectively. She already knows that this weakness has caused TEPCo to lose customers and suppliers to competitors.

You started work as an intern at TEPCo six months ago to learn more about international business while you attend college. Justin Jansen and Arti Rao have been with the firm for about five years and are Lorraine's key assistants. During this week's meeting with you, Justin, and Arti, Lorraine expressed concern that TEPCo has become internally focused and might be missing major trends that affect its worldwide suppliers. She worries that reading newspapers for market information and staying in touch with suppliers by telephone are time-consuming, ineffective strategies. She recalled the events of the last year, when bad weather in Costa Rica destroyed most of their suppliers' sapote crop and TEPCo received the reports too late to change its customer price schedule.

Justin mentioned that he knew some people who followed weather reports from all over the world using the Internet, which he explained was a worldwide collection of computers, connected together to allow communication. He also suggested that TEPCo might be able to attract new customers by creating a World Wide Web site on a computer connected to the Internet. Arti looked worried as she noted that TEPCo's five computers were not even connected to each other, much less to a worldwide network of computers. Lorraine knew that colleges and universities had been involved in the Internet for years and asked you to do some research on ways that TEPCo might use the Internet. You agreed to undertake the project so you could learn more about international business in general.

WEB 1.3

SESSION 1.1

The Internet offers anyone connected to it a vast array of communication tools and information resources. This session explains what the Internet and World Wide Web are, describes how they have grown from their beginnings in the military and research communities, and outlines some of the resources available on them.

Internet and World Wide Web: Amazing Developments

The **Internet**—a large collection of computers all over the world that are connected to one another in various ways—is one of the most amazing technological developments of this century. Using the Internet, you can communicate with other people throughout the world through **electronic mail** (or **e-mail**); read online versions of newspapers, magazines, academic journals, and books; join discussion groups on almost any conceivable topic; participate in games and simulations; and obtain free computer software. In recent years, the Internet has allowed commercial enterprises to connect. Today, all kinds of businesses provide information about their products and services on the Internet. Many of these businesses use the Internet to market and sell their products and services. The part of the Internet known as the **World Wide Web** (or the **Web**), is a subset of the computers on the Internet that are connected to each other in a specific way that makes those computers and their contents easily accessible to all computers in that subset. The Web has helped to make Internet resources available to people who are not computer experts. Figure 1-1 shows some of the tools and resources available on the Internet today.

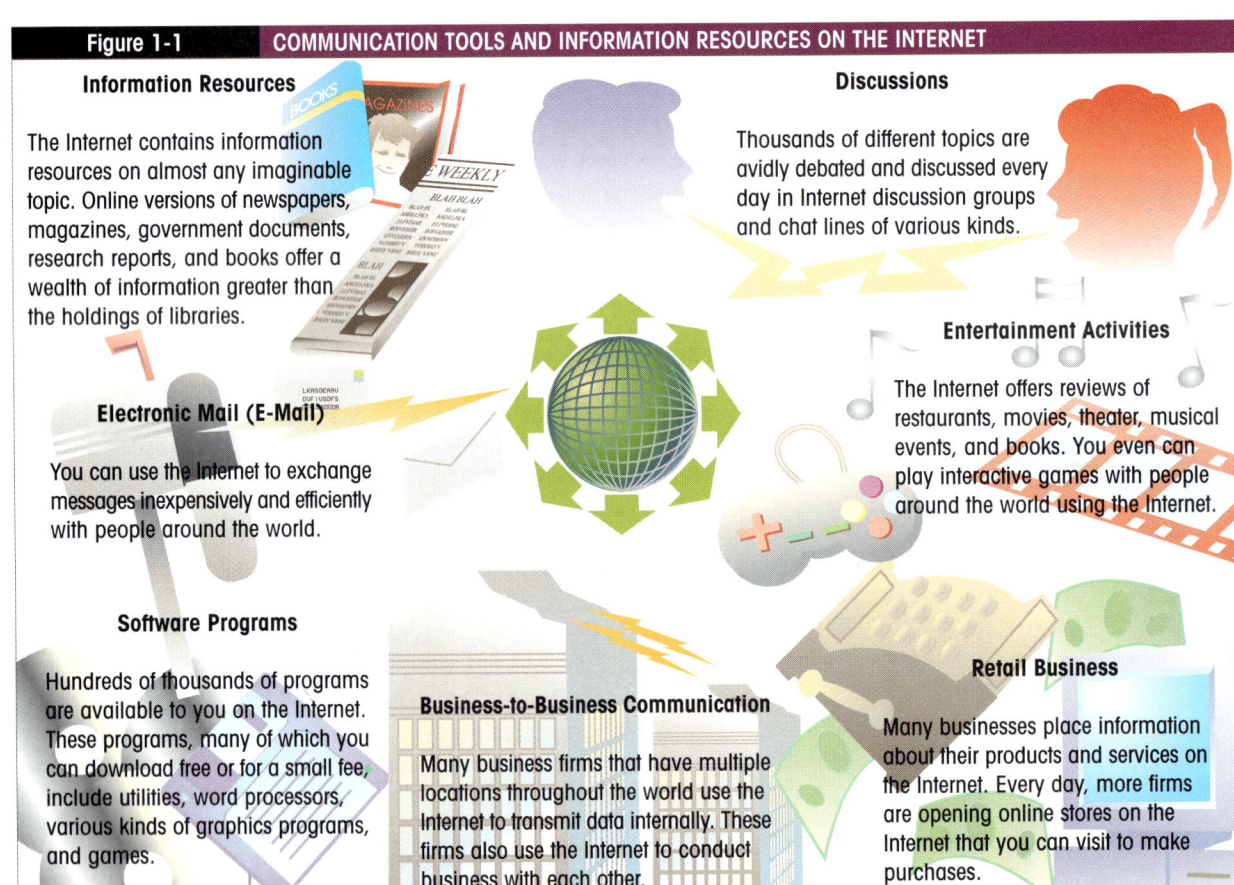

Figure 1-1 COMMUNICATION TOOLS AND INFORMATION RESOURCES ON THE INTERNET

Information Resources
The Internet contains information resources on almost any imaginable topic. Online versions of newspapers, magazines, government documents, research reports, and books offer a wealth of information greater than the holdings of libraries.

Discussions
Thousands of different topics are avidly debated and discussed every day in Internet discussion groups and chat lines of various kinds.

Electronic Mail (E-Mail)
You can use the Internet to exchange messages inexpensively and efficiently with people around the world.

Entertainment Activities
The Internet offers reviews of restaurants, movies, theater, musical events, and books. You even can play interactive games with people around the world using the Internet.

Software Programs
Hundreds of thousands of programs are available to you on the Internet. These programs, many of which you can download free or for a small fee, include utilities, word processors, various kinds of graphics programs, and games.

Business-to-Business Communication
Many business firms that have multiple locations throughout the world use the Internet to transmit data internally. These firms also use the Internet to conduct business with each other.

Retail Business
Many businesses place information about their products and services on the Internet. Every day, more firms are opening online stores on the Internet that you can visit to make purchases.

As you begin Lorraine's research project, you remember Arti's comment that TEPCo does not have its computers connected to each other. You decide to learn more about what computer networks are and how to connect computers to each other to form those networks.

Computer Networks

After talking with Adolfo Segura, the director of your school's computer lab, you realize that you will have some good news for Arti. Adolfo explained to you that he linked the lab computers to each other by inserting a network interface card into each computer and connecting cables from each card to the lab's main computer, called a server. Adolfo told you that a **network interface card (NIC)** is a card or other device used to connect a computer to a network of other computers. A **server** is a general term for any computer that accepts requests from other computers that are connected to it and shares some or all of its resources, such as printers, files, or programs, with those computers.

Client/Server Local Area Networks

The server runs software that coordinates the information flow among the other computers, which are called **clients**. The software that runs on the server computer is called a **network operating system**. Connecting computers this way, in which one server computer shares its resources with multiple client computers, is called a **client/server network**. Client/server networks commonly are used to connect computers that are located close together (for example, in the same room or building). Because the direct connection from one computer to another through NICs only works over relatively short distances (no more than a few thousand feet), this kind of network is called a **local area network (LAN)**. Figure 1-2 shows a typical client/server LAN.

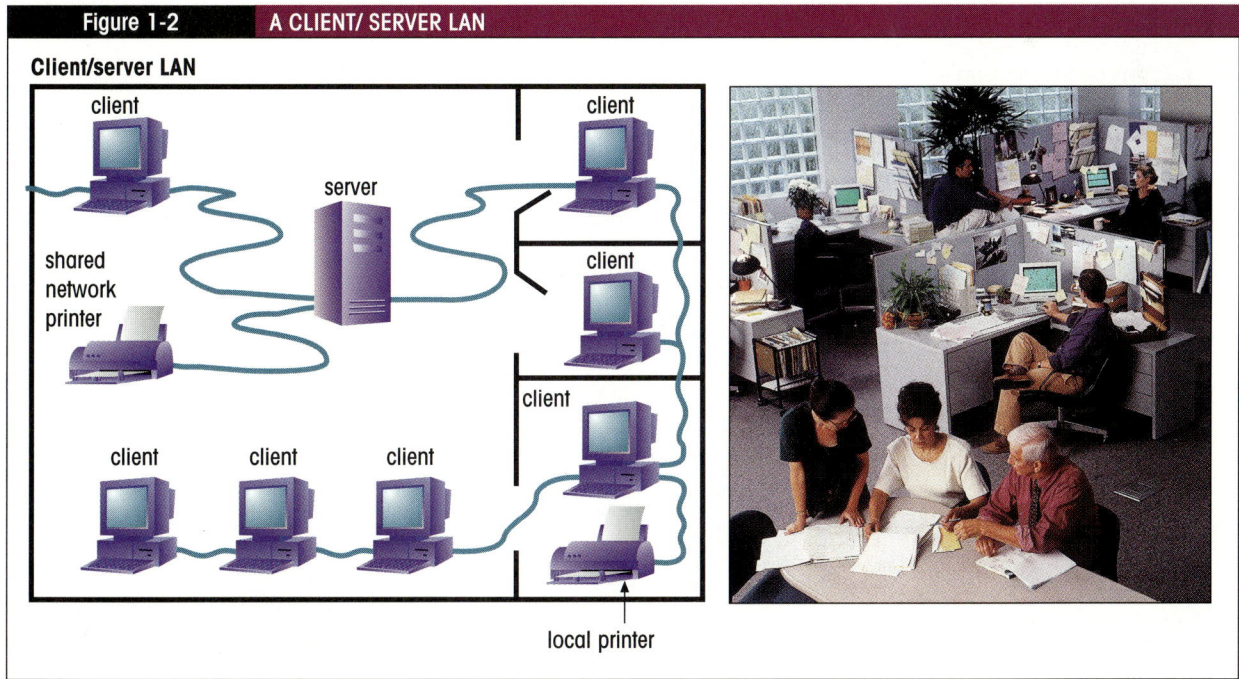

Figure 1-2 A CLIENT/ SERVER LAN

The good news for Arti is that both the NICs and the cable that connects them are fairly inexpensive. Arti's first step is to select one of TEPCo's more powerful computers to be the server. A server can be a powerful personal computer (PC) or a larger computer such as a minicomputer or a mainframe computer. **Minicomputers** and **mainframe computers** are larger, more expensive computers that businesses and other organizations use to process large volumes of work at high speeds. For many years, even the largest PCs were not powerful enough to be servers, but this has changed in the past few years.

Next, Arti will need to buy the network operating system software and have a network technician install it on the server. This software is more expensive than the operating system software for a standalone computer; however, you find that having the computers connected in a client/server network offers TEPCo some potential cost savings. For example, by connecting each computer to the server, each computer now has its own printer and its own tape drive for backups because a client/server network lets computers on the network share printers and tape drives.

Connecting Computers to a Network

As you talk with Adolfo, you learn more about computer networks. You find that not all LANs use the same kind of cables to connect their computers. The oldest cable type is called **twisted-pair**, which is the type of cable that telephone companies have used for years to wire residences and businesses. Twisted-pair cable has two or more insulated copper wires that are twisted around each other and enclosed in another layer of plastic insulation. The wires are twisted to reduce interference from other nearby current-carrying wires. Twisted-pair cable transmits information slower than the other cable types, but it is also much less expensive. **Coaxial cable** is an insulated copper wire encased in a metal shield that is enclosed with plastic insulation. The signal-carrying wire is completely shielded, so it resists electrical interference much better than twisted-pair cable. Coaxial cable also carries signals about 20 times faster than twisted-pair; however, it is considerably more expensive. You might recognize coaxial cable because most cable television connections still use coaxial cable. The most expensive cable type is **fiber-optic cable**, which does not use an electrical signal at all. Fiber-optic cable transmits information by pulsing beams of light through very thin strands of glass. Fiber-optic cable transmits signals much faster than coaxial cable and, because it does not use electricity, it is completely immune to electrical interference. Fiber-optic cable is lighter and more durable than coaxial cable, but it is harder to work with and much more expensive. Figure 1-3 shows these three types of cable.

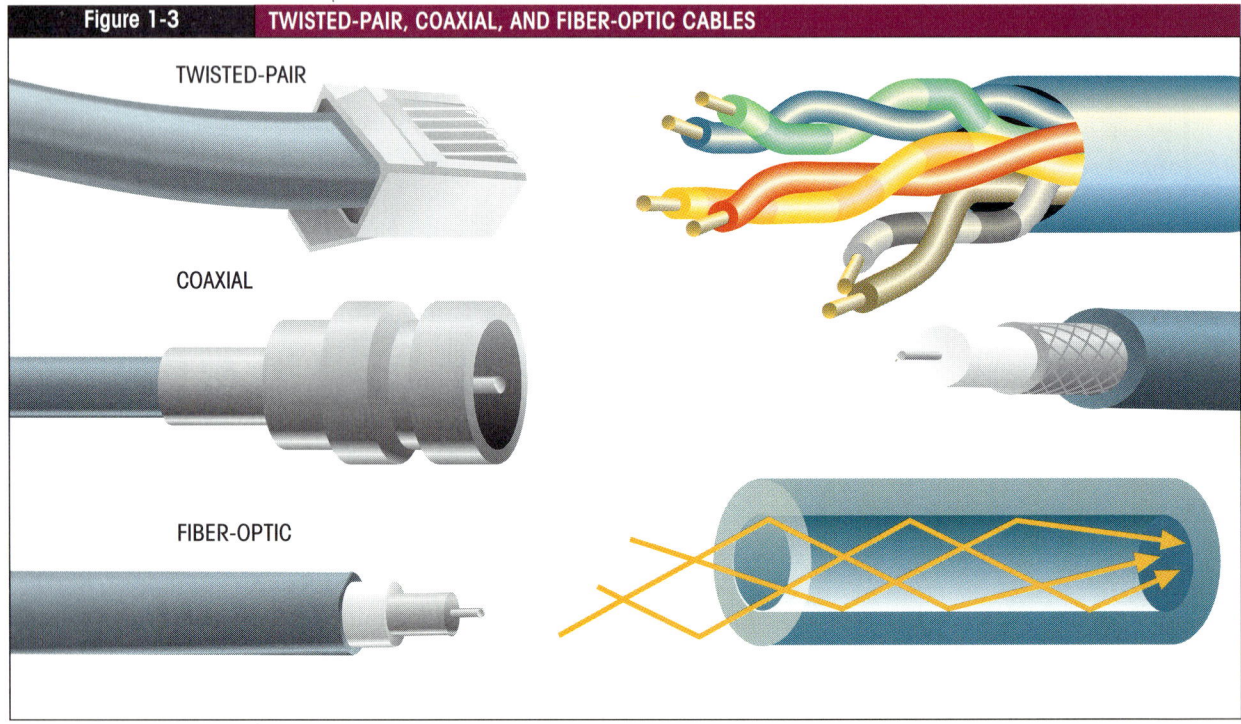

Figure 1-3 TWISTED-PAIR, COAXIAL, AND FIBER-OPTIC CABLES

Perhaps the most intriguing way to connect computers in a LAN is to avoid cable all together. **Wireless networks** are becoming more common as the cost of the wireless transmitters and receivers that plug into NICs continues to drop. Wireless LANs are especially welcome in organizations that occupy old buildings. Many cities have structures that were built before electricity and telephones were widely available. These buildings have no provision for running wires through walls or between floors, so a wireless network can be the best option for connecting resources.

Wide Area Networks

You know that your school has several computer labs in different buildings, so you ask Adolfo whether the individual labs are connected to each other as a larger LAN. Adolfo explains that each computer lab is its own client/server LAN, but that these individual networks are connected to each other as part of the school's **wide area network** (**WAN**). Adolfo remembers that you came to him with questions about the Internet and tells you that **internet** (lowercase "i") is short for **interconnected network**. The computer lab LANs are networks, and the school's WAN is a network of networks, or an internet. You look a little puzzled, so Adolfo continues to explain that *any* network of networks is called an internet. However, the school's WAN is connected to an internet called the Internet (capital "I"). The **Internet** is a specific worldwide collection of interconnected networks whose owners have voluntarily agreed to share resources and network connections with each other. You decide that your project is starting to become interesting and head toward the campus library to find out more about this huge interconnected network called the Internet.

How the Internet Began

In the early 1960s, the U.S. Department of Defense (DOD) became very concerned about the possible effects of nuclear attack on its computing facilities. The DOD realized that the weapons of the future would require powerful computers for coordination and control. The powerful computers of that time were all large mainframe computers, so the DOD began examining ways to connect these computers to each other and also to weapons installations that were distributed all over the world.

The agency charged with this task was the **Advanced Research Projects Agency**. (During its lifetime, this agency has used two acronyms, ARPA and DARPA; this book uses its current acronym, **DARPA**.) DARPA hired many of the best communications technology researchers and, for many years, funded research at leading universities and institutes to explore the task of creating a worldwide network. DARPA researchers soon became concerned about computer networks' vulnerability to attack and worked hard to devise ways to eliminate the need for network communications to rely on a central control function.

Circuit Switching vs. Packet Switching

The early models for networked computers were the telephone companies; most early WANs used leased telephone company lines for their connections. In telephone company systems of that time, a telephone call established a single connection between sender and receiver. Once the connection was established, all data then traveled along that single path. The telephone company's central switching system selected specific telephone lines, or **circuits**, that would be connected to create the single path. This centrally controlled, single-connection method is called **circuit switching**.

DARPA researchers turned to a different method of sending information, packet switching. In a **packet switching** network, files and messages are broken down into packets that are labeled electronically with codes for their origin and destination. The packets travel from computer to computer along the network until they reach their destination. The destination computer collects the packets and reassembles the original data from the pieces in each packet. Each computer that an individual packet encounters on its trip through the network determines the best way to move the packet forward to its destination. Computers that perform this function on networks are often called **routers**, and the programs they use to determine the best path for packets are called **routing algorithms**.

By 1967, DARPA researchers had published their plan for a packet switching network and in 1969, they connected the first computer switches at the University of California at Los Angeles, SRI International, the University of California at Santa Barbara, and the University of Utah. This experimental WAN, called the **ARPANET**, grew over the next three years to include over 20 computers and used the **Network Control Protocol (NCP)**. A **protocol** is a collection of rules for formatting, ordering, and error-checking data sent across a network.

Open Architecture Philosophy

As more researchers connected to the ARPANET, interest in the network grew in the academic community. The next several years saw many technological developments that increased the speed and efficiency with which the network operated. One reason for the project's success was its adherence to an **open architecture** philosophy; that is, each network could continue using its own protocols and data-transmission methods internally. Conversion to NCP occurred only when the data moved out of the local network and onto the ARPANET. The original purpose of the ARPANET was to connect computers in the field that were controlling a wide range of diverse weapons systems, so the ARPANET could not force its protocol or structure onto those individual component networks. This open approach was quite different from the closed architecture designs that companies such as IBM and Digital Equipment Corporation were using to build networks for their customers during this period. The open architecture philosophy included four key points:

- Independent networks should not require any internal changes to be connected to the Internet.
- Packets that do not arrive at their destinations must be retransmitted from their source network.
- The router computers do not retain information about the packets they handle.
- No global control will exist over the network.

One of the new developments of this time period that was rapidly adopted throughout the ARPANET was a set of new protocols developed by Vincent Cerf and Robert Kahn. These new protocols were the **Transmission Control Protocol** and the **Internet Protocol**, which usually are referred to by their combined acronym, **TCP/IP**. TCP includes rules that computers on a network use to establish and break connections; IP includes rules for routing of individual data packets. These two protocols were technically superior to the NCP that ARPANET had used since its inception and gradually replaced that protocol. TCP/IP continues to be used today in LANs and on the Internet. The term *Internet* was first used in a 1974 article about the TCP protocol written by Cerf and Kahn. The importance of the TCP/IP protocol in the history of the Internet is so great that many people consider Vincent Cerf to be the Father of the Internet.

ARPANET's successes were not lost on other network researchers. Many university and research institution computers used the UNIX operating system. When TCP/IP was included in a version of UNIX, these institutions found it easier to create networks and interconnect them. A number of TCP/IP-based networks—independent of the ARPANET—were created in the late 1970s and early 1980s. The National Science Foundation (NSF) funded the **Computer Science Network (CSNET)** for educational and research institutions that did not have access to the ARPANET. The City University of New York started a network of IBM mainframes at universities, called the **Because It's Time** (originally, "There") **Network (BITNET)**.

Birth of E-Mail: A New Use for Networks

Although the goals of ARPANET were still to control weapons systems and transfer research files, other uses for this vast network began to appear in the early 1970s. In 1972, an ARPANET researcher named Ray Tomlinson wrote a program that could send and receive messages over the network. E-mail had been born and became widely used very quickly; in 1976, the Queen of England sent an e-mail message over the ARPANET. By 1981, the ARPANET had expanded to include over 200 networks and was continuing to develop faster and more effective network technologies; for example, ARPANET began sending packets via satellite in 1976.

More New Uses for Networks Emerge

The number of network users in the military and education research communities continued to grow. Many of these new participants used the networking technology to transfer files and access computers remotely. The TCP/IP suite included two tools for performing these tasks. **File Transfer Protocol (FTP)** enabled users to transfer files between computers, and **Telnet** let users log in to their computer accounts from remote sites. Both FTP and Telnet still are widely used on the Internet today for file transfers and remote logins, even though more advanced techniques facilitate multimedia transmissions such as realtime audio and video clips. The first e-mail mailing lists also appeared on these networks. A **mailing list** is an e-mail address that takes any message it receives and forwards it to any user who has subscribed to the list.

Although file transfer and remote login were attractive features of these new TCP/IP networks, their improved e-mail and other communications facilities attracted many users in the education and research communities. For example, BITNET would run mailing list software (called **LISTSERV**) on its IBM mainframe computers that provided automatic control and maintenance for the mailing lists. In 1979, a group of students and programmers at Duke University and the University of North Carolina started **Usenet**, an acronym for **User's News Network**. Usenet allows anyone that connects with the network to read and post articles on a variety of subjects.

Usenet survives on the Internet today, with over a thousand different topic areas, called **newsgroups**. Going even farther from the initial purpose of TCP/IP networks, researchers at the University of Essex wrote a program that allowed users to assume character roles and play an adventure game. This adventure game let multiple users play at the same time and interact with each other. These games continue on the Internet today and are called **MUDs**, which originally stood for **multiuser dungeon**, although many users now consider the term an acronym for **multiuser domain**, or **multiuser dimension**.

Although the people using these networks were developing many creative applications, the number of persons who had access to the networks was limited to members of the research and academic communities. The decade from 1979 to 1989 would be the time in which these new and interesting network applications were improved and tested with an increasing number of users. The TCP/IP set of protocols would become more widely used as academic and research institutions realized the benefits of having a common communications network. The explosion of PC use during that time also would help more people become comfortable with computing.

Interconnecting the Networks

The early 1980s saw continued growth in the ARPANET and other networks. The **Joint Academic Network (Janet)** was established in the United Kingdom to link universities there. Traffic increased on all of these networks and, in 1984, the Department of Defense (DOD) split the ARPANET into two specialized networks: ARPANET would continue its advanced research activities, and **MILNET** (for **Military Network**) would be reserved for military uses that required greater security. That year also saw a new addition to CSNET, named the **National Science Foundation Network** (**NSFnet**). By 1987, congestion on the ARPANET caused by a rapidly increasing number of users on the limited-capacity leased telephone lines was becoming severe. To reduce the government's traffic load on the ARPANET, the NSFnet merged with BITNET and CSNET to form one network. The resulting NSFnet awarded a contract to Merit Network, Inc., IBM, Sprint, and the State of Michigan to upgrade and operate the main NSFnet backbone. A **network backbone** includes the long-distance lines and supporting technology that transports large amounts of data between major network nodes. The NSFnet backbone connected 13 regional WANs and six supercomputer centers. By the late 1980s, many other TCP/IP networks had merged or established interconnections. Figure 1-4 summarizes how the individual networks described in this section combined to become the Internet as we know it today.

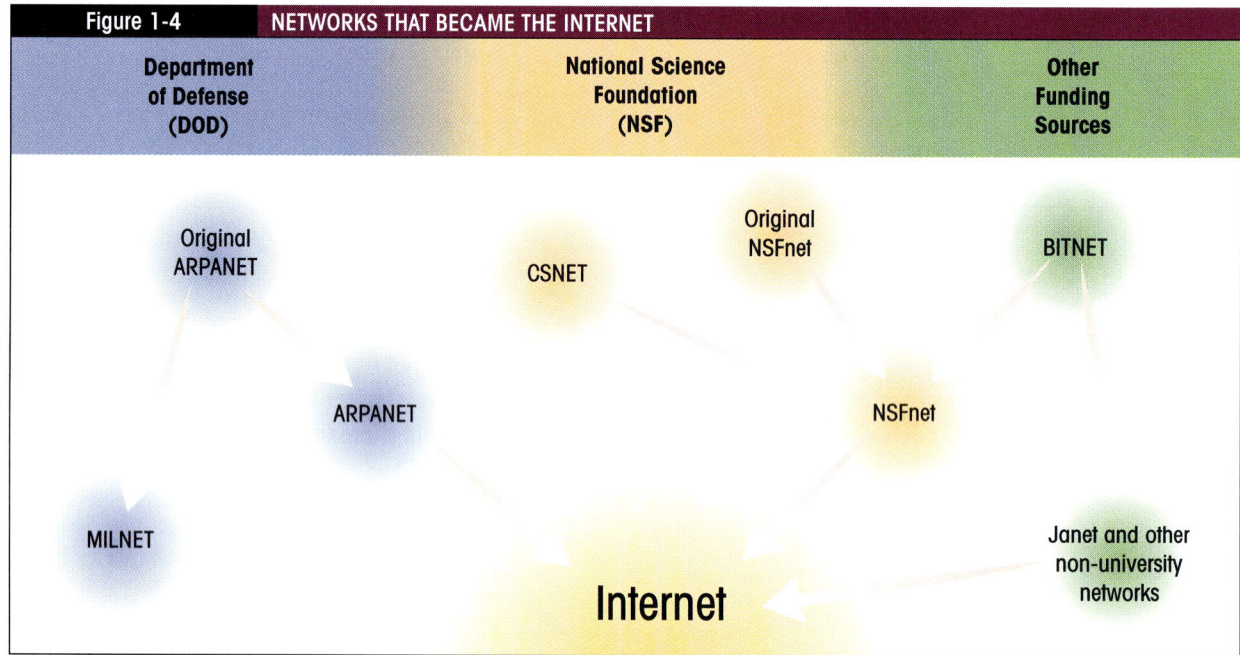

Figure 1-4 NETWORKS THAT BECAME THE INTERNET

Commercial Interest Increases

As PCs became more powerful, affordable, and available during the 1980s, firms increasingly used them to construct LANs. Although these LANs included e-mail software that employees could use to send messages to each other, businesses wanted their employees to be able to communicate with people outside their corporate LANs. The National Science Foundation (NSF) prohibited commercial network traffic on the networks it funded, so businesses turned to commercial e-mail services. Larger firms built their own TCP/IP-based WANs that used leased telephone lines to connect field offices to corporate headquarters. Today, we use the term **intranet** to describe LANs or WANs that use the TCP/IP protocol but do not connect to sites outside the firm. In 1989, the NSF permitted two commercial e-mail services, MCI Mail and CompuServe, to establish limited connections to the Internet that allowed their commercial subscribers to exchange e-mail messages with the members of the academic and research communities who were connected to the Internet. These connections allowed commercial enterprises to send e-mail directly to Internet addresses and allowed members of the research and education communities on the Internet to send e-mail directly to MCI Mail and CompuServe addresses. The NSF justified this limited commercial use of the Internet as a service that would primarily benefit the Internet's noncommercial users.

People from all walks of life—not just scientists or academic researchers—started thinking of these networks as a global resource that we now know as the Internet. Information systems professionals began to form volunteer groups such as the **Internet Engineering Task Force (IETF)**, which first met in 1986. The IETF is a self-organized group that makes technical contributions to the engineering of the Internet and its technologies. IETF is the main body that develops new Internet standards.

Just as the world was coming to realize the value of these interconnected networks, however, it also became aware of the threats to privacy and security posed by these networks. In 1988, Robert Morris launched a program called the **Internet Worm** that used weaknesses in e-mail programs and operating systems to distribute itself to over 6,000 of the 60,000 computers that were then connected to the Internet. The Worm program created multiple copies of itself on the computers it infected. The large number of program copies would consume the processing power of the infected computer and prevent it from running other programs. This event brought international attention and concern to the Internet.

Although the network of networks that is now known as the Internet had grown from four computers on the ARPANET in 1969 to over 300,000 computers on many interconnected networks by 1990, the greatest growth in the Internet was yet to come.

Growth of the Internet

A formal definition of Internet, which was adopted in 1995 by the Federal Networking Council, appears in Figure 1-5.

Figure 1-5 THE FEDERAL NETWORKING COUNCIL'S OCTOBER 1995 RESOLUTION TO DEFINE THE TERM INTERNET

RESOLUTION: The Federal Networking Council (FNC) agrees that the following language reflects our definition of the term "Internet." "Internet" refers to the global information system that—

(i) is logically linked together by a globally unique address space based on the Internet Protocol (IP) or its subsequent extensions/follow-ons;

(ii) is able to support communications using the Transmission Control Protocol/Internet Protocol (TCP/IP) suite or its subsequent extensions/follow-ons, and/or other IP-compatible protocols; and

(iii) provides, uses or makes accessible, either publicly or privately, high level services layered on the communications and related infrastructure described herein.

Source: http://www.fnc.gov/Internet_res.html

Many people find it interesting to note that a formal definition of the term did not appear until 1995. The Internet was a phenomenon that surprised an unsuspecting world. The researchers who had been so involved in the creation and growth of the Internet accepted it as part of their working environment. People outside the research community were largely unaware of the potential offered by a large interconnected set of computer networks.

From Research Project to Information Infrastructure

By 1990, the Internet had become a well-functioning grid of useful technology. Much of the funding for these networks had come from the U.S. government, through its DOD and the NSF. The NSFnet alone consumed over $200 million from 1986 to 1995 on research and development. Realizing that the Internet was no longer a research project, the DOD finally closed the research portion of its network, the ARPANET. The NSF also wanted to turn over the Internet to others so it could return its attention and funds to other research projects.

In 1991, the NSF further eased its restrictions on Internet commercial activity and began implementing plans to privatize much of the Internet eventually. The first parts of the NSFnet on which it encouraged commercial activity were the local and regional nodes, which allowed time for private firms to develop long-haul network capacity similar to that of the NSFnet national network backbone. Businesses and individuals connected to the Internet in ever-increasing numbers. Figure 1-6 shows the number of Internet host computers from 1991 through 1997. As you can see, the growth has been dramatic.

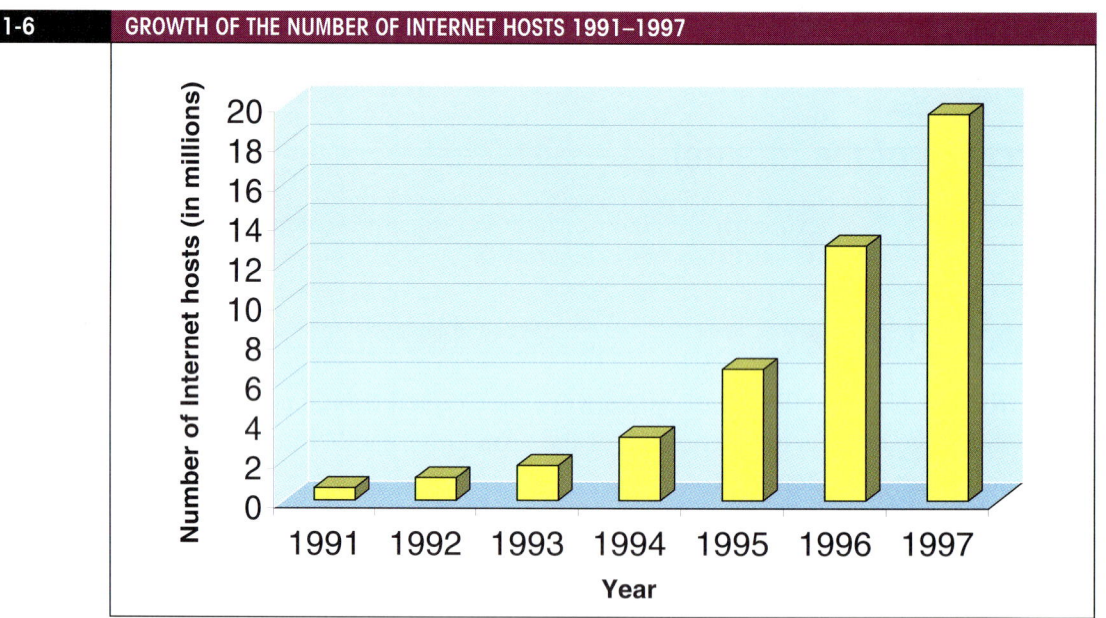

Figure 1-6 GROWTH OF THE NUMBER OF INTERNET HOSTS 1991–1997

The numbers in Figure 1-6 probably understate the true growth of the Internet in recent years for two reasons. First, the number of hosts connected to the Internet only includes directly connected computers. In other words, if a LAN with 100 PCs is connected to the Internet through only one host computer, those 100 computers appear as one host in the count. Because the number and size of LANs has increased steadily in recent years, the host count probably is understated. Second, the number of computers is only one measure of growth. Internet traffic now carries more files that contain graphics, sound, and video, so Internet files have become larger. A given number of users sending video clips will use much more of the Internet's capacity than the same number of users will use by sending e-mail messages or text files. Many people are surprised to learn that no one knows how many users are on the Internet. The Internet has no central management or coordination, and the routing computers do not maintain records of the packets they handle. Therefore, no one has the capability to know how many individual e-mail messages or files travel on the Internet.

New Structure for the Internet

As NSFnet converted the main traffic-carrying backbone portion of its network to private firms, it organized the network around the four network access points (NAPs) shown in Figure 1-7. A different company now operates each of these NAPs, as shown in Figure 1-7.

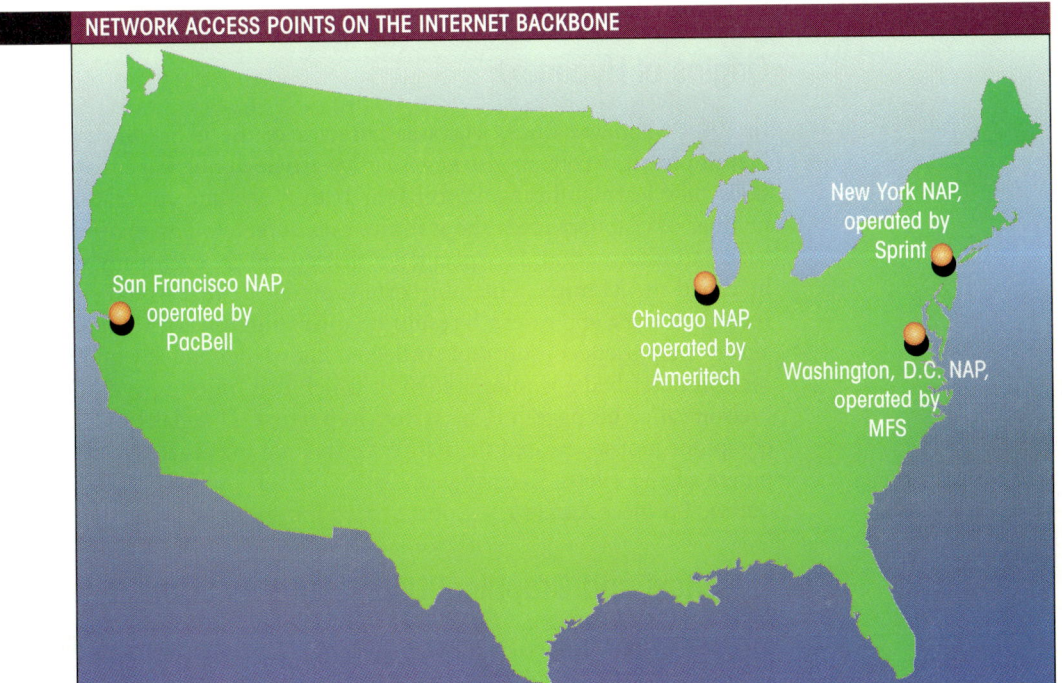

Figure 1-7   NETWORK ACCESS POINTS ON THE INTERNET BACKBONE

These four companies sell access to the Internet through their NAPs to organizations and businesses. The NSFnet still exists for government and research use, but it uses these same NAPs for long-range data transmission.

With over 20 million connected computers and an estimate of between 50 and 150 million worldwide Internet users, the Internet faces some challenges. The firms that sell network access have enough incentive to keep investing in the network architecture because they can recoup their investments by attracting new Internet users. However, the existing TCP/IP numbering system that identifies users will run out of addresses in a few years if the Internet continues its current rate of growth. Groups like the IETF are working on a new addressing scheme that will allow existing users to continue accessing the Internet while the new system is implemented.

In less than 30 years, the Internet has become one of the most amazing technological and social accomplishments of the century. Millions of people use a complex, interconnected network of computers that run thousands of different software packages. The computers are located in almost every country of the world. Over one billion dollars changes hands over the Internet in exchange for all kinds of products and services. All of this activity occurs with no central coordination point or control. Even more interesting is that the Internet began as a way for the military to maintain control while under attack.

The opening of the Internet to business enterprise helped increase its growth dramatically in recent years. However, there was another development that worked hand-in-hand with the commercialization of the Internet to spur its growth. That development was the technological advance known as the World Wide Web.

World Wide Web

The World Wide Web (the Web) is more a way of thinking about information storage and retrieval than it is a technology. Because of this, its history goes back many years. Two important innovations played key roles in making the Internet easier to use and more accessible to people who were not research scientists: hypertext and graphical user interfaces (GUIs).

Origins of Hypertext

In 1945, Vannevar Bush, who was Director of the U.S. Office of Scientific Research and Development, wrote an *Atlantic Monthly* article about ways that scientists could apply the skills they learned during World War II to peacetime applications. The article included a number of visionary ideas about future uses of technology to organize and facilitate efficient access to information. He speculated that engineers eventually would build a machine that he called the **Memex**, a memory extension device that would store all of a person's books, records, letters, and research results on microfilm. Bush's Memex would include mechanical aids to help users consult their collected knowledge quickly and flexibly. In the 1960s, Ted Nelson described a similar system in which text on one page links to text on other pages. Nelson called his page-linking system **hypertext**. Douglas Englebart, who also invented the computer mouse, created the first experimental hypertext system on one of the large computers of the 1960s. Twenty years later, Nelson published *Literary Machines*, in which he outlined project **Xanadu**, a global system for online hypertext publishing and commerce.

Hypertext and Graphical User Interfaces Come to the Internet

In 1989, Tim Berners-Lee and Robert Calliau were working at CERN-The European Laboratory for Particle Physics and were trying to improve the laboratory's research document-handling procedures. CERN had been connected to the Internet for two years, but its scientists wanted to find better ways to circulate their scientific papers and data among the high-energy physics research community throughout the world. Independently, they each proposed a hypertext development project.

Over the next two years, Berners-Lee developed the code for a hypertext server program and made it available on the Internet. A **hypertext server** is a computer that stores files written in the hypertext markup language and lets other computers connect to it and read those files. **Hypertext markup language (HTML)** is a language that includes a set of codes (or **tags**) attached to text. These codes describe the relationships among text elements. For example, HTML includes tags that indicate which text is part of a header element, which text is part of a paragraph element, and which text is part of a numbered list element. One important type of tag is the hypertext link tag. A **hypertext link**, or **hyperlink**, points to another location in the same or another HTML document. You can use several different types of software to read HTML documents, but most people use a Web browser such as Netscape Navigator or Microsoft Internet Explorer. A **Web browser** is software that lets users read (or browse) HTML documents and move from one HTML document to another through the text formatted with hypertext link tags in each file. If the HTML documents are on computers connected to the Internet, you can use a Web browser to move from an HTML document on one computer to an HTML document on any other computer on the Internet. HTML is based on **Standard Generalized Markup Language (SGML)**, which organizations have used for many years to manage large document-filing systems.

An HTML document differs from a word-processing document because it does not specify *how* a particular text element will appear. For example, you might use word-processing software to create a document heading by setting the heading text font to Arial, its font size to 14 points, and its position to centered. The document would display and print these exact settings whenever you opened the document in that word processor. In contrast, an HTML document would simply include a heading tag with the text. Many different programs can read an HTML document. Each program recognizes the heading tag and displays the text in whatever manner each program normally displays headers. Different programs might display the text differently.

A Web browser presents an HTML document in an easy-to-read format in its graphical user interface. A **graphical user interface (GUI)** is a way of presenting program output to users that uses pictures, icons, and other graphical elements instead of just displaying text. Almost all PCs today use a GUI such as Microsoft Windows or the Macintosh user interface.

Berners-Lee and Calliau called their system of hyperlinked HTML documents the World Wide Web. The Web caught on quickly in the scientific research community, but few people outside that community had software that could read the HTML documents. In 1993, a group of students led by Marc Andreessen at the University of Illinois wrote **Mosaic**, the first GUI program that could read HTML and use HTML documents' hyperlinks to navigate from page to page on computers anywhere on the Internet. Mosaic was the first Web browser that became widely available for PCs.

The Web and Commercialization of the Internet

Programmers quickly realized that a functional system of pages connected by hypertext links would provide many new Internet users with an easy way to locate information on the Internet. Businesses quickly recognized the profit-making potential offered by a worldwide network of easy-to-use computers. In 1994, Andreessen and other members of the University of Illinois Mosaic team joined with James Clark of Silicon Graphics to found Netscape Communications. Their first product, the Netscape Web browser program based on Mosaic, was an instant success. Netscape became one of the fastest growing software companies ever. Microsoft created its Internet Explorer Web browser and entered the market soon after Netscape's success became apparent. A number of other Web browsers exist, but these two products dominate the market today.

The number of **Web sites**, which are computers connected to the Internet that store HTML documents, has grown even more rapidly than the Internet itself to be between 500,000 and 800,000 sites. Each Web site might have hundreds, or even thousands, of individual Web pages, so the amount of information on the Web is astounding. Figure 1-8 shows the phenomenal growth in the Web during its short lifetime.

As more people obtain access to the Web, commercial uses of the Web and a variety of nonbusiness uses will greatly increase. Although the Web has grown rapidly, many experts believe that it will grow at an increasing rate for the foreseeable future.

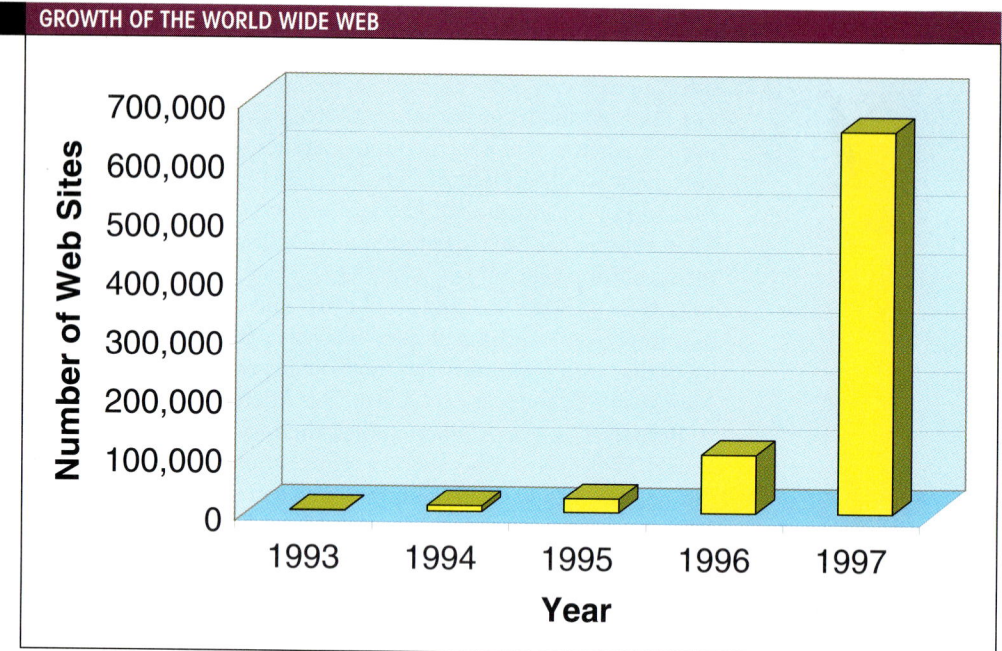

Figure 1-8   GROWTH OF THE WORLD WIDE WEB

Quick Check

1. Name three resources that computers connected to a client/server LAN can share.

2. The fastest and most expensive way to connect computers in a network is _____ cable.

3. Telephone companies use centrally controlled circuit switching to connect telephone callers and transmit data. Name and briefly describe the switching method used by the Internet.

4. What is the technical term for the collection of rules that computers follow when formatting, ordering, and error-checking data sent across a network?

5. The networks that became the Internet were originally designed to transmit files; however, early in its history, people found other uses for the Internet. Name three of those uses.

6. What is an internet?

7. Name and briefly describe two key factors that contributed to the Internet's rapid growth in the 1990s.

8. What type of software can network users run on their computers to access HTML documents that are stored on other computers?

You have obtained a good background for your report on how TEPCo might use the Internet and the Web by learning about their histories. You are convinced that the Internet can help Lorraine and her assistants manage the company better, identify new customers, and stay in contact with suppliers. You decide that the next logical step in your research is to identify ways that TEPCo can connect to the Internet. In the next session, you will learn how to evaluate Internet connection options.

SESSION 1.2

You can connect your computer to the Internet in several different ways. This session presents an overview of connection options and explains how you can choose the one that is right for you.

Connection Options

Remember that the Internet is a set of interconnected networks. Therefore, you cannot become a part of the Internet unless you are part of a communications network, whether it is a LAN, an intranet, or through a telephone connection. Each network that joins the Internet must accept some responsibility for operating the network by routing message packets that other networks pass along. As you consider your project for TEPCo, you become concerned that Justin and Arti are not going to want to become involved in something this complex. After all, they are exotic-produce experts—not computer wizards!

Business of Providing Internet Access

As you continue your research, you learn more about the NAPs (network access points) that maintain the core operations and long-haul backbone of the Internet. You find that they do not offer direct connections to individuals or small businesses. Instead, they offer connections to large organizations and businesses that, in turn, provide Internet access to other businesses and individuals. These firms are called **Internet access providers (IAPs)** or **Internet service providers (ISPs)**. Most of these firms call themselves ISPs because they offer more than just access to the Internet. ISPs usually provide their customers with the software they need to connect to the ISP, browse the Web, send and receive e-mail messages, and perform other Internet-related functions such as file transfer and remote login to other computers. ISPs often provide network consulting services to their customers and help them design Web pages. Some ISPs have developed a full range of services that include network management, training, and marketing advice. Some larger ISPs not only sell Internet access to end users, but also market Internet access to other ISPs, which then sell access and service to their own business and individual customers. This hierarchy of Internet access appears in Figure 1-9.

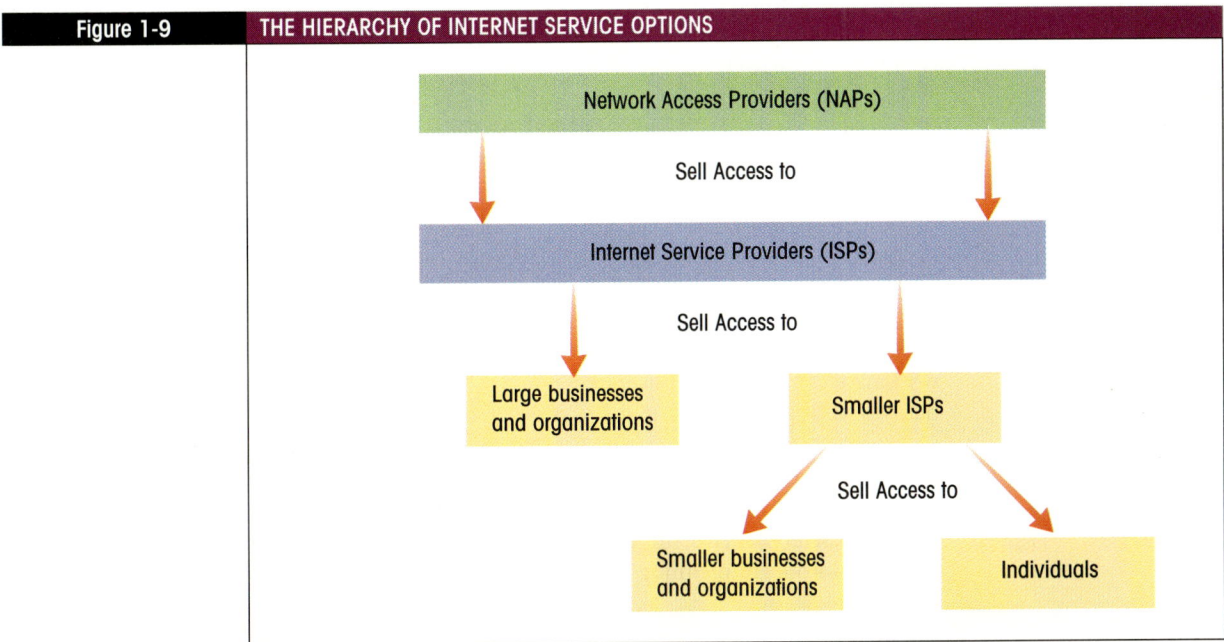

Figure 1-9 THE HIERARCHY OF INTERNET SERVICE OPTIONS

Connection Bandwidth

Of the differences that exist among service providers at different levels of the access hierarchy, one of the most important is the connection bandwidth that an ISP can offer. **Bandwidth** is the amount of data that can travel through a communications circuit in one second. The bandwidth that an ISP can offer you depends on the type of connection it has to the Internet and the kind of connection you have to the ISP.

The bandwidth for a network connection between two points always is limited to the narrowest bandwidth that exists in any part of the network. For example, if you connect to an ISP through a regular telephone line, your bandwidth is limited to the bandwidth of that telephone line, regardless of the bandwidth connection that the ISP has to the Internet. Bandwidth is measured in multiples of **bits per second** (**bps**). Discussions of Internet bandwidth often use the terms **kilobits per second** (**Kbps**), which is 1,024 bps; **megabits per second** (**Mbps**), which is 1,048,576 bps; and **gigabits per second** (**Gbps**), which is 1,073,741,824 bps. Most LANs run either an Ethernet network, which has a bandwidth of 10 Mbps, or Fast Ethernet, which operates at 100 Mbps. When you extend your network beyond a local area, the speed of the connection depends on what type of connection you use.

One way to connect computers or networks over longer distances is to use regular telephone service (sometimes referred to as **POTS**, or **plain old telephone service**). Regular telephone service to most U.S. residential and business customers provides a maximum bandwidth of between 28.8 Kbps and 56 Kbps. These numbers vary because the U.S. has a number of different telephone companies that do not all use the same technology. Some telephone companies offer a higher grade of service that uses one of a series of protocols called **Digital Subscriber Line** or **Digital Subscriber Loop** (**DSL**). The first technology that was developed using a DSL protocol is called **Integrated Services Digital Network** (**ISDN**). ISDN service has been available in various parts of the U.S. since 1984. Although considerably more expensive than regular telephone service, ISDN offers bandwidths of up to 128 Kbps. ISDN is much more widely available in Australia, France, Germany, Japan, and Singapore than in the U.S. because the regulatory structure of the telecommunications industries in these countries encouraged rapid deployment of this new technology. All technologies based on the DSL protocol require the implementing telephone company to install modems at its switching stations, which can be very expensive. New technologies that use the DSL protocol are currently being tested around the world. One of those, **Asymmetric Digital Subscriber Line** (**ADSL**), will offer transmission speeds ranging from 16 to 640 Kbps from the user to the telephone company and from 1.5 to 9 Mbps from the telephone company to the user.

Larger firms can connect to an ISP using higher-bandwidth telephone company connections called **T1** (1.544 Mbps) and **T3** (44.736 Mbps) connections. These connections are much more expensive than POTS or ISDN connections; however, organizations that must link hundreds or thousands of individual users to the Internet require the greater bandwidth of T1 and T3 connections. The NAPs currently operate the Internet backbone using a variety of connections. In addition to T1 and T3 lines, the NAPs use newer **Asynchronous Transfer Mode** (**ATM**) connections that have bandwidths of up to 622 Mbps. Improved ATM methods are being developed that will provide bandwidths exceeding 1 Gbps. NAPs also use satellite and radio communications links to transfer data over long distances. The NAPs are working with a group of universities and the National Science Foundation (NSF) to develop a network called **Internet 2** that will have backbone bandwidths that exceed 1 Gbps.

A new connection option that is just becoming available in parts of the U.S. is to connect to the Internet through a cable television company. The cable company transmits data in the same cables it uses to provide television service. Only a few cable operators around the country currently have the necessary cable installed to offer this service; however, many cable operators are planning to upgrade their facilities during the next few years. Cable can deliver up to 10 Mbps to an individual user and can accept up to 768 Kbps from an individual user. These speeds far exceed those of existing POTS and ISDN connections and are comparable to speeds that will be provided by the ADSL technologies currently being tested by telephone companies.

An option that is particularly appealing to users in remote areas is connecting via satellite. Using a satellite-dish receiver, you can download at a bandwidth of approximately 400 Kbps. Unfortunately, you cannot send information to the Internet using a satellite dish, so you must also have an ISP account to send files or e-mail. Figure 1-10 summarizes the bandwidths for various types of connections currently in use on the Internet.

Figure 1-10 BANDWIDTHS FOR VARIOUS TYPES OF INTERNET CONNECTIONS

TYPE OF SERVICE	SPEED	TYPICAL USES
Regular telephone service	28.8 Kbps to 56 Kbps	Individual and small business users connecting to ISPs
Integrated Services Digital Network (ISDN)	128 Kbps	Individual and small business users connecting to ISPs
T1 leased line	1.544 Mbps	Large businesses and other organizations connecting to ISPs and ISPs connecting to other ISPs
T3 leased line	44.736 Mbps	Large businesses and other organizations connecting to ISPs, ISPs connecting to other ISPs, ISPs connecting to NAPS, and portions of the Internet backbone
Asynchronous Transfer Mode (ATM) Line	622 Mbps	Internet backbone

As you evaluate the information you have gathered about ways Lorraine might connect TEPCo to the Internet, you realize that there are four ways that individuals or small businesses can link to the Internet. The first way, which is only for individuals, is a connection through your school or employer. The second option is to connect through an ISP. The third option is to connect through a cable television company. The fourth option is to use a combination of satellite download and an upload method. Next, you will learn about some of the advantages and disadvantages of each connection method that you have identified for your analysis and report to Lorraine.

Connecting Through Your School or Employer

One of the easiest ways to connect to the Internet is through your school or employer, if it already has an Internet connection. The connection is either free or very reasonably priced. However, by using your school or employer to connect to the Internet, you must comply with its rules. In some cases, this can outweigh the cost advantage.

Connecting Through Your School

Most universities and community colleges are connected to the Internet, and many offer Internet access to their students, faculty members, and other employees. In most schools, you can use computers in computing labs or in the library to access the Internet. Many schools provide a way to connect your own computer through the school's network to the Internet. The form of connection will depend on what your school offers. An increasing number of schools have dormitory rooms wired with LAN connections so students can connect using their own computers. Some schools even provide the computers as part of their tuition or housing charge.

Dialing in

Most schools or businesses, whether or not they have LANs in their buildings, provide telephone numbers that you can call and connect your computer through a modem. **Modem** is short for **modulator-demodulator**. When you connect your computer, which communicates using digital signals, to another computer through a telephone line, which uses analog signals, you must perform a signal conversion. Converting a digital signal to an analog signal is **modulation**; converting that analog signal back into digital form is called **demodulation**. A modem performs both functions; that is, it acts as a modulator-demodulator. If you use a modem to connect to the Internet, you will need to install software that implements a protocol that makes your modem connection appear to be a TCP/IP connection. Two of the most frequently used software packages are the **serial line Internet protocol (SLIP)** and the **point-to-point protocol (PPP)**. Usually, this software automatically chooses the correct protocol (either SLIP or PPP) when you install it, based on your description of the connection you are making.

Connecting Through Your Employer

Your employer might offer you a connection to the Internet through the computer you use in your job. This computer might be connected through a LAN to the Internet, or you might have to use a modem to connect it. Before you attempt to connect to the Internet this way, make sure that your employer permits personal use of company computing facilities. Remember, your employer owns the computers you use as an employee. In most of the world, this gives your employer the right to examine any e-mail files that you transmit or store using those computers. A number of schools retain similar rights under the law or through policies they publish in their student handbooks.

Acceptable Use Policies

Most schools and employers have an **acceptable use policy** (**AUP**) that specifies the conditions under which you can use their Internet connections. Some organizations require you to sign a copy of the AUP before they permit you to use their computing facilities; others simply include it as part of your student or employee contract. AUPs often include provisions that require you to respect copyright laws, trade secrets, the privacy of other users, and standards of common decency. Many AUPs expressly prohibit you from engaging in commercial activities, criminal activities, or specific threat-making or equipment-endangering practices.

Many provisions in AUPs are open to honest misunderstanding or disagreement in interpretation. It is extremely important for you to read and understand any AUP with which you must comply when you use computing facilities at your school or employer. AUPs often include punitive provisions that include revocation of user accounts and all rights to use the network. Some AUPs state that a user can be expelled or fired for serious violations.

Advantages and Disadvantages

Although accessing the Internet through your school or employer might be the least expensive option, you might decide that the restrictions on your freedom of expression and actions are too great. For example, if you wanted to start a small business on the Web, you would not want to use your school account if its AUP has a commercial-activity exclusion. An important concern when using your employer's computing facilities to connect to the Internet is that the employer generally retains the right to examine any files or e-mail messages that you transmit through those facilities. Carefully consider whether the limitations placed on your use of the Internet are greater than the benefits of the low cost of this access option.

Connecting Through an Internet Service Provider

Depending on where you live, you might find that an ISP is the best way for you to connect to the Internet. In major metropolitan areas, many ISPs compete for customers and, therefore, connection fees often are reasonable. Smaller towns and rural areas have fewer ISPs and, therefore, might be less competitive. When you are shopping for an ISP, you will want to find information such as:

- The monthly base fee and number of hours it provides
- The hourly rate for time used over the monthly base amount
- Whether the telephone access number is local or long distance
- Which specific Internet services are included
- What software is included
- What user-support services are available

Advantages and Disadvantages

ISPs are the best option for many Internet users, in part because they usually provide reliable connectivity at a reasonable price. The terms of their AUPs often are less restrictive than those imposed by schools on their students or employers on their employees. You should examine carefully the terms of the service agreement, and you always should obtain references from customers who use an ISP before signing any long-term contract.

Some ISPs limit the number of customers they serve, whereas others guarantee that you will not receive a busy signal when you dial in. These are significant factors in the quality of service you will experience. Remember, each ISP has a limited amount of bandwidth in its connection to the Internet. If your ISP allows more new customers to subscribe to its service than leave each month, each remaining user will have proportionally less bandwidth available. Be especially wary of ISPs that offer a large discount if you sign a long-term agreement. The quality of service might deteriorate significantly over time if the ISP adds many new customers without expanding its bandwidth.

You also should find out whether the ISP has an AUP and, if so, you should examine its terms carefully. Some ISPs have restrictive policies. For example, an ISP might have an entirely different fee structure for customers who use their Internet access for commercial purposes. Carefully outline how you plan to use your Internet connection and decide what services you want before signing any long-term contract with an ISP.

Connecting Through Your Cable Television Company

One of the more recent developments in the Internet access business is the cable modem. A **cable modem** performs a function similar to that of a regular modem; that is, it converts digital computer signals to analog signals. However, instead of converting the digital signals into telephone-line analog signals, a cable modem converts them into radio-frequency analog signals that are similar to television transmission signals. The converted signals travel to and from the cable company on the same lines that carry your cable television service. The cable company maintains a connection to the Internet and otherwise operates much like the ISPs discussed previously, which deliver an Internet connection through telephone lines.

To install a cable modem, the cable company first installs a **line-splitter**, a device that divides the combined cable signals into their television and data components, and then connects the television (or televisions) and the cable modem to the line-splitter. Most cable companies that offer this service rent the required line-splitter and cable modem to each customer.

Advantages and Disadvantages

The main advantage of a cable television connection to the Internet is its high bandwidth. A cable connection can provide very fast downloads to your computer from the Internet, as much as 170 times faster than a telephone line connection. Although upload speeds are not as fast, they are still about 14 times faster than a telephone line connection. The cost usually is higher than—and often more than double—what competing ISPs charge. However, if you consider that the cable connection might save you the cost of a second telephone line, the net benefit can be significant. The greatest disadvantage for most people right now is that the cable connection is simply not available in their area yet. Because cable companies must invest in expensive upgrades to offer this service, it might not become available in many parts of the U.S. for many years. You should remember that, other than the nature of the connection, a cable company is the same as any other ISP. Therefore, all of the issues outlined in the previous section about contracting with ISPs apply equally to dealing with your cable company.

Connecting Via Satellite

Many rural areas in the U.S. do not have cable television service and never will because their low population density makes it too expensive: A cable company cannot afford to run miles of cable to reach one or two isolated customers. People in these areas often buy satellite receivers to obtain television signals. Recently, Internet connections via satellite became available. The satellite connection is downlink only, so you also must have another connection through an ISP that uses telephone lines to handle the uplink half of the connection.

Advantages and Disadvantages

The major advantage of a satellite connection is speed. Although the speeds are not as great as those offered by cable modems, they are about five to 10 times greater than telephone connections. The speed increase is in one direction only, so you still send information to the Internet through a modem and telephone lines to an ISP. An ISP still is involved in this connection option, so all of the advantages and disadvantages outlined earlier also apply to a satellite connection. The cost of the satellite dish antenna and receiver still is fairly high, but prices are slowly dropping as more people become aware of this connection option. For users in remote areas, this technology often offers the best connection solution.

QUICK CHECK

1. To connect to the Internet, your computer must be part of a(n) _____.
2. What services do ISPs usually offer their customers?
3. How much greater bandwidth does ISDN offer over telephone service?
4. The Internet backbone today uses a combination of technologies to transmit data over long distances. Name and briefly describe three of these technologies.
5. Explain briefly how a modem enables a computer to transmit information over regular telephone lines.
6. Many schools and businesses have adopted acceptable use policies (AUPs). Describe the purpose of an AUP.
7. What conditions would lead you to consider connecting to the Internet via satellite?

You now have collected a great deal of information about the origins and history of the Internet and the Web. As you conducted your research project for TEPCo, you learned about some of the information and tools that exist on the Internet. You also gathered information about ways to connect to the Internet. Now you are ready to prepare your report for Lorraine and recommend a plan of action for connecting TEPCo to the Internet.

PROJECTS

1. **Diagramming School Networks**   Your school probably has a number of computer networks. At most schools, you can find information about computing facilities from the department of academic computing or the school library. Identify what LANs and WANs you have on your campus, and determine whether any or all of them are interconnected. Draw a diagram that shows the networks, their connections to each other, and their connection to the Internet.

2. **DARPA Alternatives**   The DARPA researchers that laid the foundation for the Internet were conducting research on ways to coordinate weapons control. They chose to develop a computer network that could operate without a central control mechanism. Think about alternative directions that the DARPA researchers might have taken to achieve their objective. Select one of these alternative directions, and discuss whether you think that approach would have given birth to something like the Internet. Describe how you think it would differ from the Internet and Web that exist today.

3. **School Cabling Choices**   Select two or three buildings on your campus that have computers in offices, dormitory rooms, or computing labs. Find out from the appropriate office administrator, dormitory official, or lab supervisor what kind of computer cable the school uses to connect the computers. Evaluate the school's cabling choices. Would you make the same decisions? Why or why not?

4. **Using the Web and E-mail**   Describe three ways in which you might use the Web or e-mail to identify part-time job and internship opportunities that relate to your major.

5. **Acceptable Use Policy Evaluation**   Obtain a copy of your school's or employer's acceptable use policy (AUP). Outline the main restrictions it places on student (or employee) activities. Compare those restrictions with the limits it places on faculty (or employer) activities. Analyze and evaluate any differences in treatment. If there are no differences, discuss whether the policy should be rewritten to include differences. If your school or employer has no policy, outline the key elements that you believe should be included in such a policy for your school or employer.

6. **Commercialization of the Internet**   Many people who have been involved with the Internet for many years believe that the National Science Foundation (NSF) made a serious mistake when it opened the Internet to commercial traffic. Discuss the advantages and disadvantages of this policy decision. Do you think that the Internet would be as successful as it is today if no commercial activity were allowed?

7. **The Web and the Memex Machine**   Vannevar Bush died before the Web came into existence. Speculate on what he would have thought about the Web. Would he have seen it as the embodiment of his Memex machine? Why or why not?

8. **Evaluating ISPs** Contact three ISPs in your area and obtain information about their Internet access and related services. You can find ISPs in your local telephone directory (try headings such as "Internet Services," "Computer Networks," or "Computer On-Line Services"), or look for advertisements in your local or student newspaper. Summarize the services and the charges for each service by ISP. Which ISP would you recommend for an individual? Why? Which ISP would you recommend for a small business? Why?

QUICK CHECK ANSWERS

Session 1.1

1. Printers, scanners, digital cameras, data files, programs, and so forth.
2. fiber-optic
3. The Internet uses packet switching, a method in which files and messages are broken down into packets that are labeled electronically with codes for their origin and destination. The packets travel along the network until they reach the destination computer, which collects the packets and reassembles the original data from the pieces in each packet.
4. protocol
5. e-mail, mailing lists, Usenet newsgroups, and adventure gaming
6. A LAN or WAN that uses the TCP/IP protocol but does not connect to sites outside a particular business firm or other organization.
7. Commercialization and the development of the WWW. Commercialization opened the Internet's potential to persons outside the academic and research communities, and the WWW graphical user interface (GUI) helped these new participants effectively use and add value to the Internet.
8. Web browser software

Session 1.2

1. network
2. Software to connect to the ISP, browse the Web, send and receive e-mail messages, transfer files, and log in to remote computers. Also, some ISPs provide network-consulting services and network management, training, and marketing advice.
3. two to four times
4. Leased telephone lines, satellite links, and radio communications links. Leased telephone lines include T1 lines, T3 lines, and Asynchronous Transfer Mode (ATM) connections. Satellite and radio links are used for the parts of the Internet that cross oceans and connect to remote locations.
5. A modem converts a computer's digital signals into analog signals that will travel over regular telephone lines (modulation). When the analog signal arrives at its destination, another modem converts the analog signals back into digital signals (demodulation).
6. An AUP specifies the conditions under which you can use your school's or your employer's Internet connection. AUPs often prohibit users from engaging in commercial activities, criminal activities, or specific threat-making or equipment-endangering practices.
7. Persons who live in remote areas that are not served by cable television providers would consider connecting to Internet via satellite if they desired a faster connection than that available through regular telephone lines.

TUTORIAL 2

OBJECTIVES

In this tutorial you will:

- Learn about e-mail and how it works
- Set up and use two popular e-mail programs
- Send and receive e-mail messages
- Print an e-mail message
- Forward and reply to e-mail messages
- Create folders to save your e-mail messages
- File and delete e-mail messages and folders
- Create and maintain an electronic address book

LAB

E-mail

BASIC E-MAIL: INTEGRATED BROWSER E-MAIL SOFTWARE

Evaluating E-Mail Alternatives

CASE

Sidamo's Magic Carpets

Sidamo's Magic Carpets is a large retail store that has been selling fine Oriental rugs since 1930. Ifram Sidamo opened his store on one floor of a large department store in Syracuse, New York. In the early days, Sidamo's sold all of its rugs to walk-in customers. Most new customers learned about Sidamo's through other customers who raved about Sidamo's high quality and variety of handmade rugs from Iran, India, Pakistan, and China.

Sidamo's Magic Carpets has grown considerably over the years, both in terms of size and sales volume. Today, Sidamo's boasts of customers from all over the United States as well as from many other countries. No longer a regional company, Sidamo's is now housed in a single, large store on the outskirts of Syracuse. With over 7,000 Oriental rugs in stock, Sidamo's offers a complete line of Oriental rugs that range in size from small mat and scatter rugs to large carpets. Over the past three years, Sidamo's has used extensive advertising campaigns to broaden its visibility. Barbara Goldberg, Sidamo's vice president of marketing, estimates that more than half of Sidamo's sales are from customers who have never visited Sidamo's showroom. Interestingly, 42 percent of all sales are to repeat customers.

Typically, a customer would see a Sidamo's advertisement in a magazine and then call the toll-free number to inquire about available rugs. This system has worked well so far, but Barbara believes that Sidamo's could serve a growing number of customers better—especially repeat customers—if it provided e-mail as an alternative way of contacting the Sidamo's sales staff. Barbara has hired you to put the new e-mail system in place. Your job includes evaluating available e-mail systems and overseeing the software's installation. Eventually, you will train the sales staff so they can use the new e-mail system efficiently and effectively.

SESSION 2.1

In this session, you will learn what e-mail is, how it travels to its destination, and the parts of a typical e-mail message. You will find out about signature files and how to use them. You will set up an e-mail client program to send, receive, print, delete, file, forward, reply to, and respond to e-mail messages. Finally, you will use an address book to manage your e-mail addresses.

What Is E-Mail and How Does It Work?

Electronic mail, or **e-mail**, is one of the most prevalent forms of business communication and the most popular use of the Internet. In fact, many people view the Internet as an electronic highway that transports e-mail messages, without realizing that the Internet provides a wide variety of services. E-mail travels across the Internet to its destination and is deposited in the recipient's electronic mailbox. While similar to other forms of correspondence, including letters and memos, e-mail has the added advantage of being fast and inexpensive. Instead of traveling through a complicated, expensive, and frequently slow mail delivery service such as a postal system, e-mail travels quickly, efficiently, and inexpensively to its destination across the city or around the world. You can send a message any time you want, without worrying about when the mail is picked up or delivered or adding any postage. In business and recreation today, people rely on e-mail as an indispensable way of sending messages and data to each other. Businesses today depend on e-mail to deliver mission-critical and time-sensitive information to other businesses, customers, and employees internal to the organization.

E-mail travels across the Internet like other forms of information—that is, in small packets, which are reassembled at the destination and delivered to the addressee, whose address you specify in the message. When you send an e-mail message to its addressee, the message is sent to a **mail server**, which is a hardware and software system that determines from the recipient's address one of several electronic routes to send your message. When you send an e-mail message to another person, the message is routed from one computer to another and is passed through several mail servers. Each mail server determines the next leg of the journey for your message until it finally arrives at the recipient's electronic mailbox.

Sending e-mail uses one of the many technologies used on the Internet. Special **protocols**, or rules that determine how the Internet handles message packets flowing on it, are used to interpret and transmit e-mail. **SMTP (Simple Mail Transfer Protocol)** decides which paths your e-mail message takes on the Internet. SMTP handles outbound mail; another protocol called **POP (Post Office Protocol)** takes care of incoming messages. POP is a standard, extensively used protocol that is part of the Internet suite of recognized protocols. Other protocols used to deliver mail include **IMAP (Internet Message Access Protocol)** and **MIME (Multipurpose Internet Mail Extensions)**. IMAP is a protocol for retrieving mail messages from a server, and MIME protocol specifies how to encode nontext data, such as graphics and sound, so they can travel over the Internet.

When an e-mail message arrives at its destination mail server, the mail server's software handles the details of distributing the e-mail locally, much like a mail-room worker unbundles a bag of mail and places letters and packages into individual departmental or personal mail slots. When the server receives a new message, it is not saved directly on the recipient's individual computer, but rather, it is held on the mail server. When you check for new e-mail messages, you use a program stored on your personal computer (PC) to request the mail server to deliver any stored mail to your PC. The software that requests mail delivery from the mail server to your PC is known as **mail client software**. You will learn about two popular e-mail client programs—Netscape Messenger and Microsoft Outlook Express—in Sessions 2.2 and 2.3, respectively.

Anatomy of an E-Mail Message

An e-mail message consists of two major parts: the message header and the message body. The **message header** contains all the information about the message, and the **message body** contains the actual message. A message header contains the recipient's e-mail address (To), the sender's e-mail address (From), and a subject line (Subject), which indicates the topic of the message. In addition, the message header can contain a carbon copy (or courtesy copy) address (Cc), a blind carbon copy (or blind courtesy copy) address (Bcc), and, sometimes, an attachment filename. Normally, your name automatically appears in the From line when you send a message. When you receive an e-mail message, the date and time it was sent and other information is added to the message automatically.

Figure 2-1 shows a message that Barbara Goldberg wrote to Ifram Sidamo, the company president. The memo contains an attached file named 800LineSales.xls, which is a spreadsheet composed using a spreadsheet program that was embedded to the message. Notice that Ifram's e-mail address appears in the To line. When Ifram receives Barbara's message, Barbara's name and e-mail address will appear in the From line. Following good e-mail etiquette, Barbara included a short Subject line so Ifram can determine the content of the message quickly. The Cc line indicates that the marketing department will receive a copy of the message. Sylvia Sidamo, Ifram's vice president of sales, also will receive a copy of the message, but Sylvia's e-mail address is on the Bcc line, so neither Ifram nor the marketing department will know that she also received a copy of the message. Each of the message parts is described next.

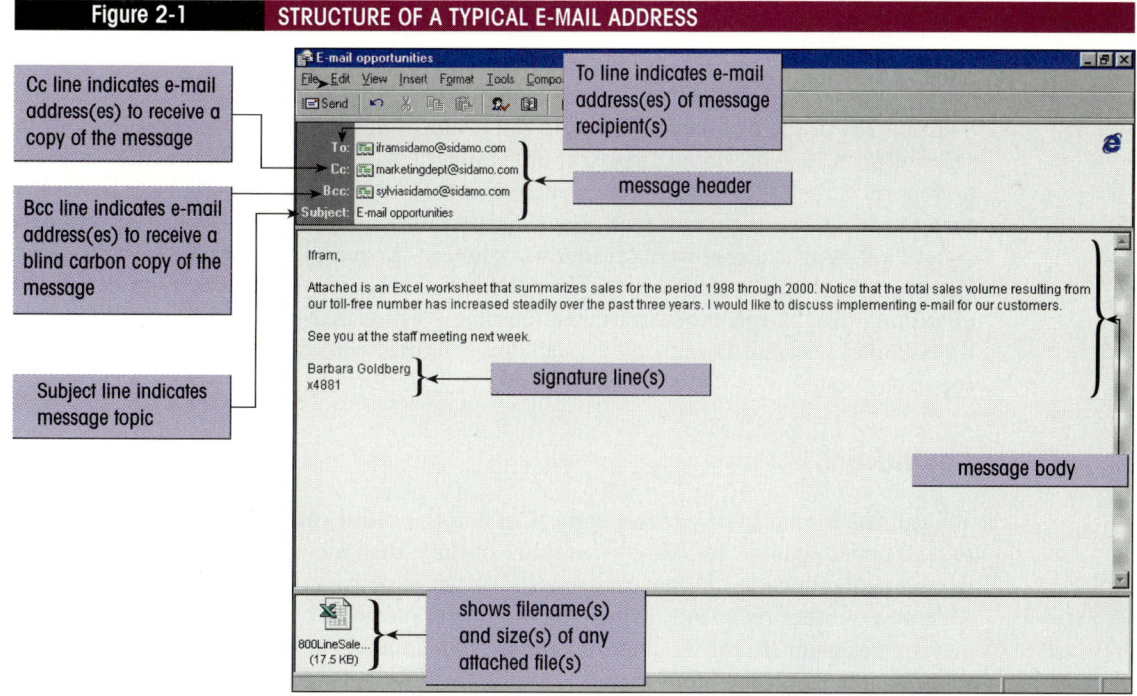

Figure 2-1 STRUCTURE OF A TYPICAL E-MAIL ADDRESS

To

You type the recipient's full e-mail address in the **To line** of an e-mail header. Usually, the To line is at the top of the header. Be careful to type the address correctly; otherwise, the e-mail cannot be delivered. You can send mail to multiple people by typing a comma between the individual e-mail addresses. There is no real limit on the number of addresses you can type in the To line or in the other parts of the e-mail header that require an address. Figure 2-2 shows the message header for a message that Barbara is sending to three people.

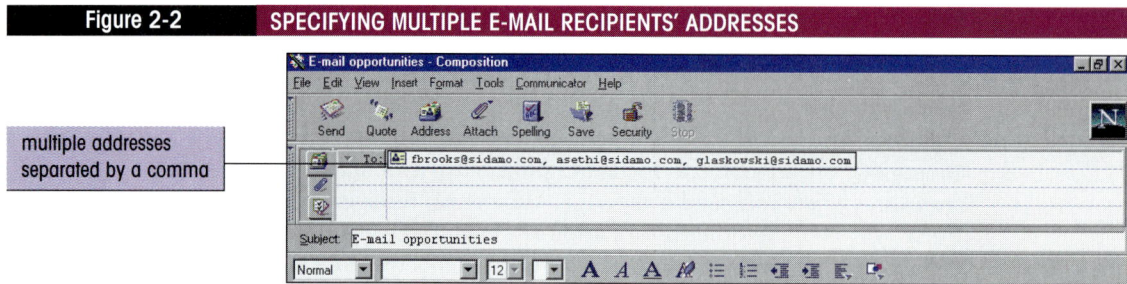

Figure 2-2 SPECIFYING MULTIPLE E-MAIL RECIPIENTS' ADDRESSES

multiple addresses separated by a comma

Sometimes, the To address contains one physical mailing address that is not one person's address, but rather, a message to a special service called a **mailing list**. In a mailing list, the single e-mail address contains dozens or even thousands of individual e-mail addresses.

From

The **From line** of an e-mail message includes the sender's e-mail address. Most e-mail programs automatically insert the sender's e-mail address into all messages. Even if you don't insert your e-mail address in an outgoing message, the recipient *always* sees the sender's e-mail address in the message—in other words, you cannot send anonymous e-mail.

Subject

The content of the **Subject line** is very important. Often, the person receiving your message will scan an abbreviated display of incoming messages, looking for the most interesting or important messages based on the contents of the Subject line. If the Subject line is blank, then the recipient might not read the associated message immediately. It is always best to include a message subject so the reader has a hint of the message's contents and importance. For example, a subject line such as "Just checking" is far less informative and certainly less interesting than "Urgent: new staff meeting time." The e-mail message shown in Figure 2-1, for example, contains the subject "E-mail opportunities" and thus indicates that the message concerns e-mail.

Cc and Bcc

You can use the optional **carbon copy (Cc)** and the **blind carbon copy (Bcc)** header lines to send mail to people who should be aware of the e-mail message but who are not the message's main addressees. When an e-mail message is delivered, every recipient can see the addresses of other recipients, except for those who receive a blind carbon copy. Neither the primary recipient (in the To line) nor those recipients on the carbon copy list are aware of those recipients on the blind carbon copy list because Bcc addresses are hidden from messages sent to people on the To and Cc lists. However, recipients on the Bcc list are aware of others who receive blind copies. For example, if you send a thank you message to a salesperson for performing a task especially well, you might consider sending a blind carbon copy to that person's supervisor. That way, the supervisor knows a customer is happy and that the praise was unsolicited.

Attachments

Because of the way the messaging system is set up, you can send only plain-text messages using SMTP—the protocol that handles outgoing e-mail. When you need to send a more complex document, such as a Word document or an Excel worksheet, you send it along as an attachment. An **attachment** is encoded so that it can be carried safely over the Internet, to "tag along" with the message. Frequently, the attached file is the most important part of the e-mail message, and the message body contains a brief statement such as "The worksheet you requested is attached." Barbara's e-mail message contains an attachment whose location and filename (on Barbara's computer) appear in the Attached line in the header. The attachment is stored on Barbara's computer on drive C with the filename 800LineSales.xls. You can attach more than one file to an e-mail message, and files can be delivered to more than one recipient at the same time. E-mail attachments provide a convenient way of transmitting electronic documents of various types to a colleague down the hall or around the world.

When you receive an e-mail message with an attached file, you can preview it within the message or save it and review it later. E-mail programs differ in how they handle and display attachments. Several e-mail programs represent an attached file with an icon that represents the program associated with that file type. In addition to an icon, several programs also display an attached file's size in kilobytes (a **kilobyte** is approximately 1,000 characters) and indicate the attached file's name. Other e-mail programs display an attached file in a preview window when they recognize the attached file's format and can start a program to display the file. In any case, you can always save the file and later execute a program associated with the file type.

With most e-mail client programs, you can easily detach an attached file, examine the file, and save it. An icon representing an attached file accompanies the file. To open the attached file, you click the icon. If a worksheet is attached to an e-mail message, for example, a spreadsheet program on your computer starts and opens the worksheet. Similarly, a Word file opens inside the Word program when you click the icon representing the Word file inside your e-mail message. Saving an open attachment is simple. Usually, you click File on the menu bar, and then click Save or Save As in the program displaying the attached file. Then, you indicate the disk and folder into which you want to save the attached file.

Message Body and Signature Files

Most often, people use e-mail to write short, quick messages. However, e-mail messages can be dozens or hundreds of pages long, although the term *pages* has little meaning in the e-mail world. Few people using e-mail think of a message in terms of page-sized chunks; e-mail is more like an unbroken scroll with no physical page boundaries.

Frequently, an e-mail message includes an optional **signature** that identifies more detailed information about the sender. You can sign a message by typing your name and other information at the end of the message for each message you send, or you can create a signature file. A **signature file** contains the information you routinely type at the end of your e-mail messages. You can instruct your e-mail program to insert the signature file into every message automatically to save a lot of time. The signature usually contains the sender's name, title, and company name. Signature files often contain a complete nonelectronic address, facsimile telephone number, and a voice phone number. Periodically, signature files include graphics, such as a company logo, or the sender's favorite quotation or saying. Enclosing a signature file in an e-mail message ensures that e-mail recipients can contact you in a variety of ways besides using your e-mail address. For example, in Figure 2-1, Barbara's signature file contains her full name and her internal company phone extension.

Signatures can be either formal or informal, or a hybrid. A **formal signature** typically contains the sender's name, title, company name, company address, telephone and fax numbers, and e-mail address. **Informal signatures** can contain graphics or quotations that express a more casual style found in correspondence between friends and acquaintances. Most e-mail software programs automatically include a signature at the end of each e-mail message you send. You can modify your signature easily or choose not to include it in selected messages. Most e-mail programs allow you to create multiple signature files so you can choose which one to include when sending a message.

When you create a signature, don't overdo it. A signature that is extremely long is in bad taste—especially if it is much longer than the message. It is best to keep a signature to a few lines that identify alternative ways to contact you. Figure 2-3 shows two examples of signatures. The top signature is informal and typical of one you might send to a friend. The bottom signature is Barbara's formal signature that she uses for all external business correspondence to identify herself, her title, and her mailing and telephone information.

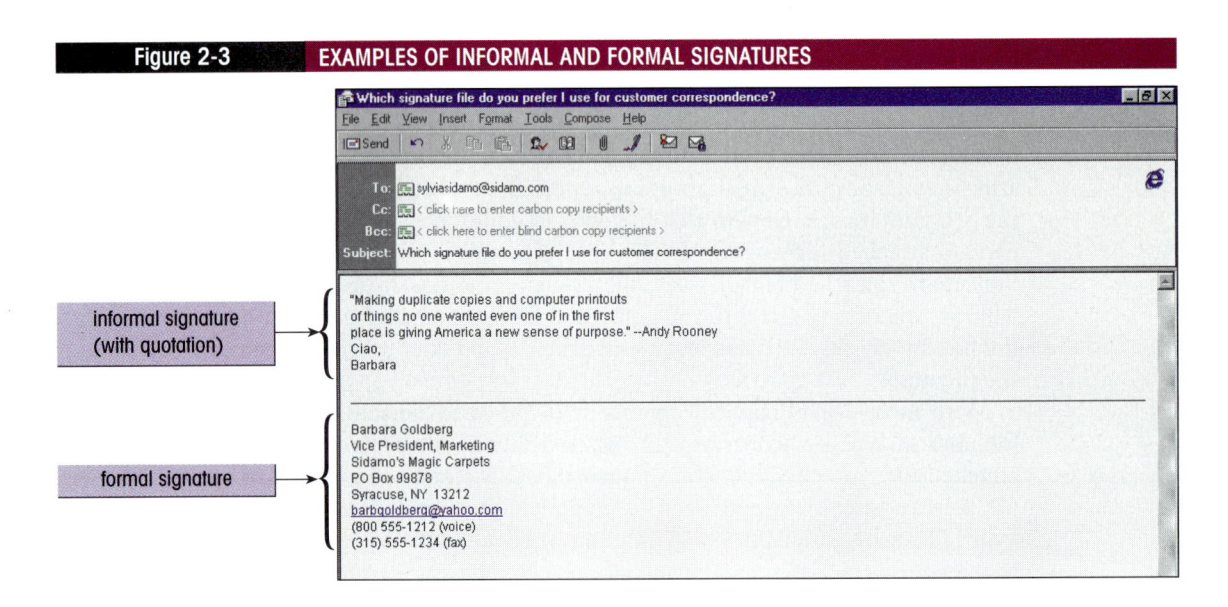

Figure 2-3 EXAMPLES OF INFORMAL AND FORMAL SIGNATURES

informal signature (with quotation):
"Making duplicate copies and computer printouts of things no one wanted even one of in the first place is giving America a new sense of purpose." --Andy Rooney
Ciao,
Barbara

formal signature:
Barbara Goldberg
Vice President, Marketing
Sidamo's Magic Carpets
PO Box 99878
Syracuse, NY 13212
barbgoldberg@yahoo.com
(800) 555-1212 (voice)
(315) 555-1234 (fax)

E-Mail Addresses

E-mail addresses, also called Internet addresses, uniquely identify an individual or organization that is connected to the Internet. They are like telephone numbers—when you want to call anyone in the world, you dial a series of numbers that route your call through a series of switchboards until your call reaches its destination. For example, calling a friend in San Diego from another country requires you to dial the country code for the United States first (the country code varies according to the country from which you are calling). Then, you must know the area code for the part of San Diego in which your friend lives, and dial that three-digit number. Finally, you dial the final seven digits of your friend's local number. Like telephone numbers, e-mail addresses consist of a series of numbers. Usually, addresses consist of three or four groups of numbers that are separated by periods. For instance, the number 192.55.87.1 is an **Internet Protocol address**, or more commonly an **IP address**, which corresponds to a single computer connected to the Internet. The IP address uniquely identifies the computer at the organization you want to contact. To route an e-mail message to an *individual* whose mail is stored on a particular computer, you must identify that person by his or her account name, or **username**, and also by the computer on which mail is stored. The two parts of an e-mail address—the username and the computer name—are separated by an at sign (@). Barbara Goldberg, for example, uses the username *barbgoldberg* to access her e-mail. If her account were stored on a Sidamo computer whose address is 123.404.678.9, then one form of her e-mail address would be barbgoldberg@123.404.678.9.

Fortunately, you rarely have to use numeric IP addresses. Instead, you use **host names**, which are unique names that are equivalent to IP addresses. By using a host name, Barbara

Goldberg's address is simply *barbgoldberg@sidamo.com*, which is much easier to remember and certainly less errorprone. A full e-mail address consists of your username, followed by an @ sign, followed by the host name (or address). A username usually specifies a person within an organization, although it can sometimes refer to an entire group. Sometimes, you can select your own username, but frequently the organization through which you obtain an e-mail account has rules about acceptable usernames. Some organizations insist that the username consist of a person's first initial followed by up to seven characters of the person's last name. Other institutions prefer that your username contain your full first and last names separated by an underscore character (for example, Barbara_Goldberg). Occasionally, you can pick a nickname such as "ziggy" or "bigbear" as your username. When typing e-mail addresses, the usage of upper- and lower-case letters does matter and the *spelling* is important. When mail cannot be delivered, the electronic postmaster sends the mail back to you and indicates the addressee is unknown—just like conventional mail.

The host name (or host address) is the second part of an e-mail address. The host name specifies the computer to which the mail is to be delivered on the Internet. Host names contain periods, which usually are pronounced "dot," to divide the host name. The most specific part of the host name appears first in the host address followed by more general destination names. Barbara's host name, sidamo.com (and pronounced "sidamo dot com"), contains only two names separated by a period. The suffix *com* in the address indicates that this company falls into the large, general class of commercial locations.

Host names can consist of more than two parts. For example, Figure 2-4 shows that the host name *condor.cs.missouri.edu* contains four parts. Clusters of related computers are sometimes given related names such as earth, wind, and fire. In this address, *condor* is one of several related computers. Where is this computer located? The second name, *cs*, is a common abbreviation for computer science. In all likelihood, the computer belongs to the computer science department. Judging by the third part of the host name, *missouri*, it's a good bet that the institution is located in Missouri or at the University of Missouri. The *edu* host name suffix indicates the organization is an educational institution of some sort. Taken together, the host name parts strongly point to the University of Missouri's computer science department. With a little imagination and experience, you can decipher most host names and determine the location of the computers to which the names refer.

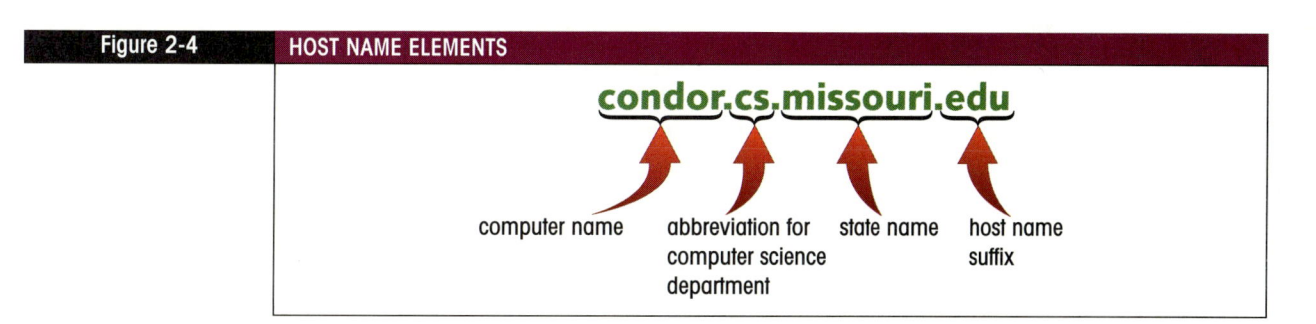

Figure 2-4   HOST NAME ELEMENTS

condor.cs.missouri.edu

- condor → computer name
- cs → abbreviation for computer science department
- missouri → state name
- edu → host name suffix

E-Mail Programs

Several programs for managing e-mail are available today because no single program works on all computers. The good news is that you can use any e-mail program to send mail to people with different e-mail clients. The recipient will be able to read your mail and you will be able to read mail from other people, regardless of which e-mail programs are used. If you have an Internet service provider (ISP) with a PPP or SLIP connection, then you can choose from a large selection of e-mail client programs that run on your PC and periodically check the mail server for incoming mail. On the other hand, you might have to use the e-mail program provided by your college or university if you have a dial-up connection that does not provide access to the Internet. Some e-mail programs—called **shareware**—are free or very inexpensive, and others are not. Some e-mail programs are software clients that run on your computer and receive the mail from the mail server. Other e-mail programs run strictly on a server machine that you access from your personal computer, which acts as a dumb terminal. A **dumb terminal** is an otherwise "smart" computer that passes all your keystrokes to another computer to which you are connected and does not attempt to do anything else during the e-mail session. Examples of popular e-mail clients operating in the Windows environment are Netscape Messenger, Microsoft Outlook Express, and Eudora. A widely used e-mail program running on larger, multiuser computers is Pine. Especially popular on university campuses, Pine is a simple system that accepts and displays only plain-text messages. In your future personal and professional life, chances are good that you will encounter a different system from the one you are currently using, so it's a good idea to learn about different e-mail clients.

Free E-Mail Clients

Several free e-mail programs are available on the Internet. Some free programs require you to access e-mail through the Web, and others have a proprietary program that you install on your computer. Examples of free e-mail programs that you access from any Web browser include Yahoo!Mail, ExciteMail, and HotMail. Another program is Juno, which is an example of a free proprietary e-mail program that was one of the earliest free e-mail services. One advantage that these e-mail services share is that you can have e-mail service without being affiliated with an organization. Before these free e-mail services came to the Internet, many people who were not students or employees of a company could not use e-mail. Now, anyone with an Internet connection can use these services to send and receive e-mail messages.

To use e-mail provided by HotMail, ExciteMail, or Yahoo!Mail, you apply for an e-mail account. In order to apply for an e-mail account, you visit the Web site of the company offering free e-mail with your Web browser. (You will learn about Web browsers in Tutorial 3.) When you apply for free e-mail, you probably will be asked to supply a small amount of information about yourself. Then, you choose a username and secret password. Next, the e-mail service checks to see that no one else has applied for the same username you requested. If the username is available, then you are immediately enrolled in the e-mail service. On the other hand, if someone already has the username you selected, the service will ask you to try a different username or change the one you chose slightly by adding digits to the end of it.

Once you have one of the Web-based e-mail accounts, such as Yahoo!Mail, you can send and receive e-mail. A big advantage of Web-based e-mail accounts is that you can get your e-mail from any computer with a Web browser and Internet access. In other words, you can access your e-mail account in Mexico City, Hong Kong, or any other place where there is public access to a Web browser. This is an advantage for people who travel a lot and do not want to incur long-distance telephone charges when accessing their own e-mail server from another city or country.

Juno and other similar services offer a different type of free e-mail service. First, you must install its free software on your computer, and then you activate a Juno e-mail account. The program automatically dials the Juno computer and establishes an e-mail account with a username and password of your choosing—subject to the username not being assigned already. Subsequently, you can access your e-mail from the same computer on which you installed it. The big disadvantage of Juno and systems like it is that you must install the Juno program on any computer on which you want to access your e-mail, which is sometimes impractical for people who travel a lot and use different computers to access their e-mail.

You might wonder how these companies can provide free e-mail—after all, nothing is free! The answer is advertising. With each e-mail message you receive, you also receive some sort of advertisement—either large or small—in the message itself or stored on your computer. Advertising revenues pay for free e-mail. So, you must decide whether you are willing to put up with a little advertising for the free e-mail service. Most users of these free services agree that seeing some ads is a small price to pay for the great convenience e-mail provides.

Setting Up and Using Your E-Mail Client

Many ISPs support POP (Post Office Protocol) or SMTP (Simple Mail Transfer Protocol), whereby the mail server receives mail and stores it until you use your mail client software to request the mail server to deliver mail to your computer. Similarly, when you send e-mail from your computer, that mail is forwarded across the Internet until it reaches its destination. Once e-mail reaches the mail server at the addressee's location, it is stored. Subsequently, e-mail is downloaded from the server to a user on request. In either case—sending or receiving and reading e-mail—a client program must notify the mail server to deliver the mail or accept outgoing mail.

Your message might not be sent to the mail server immediately, depending on how the e-mail client is configured on your computer. A message can be **queued**, or temporarily held with other messages, and sent when you either exit the program or check to see if you received any new e-mail.

Remember, e-mail correspondence can be formal or informal, but you still should follow the rules of good writing and grammar. After typing the content of your message—even a short message—it is always a good idea to check your typing and spelling. Most mail systems do not allow you to retract mail after you send it, so you should examine your messages carefully *before* sending them. Always exercise politeness and courtesy in your messages. Don't write anything in an e-mail message that you wouldn't want someone else to post on a public bulletin board.

Receiving Mail

The mail server is always ready to process mail; in theory, it never sleeps. That means that when you receive e-mail, it is held on the mail server until you start the e-mail client on your PC and ask the server to retrieve your mail. Most clients allow you to save delivered mail in any of several standard or custom mailboxes or folders on your PC. However, the mail server is a completely different story. Once the mail is delivered to your PC, one of two things can happen to it on the server: either the server's copy of your mail is deleted, or it is preserved and marked as delivered or read. Marking mail as **delivered** or **read** is the server's way of identifying new mail from mail that you have read. For example, when Barbara receives mail on the Sidamo mail server, she might decide to save her accumulated mail—even after she reads it—so she has an archive of all of her received e-mail messages. On the other hand, Barbara might want to delete old mail to save space on the mail server. Both methods have advantages—saving old mail on the server lets you access your mail from *any* PC that can connect to your mail server. If you automatically delete mail after reading it, you don't have to worry about storing and organizing messages that you don't need, which requires less effort.

Printing a Message

Reading mail on the computer is fine, but there are times when you will need to print a copy of some or all of your messages. Other times, you need to file your mail in an appropriate mailbox and deal with it later or simply file it for safekeeping. You also might find that you don't need to keep or file certain messages, so you can read and immediately delete them. Most client programs provide these facilities to help you manage your electronic correspondence.

The majority of programs let you print a message during or after you compose it or after mail has been received or sent. The Print command usually appears on the File menu in a GUI program, or there is a Print button on the toolbar. In a character-based program, the Print command usually is a key combination, such as Ctrl + P.

Filing a Message

Most clients let you create separate mailboxes or folders in which to store related messages. You can create new mailboxes or folders when needed, rename existing mailboxes and folders, or delete folders and their contents when you no longer need them. You can move mail from the incoming mailbox or folder to any other mailbox or folder to file it. Some programs let you use a **filter** to move incoming mail into one or several mailboxes or folders automatically based on the content of the message. If your client does not allow the use of filters, you can filter the messages manually by reading them and filing them in the appropriate folder.

Forwarding a Message

You can forward any message that you receive to one or more recipients. When you **forward** a message to another recipient, a copy of the original message is sent to the new recipient you specify, without the original sender's knowledge. You can forward a misdirected message to another recipient, or you can forward a message to someone who was not included in the original message routing list.

For example, suppose you receive a message intended for someone else, or the message requests information that you do not have but you know a colleague who does know the information. In either case, you can forward the message you received to the person who can deal with the request best. When you forward a message, your e-mail address and name appear automatically on the From line, and most e-mail clients amend the Subject line with the text "Fwd," "Forward," or something similar to indicate that the message is being forwarded. You simply fill in the To line and then send the message. Optionally, the message you received is quoted. A **quoted** message is a copy of the sender's original message that is returned to the sender with your comments added. Each line of the quoted message is preceded by a special mark (usually the greater than symbol, >). When you respond to a message someone sent to you, it is a good idea to include parts of the sender's message, or the quoted message. That way, the receiver can recall his or her original statement or question and therefore better understand your "yes, I agree with you" response.

Replying to a Message

When you **reply** to a message, the e-mail client automatically formats a new, blank message and addresses it to the sender. Replying to a message is a quick way of sending a response to someone who sent a message to you. When you reply to a message, the client automatically addresses a new message to the sender of the original message. Most clients will copy the entire message from the original message and place it in the response window. Usually, a special mark, such as >, appears at the beginning of each line of the response to indicate the text of the original message. When you are responding to more than one question, it is a good idea to type your responses below the original questions. That way, the recipient can understand the context of your responses better. When you respond to a message that has been sent to a number of people—perhaps some people received the message as a carbon copy—be careful about responding. You can choose to respond to all the original recipients or just to the sender.

Deleting a Message

On most e-mail clients, deleting a message is a two-step process, to avoid accidental deletions of important messages. First, you temporarily delete a message by placing it in a "trash" folder or by marking it for deletion. Then, you permanently delete the trash or marked messages by emptying the trash or by indicating to the client to delete the messages. It is a good idea to delete unneeded mail.

Maintaining an Address Book

E-mail addresses sometimes are difficult to remember and type, especially when you send many e-mail messages to the same recipients. You can use an **address book** to save e-mail addresses and convenient nicknames to remember them by. The features of an e-mail address book vary by e-mail client. Usually, you can organize information about individuals or companies. Each entry in the address book can contain an individual's full e-mail address (or a group e-mail address that represents several individual addresses), a person's real name, and the person's complete contact information. In addition, some e-mail clients allow you to include notes for each address book entry. You can assign a unique nickname to each entry so it is easier to refer to e-mail addresses when you need them.

After saving entries in your address book, you can refer to them at any point while you are composing, replying to, or forwarding a message. You can review your address book and sort the entries in alphabetical order by nickname, or you can view them in last name order. Of course, you can switch between several sort orders any time you want—even as you are creating a message.

Creating a Multi-Address Entry

What happens if you need to send the same e-mail message to different recipients? You could send the message to all recipients by typing their nicknames in the To line and separating them with a comma. But what if you need to send a message to an entire department or the entire sales staff? You can create a handy address entry called a distribution list. A **distribution list**, or a **group mailing list**, is a single nickname that represents more than one individual e-mail address. For example, you might use the nickname "Web Site" to save the e-mail addresses of your partners on a Web site project. When you need to send a message to your partners, you just type "Web Site" in the To line, and then the client will send the same message to each individual's e-mail address.

QUICK CHECK

1. True or False: E-mail travels across the Internet in small clusters.
2. The special rules governing how information is handled on the Internet are collectively called _____ .
3. An e-mail message consists of two parts: the message _____ and the message _____ .
4. Explain why it is a good practice to include a Subject line in your e-mail messages.
5. True or False: You use the Bcc line in an e-mail message to send copies of a message to others without the principal addressee knowing who received a copy.
6. Can you send a spreadsheet file over the Internet? If so, how?
7. The four-part number comprising an Internet address is known as a(n) _____ address.
8. Why is it important to include part of the sender's message in your reply?
9. What advantage(s) does a distribution list or mailing list provide when sending a message to many recipients?

Now that you understand some basic information about e-mail and e-mail client software, you are ready to start using your e-mail client. If you are using Netscape Messenger, your instructor will assign Session 2.2; if you are using Microsoft Outlook Express, your instructor will assign Session 2.3. The authors recommend, however, that you read both sessions so you are familiar with both e-mail clients. In the future, you might encounter a different e-mail client on a public or employer's computer, so it is important to be familiar with both clients. Fortunately, most e-mail clients work the same so it is easy to use other programs once you master the basics.

SESSION 2.2

In this session you will learn how to use Netscape Messenger to send and receive e-mail. You will learn how to print, file, save, delete, respond to, and forward e-mail messages. Finally, you will organize your e-mail addresses in an address book.

Netscape Messenger Client

You continue to express your enthusiasm for your newly assigned task of evaluating e-mail software. **Netscape Messenger**, or simply **Messenger**, is the e-mail client that is an integral part of the Netscape Communicator suite. You installed Netscape Communicator and are anxious to start using Messenger. Barbara stopped by to ask you a few questions about the program and wants you to use Messenger to e-mail items, such as the weekly marketing meeting agenda, to members of the marketing department staff. You start Messenger by using the Start menu or by double-clicking a desktop icon, if one was installed. Figure 2-5 shows the Message List window.

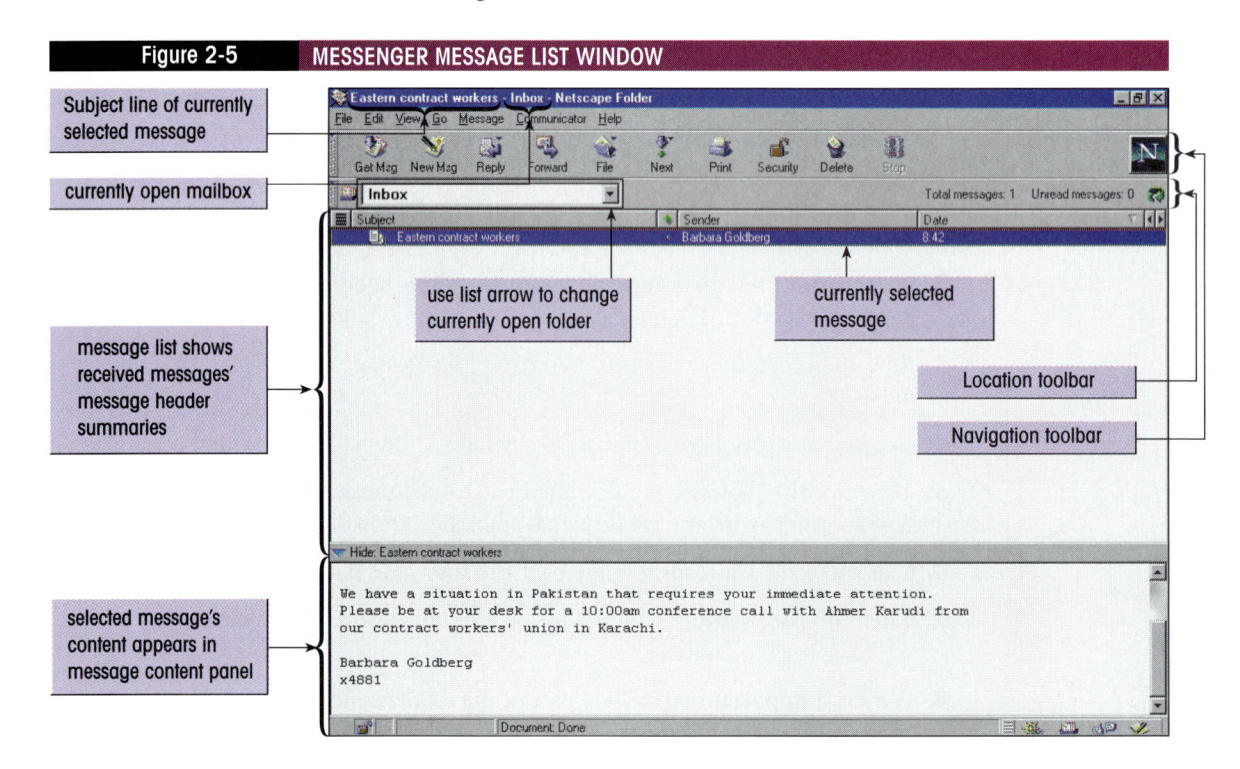

Figure 2-5   MESSENGER MESSAGE LIST WINDOW

- Subject line of currently selected message
- currently open mailbox
- use list arrow to change currently open folder
- currently selected message
- Location toolbar
- Navigation toolbar
- message list shows received messages' message header summaries
- selected message's content appears in message content panel

Messenger uses four different windows to furnish the tools you need to manage your e-mail: the Message List, Netscape Message Center, Netscape Message, and Composition windows. When you start Messenger, the Message List window shown in Figure 2-5 opens. The

Message List window opens the **Inbox,** which is one of several mailboxes, and displays its contents in two panels. The top panel shows a summary of messages, called **message header summaries**. The lower panel, or the **message content panel**, shows the contents of a selected message header summary.

The **Netscape Message Center window** contains a list of your mailboxes, mail folders, and discussion groups. You open the Netscape Message Center window by clicking Communicator on the menu bar and then clicking Message Center. When you open the Netscape Message Center window, you can see the mailboxes on your computer (see Figure 2-6). Mailboxes in the list shown in Figure 2-6 include Inbox, Unsent Messages, Drafts, Sent, Trash, and Samples. News, another item on the Local Mail list, contains mail from **newsgroups**, which are Internet discussion groups on a specified topic. The Inbox contains your incoming mail messages.

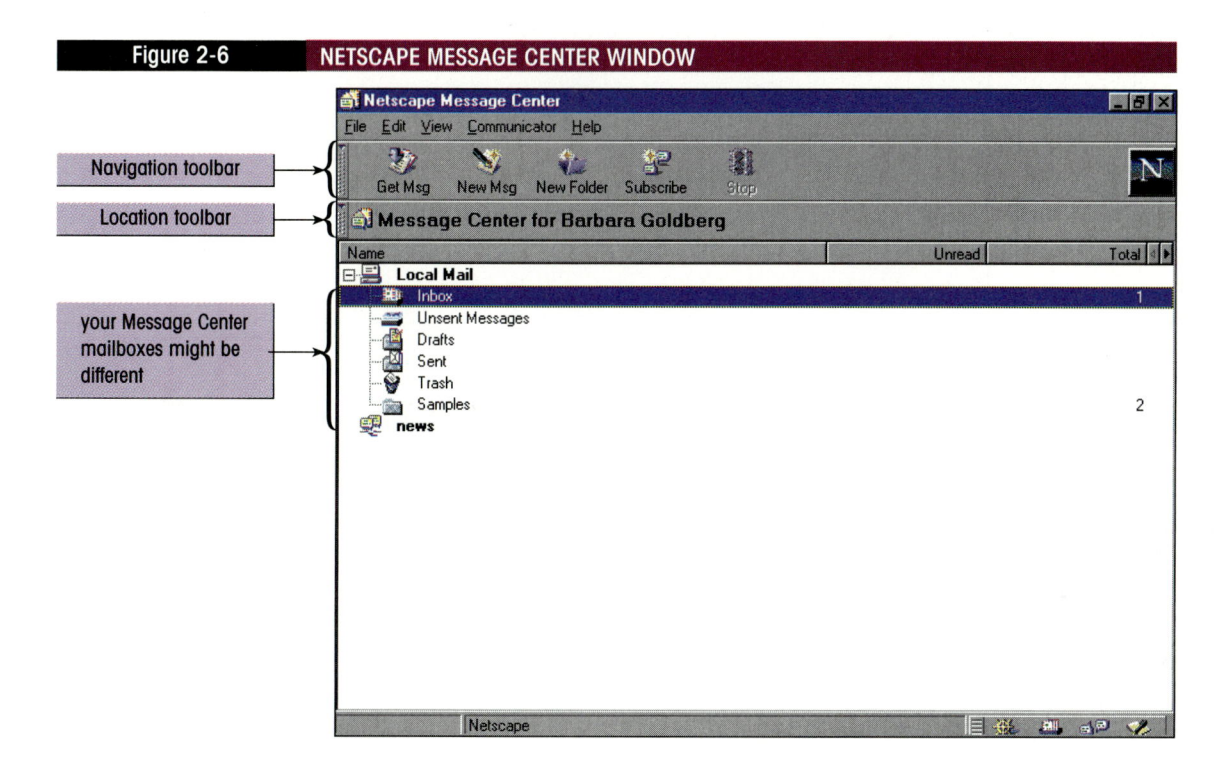

Figure 2-6 NETSCAPE MESSAGE CENTER WINDOW

The **Netscape Message window** shown in Figure 2-7 shows your individual messages. You use the Netscape Message window to respond to a message, file it in one of several mailboxes, forward a message to someone else, print a message, or delete it. You open the Netscape Message window by double-clicking any message header summary in the Message List window.

You use the **Composition window** shown in Figure 2-8 to create messages. You open the Composition window by clicking the New Message button on the Navigation toolbar in the Message List or Netscape Message windows. The Composition window toolbar contains buttons to send e-mail, quote (paste) information from another person's e-mail message, use the address book to find someone's e-mail address, attach files, check spelling, save an e-mail message as a draft, or stop a current message after sending it. When you start a new message, you will see the To, From, Cc, and Bcc lines in the Composition window.

Figure 2-7 NETSCAPE MESSAGE WINDOW

- Navigation toolbar
- Location toolbar
- message's subject appears in the title bar

Figure 2-8 COMPOSITION WINDOW

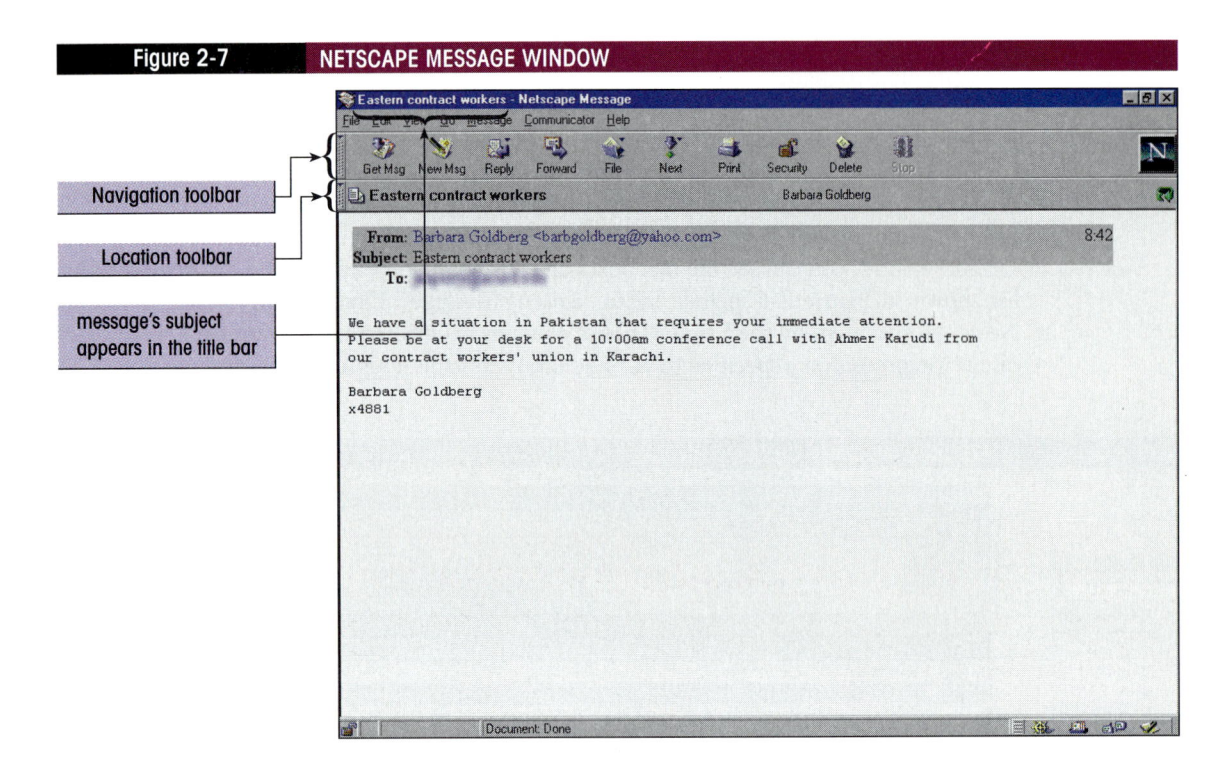

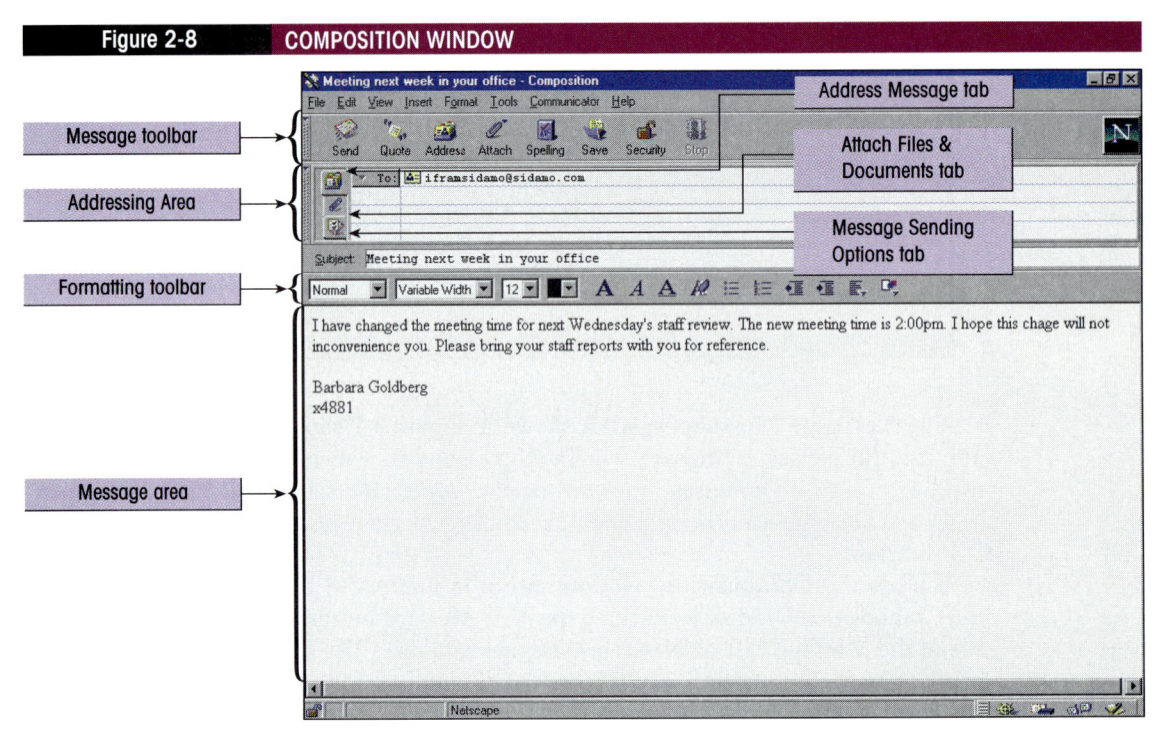

- Message toolbar
- Addressing Area
- Formatting toolbar
- Message area
- Address Message tab
- Attach Files & Documents tab
- Message Sending Options tab

Setting Up E-Mail

You are eager to start using Messenger to see if Sidamo's customers can use it to contact sales representatives. Cost is not a consideration because the Netscape Communicator suite—including Netscape Messenger—is free. Your first step is to start and configure Messenger so it fetches and sends *your* e-mail.

TUTORIAL 2 BASIC E-MAIL: INTEGRATED BROWSER E-MAIL SOFTWARE   WEB 2.15

To start and initialize Messenger for use on a public computer:

1. Click the **Start** button on the Windows taskbar, point to **Programs**, point to **Netscape Communicator**, and then click **Netscape Messenger** to start the program. The Message List window opens (see Figure 2-5).

2. Click the **New Msg** button on the Navigation toolbar to open the Composition window (see Figure 2-8). If necessary, click the **Maximize** button on the Composition window title bar so the window fills the desktop.

3. Click **Edit** on the menu bar, and then click **Preferences**. The Preferences window opens and shows the preferences for the Mail & Groups category.

4. If necessary, click the **plus sign** to the left of the Mail & Groups category to show the different settings that you can change. (After you click the plus sign, it changes to a minus sign.) To set up your e-mail information, you will change the settings in the Mail Server category. See Figure 2-9.

Figure 2-9   PREFERENCES WINDOW

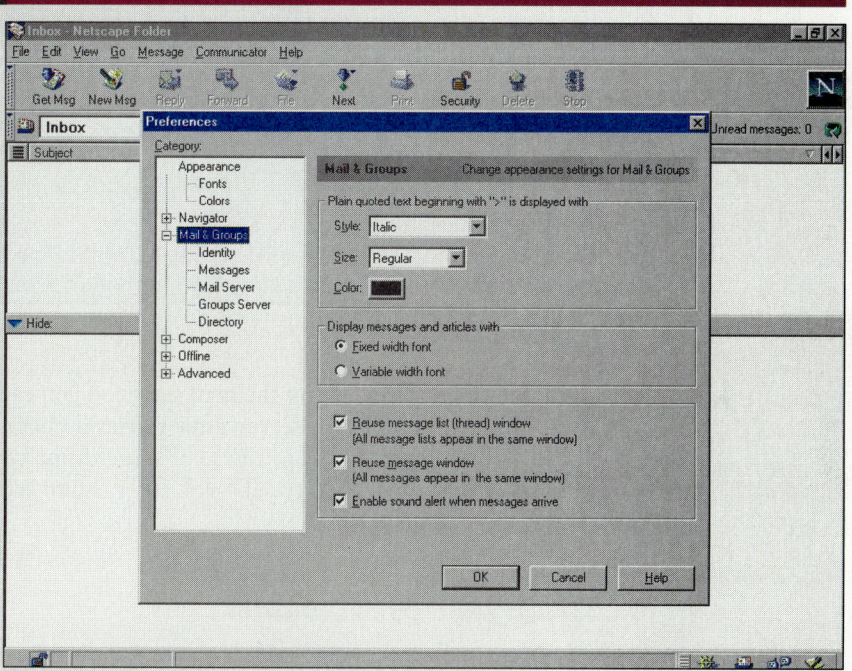

5. Click **Mail Server** in the Category list to open the Mail Server settings on the right side of the window.

    TROUBLE? If you (or someone else) already set up your account, then go to Step 4 in the next set of steps ("To change your e-mail name").

6. Type your e-mail address (or login name) in the Mail server user name text box, and then press the **Tab** key to go to the Outgoing mail (SMTP) server text box.

7. Type the name of the server that processes your outgoing mail. Your instructor or technical support person will provide you with this name. Usually, your outgoing mail server name is either SMTP or MAIL followed by a domain name.

8. Press the **Tab** key to move the insertion point to the Incoming mail server text box, and then type the name of the server that processes your incoming mail. (Your instructor or lab manager will provide you with this name.) Usually, your incoming mail server name is POP, POP3, or IMAP followed by a domain name. Figure 2-10 shows Barbara Goldberg's information.

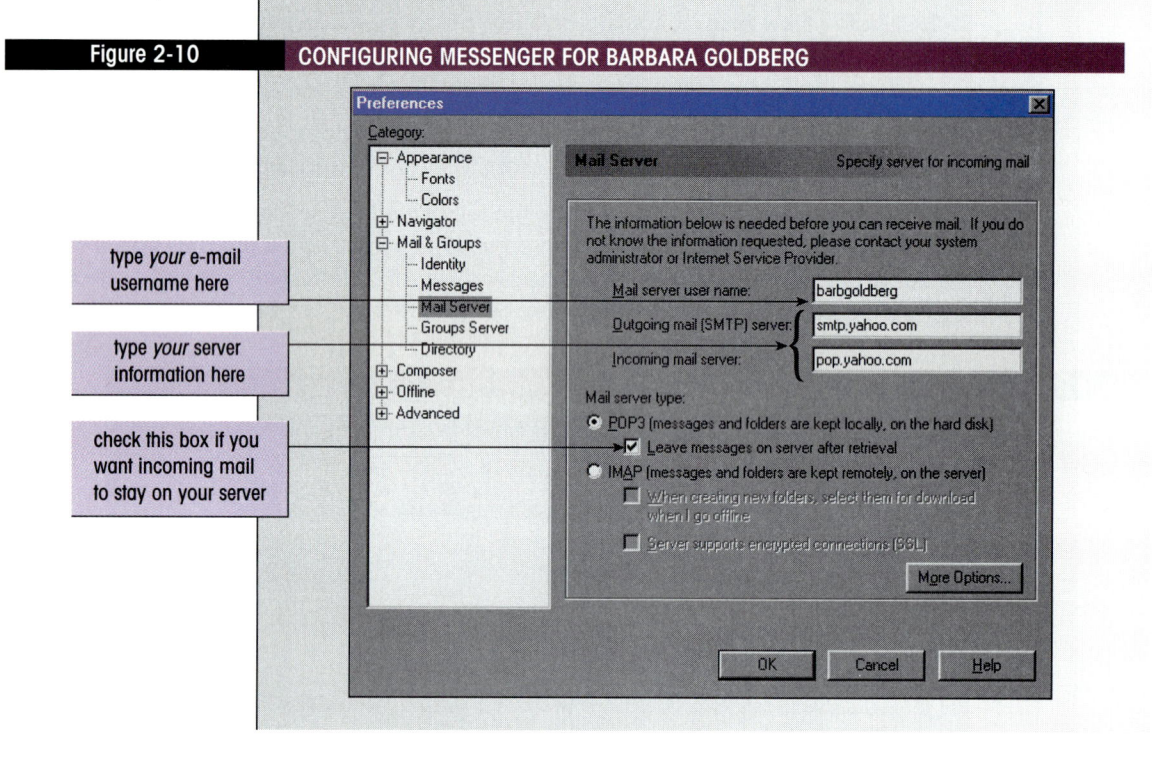

Figure 2-10 — CONFIGURING MESSENGER FOR BARBARA GOLDBERG

- type *your* e-mail username here
- type *your* server information here
- check this box if you want incoming mail to stay on your server

If you want your mail to remain on the mail server so you can read it from any computer, then check the Leave messages on server after retrieval check box. Otherwise, the server will delete your e-mail messages from the mail server after you retrieve your e-mail. You aren't finished configuring Messenger yet—you still need to set up the way that your e-mail is identified to its recipients.

To change your e-mail name:

1. Click **Identity** in the Category list to open the Identity settings in the right side of the window.

2. If necessary, click in the Your name text box, and then type your first and last names. Type your name the way you want it to appear in the message summary header when recipients receive your messages.

3. Press the **Tab** key to move the insertion point to the Email address text box, and then type your full e-mail address. Figure 2-11 shows the Identity tab for Barbara Goldberg. The values you enter in the Identity panel have no affect on your ability to send or receive e-mail; these text boxes only identify a name and associated address in the From text box of your outgoing e-mail messages.

4. Click the **OK** button to close the Preferences window.

TUTORIAL 2 BASIC E-MAIL: INTEGRATED BROWSER E-MAIL SOFTWARE   WEB 2.17   INTERNET

| Figure 2-11 | ADDING YOUR IDENTITY INFORMATION |

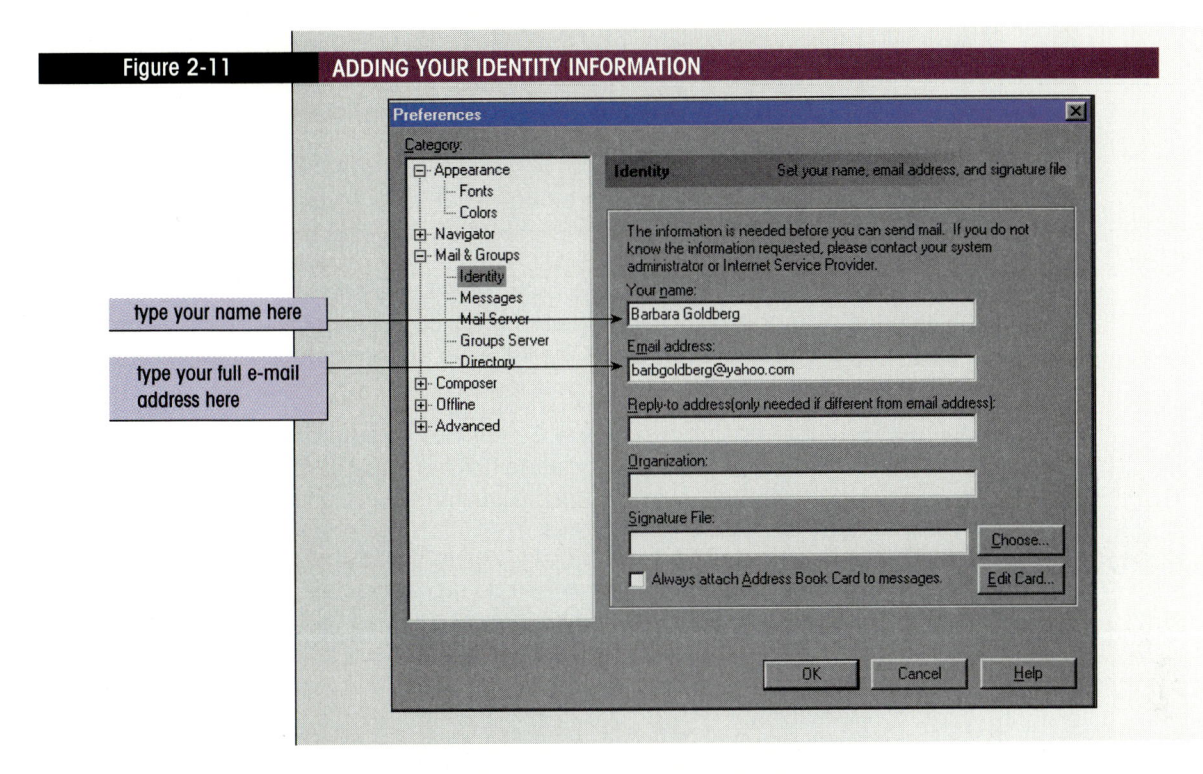

type your name here → Your name: Barbara Goldberg

type your full e-mail address here → E-mail address: barbgoldberg@yahoo.com

Now your copy of Messenger is set up to send and receive messages, so you are ready to send a message to Barbara.

Note: In this tutorial, you will send messages to a real mailbox with the address barbgoldberg@yahoo.com. Follow the instructions carefully so you use the correct address. Messages sent to this mailbox are deleted without being opened or read, so do not send important messages to this address.

Sending a Message Using Messenger

You decide to use Messenger to send a message with an attached file to Barbara. You will send a carbon copy of the message to your own e-mail address to make sure that the message and attached file are sent correctly. The Composition window is open, so you are ready to start typing Barbara's e-mail address.

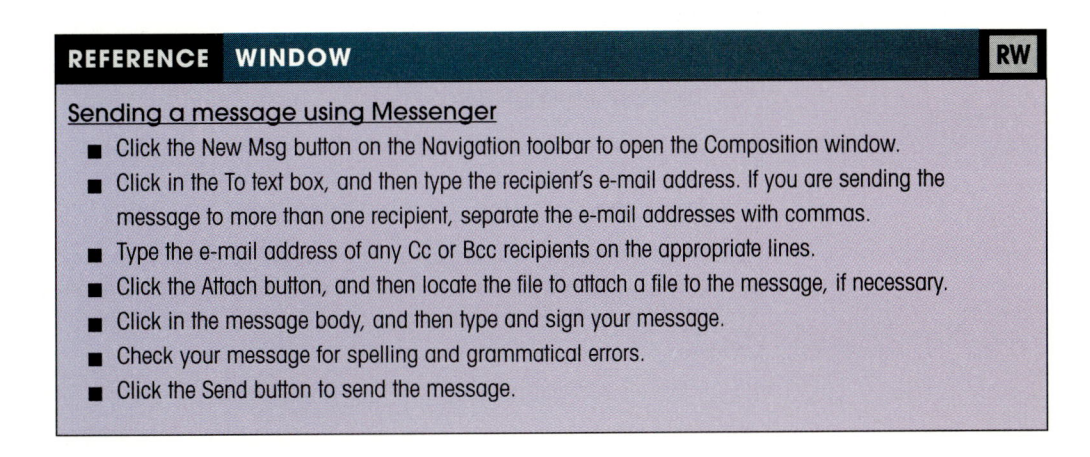

REFERENCE WINDOW

Sending a message using Messenger
- Click the New Msg button on the Navigation toolbar to open the Composition window.
- Click in the To text box, and then type the recipient's e-mail address. If you are sending the message to more than one recipient, separate the e-mail addresses with commas.
- Type the e-mail address of any Cc or Bcc recipients on the appropriate lines.
- Click the Attach button, and then locate the file to attach a file to the message, if necessary.
- Click in the message body, and then type and sign your message.
- Check your message for spelling and grammatical errors.
- Click the Send button to send the message.

To send a message with an attachment:

1. Click in the To text box, and then type **barbgoldberg@yahoo.com**.

   TROUBLE? Make sure that you use the address barbgoldberg@yahoo.com, instead of barbgoldberg@sidamo.com. If you type Barbara's e-mail address incorrectly, your message will be returned with an error message attached.

2. Click the empty box below the To button in the message header. When the second To button appears (below the first one), click it to show a list of alternate text boxes, and then click **Cc:** in the list. A Cc button replaces the To button on the second line of the message header.

3. Type your full e-mail address in the Cc text box so you will receive a copy of your own message. It is a good idea to have a copy of all electronic correspondence as a reference. Most e-mail programs allow you to choose whether to save a copy of messages you send.

   TROUBLE? If you make a typing mistake on a previous line, use the arrow keys or click the insertion point to return to a previous line so you can correct your mistake. If the arrow keys do not move the insertion point backward or forward in the header block, then press Shift + Tab or the Tab key to move backward or forward, respectively.

4. Click in the **Subject** text box, and then type **Test message**.

5. Click the **Attach** button on the Message toolbar, and then click **File** in the drop-down list. The Enter file to attach dialog box opens.

6. Make sure your Student Disk is in drive A. Click the **Look in** list arrow, and select **3½ Floppy (A:)** to display the list of folders on your Student Disk.

7. Double-click the **Tutorial.02** folder to open it, and then double-click the file named **Market.wri** to close the dialog box. The Attach Files & Documents tab changes color, and the filename appears on the first line of the Addressing Area. The color change indicates one or more files are attached to the message.

8. Click the **Address Message** tab to see the message recipients' addresses again.

9. Click in the message body, and then type **Please let me know that this message arrived safely and that you are able to read it and the attached file with no difficulty. I'm testing Netscape Messenger and want to make sure that it is working properly.**

10. Press the **Enter** key twice, and then type your first and last name to sign your message. See Figure 2-12.

11. Click the **Spelling** button on the Message toolbar to check your spelling before sending the message. If necessary, correct any typing errors. When you are finished, click the **Done** button to close the Check Spelling dialog box.

12. Click the **Send** button on the Message toolbar to send the message. The Composition window closes, and the message is sent to the mail server for delivery to Barbara. The Message List window reappears.

TUTORIAL 2 BASIC E-MAIL: INTEGRATED BROWSER E-MAIL SOFTWARE   WEB 2.19   INTERNET

TROUBLE? If you see a message that says "No SMTP server has been specified in the Mail and Groups Preferences," then you did not provide enough information about your mail server and your login name. Return to the Composition window, click Edit on the menu bar, click Preferences, click the Mail & Groups category, click the Mail Server category, and then ask your instructor or technical support person for the correct mail server user name, outgoing mail (SMTP) server name, and incoming mail server. After entering this information, click the OK button and repeat Step 12 to continue.

Figure 2-12 **SENDING A TEST MESSAGE USING MESSENGER**

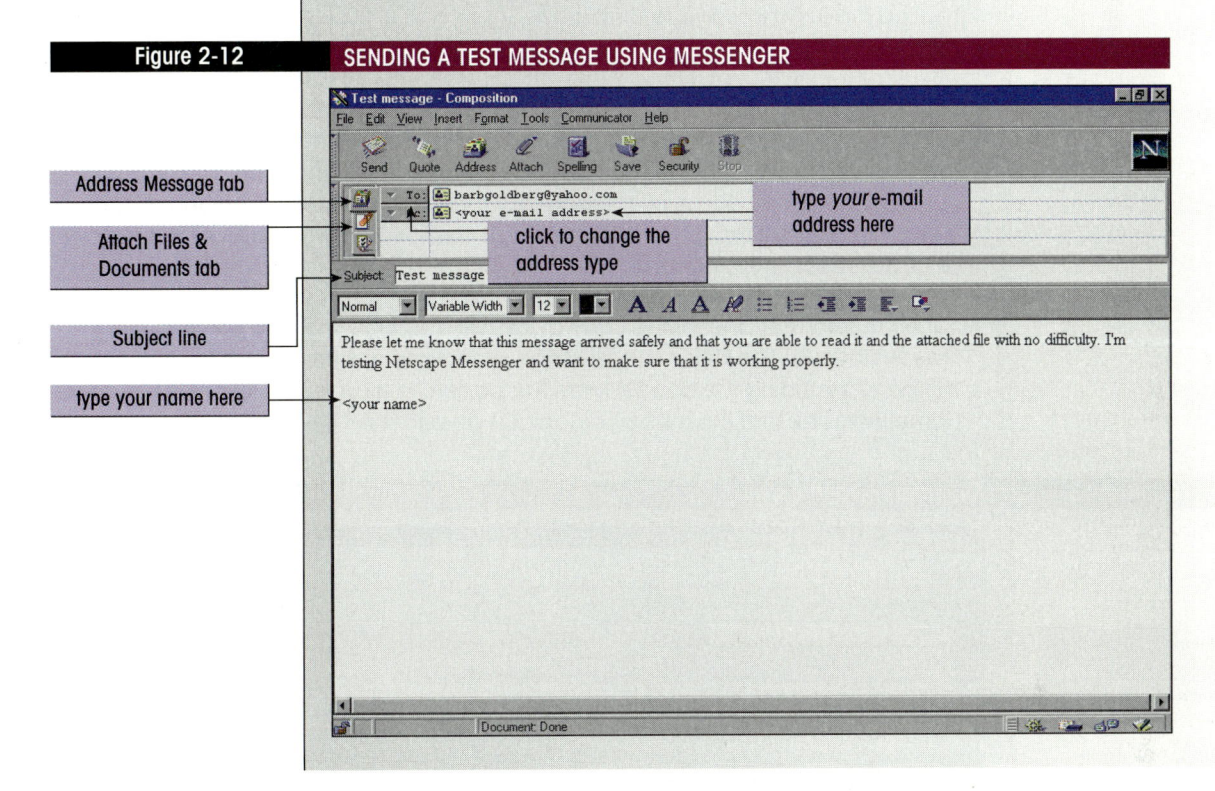

- Address Message tab
- Attach Files & Documents tab
- Subject line
- type your name here
- type *your* e-mail address here
- click to change the address type

Depending on your system configuration, Messenger might not send your message immediately. Instead, it might queue (hold) the message until you connect to your Internet service provider (ISP). When you are ready to send your messages, you can send all the queued messages at once when you connect to your ISP.

Receiving and Reading a Message

When you receive new mail, messages that you have not opened have a closed envelope to their left in the message list summaries, and messages that you have opened have an open envelope next to them. Messages that have an attached file have a paperclip icon in their message summaries. Next, you will check your e-mail to see if you received the Cc copy of the message you sent to Barbara.

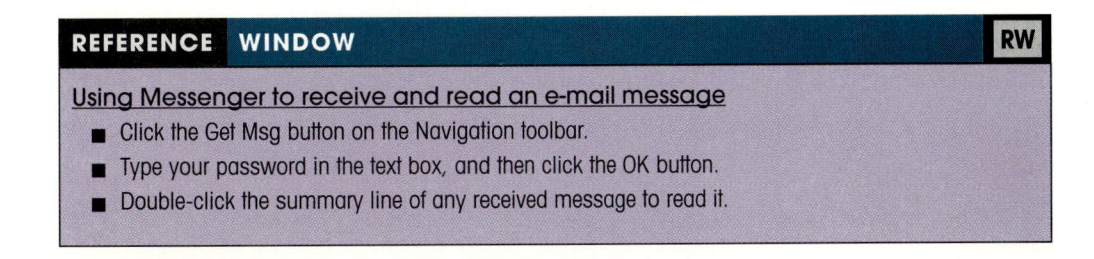

REFERENCE WINDOW   RW

Using Messenger to receive and read an e-mail message
- Click the Get Msg button on the Navigation toolbar.
- Type your password in the text box, and then click the OK button.
- Double-click the summary line of any received message to read it.

To check for incoming mail:

1. Click the **Get Msg** button on the Navigation toolbar in the Message List window. The Password Entry Dialog dialog box opens.

2. Type your password in the text box, and then click the **OK** button. Depending on your system configuration, you might have to connect to your ISP to get your new mail. Within a few moments, your mail server transfers all new mail to your Inbox. You should see the Cc message that you sent to yourself when you mailed the test message to Barbara.

    TROUBLE? If you do not see any incoming messages in your Inbox, then you either did not receive any new mail or you might be looking in the wrong mailbox. If necessary, click the list arrow next to the mailbox name on the Location toolbar, which is just above the message summary list, and then click Inbox. If you still don't have any mail messages, wait a few moments and then repeat Steps 1 and 2 until you receive a message. Sometimes mail delivery slows down at peak times during the day.

3. Click the summary line for the copy of the test message that you just received in the message list. The Netscape Message window opens and shows the full message, including the header lines. The paperclip icon to the right of the sender's name indicates that the message contains an attached file. See Figure 2-13.

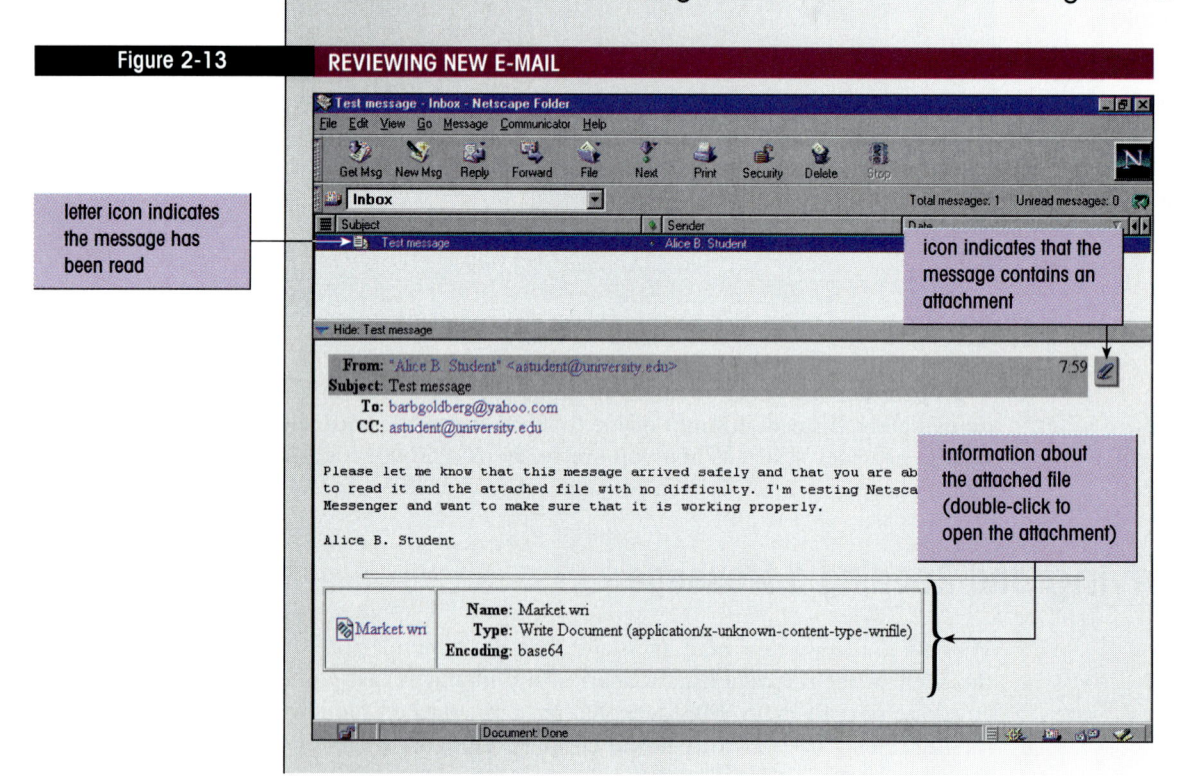

Figure 2-13   REVIEWING NEW E-MAIL

- letter icon indicates the message has been read
- icon indicates that the message contains an attachment
- information about the attached file (double-click to open the attachment)

You received your Cc copy of the test message that you sent to Barbara, and the paperclip icon indicates that you received an attached file with the message. Now you can open the attachment in a preview window, or save it for viewing later. Open the attachment next.

Opening and Saving an Attached File

You want to make sure that your attached file was sent properly, so you decide to open it in the preview window. After you are finished looking at an attached file, you can decide whether to save or delete it from your system.

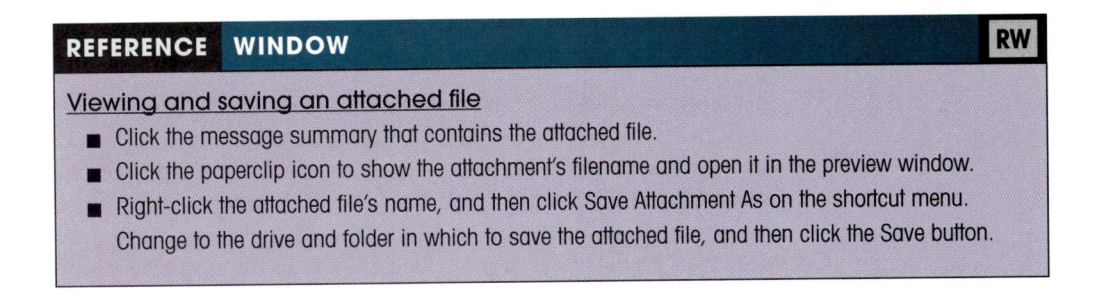

REFERENCE WINDOW — RW

Viewing and saving an attached file
- Click the message summary that contains the attached file.
- Click the paperclip icon to show the attachment's filename and open it in the preview window.
- Right-click the attached file's name, and then click Save Attachment As on the shortcut menu. Change to the drive and folder in which to save the attached file, and then click the Save button.

To view an e-mail attachment:

1. Click the paperclip icon in the Netscape Message window to show the attachment's filename.

2. Right-click the attachment name **Market.wri** icon near the bottom of the screen. (You might need to scroll down the window to see the icon.) A shortcut menu opens.

3. Click **Save Attachment As** on the shortcut menu to open the Save Messages As dialog box.

4. Click the **Save in** list arrow, and then select the drive that contains your Student Disk.

5. Double-click the **Tutorial.02** folder to open it. Change the suggested filename to **Memo1.wri** (see Figure 2-14).

Figure 2-14 — SAVING AN ATTACHED FILE

- Tutorial.02 folder is open
- type new filename here

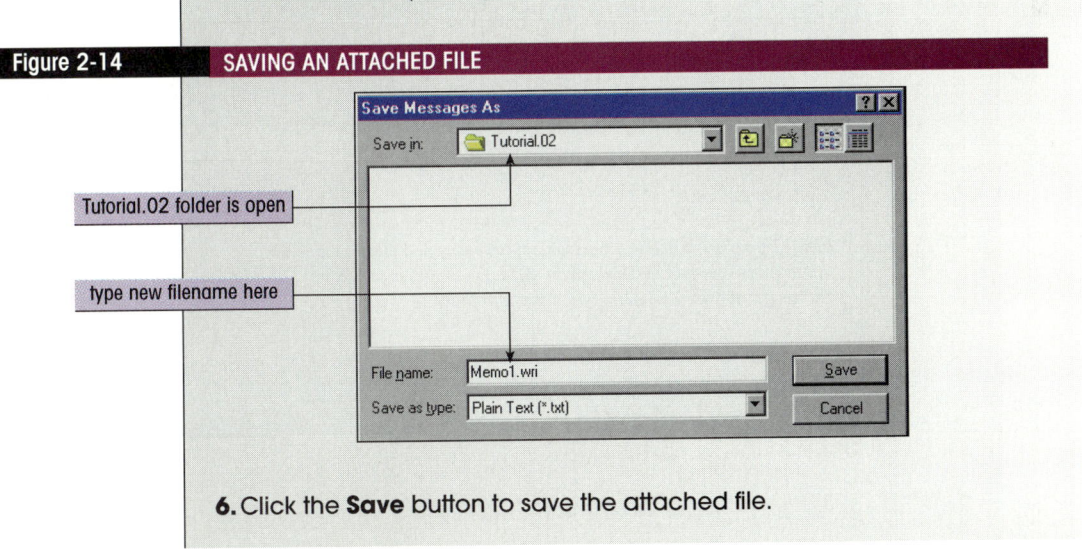

6. Click the **Save** button to save the attached file.

Replying to and Forwarding Messages

You can forward any message you receive to someone else. Similarly, you can respond to the sender of a message quickly and efficiently to respond to a sender's message. You will reply to and forward messages extensively as you use e-mail.

Replying to an E-Mail Message

To reply to a message, select the message summary line in the Message List window and click the Reply button on the Navigation toolbar. Click Reply to Sender or Reply to Sender and All Recipients, whichever is appropriate. Messenger opens a Composition window and places the original sender's address in the message header To text box. You can leave the Subject line as is or modify it. Most systems, including Messenger, will copy the entire message from the original message and place it in the response window. Usually, a special mark in one edge of the response indicates what part is the original message. After typing your response, you click the Composition window Send button to send your response to the original message's author.

If you are responding to a question, it is a good idea to intersperse your responses below each question from the original message so the recipient can better understand the context of your responses. When you respond to a message that was sent to a number of people—perhaps some people received the message as a carbon copy—be careful how you respond. You can choose to respond to all the original recipients or just to the sender. Figure 2-15 shows the Composition window that opens when you reply to a message sent by Alice B. Student.

Figure 2-15 REPLYING TO A MESSAGE

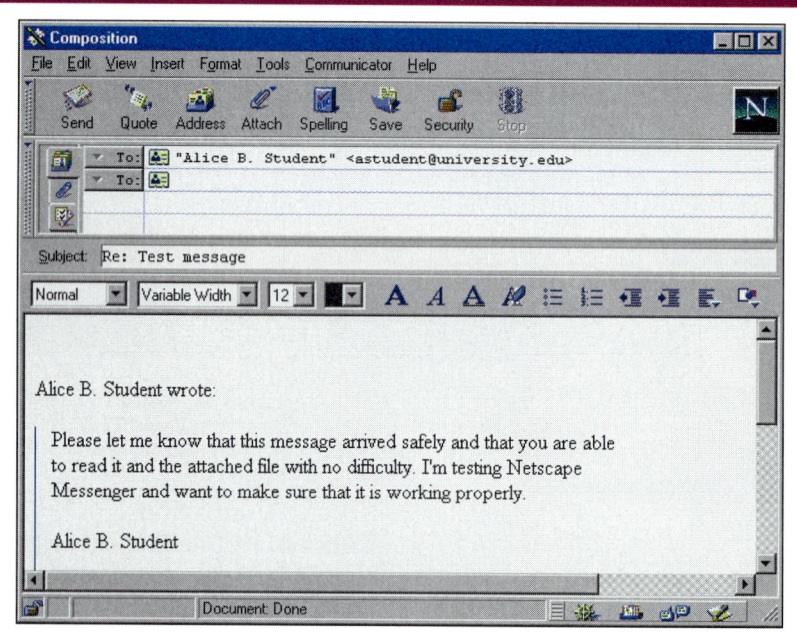

> **REFERENCE WINDOW**
>
> **Replying to a sender's message**
> - Click the message summary of the message to which you want to reply to select it.
> - Click the Reply button on the Navigation toolbar. A menu will appear so you can select an option to reply only to the sender, or to the sender and all other recipients. Click one of these options to open the Composition window. The Composition window will include a To line with the address of the sender or the sender and all recipients, depending on your selection. You can type other recipients' e-mail addresses in the message header as needed.
> - The Subject line includes the subject of the original message, plus "Re:" to indicate that this is a reply message. You can change the Subject line by editing it, if necessary.
> - The message body includes one blank line at the top of the window, and the text of the original message, which is indicated with a vertical blue line in the left margin. You can type a message on the blank line (use as much space as you require). You also can delete any of the original message that you don't need. For example, you might type a message such as, "I received your message today, thank you." at the top of your reply message.
> - Send the message by clicking the Send button on the Message toolbar.

Forwarding an E-Mail Message

When you forward a message, it is removed from your Inbox folder and travels to the person to whom you are forwarding the message. To forward an existing mail message to another user, open the folder containing the message (usually, the Inbox folder) in the Message List window, double-click the message summary to open a full Message window, and click Message on the menu bar, and then click Forward Quoted. The Composition window opens and displays the message to forward along with a full message header. The forwarded message is marked with a line to the left side. You can include your own comments along with the message itself. Figure 2-16 shows the Composition window for forwarding a message. You can forward a message to more than one person by including each e-mail address in the To, Cc, or Bcc text boxes as necessary.

> **REFERENCE WINDOW**
>
> **Forwarding an e-mail message**
> - Click the message summary for the message that you want to forward to another person.
> - Click the Forward button on the Navigation toolbar to open the Composition window.
> - If you want to include the text from the original message, click Message on the menu bar, and then click Forward Quoted. The Subject line changes to include "Fwd:" and the original message's subject so the recipient knows that this is a forwarded message.
> - Click in the To text box, and then type the e-mail address of the recipient. You can forward one message to multiple recipients or Cc and Bcc recipients by including the recipients' e-mail addresses on these lines.
> - The message body includes one blank line at the top of the window, and the text of the original message if you are sending a quoted message, which is indicated with a vertical blue line in the left margin. You can type a message on the blank line (use as much space as you require). Also, you can delete any of the original message that you don't need. For example, you might type a message such as, "I thought you might be interested in this message that I received." at the top of your forwarded message. If you do not see in your reply the message you received, then click the Quote button on the Message toolbar. The message will appear.
> - Send the message by clicking the Send button on the Message toolbar.

INTERNET   WEB 2.24   TUTORIAL 2   BASIC E-MAIL: INTEGRATED BROWSER E-MAIL SOFTWARE

Figure 2-16   FORWARDING A MESSAGE

[Screenshot of Composition window showing a forwarded message. To: Sylvia@sidamo.com, Ifram@sidamo.com, billg@microsoft.com. Subject: [Fwd: Eastern contract workers]. Body: "Barbara Goldberg wrote: We have a situation in Pakistan that requires your immediate attention. Please be at your desk for a 10:00am conference call with Ahmer Karudi from our contract worker's union in Karachi. Barbara Goldberg x4881"]

Filing an E-Mail Message

You can use Messenger mail folders to file your e-mail messages by category. When you file a message, you move it from the Inbox to another folder. You also can make a *copy* of a message in the Inbox and save it in another folder. You will make a copy of your Cc message and save it in a folder named "Marketing" for safekeeping. You can create other folders to suit your individual working style.

To create a new folder:

1. Click **File** on the menu bar in the Message List window, and then click **New Folder**. The New Folder dialog box opens.

2. Type **Marketing** in the Name text box to name the new folder. You will create this folder as a sub-folder of the Inbox folder.

3. Make sure that the Create as a subfolder of list box shows the Inbox. If it doesn't, then click the list arrow and click **Inbox**. See Figure 2-17.

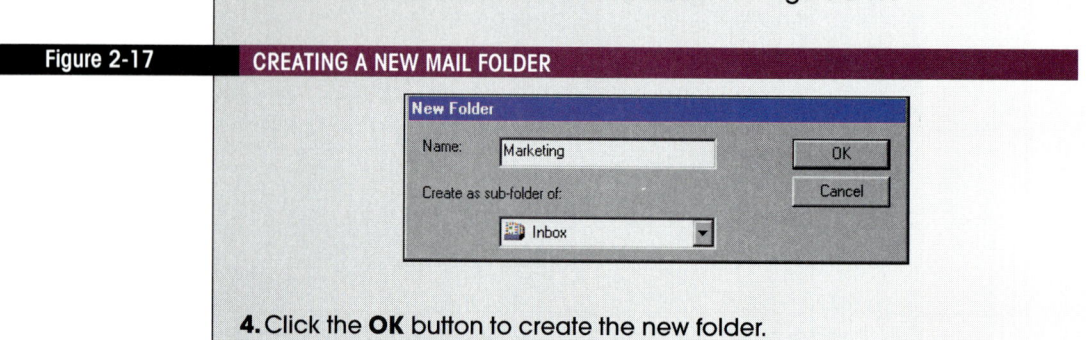

Figure 2-17   CREATING A NEW MAIL FOLDER

[Screenshot of New Folder dialog box. Name: Marketing. Create as sub-folder of: Inbox. Buttons: OK, Cancel.]

4. Click the **OK** button to create the new folder.

After you create the Marketing folder, you can transfer messages to it. Besides copying or transferring mail from the Inbox, you can select any other mail folder's messages for transfer to another folder.

To send a copy of a message to another folder:

1. Click the message summary for your Cc message in the Message List window to select it.

2. Click **Message** on the menu bar, point to **Copy Message**, point to **Inbox**, and then click **Marketing**. Your Cc message still appears in the Inbox. Now, make sure that you have copied and filed your Cc message correctly.

   TROUBLE? If you make a mistake and move or copy messages to the wrong folder, click Edit on the menu bar, and then click Undo to cancel the action.

3. Click the **list arrow** on the Location toolbar, and then click **Marketing** to open that mailbox. Your Cc message appears in the Marketing mailbox.

When you need to file a message, you follow a similar procedure.

To file a message in another folder:

1. Select the message summary for your Cc message in the Marketing folder.

2. Click the **File** button on the Navigation toolbar, and then click **Trash**. The message is deleted from the Marketing folder and is transferred to the Trash folder.

Moving or copying several messages at once is a snap. Hold down the Ctrl key and click each message summary in the Message List window that you want to move. Then click Message on the menu bar. Next, point to either File Message or Copy Message and then click the folder to which you want to move the group of messages.

You might need to print important messages in the future, so you want to make sure that you can print and file messages in a safe place.

To print an e-mail message:

1. Click the **list arrow** on the Location toolbar, and then click **Inbox** to return to that folder.

2. Right-click the message summary for your Cc message in the Inbox window to open the shortcut menu that shows the actions you can take.

3. Click **Print Message** on the shortcut menu, and then click the **OK** button in the Print dialog box to send the message to the printer.

You can print a message at any time—when you receive it, before you send it, or after you file it.

Deleting an E-Mail Message

You saved and printed your Cc message, so now you can delete the message and the Marketing folder that you created. Deleting messages in the Inbox mailbox and other mailboxes is easy. When you delete a message, you are really just moving it to the Trash mailbox. To remove messages permanently, click File on the menu bar, and then click Empty Trash Folder. If you are using a public PC in a university computer laboratory, it is always a good idea to delete all your messages and then empty the trash before you leave the computer. Otherwise, the next person who uses Messenger will be able to access and read your messages.

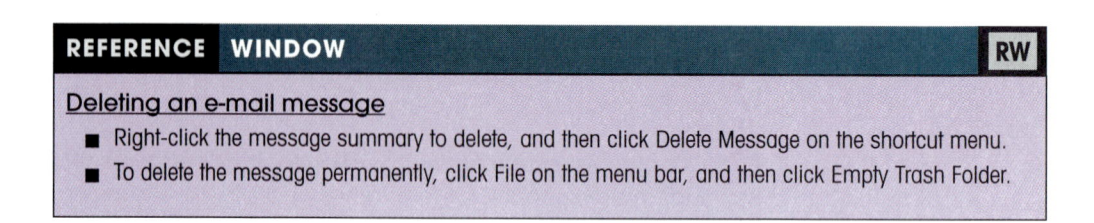

REFERENCE WINDOW

Deleting an e-mail message
- Right-click the message summary to delete, and then click Delete Message on the shortcut menu.
- To delete the message permanently, click File on the menu bar, and then click Empty Trash Folder.

To delete a message and empty the trash:

1. Right-click the message summary line for your Cc message. See Figure 2-18.

Figure 2-18   DELETING A MESSAGE

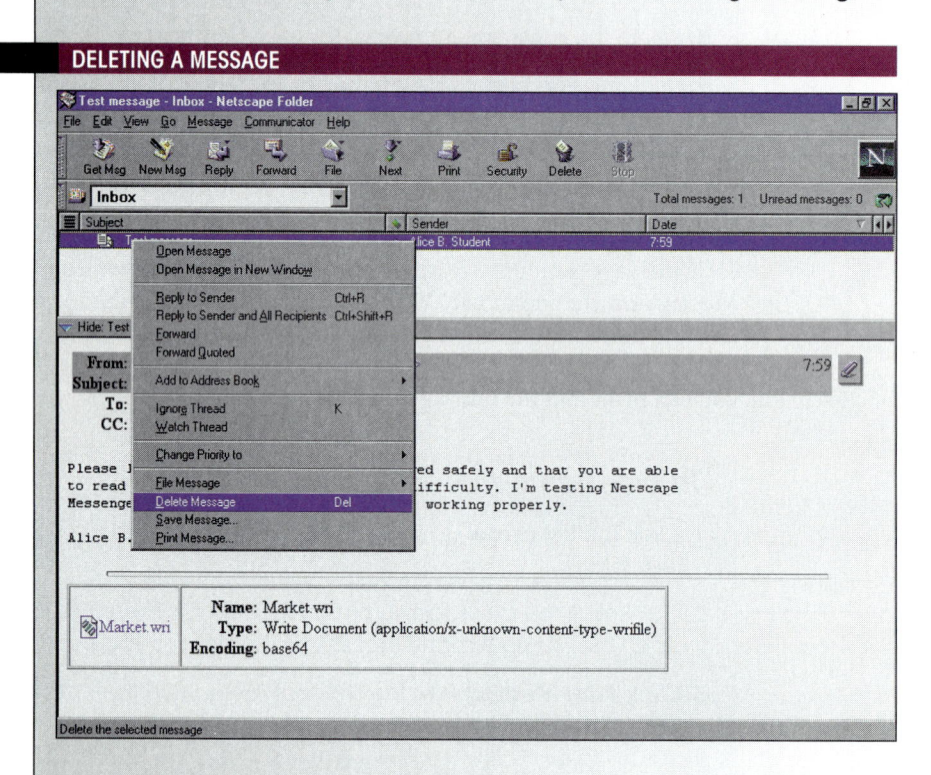

2. Click **Delete Message** on the shortcut menu to delete the message. The message is moved from the Inbox to the special folder named Trash.

TROUBLE? If you deleted a message you wanted to keep, you can recover it by clicking Edit on the menu bar and then clicking Undo.

To remove the message completely, you empty the contents of the Trash folder.

TUTORIAL 2 BASIC E-MAIL: INTEGRATED BROWSER E-MAIL SOFTWARE WEB 2.27 INTERNET

> 3. Click **File** on the menu bar, and then click **Empty Trash Folder**. Any deleted messages or folders are permanently removed.

To delete a folder, you follow the same process.

> ### To delete a user-created folder:
> 1. Click the **list arrow** on the Location toolbar, and then click **Local Mail** to open the parent folder of all your mail folders.
> 2. Right-click the **Marketing** folder.
> 3. Click **Delete Folder** on the shortcut menu. The folder moves to the Trash folder.
>
>   **TROUBLE?** If you deleted a folder you wanted to keep, you can recover it by clicking Edit on the menu bar and then clicking Undo.
>
> 4. To remove the folder completely, click **File** on the menu bar, click **Empty Trash Folder**, and then click the **OK** button to delete the folder and its contents. Any deleted messages or folders are permanently removed.

Maintaining an Address Book

As you send e-mail to different people, you probably will find it burdensome and sometimes errorprone to type their e-mail addresses, especially long and difficult ones. As you use e-mail to contact business associates and friends, you will want to save their addresses in an address book.

Adding an Address to the Address Book

You can access the address book by clicking Communicator on the menu bar and then clicking Address Book. To create a new address, you open the address book and then click the New Card button so you can enter information into the text boxes in the New Card dialog box for each person, including the person's first and last names and complete e-mail address information. If you enter a short name in the Nickname text box, then you can use that name to address a new message. After you click the OK button in the New Card dialog box, Messenger adds the new contact information to your address book.

You are eager to add information to your address book. Begin by entering Barbara Goldberg's contact information into your Messenger address book.

> **REFERENCE WINDOW** RW
>
> Adding an address to the address book
> - Open the address book by clicking Communicator on the menu bar in the Message List window and then clicking Address Book. Make sure that the Personal Address Book is selected.
> - Click the New Card button on the Address Book toolbar.
> - Enter the person's name, nickname, and e-mail address.
> - Click the OK button to save the new entry.
> - Continue adding names and addresses, or click the Close button to close the Address Book window.

To add an e-mail address to the address book:

1. Click **Communicator** on the menu bar in the Message List window, and then click **Address Book** to open the Address Book window. If necessary, click the **Maximize** button on the Address Book window. See Figure 2-19.

Figure 2-19

ADDRESS BOOK WINDOW

Personal Address Book selected

you might see address book entries in this window if you have used Messenger to save addresses

2. Make sure that the **Personal Address Book** is selected in the list box that appears below the Address Book toolbar. If it is not selected, click the list arrow, and then click Personal Address Book.

3. Click the **New Card** button on the Address Book toolbar. The New Card dialog box opens. You use this dialog box to add addresses to your address book. The Name tab stores information about a person's e-mail address. You can use the Contact tab to store postal mail address information and other personal information.

4. Type **Barbara** in the First Name text box, and then press the **Tab** key to go to the Last Name text box.

5. Type **Goldberg**, and then press the **Tab** key three times to go to the Email Address text box.

6. Type **barbgoldberg@yahoo.com**, press the **Tab** key to go to the Nickname text box, and then type **Barbara**. Your New Card dialog box looks like Figure 2-20.

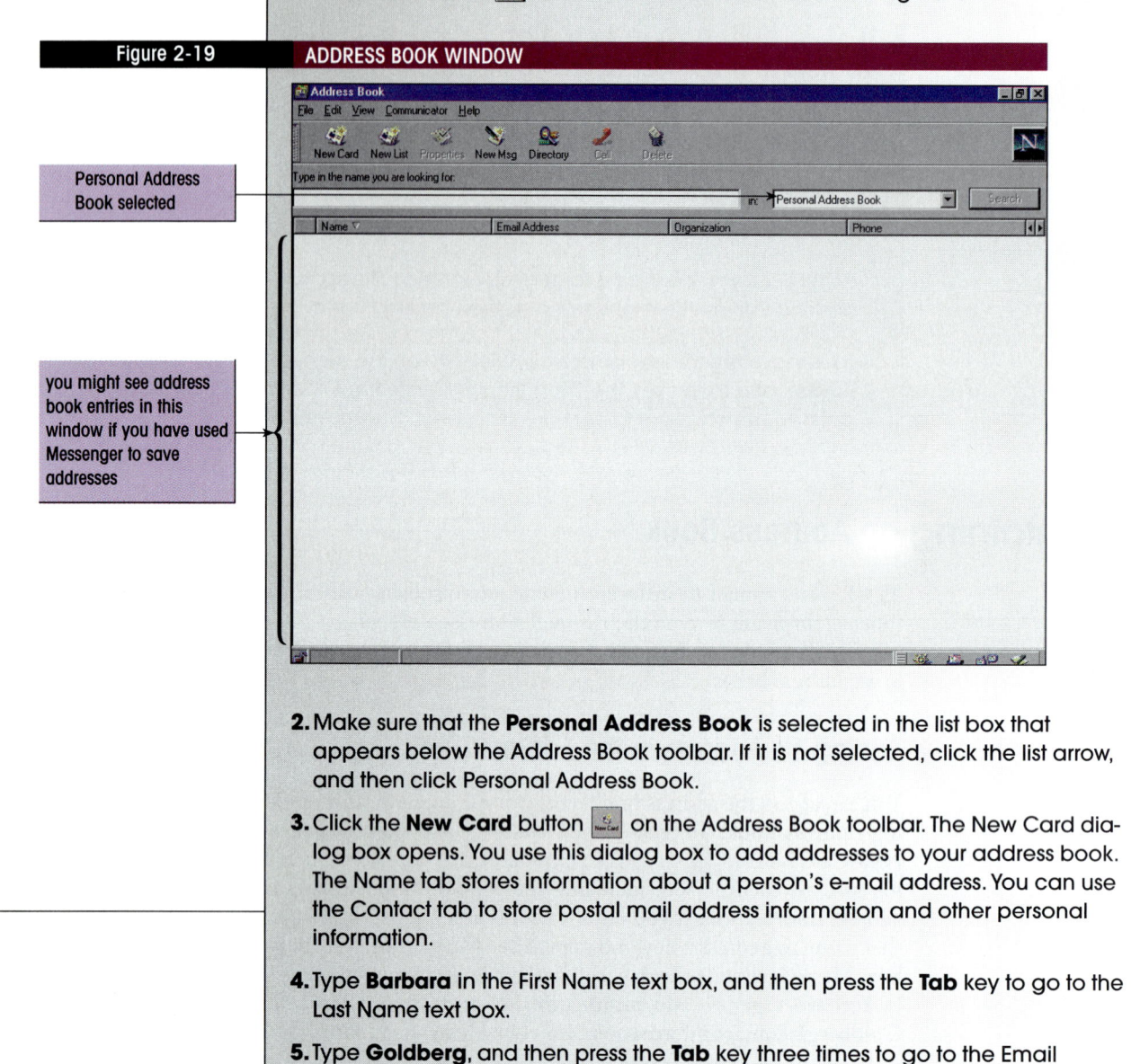

Figure 2-20   ENTERING A NEW ADDRESS IN THE ADDRESS BOOK

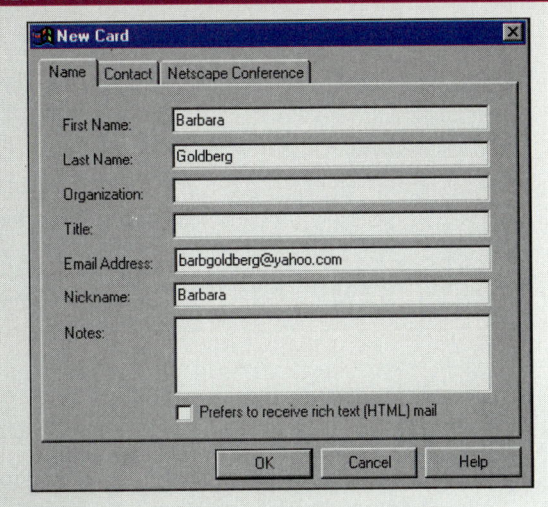

[Screenshot of New Card dialog box with Name tab selected, showing fields: First Name: Barbara, Last Name: Goldberg, Organization: (blank), Title: (blank), Email Address: barbgoldberg@yahoo.com, Nickname: Barbara, Notes: (blank), with a checkbox "Prefers to receive rich text (HTML) mail" and OK, Cancel, Help buttons.]

7. Click the **OK** button to store your new address entry.

8. Repeat Steps 3 through 7 to create address cards for the following members of the marketing department:

First Name	Last Name	E-mail Address	Nickname
Gary	**Kildare**	**gkildare@sidamo.com**	**Gary**
Faye	**Borthman**	**fborthman@sidamo.com**	**Faye**
Fran	**Brooks**	**fbrooks@sidamo.com**	**Fran**

9. When you are finished adding the addresses, click the **Close** button ☒ on the Address Book window title bar to close it.

With these entries now in your address book, you can easily insert even the most complicated e-mail address in any of the message text boxes as you compose a message. To insert an e-mail address into a new message's address line, open the address book, select the address, and then click the To, Cc, or Bcc buttons as needed. You can edit an address book entry while viewing the address book by either double-clicking the name or right-clicking the name and then clicking Properties. Another handy facility lets you add new names to your address book easily. Whenever you receive mail from someone not in your address book, right-click the message summary line in the Message List window, and then click Add to Address Book on the shortcut menu to add the sender's e-mail address to your address book.

Creating a Multi-Address Entry

You can use Messenger to create a distribution list, or a **mailing list**, which is an address entry consisting of more than one e-mail address in a single group. A mailing list is helpful when you want to send one message to several people simultaneously.

Barbara sends messages to each member of the marketing department frequently. She asks you to create a mailing list entry in her address book so she can type one nickname for the group of e-mail addresses, instead of typing each address separately.

> **REFERENCE WINDOW**
>
> **Creating a mailing list**
> - Click Communicator on the menu bar in the Message List window, and then click Address Book to open the Address Book window.
> - Click the New List button on the Address Book toolbar.
> - Enter the mailing list's name in the List Name text box.
> - Enter the mailing list's nickname in the List Nickname text box.
> - Enter the individual nicknames or e-mail address information of the individual group members.
> - Click the OK button to create the list.

To create a mailing list address entry:

1. Click **Communicator** on the menu bar in the Message List window, and then click **Address Book** to open the Address Book window. Maximize the Address Book window, if necessary.

2. Click the **New List** button on the Address Book toolbar. The Mailing List dialog box opens. You will add a group name, a nickname, and the individual e-mail addresses for the group to your mailing list entry.

3. Type **Marketing List** in the List Name text box, and then press the **Tab** key to go to the List Nickname text box.

4. Type **mkt** in the List Nickname text box. Now, when Barbara needs to send a message to every member of the marketing department, she can type "mkt" on the To line. Next, add the individual e-mail addresses to the mailing list.

5. Press the **Tab** key twice to move to the address list, and then start typing **Fran Brooks**. You already added Fran's address to the address book. After you start typing Fran's name, Messenger recognizes it. Press the **Enter** key to add Fran's address to the list.

6. Repeat Step 5 to add Faye Borthman and Gary Kildare to the mailing list. Press the **Enter** key after entering each name to add the name to the mailing list and to move to the next line in the address list. Figure 2-21 shows the marketing list after three names have been entered.

7. Click the **OK** button to close the Mailing List dialog box. Now, the Marketing List entry appears in the Address Book window. See Figure 2-22.

8. Close the Address Book by clicking the **Close** button.

9. Close all open Netscape windows, and then close your dial-up connection, if necessary.

TUTORIAL 2 BASIC E-MAIL: INTEGRATED BROWSER E-MAIL SOFTWARE   WEB 2.31

| Figure 2-21 | CREATING A MAILING LIST |

| Figure 2-22 | COMPLETED MARKETING LIST ADDRESS ENTRY |

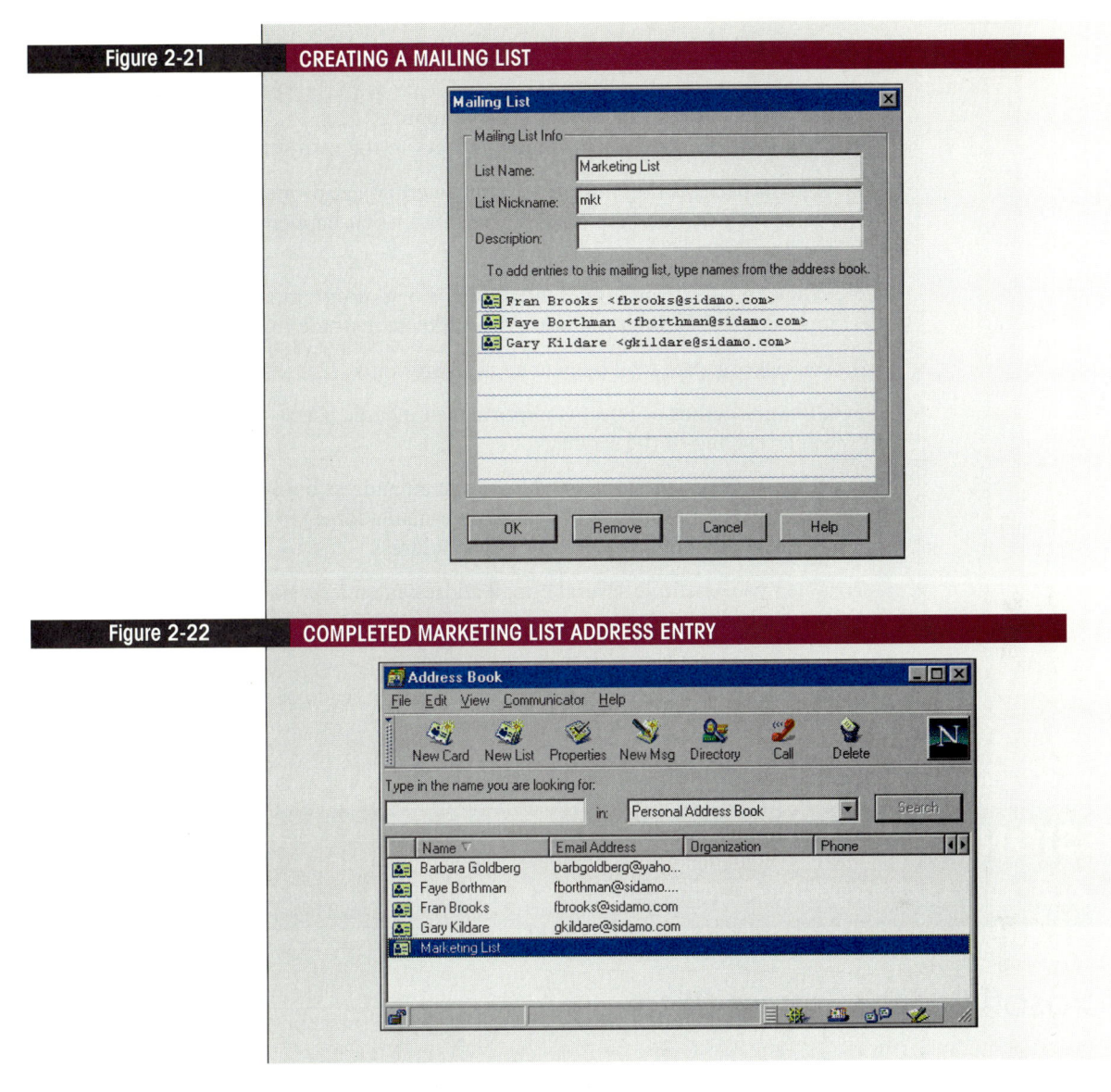

When you need to modify a mailing list, you can delete one or more members from the group by opening the address book, double-clicking the list name, and then deleting a member's name by selecting it and clicking the Remove button. You can add members to an existing list by opening the mailing list and typing the new member's name.

QUICK CHECK

1. Netscape Messenger is known as an e-mail _____ because it runs on a PC and it sends requests for mail delivery to the mail server.

2. What is perhaps the most important potential disadvantage of using mail programs such as Netscape Messenger? *Hint:* What happens when you read mail in another location?

3. When you delete an e-mail message in a mail program, are the messages deleted immediately? If not, then how do you delete mail messages permanently?

4. You can organize mail by placing messages into _____ .

5. Discuss whether or not it is important to include parts of the original message when replying to the sender.

6. If you store people's e-mail addresses in an address book, then you can type a(n) _____ in place of a person's e-mail address and Netscape Messenger will automatically fill in the correct e-mail address.

7. When you assemble several e-mail addresses under a single address book entry, you are creating a(n) _____ list.

If your instructor assigns Session 2.3, continue reading. Otherwise, complete the Tutorial Assignments at the end of this tutorial.

SESSION 2.3

In this session you will learn how to use Microsoft Outlook Express to send and receive e-mail. You will learn how to print, file, save, delete, respond to, and forward e-mail messages. Finally, you will organize your e-mail addresses in an address book.

Microsoft Outlook Express Client

Microsoft Outlook Express, or simply **Outlook Express**, is an e-mail client that supports all the standard e-mail functions you learned about in Session 2.1 to send and receive mail. You can execute Outlook Express from within a Web browser or any Microsoft Office program.

You are eager to continue your evaluation of e-mail software. You start Outlook Express by double-clicking its icon on the Windows desktop or by using the Start menu. Figure 2-23 shows the Outlook Express Inbox window.

Three panels appear on the screen: the Folder list on the left side, the Message list in the upper-right pane, and the Preview pane in the lower-right pane. The **Folder list** displays a list of folders for receiving, saving, and deleting mail messages; your folders might be different from what appears in Figure 2-23. The **Inbox** folder holds messages you have received, the **Outbox** folder holds messages waiting to be sent, the **Sent Items** folder contains copies of messages you sent, and the **Deleted Items** folder contains messages you deleted from other folders.

The Message list contains summary information for each message that you receive, including the message priority, an indication for an attached file, the sender's name, and the message's subject. The message summary that is selected in the Message list appears in the Preview pane. The Preview pane normally is located below the message list and reveals part of the message's contents. You can customize each of the panels to display different information, so Figure 2-23 might be slightly different from what you see in your copy of Outlook Express.

Figure 2-23   OUTLOOK EXPRESS INBOX WINDOW

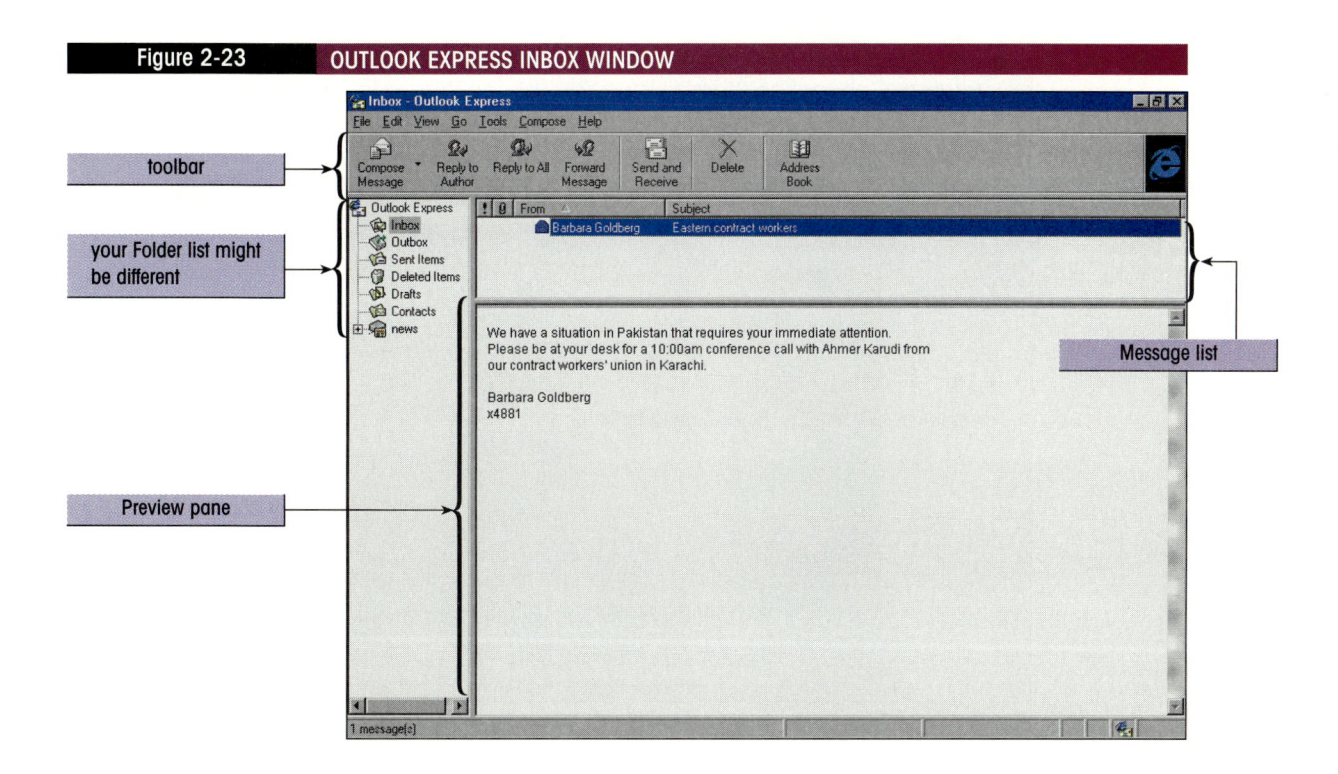

- toolbar
- your Folder list might be different
- Preview pane
- Message list

Setting Up E-Mail

You are eager to get started using Outlook Express. These steps assume that Outlook Express already is installed on your computer. First, you want to set up Outlook Express so it will retrieve your mail from a publicly accessible computer. Cost is not a consideration because the Microsoft Outlook Express program is free. Your first step is to start and configure Outlook Express so it fetches and sends *your* e-mail.

> ### To start and initialize Outlook Express for use on a public computer:
>
> 1. Click the **Start** button on the Windows taskbar, point to **Programs**, point to **Internet Explorer**, and then click **Outlook Express** to start the program. The Inbox folder opens (see Figure 2-23).
>
>   **TROUBLE?** If a graphic Microsoft Outlook Express screen appears when you start Outlook Express, click the Read Mail icon to go directly to your Inbox.
>
>   **TROUBLE?** If a Browse for Folder dialog box opens when you first try to start Outlook Express, click the Outlook Express folder, and then click the OK button.
>
>   **TROUBLE?** If the Internet Connection Wizard starts, click the Cancel button.
>
>   **TROUBLE?** If you cannot find the Outlook Express program on your computer, ask your instructor or technical support person for assistance.
>
> 2. Click **Tools** on the menu bar, click **Accounts**, and then, if necessary, click the **Mail** tab so you can set up your mail account settings.
>
>   **TROUBLE?** If you (or someone else) already set up your account, then skip to Step 11.

3. Click the **Add** button on the Mail tab, and then click **Mail**, if necessary. The Internet Connection Wizard starts. You use the Wizard to identify yourself and the settings for your mail server and username. See Figure 2-24.

Figure 2-24   **INTERNET CONNECTION WIZARD DIALOG BOX**

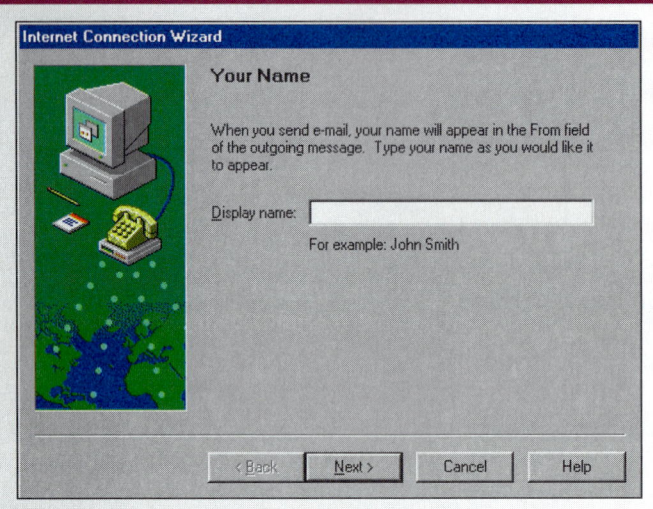

4. Type your first and last name in the Display name text box, and then click the **Next** button to go to the next dialog box, where you enter your e-mail address.

5. Type your full e-mail address (such as student@university.edu) in the E-mail address text box, and then click the **Next** button. The next dialog box asks you for your incoming and outgoing mail server names.

6. Enter the name of your incoming and outgoing mail servers in the text boxes where indicated. Your instructor or technical support person will provide you with this information. Usually, your outgoing mail server name is either SMTP or MAIL followed by a domain name. Your incoming mail server name typically is POP, POP3, or IMAP followed by a domain name. When you are finished, click the **Next** button to continue.

7. Type your Internet mail logon, as supplied by your instructor or technical support person. You might enter a password, depending on your configuration. Make sure that you type only the login name and not the domain name. Click the **Next** button.

8. Type an alias, or friendly name, for your account. You might use your first name or your nickname—whichever is easier for you to remember—and then click the **Next** button.

9. Click the option button that reflects your Internet connection, as provided by your instructor or technical support person. If you connect using a modem, click the Connect using my phone line option button. If you are in a computer lab, you probably will click the Connect using my local area network (LAN) option button. If you do not have an ISP yet, click the I will establish my Internet connection manually option button. When you are finished, click the **Next** button.

TROUBLE? Depending on your selections in the Choose Connection Type dialog box, you might see additional dialog boxes to provide information about your LAN or ISP. Follow these directions carefully, and then continue.

10. Click the **Finish** button to save the mail account information and close the Internet Connection Wizard. The Internet Accounts dialog box reappears, and your account is listed on the Mail tab. Figure 2-25 shows Barbara Goldberg's information.

Figure 2-25 INTERNET ACCOUNTS INFORMATION FOR BARBARA GOLDBERG

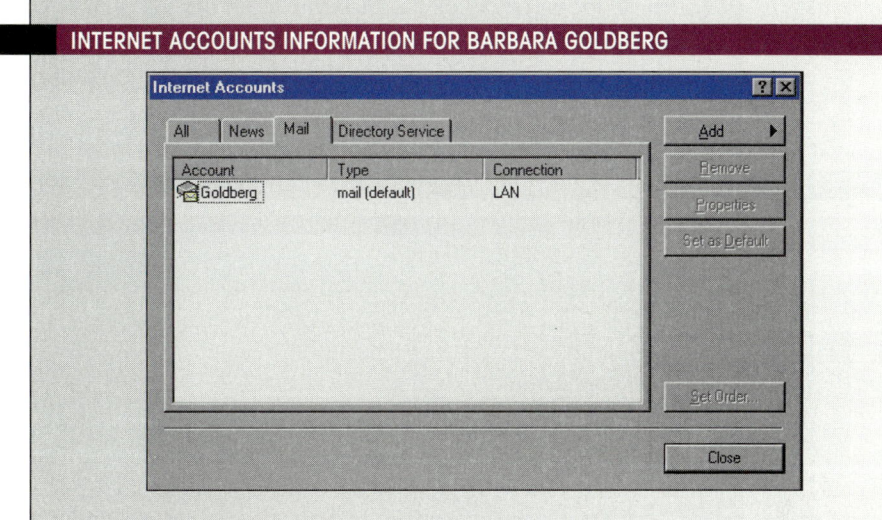

11. Click the **Close** button in the Internet Accounts dialog box to close it.

Now, your copy of Outlook Express is set up to send and receive messages, so you are ready to send a message to Barbara. *Note*: In this tutorial, you will send messages to a real mailbox with the address barbgoldberg@yahoo.com. Follow the instructions carefully so you use the correct address. Messages sent to this mailbox are deleted without being opened or read, so do not send important messages to this address.

Sending a Message Using Outlook Express

You decide to use Outlook Express to send a message with an attached file to Barbara. You will send a carbon copy of the message to your own e-mail address to make sure that the message and attached file are sent correctly.

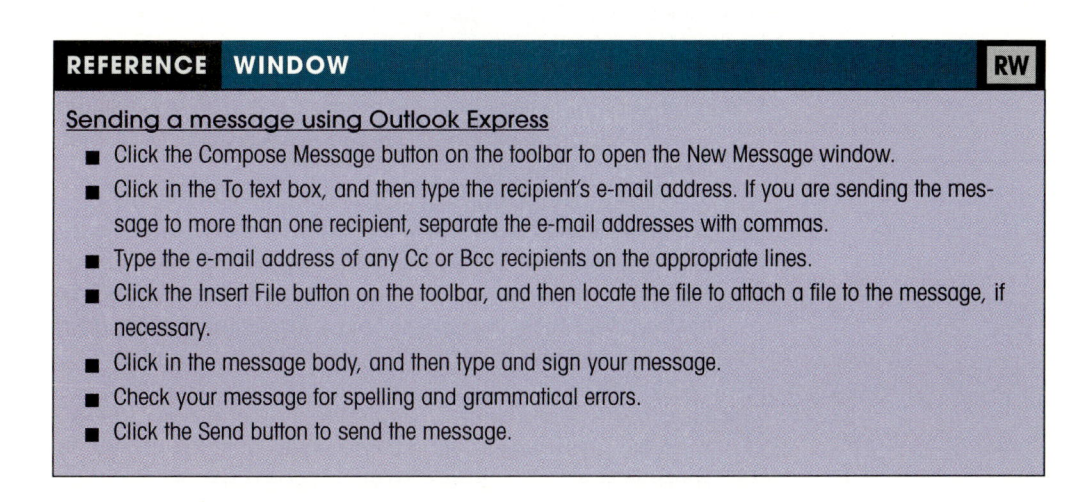

REFERENCE WINDOW	RW

Sending a message using Outlook Express
- Click the Compose Message button on the toolbar to open the New Message window.
- Click in the To text box, and then type the recipient's e-mail address. If you are sending the message to more than one recipient, separate the e-mail addresses with commas.
- Type the e-mail address of any Cc or Bcc recipients on the appropriate lines.
- Click the Insert File button on the toolbar, and then locate the file to attach a file to the message, if necessary.
- Click in the message body, and then type and sign your message.
- Check your message for spelling and grammatical errors.
- Click the Send button to send the message.

To send a message:

1. Make sure that the Inbox is selected in the folder list, and then click the **Compose Message** button on the toolbar to open the New Message window. If necessary, click the **Maximize** button on the New Message window. See Figure 2-26. The New Message window contains its own menu bar, toolbar, message display area, and text boxes in which you enter address and subject information.

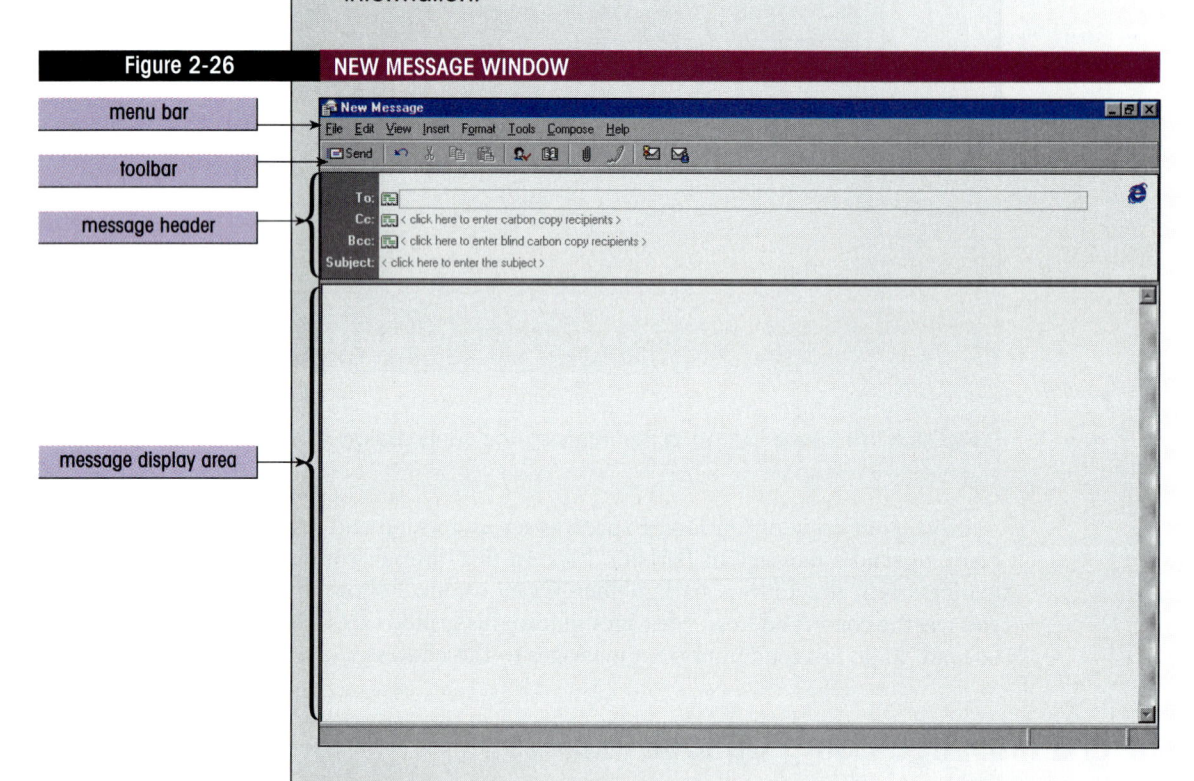

Figure 2-26 NEW MESSAGE WINDOW

- menu bar
- toolbar
- message header
- message display area

2. Type **barbgoldberg@yahoo.com** in the To text box, and then press the **Tab** key to move to the Cc line.

   TROUBLE? Make sure that you use the address barbgoldberg@yahoo.com, instead of barbgoldberg@sidamo.com. If you type Barbara's e-mail address incorrectly, your message will be returned with an error message attached.

3. Type your full e-mail address on the Cc line so you will receive a copy of your own message. It is a good idea to have a copy of all electronic correspondence as a reference.

   TROUBLE? If you make a typing mistake on a previous line, use the arrow keys or click the insertion point to return to a previous line so you can correct your mistake. If the arrow keys do not move the insertion point backward or forward in the header block, then press Shift + Tab or the Tab key to move backward or forward, respectively.

4. Press the **Tab** key twice to move the insertion point to the Subject line, and then type **Test message**. Notice that the title bar now shows "Test message" as the window title.

TUTORIAL 2 BASIC E-MAIL: INTEGRATED BROWSER E-MAIL SOFTWARE   WEB 2.37

5. Click the **Insert File** button on the New Message window toolbar. The File Attachment dialog box opens.

6. Make sure your Student Disk is in drive A. Click the **Look in** list arrow, and then click **3 ½ Floppy (A:)** to display the contents of your Student Disk.

7. Double-click **Tutorial.02** to open that folder, and then double-click the **Market.wri** file. The Insert Attachment dialog box closes, and the attached file's icon appears in the message.

8. Click the insertion point in the message display area, and then type **Please let me know that this message arrived safely and that you are able to read it and the attached file with no difficulty. I'm testing Outlook Express and want to make sure that it is working properly.**

9. Press the **Enter** key twice, and then type your first and last name. See Figure 2-27.

Figure 2-27   SENDING AN E-MAIL MESSAGE

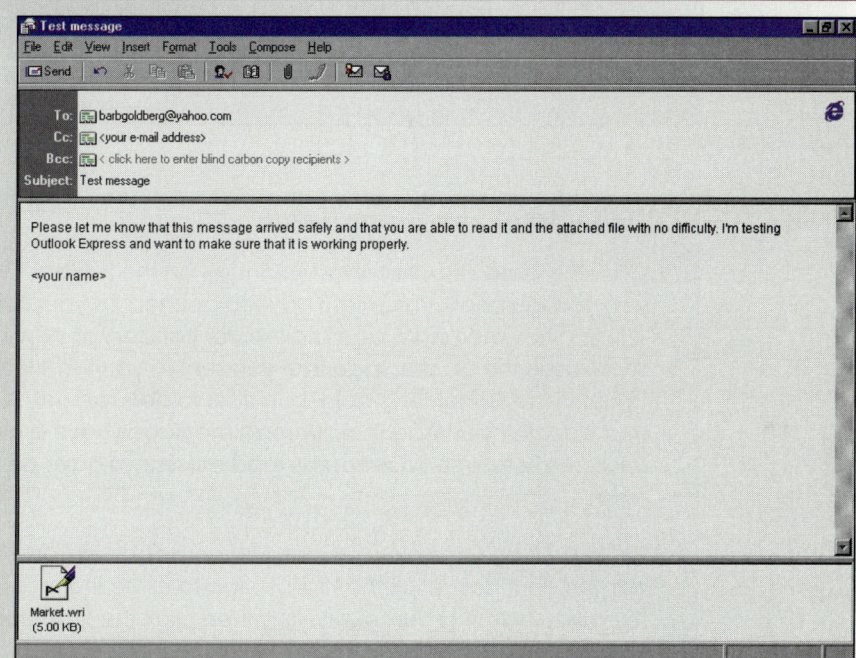

10. Click **Tools** on the menu bar, and then click **Spelling** to check your spelling before sending the message. If necessary, correct any typing errors. When you are finished, click the **OK** button to close the Check Spelling dialog box.

    TROUBLE? If the Spelling command is dimmed on the Tools menu, then your computer does not have the spelling feature installed. Press the Esc key to close the menu, and then continue with Step 11.

11. Click the **Send** button on the toolbar to mail the message. The Test message window closes and the message is placed in the Outbox. The Outlook Express window reappears.

Depending on your system configuration, Outlook Express might not send your message(s) immediately. It might queue (hold) the message(s) until you connect to your Internet service provider (ISP). If you want to examine the setting and change it, click Tools on the menu bar, and then click Options. Select the Send tab. If the Send messages immediately check box has a check mark, then mail goes out as soon as you click the Send button on the toolbar. Otherwise, the message is held and sent when you connect again.

Receiving and Reading a Message

When you receive new mail, messages that you have not opened have a closed envelope to their left in the message list summaries, and messages that you have opened have an open envelope next to them. You will check for new mail next.

REFERENCE WINDOW

Using Outlook Express to receive and read an e-mail message
- Click the Send and Receive button on the toolbar.
- Double-click the summary line of any received message to read it.

To check for incoming mail:

1. Click the **Send and Receive** button on the toolbar. Depending on your system configuration, you might have to connect to your ISP to get your new mail. Within a few moments, your mail server transfers all new mail to your Inbox. You should see the Cc message that you sent to yourself. Notice that the Inbox folder in the Folder list is bold, but other folders are not. A bold folder indicates that it contains unread mail. Unread messages have a closed envelope to their left in the Message list, whereas read messages have an open envelope next to them.

    TROUBLE? If an Outlook Express message box opens and tells you that it could not find your host, click the Hide button to close the message box, click Tools on the menu bar, click Accounts, and then click the Properties button. Verify that your incoming and outgoing server names are correct, and then repeat Step 1. If you still have problems, ask your instructor or technical support person for help.

    TROUBLE? If you do not see any incoming messages in your Inbox, then you either did not receive any new mail or you might be looking in the wrong mailbox. If necessary, click the Inbox folder in the Folder list. If you still don't have any mail messages, wait a few moments, and then repeat Step 1 until you receive a message.

2. Click the message summary for your Cc message in the Message list pane to open it in the Preview pane. See Figure 2-28.

3. Now, double-click the message summary for your Cc message in the Message list to open the Test message window with the full message content.

4. Click the **Close** button on the Test message title bar to close the window. You return to the Inbox window.

Figure 2-28 RECEIVING A NEW MESSAGE

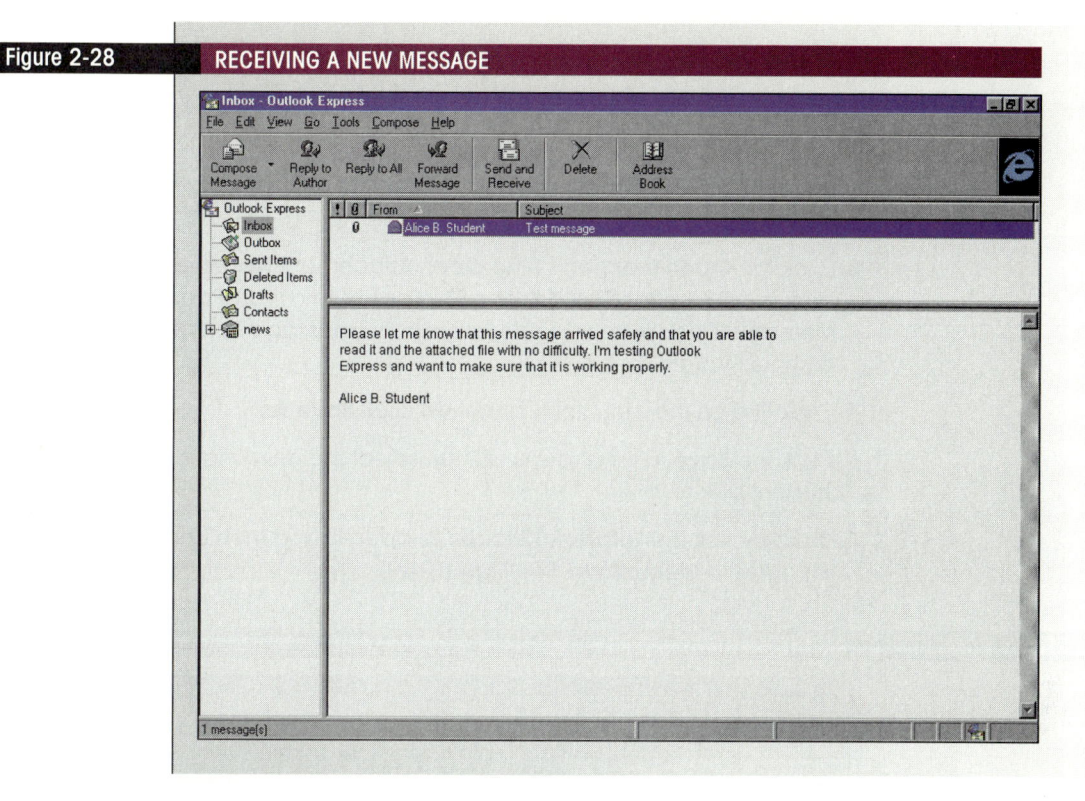

You received your Cc copy of the test message that you sent to Barbara, and the paperclip icon indicates that you received an attached file with the message. Either open the attachment in a preview window, or save it for viewing later. Open the attachment next.

Opening and Saving an Attached File

You want to make sure that your attached file was sent properly, so you decide to open it in the preview window. After you are finished looking at an attached file, you can decide whether to save or delete it from your system.

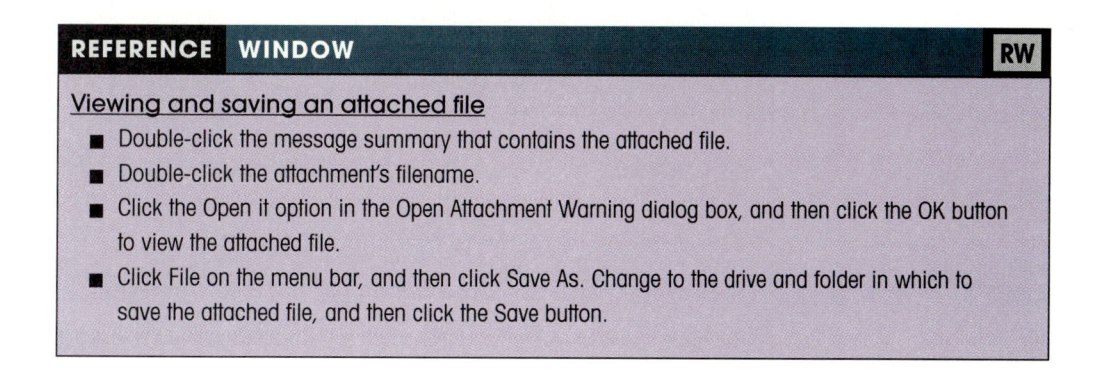

REFERENCE WINDOW

Viewing and saving an attached file
- Double-click the message summary that contains the attached file.
- Double-click the attachment's filename.
- Click the Open it option in the Open Attachment Warning dialog box, and then click the OK button to view the attached file.
- Click File on the menu bar, and then click Save As. Change to the drive and folder in which to save the attached file, and then click the Save button.

To view an e-mail attachment:

1. Double-click the message summary for your Cc message in the Message list to open the message.

2. Double-click the attachment icon name **Market.wri** located in the third panel of your message.

3. Click the **Open it** option of the Open Attachment Warning dialog box, and then click the **OK** button. The attached file opens in a WordPad window on top of the Message window. You decide to keep the message from Barbara and save it on your Student Disk.

4. Click **File** on the menu bar, and then click **Save As**.

5. Click the **Save in** list arrow, and then select the drive that contains your Student Disk.

6. Double-click the **Tutorial.02** folder to open it, and then change the suggested filename to **Memo2.wri**. See Figure 2-29.

Figure 2-29 SAVING AN ATTACHED FILE

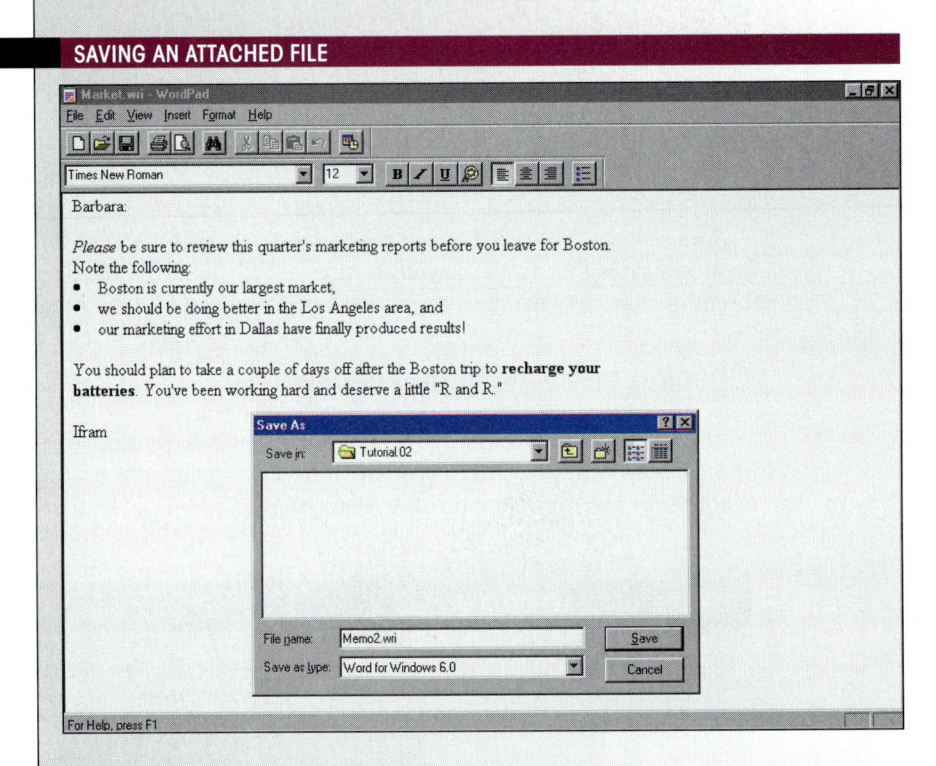

7. Click the **Save** button to save the attached file.

8. Click the WordPad **Close** button ⊠ to close WordPad.

9. Click the **Close** button ⊠ on the Outlook Express message window title bar to close it.

Replying to and Forwarding Messages

You can forward any message you receive to someone else. Similarly, you can respond to the sender of a message quickly and efficiently by replying to a message. You will use both extensively as you use e-mail.

Replying to an E-Mail Message

To reply to a message, select the message in the message summary list (or from any folder), and then click the Reply to Author button on the toolbar. Outlook Express will open a new message window and place the original sender's address in the To text box. You can leave the Subject line as is or modify it. Most systems, including Outlook Express, will copy the entire message from the original message and place it in the response window. Usually, a special mark in one edge of the response indicates what part is the original message. You click the Send button in the Reply window to send the message to the original author.

If you are responding to a question, it is a good idea to type your responses below each question from the original message to help the recipient better understand the context of your responses. When you respond to a message that was sent to a number of people—perhaps some people received the message as a carbon copy—be careful how you respond. You can choose to respond to all the original recipients or just to the sender. Figure 2-30 shows the window that you would use to reply to a message sent by Alice B. Student.

Figure 2-30 REPLYING TO A MESSAGE

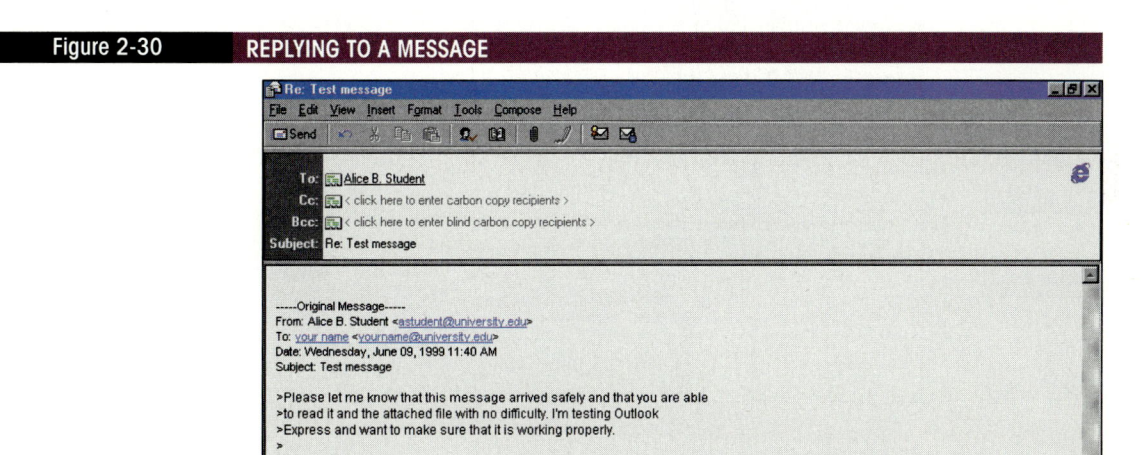

REFERENCE WINDOW

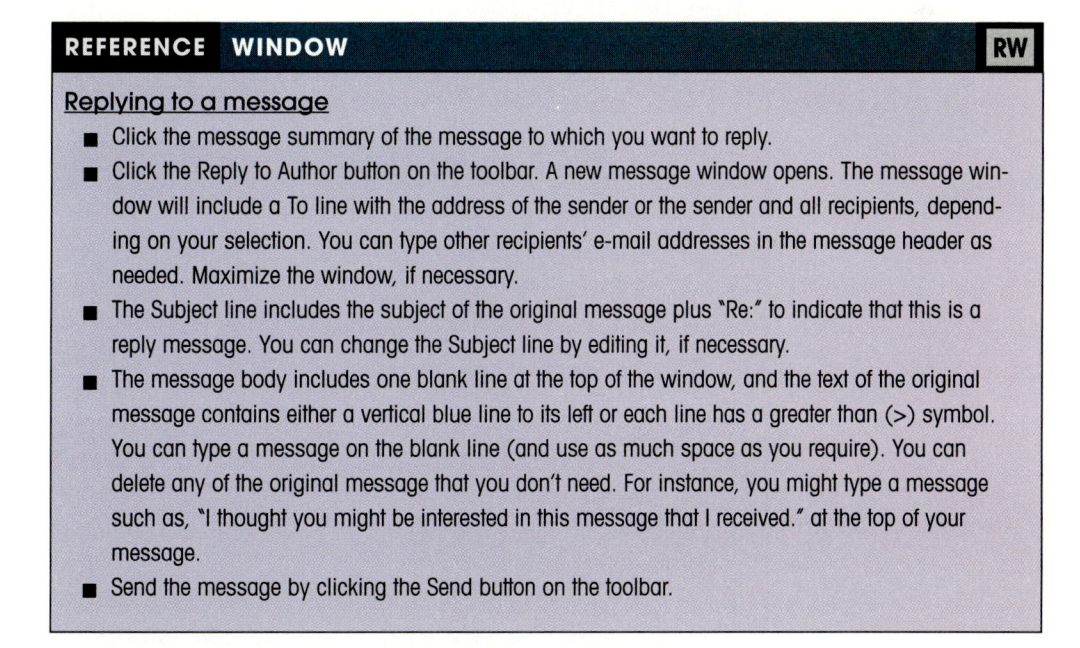

Replying to a message
- Click the message summary of the message to which you want to reply.
- Click the Reply to Author button on the toolbar. A new message window opens. The message window will include a To line with the address of the sender or the sender and all recipients, depending on your selection. You can type other recipients' e-mail addresses in the message header as needed. Maximize the window, if necessary.
- The Subject line includes the subject of the original message plus "Re:" to indicate that this is a reply message. You can change the Subject line by editing it, if necessary.
- The message body includes one blank line at the top of the window, and the text of the original message contains either a vertical blue line to its left or each line has a greater than (>) symbol. You can type a message on the blank line (and use as much space as you require). You can delete any of the original message that you don't need. For instance, you might type a message such as, "I thought you might be interested in this message that I received." at the top of your message.
- Send the message by clicking the Send button on the toolbar.

Forwarding an E-Mail Message

When you forward a message, it is removed from your Inbox folder and travels to the person to whom you are forwarding the message. To forward an existing mail message to another user, open the folder containing the message (the Inbox folder usually), select the message in the Message list, and then click the Forward Message button on the toolbar. The Fw: window opens. Type the address of the recipient in the To text box. If you want to forward the message to several people, type their addresses in the To text box (or Cc text box) and separate each e-mail address with a semicolon or comma. Finally, click the Send button on the toolbar to send the message. Figure 2-31 shows the window that you use to forward a message.

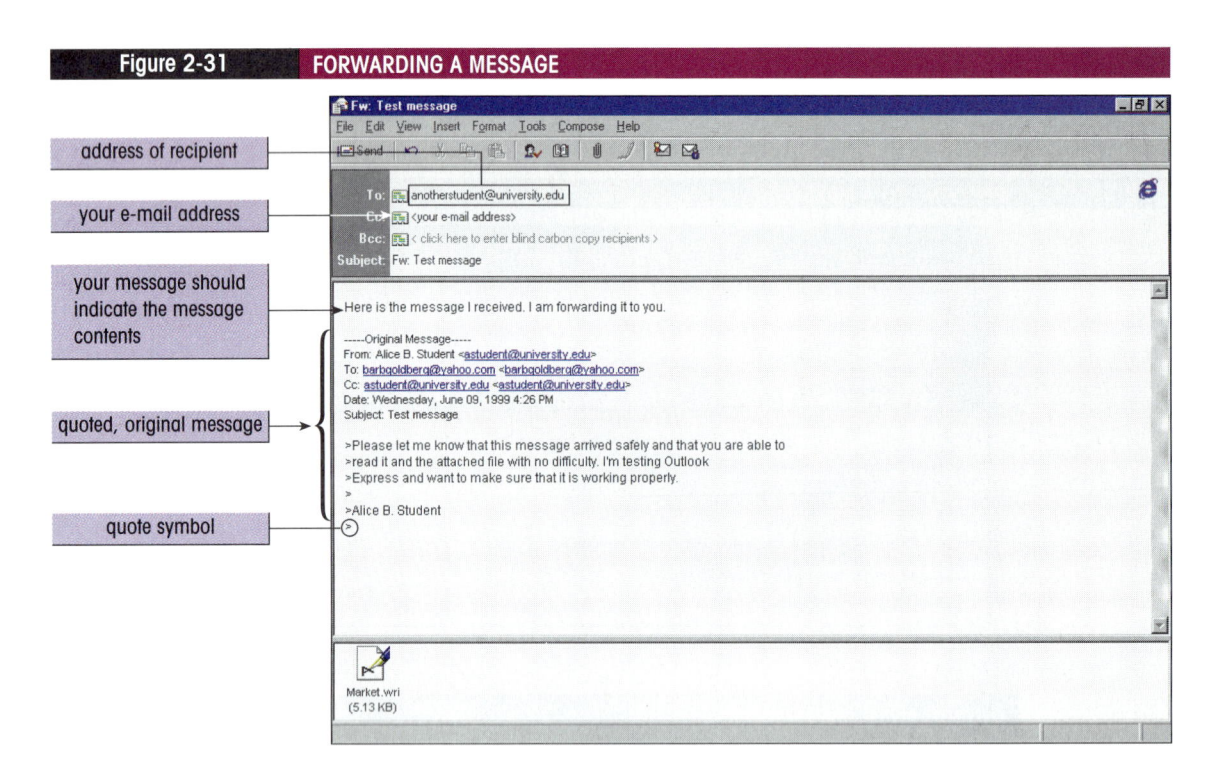

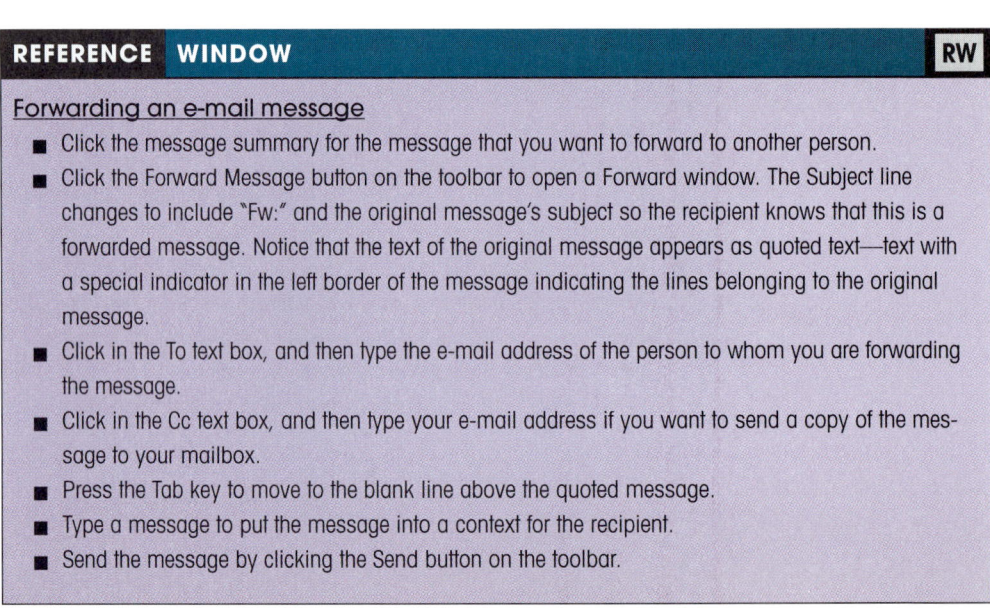

Figure 2-31 FORWARDING A MESSAGE

Callouts:
- address of recipient
- your e-mail address
- your message should indicate the message contents
- quoted, original message
- quote symbol

Window contents:
- To: anotherstudent@university.edu
- Cc: <your e-mail address>
- Bcc: < click here to enter blind carbon copy recipients >
- Subject: Fw: Test message

Here is the message I received. I am forwarding it to you.

-----Original Message-----
From: Alice B. Student <astudent@university.edu>
To: barbgoldberg@yahoo.com <barbgoldberg@yahoo.com>
Cc: astudent@university.edu <astudent@university.edu>
Date: Wednesday, June 09, 1999 4:26 PM
Subject: Test message

>Please let me know that this message arrived safely and that you are able to
>read it and the attached file with no difficulty. I'm testing Outlook
>Express and want to make sure that it is working properly.
>
>Alice B. Student
>

Market.wri
(5.13 KB)

REFERENCE WINDOW

Forwarding an e-mail message
- Click the message summary for the message that you want to forward to another person.
- Click the Forward Message button on the toolbar to open a Forward window. The Subject line changes to include "Fw:" and the original message's subject so the recipient knows that this is a forwarded message. Notice that the text of the original message appears as quoted text—text with a special indicator in the left border of the message indicating the lines belonging to the original message.
- Click in the To text box, and then type the e-mail address of the person to whom you are forwarding the message.
- Click in the Cc text box, and then type your e-mail address if you want to send a copy of the message to your mailbox.
- Press the Tab key to move to the blank line above the quoted message.
- Type a message to put the message into a context for the recipient.
- Send the message by clicking the Send button on the toolbar.

TUTORIAL 2 BASIC E-MAIL: INTEGRATED BROWSER E-MAIL SOFTWARE   WEB 2.43

Occasionally, you will receive important messages, so you want to make sure that you print them and then file them in a safe place.

Filing an E-Mail Message

You can use the Outlook Express mail folders to file your e-mail messages by category. When you file a message, you move it from the Inbox to another folder. You also can make a *copy* of a message in the Inbox and save it in another folder. You will make a copy of Barbara's message and save it in a folder named "Marketing" for safekeeping. Later, you can create other folders to suit your style and working situation.

To create a new folder:

1. Click **File** on the menu bar, point to **Folder**, and then click **New Folder**. The Create Folder dialog box opens.

2. Click the first folder at the top of the list, which usually is named **Outlook Express**, in the Select the folder in which to create the new folder list box. You will create the new Marketing folder below the Outlook Express folder, so it is on the same level as the Inbox folder.

3. Type **Marketing** in the Folder name text box. See Figure 2-32.

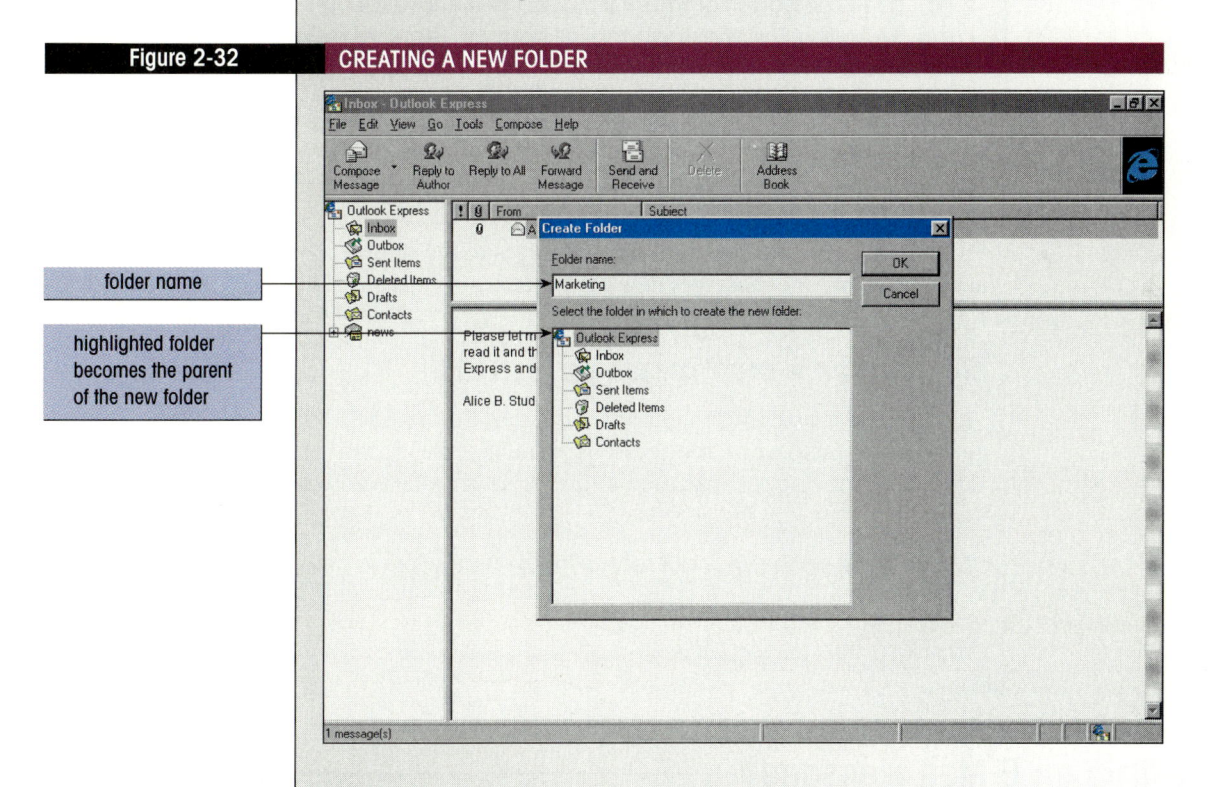

Figure 2-32   CREATING A NEW FOLDER

- folder name
- highlighted folder becomes the parent of the new folder

4. Click the **OK** button to create the folder and close the Create Folder dialog box. The new Marketing folder appears in the Folder list.

After you create the Marketing folder, you can transfer messages to it. Besides copying or transferring mail from the Inbox, you can select messages in any other folder and then transfer them to another folder.

To send a copy of a message to another folder:

1. Click the message summary for Barbara's message in the Message list to select it.

2. Click **Edit** on the menu bar, click **Copy to Folder**, click **Marketing**, and then click the **OK** button. Your Cc message still appears in the Inbox. Now, make sure that you copied and filed your Cc message correctly.

   TROUBLE? If you make a mistake and move or copy messages to the wrong folder, click Edit on the menu bar and then click Undo to cancel the action.

3. Click the **Marketing** folder in the Folder list to open that folder. Your Cc message appears in the Marketing folder.

When you need to file a message, you follow a similar procedure.

To file a message in another folder:

1. Click the message summary for your Cc message in the Message list.

2. Click and hold down the mouse button, and then drag the message summary for your Cc message from the Marketing folder to the **Deleted Items** folder. When the message summary is on top of the Deleted Items folder, release the mouse button. The message moves from the Inbox to the Deleted Items folder.

Moving or copying several messages at once is a snap. Hold down the Ctrl key, and click each message summary in the Message list that you want to move. Then drag the selected messages to the correct folder, or use the menu commands to copy the messages and save them in a folder.

You might need to print important messages in the future, so you want to make sure that you can print and file messages in a safe place.

To print an e-mail message:

1. Open the Inbox, and then right-click your Cc message summary in the Message list to open the shortcut menu that shows the actions you can take, such as moving messages to folders, replying to a message, and other similar tasks.

2. Click **Print** on the shortcut menu. The message prints within a few seconds.

You can print a message at any time—when you receive it, before you send it, or after you file it.

Deleting an E-Mail Message

When you don't need a message any longer, select the message and then click the Delete button on the toolbar. You can select multiple messages using the Ctrl key and delete them simultaneously. Also, you can delete a folder by selecting it in the Folder list, and then clicking the Delete button. When you delete a message, you are simply moving it to the Deleted Items folder. To remove messages permanently, delete them from the Deleted

TUTORIAL 2 BASIC E-MAIL: INTEGRATED BROWSER E-MAIL SOFTWARE   WEB 2.45   INTERNET

Items folder using the same procedure. When you delete a folder, the deletion is permanent, but you receive a warning dialog box giving you a chance to cancel your proposed folder deletion. If you are using a public PC in a university computer laboratory, it is always a good idea to delete all your messages from the Inbox and then delete them again from the Deleted Items folder before you leave the computer. Otherwise, the next person who uses Outlook Express will be able to access and read your messages.

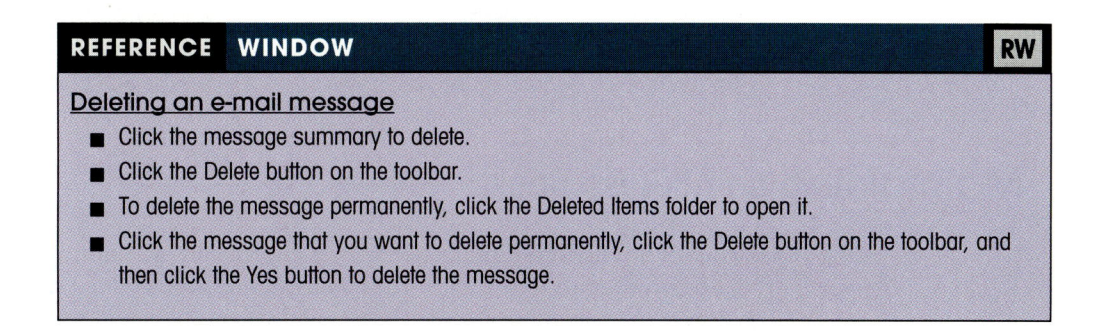

REFERENCE WINDOW

Deleting an e-mail message
- Click the message summary to delete.
- Click the Delete button on the toolbar.
- To delete the message permanently, click the Deleted Items folder to open it.
- Click the message that you want to delete permanently, click the Delete button on the toolbar, and then click the Yes button to delete the message.

To delete a message permanently:

1. Select the message summary for the message you received as a carbon copy.

2. Click the **Delete** button on the toolbar. The message is moved to the Deleted Items folder.

3. Click the **Deleted Items** folder to open it.

4. Click the message summary for the message you received that is now in the Deleted Items folder. You can press Ctrl and click more than one message summary to delete them permanently. Click the **Delete** button on the toolbar. A dialog box opens warning you that the deletion will be permanent (see Figure 2-33).

Figure 2-33   DELETING A MESSAGE

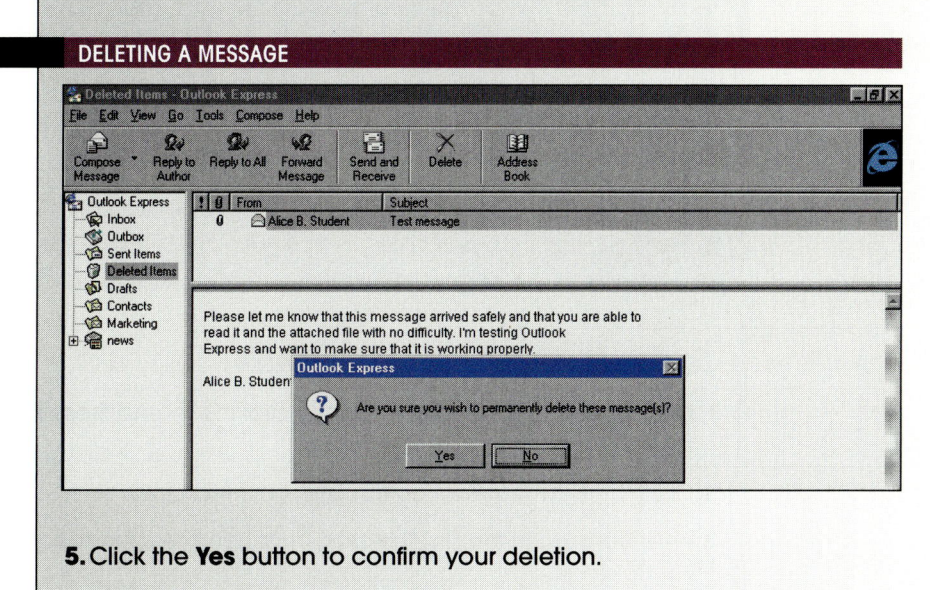

5. Click the **Yes** button to confirm your deletion.

To delete a folder, you follow the same process.

To delete a user-created folder:

1. Right-click the **Marketing** folder in the folder list.
2. Click **Delete** from the shortcut list of commands. A dialog box opens and warns that the deletion will be permanent.
3. Click the **Yes** button to confirm the delete.
4. Click the **Inbox** folder to re-display your list of mail folders and the message summary and preview panels.

Maintaining an Address Book

As you send e-mail to different people, you probably will find it burdensome and sometimes errorprone to type their e-mail addresses, especially long and difficult ones. As you use e-mail to contact business associates and friends, you will want to save their addresses in an address book.

Adding an Address to the Address Book

You can access the address book by clicking the Address Book button on the toolbar. To create a new address, you open the address book, click the New Contact button on the toolbar, and then enter information into the Properties dialog box for that contact. You can enter first and last names and e-mail address information. If you enter a short name in the Nickname text box, then you can use that shortened name when you create a new message.

You are eager to add information to your address book. Begin by entering Barbara Goldberg's contact information into your Outlook Express address book.

REFERENCE WINDOW — RW

Entering a new e-mail address in the address book
- Click the Address Book button on the toolbar to open the Address Book window.
- Click the New Contact button on the toolbar.
- Enter the person's name, e-mail address, and other information, as necessary.
- Click the Add button and then click the OK button to add the entry to the address book.
- Repeat the steps to add more addresses, or click the Close button to close the Address Book window.

To create an address book entry:

1. Open the Address Book window by clicking the **Address Book** button on the toolbar.
2. Click the **New Contact** button on the toolbar.
3. Type **Barbara** in the First text box, and then press the **Tab** key twice to go to the Last text box.

TUTORIAL 2 BASIC E-MAIL: INTEGRATED BROWSER E-MAIL SOFTWARE   WEB 2.47

4. Type **Goldberg** in the Last text box, and then press the **Tab** key twice to go to the Nickname text box.

5. Type **Barbara** in the Nickname text box, and then press the **Tab** key to go to the Add new text box.

6. Type **barbgoldberg@yahoo.com** in the Add new text box. See Figure 2-34.

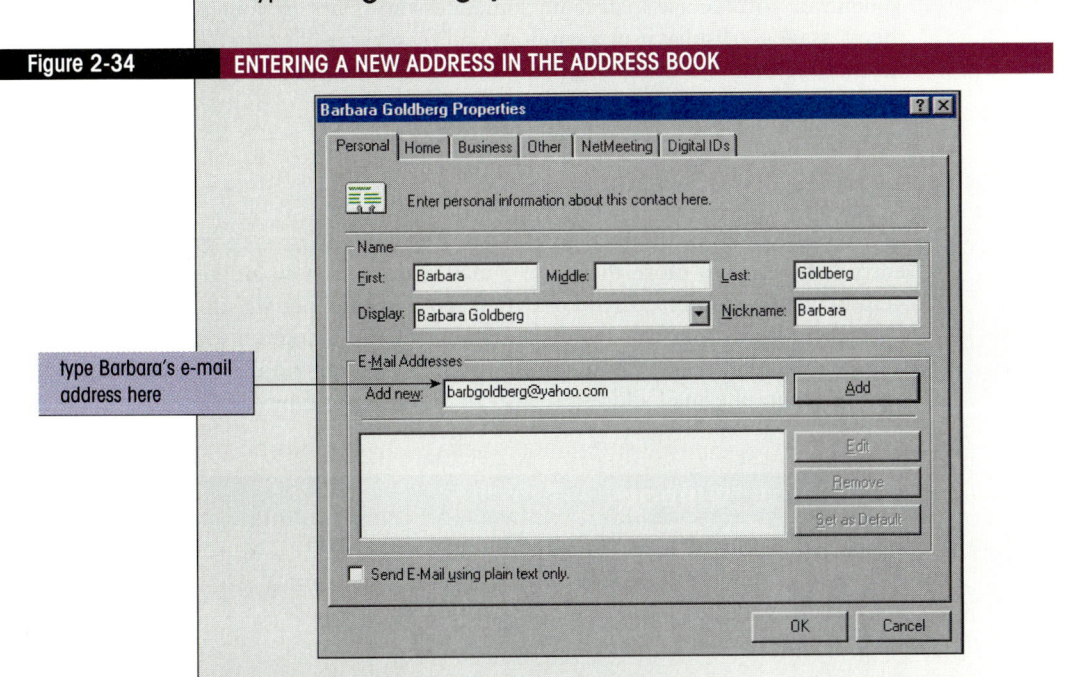

| Figure 2-34 | ENTERING A NEW ADDRESS IN THE ADDRESS BOOK |

type Barbara's e-mail address here

7. Click **Add** button and then click the **OK** button to close the Properties dialog box and return to the Address Book window.

8. Repeat Steps 2 through 7 to create address cards for the following members of the marketing department:

First Name	Last Name	E-mail Address	Nickname
Gary	**Kildare**	gkildare@sidamo.com	**Gary**
Faye	**Borthman**	fborthman@sidamo.com	**Faye**
Fran	**Brooks**	fbrooks@sidamo.com	**Fran**

9. When you are finished adding the addresses, click the **Close** button ⊠ on the Address Book window title bar to close it.

With these entries in your address book, you can easily insert even the most complicated e-mail address in any of the message text boxes as you compose a message by typing the first few letters of the addressee's e-mail address. As you type one, two, or three of the first letters of the e-mail address, full addresses from the address book appear in the address text box. Edit a name by either double-clicking the name or clicking the name and clicking Properties. Another handy facility lets you add new names to your address book easily. Whenever you receive mail from someone who is not in your address book, double-click the message to display it in a window, and then right-click the "From" name. Finally, click the Add To Address Book command on the shortcut menu. The sender's e-mail address is added to your address book.

Creating a Multi-Address Entry

You can use Outlook Express to create a distribution list, or a **group**, which is an address entry consisting of more than one e-mail address in a single group. A distribution list is helpful when you want to send one message to several people simultaneously.

Barbara sends messages to each member of the marketing department frequently. She asks you to create a distribution list entry in her address book so she can type one nickname for the group of e-mail addresses, instead of having to type each address separately.

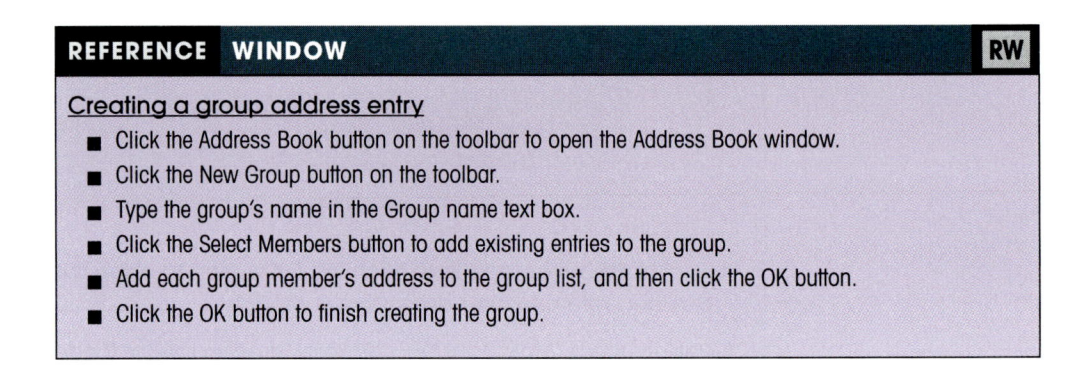

REFERENCE WINDOW

Creating a group address entry
- Click the Address Book button on the toolbar to open the Address Book window.
- Click the New Group button on the toolbar.
- Type the group's name in the Group name text box.
- Click the Select Members button to add existing entries to the group.
- Add each group member's address to the group list, and then click the OK button.
- Click the OK button to finish creating the group.

To create a group address entry:

1. Click the **Address Book** button on the toolbar to open the address book.

2. Click the **New Group** button on the toolbar to open the New Group dialog box.

3. Type **mkt** in the Group name text box to establish the group's name.

4. Click the **Select Members** button to add existing entries to the group. The Select Group Members dialog box opens so you can choose which names to add to the marketing group list.

5. Select Faye's name in the left panel, and then click the **Select** button to add it to the Members panel.

TUTORIAL 2 BASIC E-MAIL: INTEGRATED BROWSER E-MAIL SOFTWARE   WEB 2.49

6. Repeat Step 5 to select Fran and Gary to add them to the group list. Remember to click the **Select** button after selecting each name. Figure 2-35 shows the completed group.

7. Click the **OK** button to close the Select Group Members dialog box.

8. Click the **OK** button to close the mktProperties dialog box. Notice the new group, mkt, appears in the address book, sorted alphabetically by the Name column.

9. Close the Address Book by clicking the **Close** button ☒.

10. Close Outlook Express, and close your dial-up connection, if necessary.

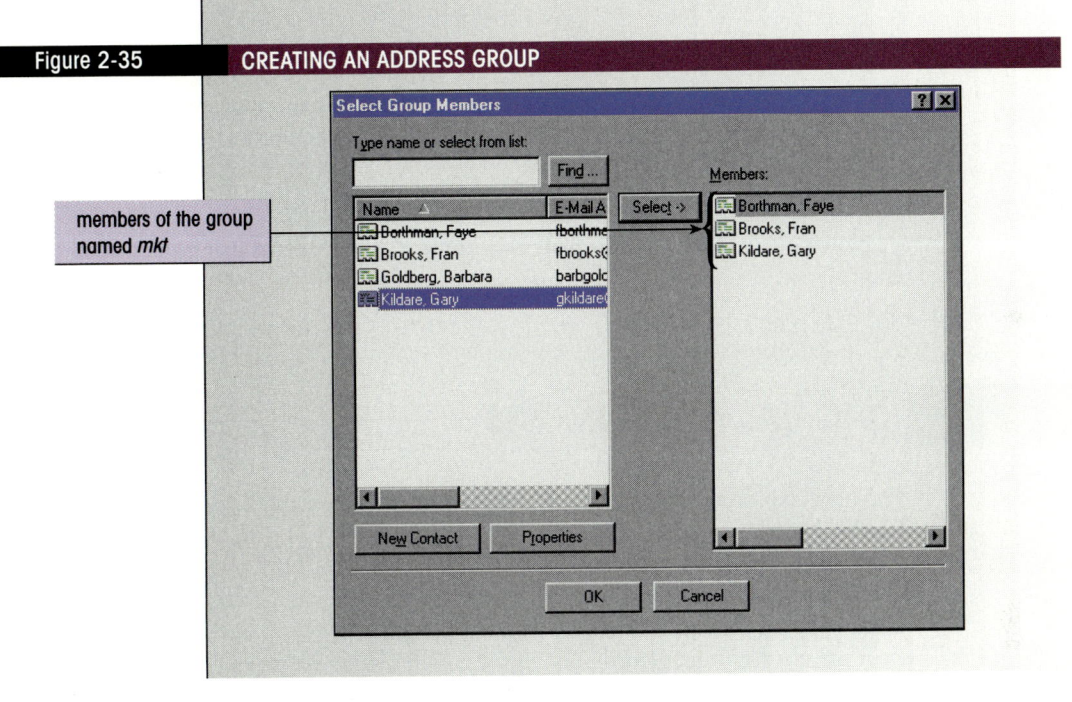

Figure 2-35   **CREATING AN ADDRESS GROUP**

members of the group named *mkt*

When you need to modify a group's members, you can delete one or members from the group by opening the address book, right-clicking the group name, and then deleting a member's name by clicking the Remove button. Similarly, you can add members by clicking the Select Members button on the group's Properties dialog box. Now, whenever Barbara Goldberg wants to send mail to the marketing department members, she can select the group name *mkt* from the address book for any of a message's address text boxes (To, Cc, or Bcc for example). Clearly, group addresses are very convenient.

QUICK CHECK

1. True or False: It is good etiquette to include a Subject line in your e-mail message so the recipient has a summary of a message's contents before reading it.

2. You use the _____ line to send copies of a message to other recipients without the principal addressee's knowledge.

3. When you want to send a complex document, such as a spreadsheet, it should be included in the message as a(n) _____.

4. What should you include in a message so that the receiver can contact you non-electronically?

5. Discuss the advantages of using an electronic address book.

6. When you send the same group of people e-mail messages frequently, you can create a(n) _____ list by which you can refer to the group with a single nickname.

Now you are ready to complete the Tutorial Assignments using the e-mail client of your choice.

TUTORIAL ASSIGNMENTS

You have explored two different e-mail clients, so you are ready to make a recommendation and send it to your instructor. Your status report will give an overview of either Netscape Messenger or Microsoft Outlook Express (or both programs, depending on your instructor's preferences), and then you will use your e-mail client to send the report, as a blind copy, to three classmates. You will send a carbon copy of the report to yourself and then print it for your records. Finally, you will delete the message.

1. Start Messenger or Outlook Express and set up yourself as a user, if necessary.

2. Add your instructor's name and full e-mail address to the address book. Use an appropriate nickname that will be easy for you to remember.

3. Add a distribution list that consists of three classmates' e-mail addresses. Enter your classmates' full names and e-mail addresses, and assign each individual a unique nickname.

4. Create a new message.

5. Type "E-mail evaluation status report 1" on the Subject line.

6. Click the To line, and then type your instructor's nickname.

7. Click the Cc line, and then type your full e-mail address.

8. Click the Bcc line, and then type the nickname of your distribution list for your classmates so they also receive a copy of the report.

9. Select the message area, and then type three or more sentences describing your overall impressions about Messenger and/or Outlook Express.

10. Attach the file named Security.wri from the Tutorial.02 folder on your Student Disk to the message.

11. Leave a blank line after the end of your message, and then type your name, class name, class section, and e-mail address on four separate lines.

12. Check your spelling before you send the message and correct any mistakes.

13. Carefully proofread your message for errors, make sure that the correct recipients are indicated, and then correct any problems.

14. Send the message.

15. Wait about 15 to 30 seconds, and then manually check for new mail to see if your message arrived on the server. Retrieve your new mail, and open the new message.

16. Print the new message.

17. Permanently delete the new message from your program.

18. Exit the e-mail client.

CASE PROBLEMS

1. Grand American Appraisal Company You work as an office manager for Grand American Appraisal Company, which is a national real-estate appraisal company with its corporate headquarters in Los Angeles. Grand American handles real-estate appraisal requests from all over the United States and maintains a huge inventory of approved real-estate appraisers located throughout the country. When an appraisal request is phoned into any regional office, an office staff member phones or faxes the national office to start the appraisal process. The appraisal order desk in Los Angeles receives the request and is responsible for locating a real-estate appraiser in the community in which the target property (i.e., the one to be appraised) is located. After the Los Angeles office identifies and contacts an appraiser by phone, the appraiser has two days to perform the appraisal and either phone or fax the regional office with a preliminary estimate of value for the property. The entire process of phoning the regional office and then phoning or faxing the national office is both cumbersome and expensive.

Your supervisor asks you to investigate alternatives to reduce the number of phone calls necessary to complete the appraisal cycle. You discover that Grand American requires all independent appraisers to have e-mail access and addresses. Nearly every Grand American employee has a PC connected on a LAN that ties into the larger computer on the Internet. Your job is to reduce the number of phone calls needed to set up an appraisal. You think e-mail is the solution, and you will be working with the existing e-mail system at Grand American to experiment with feasible alternatives.

Do the following:

1. Start Messenger or Outlook Express and ensure that the e-mail program has the correct settings for your mail server, your e-mail address, and your username.

Explore

2. Use the Help system to learn how to create a signature file. Then create a personal signature file that has three lines with your first and last name (line 1), your class and section (line 2), and your e-mail address (line 3). Save your signature file as Mysig.txt in the Tutorial.02 folder on your Student Disk.

3. Find a classmate and get his or her e-mail address. Your classmate will play the role of the Los Angeles order desk. Enter your classmate's nickname, full name, and e-mail address in the address book.

4. Enter your instructor's nickname, full name, and e-mail address in the address book.

5. Compose a message to your classmate. Type your classmate's nickname on the To line, type your e-mail address and your instructor's nickname on the Cc line, and then type "Request for appraisal" on the Subject line.

6. Type a short message that requests the assignment of an appraiser. Include your street address and the request date in the message.

Explore

7. Include your signature file in the message you are about to send.

8. Send the message immediately, without queuing it.

9. Wait a few seconds, and then retrieve the message that you sent to yourself.

10. Print a copy of your message, and then delete it permanently from the server and the PC.

11. Exit the e-mail client.

2. Bridgefield Engineering Company   Bridgefield Engineering Company (BECO) is a small engineering firm in Somerville, New Jersey that manufactures and distributes heavy industrial machinery for factories worldwide. Because BECO has trouble reaching its customers around the world in different time zones, the company decided to implement an e-mail system to facilitate contact between BECO employees and their customers. BECO hired you to help employees set up and use their e-mail system to reach their customers. Your first task is to compile a list of typical industrial machines that BECO can manufacture and send it to several of BECO's marketing staff located throughout the country.

Do the following:

1. Start Messenger or Outlook Express and ensure that the e-mail program has the correct settings for your mail server, your e-mail address, and your username.

2. Add your instructor and two classmates to the address book. Use an appropriate nickname for each person.

3. Start a new message. Use the To line to address the message to three people: yourself, your instructor, and to one of the classmates that you added to the address book in Step 2.

4. Send a blind carbon copy of the message to the second classmate that you added to the address book in Step 2.

5. In the message body, type "Bridgefield manufactures machines to your specifications. We can build borers, planers, horn presses, and a variety of other machines. E-mail us for further information."

6. Send the message.

Explore

7. Save the message in the Tutorial.02 folder on your Student Disk as BECO.txt.

8. Create a mail folder or mailbox named BECO on your client, in which you will store all mail for BECO.

9. Save the message you mailed to yourself in the BECO mail folder.

10. Create a distribution list address book entry using only the nicknames of the people that you added to the address book in Step 2. The nickname for the distribution list is classinfo.

11. Close and save the changes to your address book.

12. Delete the BECO folder and its contents from your PC.

13. Exit the e-mail client.

3. Recycling Awareness Campaign You are an assistant in the mayor's office in Cleveland. The mayor has asked you to help with the recycling awareness campaign. Your job is to use e-mail to increase awareness of the recycling centers throughout the city and to encourage Cleveland's citizens and businesses to participate in the program. As it happens, you know that over 45 percent of the city's registered voters have subscribed to a particular television cable service. Of those, over 8 percent have e-mail addresses and cable modems. You decide to send an e-mail message to several key businesspeople with an invitation to help increase awareness of the program by forwarding the recycle message to their employees and colleagues. Your message includes an attached file that explains the program in detail and how to use it.

Do the following:

1. Start Messenger or Outlook Express, and ensure that the e-mail program has the correct settings for your mail server, your e-mail address, and your username.

2. You will use the e-mail addresses of five classmates to act as the city's key businesspeople. Obtain and add the nicknames, full names, and e-mail addresses of five classmates as a distribution list named "council" in your address book. Then add the nickname, fullname, and e-mail address of your instructor as a single-entry address.

3. Create a new message. Type the distribution list nickname on the To line, your e-mail address on the Cc line, and your instructor's nickname on the Bcc line. Add an appropriate subject on the Subject line.

Explore

4. Create a signature file, and save it with the filename Mayor.txt in the Tutorial.02 folder on your Student Disk. Your signature should include your name on line 1, your new title of "Assistant to the mayor" on line 2, and your real e-mail address on line 3.

5. Write a two- or three-line message urging the council members to encourage recycling in their districts by forwarding the attached file to their local business contacts. Thank them for reading your e-mail.

6. Attach the file named Recycle.wri that is saved in the Tutorial.02 folder on your Student Disk to the message.

7. Make sure that your signature file is added automatically to the outgoing message, proofread and spell-check your message, and then send your message.

8. After a few moments, retrieve your e-mail message from the server and print it.

9. Forward the message to any one of the classmates in your address book. Add a message to the forwarded message that asks the recipient to forward the message to appropriate business leaders per your program objectives.

10. Save a copy of your message in a new folder named "Recycling," and then delete the original message.

11. Delete the Recycling folder and your message.

12. Exit the e-mail client.

4. Student Birds-of-a-Feather Group In two weeks, you have a midterm exam and you want to organize a study group with your classmates. Everyone in your class has an e-mail account on the university's computer. You want to contact some classmates to find out when they might be available to get together in the next week to study for the exam. To reach these students to create a study group, you decide to use e-mail.

Do the following:

1. Start Messenger or Outlook Express and ensure that the e-mail program has the correct settings for your mail server, your e-mail address, and your username.

2. Type the e-mail addresses of at least four group members—people in your class or friends' e-mail addresses who won't mind getting an e-mail message from you—on the To line of the new message.

3. Type your e-mail address on the Bcc line and your instructor's e-mail address on the Cc line.

4. In the message body, tell your classmates about your study group. Ask your recipients to respond to you through e-mail by a specified date so you can see who is interested.

5. Sign the message at the bottom with your full name, your course name and section number, and your e-mail address.

6. Send the message.

7. Create a new mailbox or folder named "Studygroup."

8. Check your mail for a copy of your message. When the message arrives, file a copy of the message in the Studygroup folder, and then delete the original message.

9. Print a copy of the message.

10. Delete the Studygroup folder and your message.

11. Exit the e-mail client.

LAB ASSIGNMENTS

E-Mail E-mail that originates on a local area network with a mail gateway can travel all over the world. That's why it is so important to learn how to use it. In this Lab you will use an e-mail simulator, so even if your school's computers don't provide you with e-mail service, you will learn the basics of reading, sending, and replying to electronic mail. See the Read This Before You Begin page for information on installing and starting this Lab.

1. Click the Steps button to learn how to work with E-mail. As you proceed through the Steps, answer all of the Quick Check questions that appear. After you complete the Steps, you will see a Quick Check summary report. Follow the instructions on the screen to print this report.

2. Click the Explore button. Write a message to re@films.org. The subject of the message is "Picks and Pans." In the body of your message, describe a movie you have recently seen. Include the name of the movie, briefly summarize the plot, and give it a thumbs up or a thumbs down. Print the message before you send it.

3. Look in your In Basket for a message from jb@music.org. Read the message, then compose a reply indicating that you will attend. Carbon copy mciccone@music.org. Print your reply, including the text of JB's original message before you send it.

4. Look in your In Basket for a message from leo@sports.org. Reply to the message by adding your rating to the text of the original message as follows:

Equipment:	Your rating:
Rollerblades	2
Skis	3
Bicycle	1
Scuba gear	4
Snowmobile	5

   Print your reply before you send it.

5. Go into the lab with a partner. You should each log into the E-mail Lab on different computers. Look at the Addresses list to find the user ID for your partner. You should each send a short e-mail message to your partner. Then, you should check your mail message from your partner. Read the message and compose a reply. Print your reply before you send it. *Note: Unlike a full-featured mail system, the e-mail simulator does not save mail in mailboxes after you log off.*

Quick Check Answers

Session 2.1

1. True
2. protocols
3. header, body
4. A recipient can quickly prioritize messages by reading the Subject line and decide when or if to read the message.
5. True
6. Yes; you can send it as an attachment to an e-mail message.
7. IP or Internet Protocol
8. So the receiver has a context for your responses.
9. It is easier and faster to type a short distribution list name than several individual e-mail addresses.

Session 2.2

1. client
2. Mail messages are (optionally) deleted from the mail server and downloaded to the PC where you are located, so unless you save the messages on a disk, you won't be able to retrieve them from the server.
3. No. Most mail clients simply put the deleted messages in a special "trash" folder where they remain on the computer until the user empties the trash.
4. folders or mailboxes
5. Yes, it is important so your recipient has a context for your message.
6. nickname
7. distribution or mailing

Session 2.3

1. True
2. Bcc or blind carbon copy
3. attachment
4. A signature file with a phone number or an address.
5. It makes entering e-mail addresses faster and more error-free. It also serves as a repository for address and phone information, which is another form of electronic organizer.
6. distribution or mailing

TUTORIAL 3

OBJECTIVES

In this tutorial you will:

- Learn about Web browser software and Web pages
- Learn about Web addresses and URLs
- Save and organize Web addresses
- Navigate the Web
- Use the Web to find information
- Configure and use the Netscape Navigator Web browser
- Configure and use the Microsoft Internet Explorer Web browser

LAB

The Internet: World Wide Web

BROWSER BASICS

Introduction to Netscape Navigator and Microsoft Internet Explorer

CASE

Sunset Wind Quintet

The Sunset Wind Quintet is a group of five musicians who have played together for eight years. At first, the group began by playing free concerts for local charitable organizations. As more people heard the quintet and its reputation grew, the musicians were soon in demand at art gallery openings and other functions.

Each member of the quintet is an accomplished musician. The instruments in a wind quintet include flute, oboe, clarinet, bassoon, and French horn, which are all orchestral instruments. Each quintet member has experience as a player in a symphony orchestra as well. Three quintet members—the flutist, bassoonist, and the French horn player—currently hold positions with the local orchestra. The other two quintet members—the clarinetist and the oboist—teach classes in their respective instruments at the local university.

This past summer, a booking agent asked the quintet to do a short regional tour. Although the tour was successful, the quintet members realized that none of them had any business-management skills. Marianna Rabinovich, the clarinetist, handles most of the business details for the group. The quintet members realized that business matters related to the tour were overwhelming Marianna and that they wanted to do more touring, so they hired you as their business manager.

One of your tasks will be to help market the Sunset Wind Quintet. To do this, you must learn more about how other wind quintets operate and sell their services. At one of your early meetings with the group, you found that each member of the quintet had different priorities. In addition to marketing the quintet's performances, some members felt it would be a good idea to record and sell CDs, whereas others were concerned about finding instrument-repair facilities on the road when tours extended beyond the local area.

As you discussed these issues with the quintet members, you started thinking of ways to address their concerns. Your first idea was to find trade magazines and newspapers that might describe what other small classical musical ensembles were doing. As you considered the time and cost of this alternative, you realized that the Internet and World Wide Web might offer a better way to get started.

SESSION 3.1

In this session, you will learn how Web pages and Web sites make up the World Wide Web. You will find out about things to consider when you select and use a specific software tool to find information on the Web. Finally, you will learn about some basic browser concepts.

Web Browsers

As you started considering how you might use the Web to gather information for the Sunset Wind Quintet, you remember that one of your college friends, Maggie Beeler, earned her degree in library science. You met with Maggie at the local public library, where she is working at the reference desk. She is glad to assist you.

Maggie begins by explaining that the Web is a collection of files that reside on computers, called **Web servers**, that are located all over the world and are connected to each other through the Internet. Most computer files connected to the Internet are private; that is, only the computer's users can access them. The owners of the files that make up the Web have made their files publicly available so you can obtain access to them if you have a computer connected to the Internet.

Client/Server Structure of the World Wide Web

When you use your Internet connection to become part of the Web, your computer becomes a **Web client** in a worldwide client/server network. A **Web browser** is the software that you run on your computer to make it work as a Web client. The Internet connects many different types of computers running different operating system software. Web browser software lets your computer communicate with all of these different types of computers easily and effectively.

Computers that are connected to the Internet and contain files that their owners have made available publicly through their Internet connections are called **Web servers**. Figure 3-1 shows how this client/server structure uses the Internet to provide multiple interconnections among the various kinds of client and server computers.

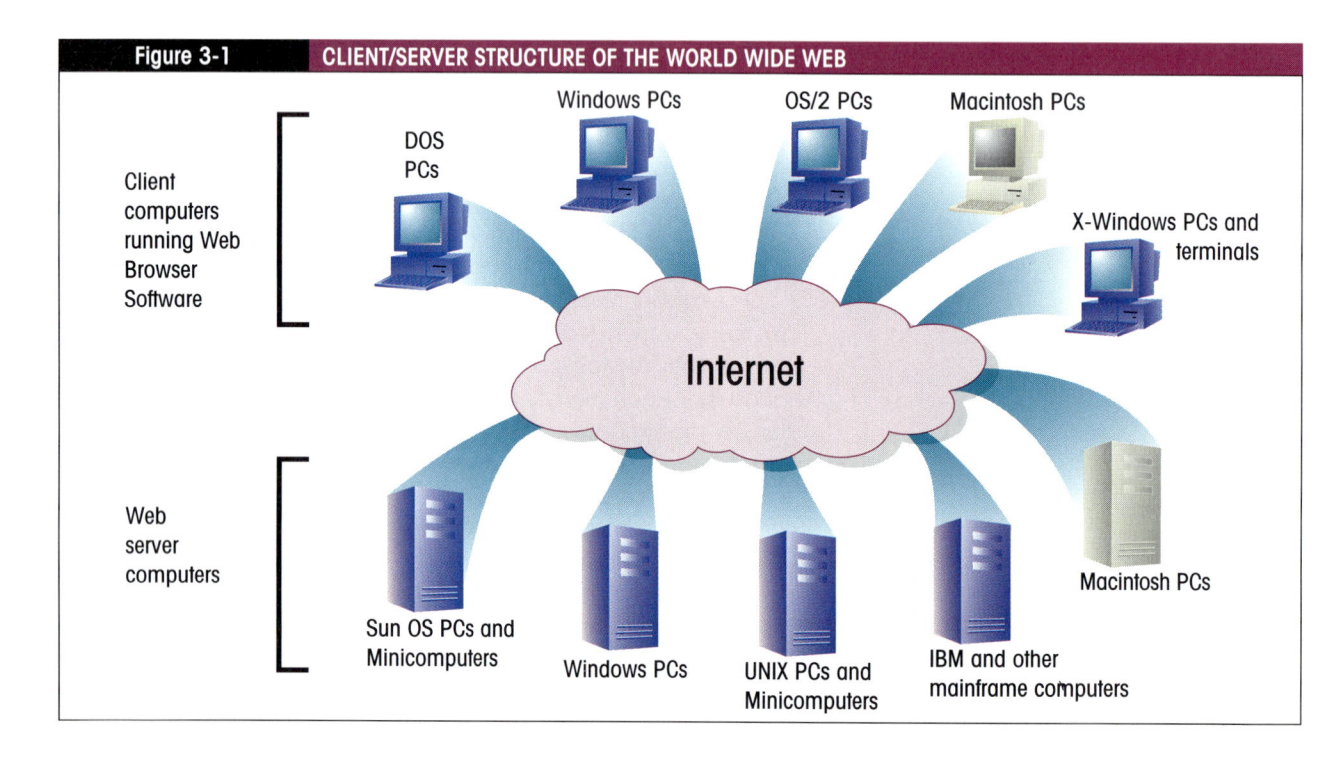

Figure 3-1 CLIENT/SERVER STRUCTURE OF THE WORLD WIDE WEB

Hypertext, Links, and Hypermedia

The public files on Web servers are ordinary text files, much like the files used by word-processing software. To allow Web browser software to read them, however, the text must be formatted according to a generally accepted standard. The standard used on the Web is **Hypertext Markup Language (HTML)**. HTML uses codes, or **tags**, to tell the Web browser software how to display the text contained in the document. For example, a Web browser reading the following line of text:

<B>A Review of the Book <I>Wind Instruments of the 18th Century</I></B> recognizes

the <B> and </B> tags as instructions to display the entire line of text in bold and the <I> and </I> tags as instructions to display the text enclosed by those tags in italics. Different Web clients that connect to this Web server might display the tagged text differently. For example, one Web browser might display text enclosed by bold tags in a blue color instead of displaying the text as bold.

HTML provides a variety of text formatting tags that you can use to indicate headings, paragraphs, bulleted lists, numbered lists, and other useful text formats in an HTML document. The real power of HTML, however, lies in its anchor tag. The **HTML anchor tag** enables you to link multiple HTML documents to each other. When you use the anchor tag to link HTML documents, you create a **hypertext link**. Hypertext links also are called **hyperlinks**, or **links**. Figure 3-2 shows how these hyperlinks can join multiple HTML documents to create a web of HTML text across computers on the Internet.

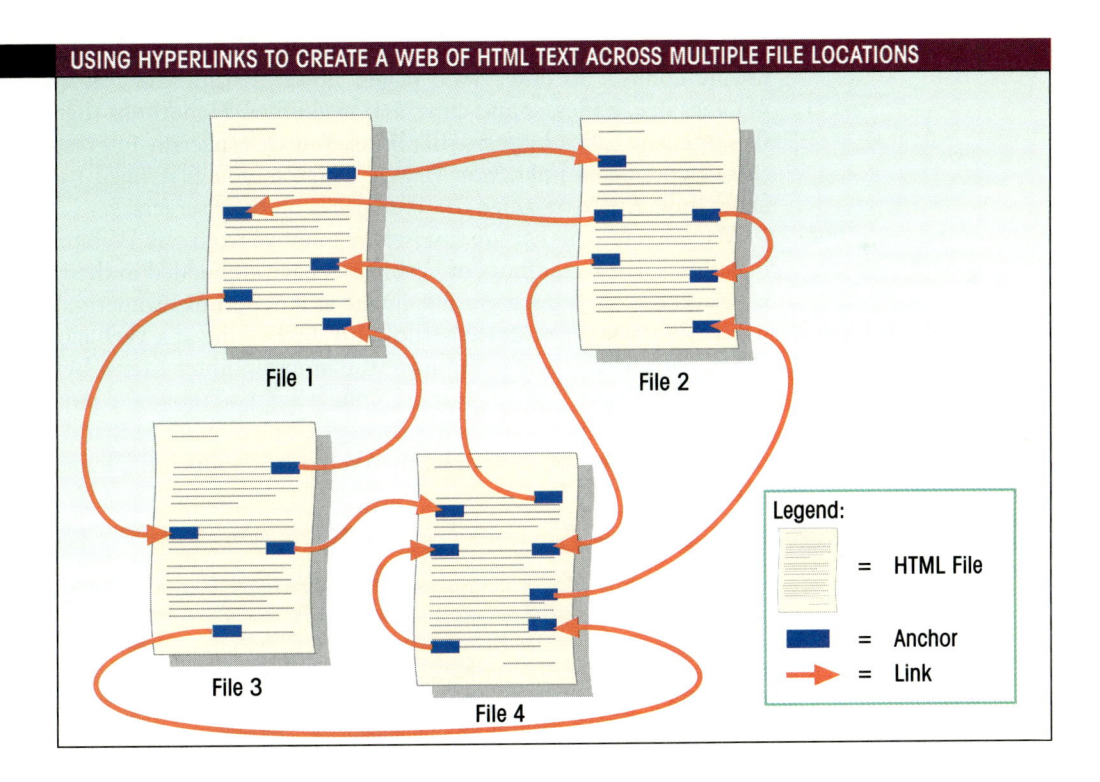

Figure 3-2 USING HYPERLINKS TO CREATE A WEB OF HTML TEXT ACROSS MULTIPLE FILE LOCATIONS

Most Web browsers display hyperlinks in a different color than other text and underline them so they are easily distinguished in the HTML document. When a Web browser displays an HTML document, people usually call the file a **Web page**. Maggie shows you the Web page that appears in Figure 3-3 and suggests that it might be interesting to the Sunset Wind Quintet. The hyperlinks on this Web page are easy to identify because the Web browser software that displayed this page shows the hyperlinks as red, underlined text.

Figure 3-3   WEB PAGE WITH HYPERLINKS

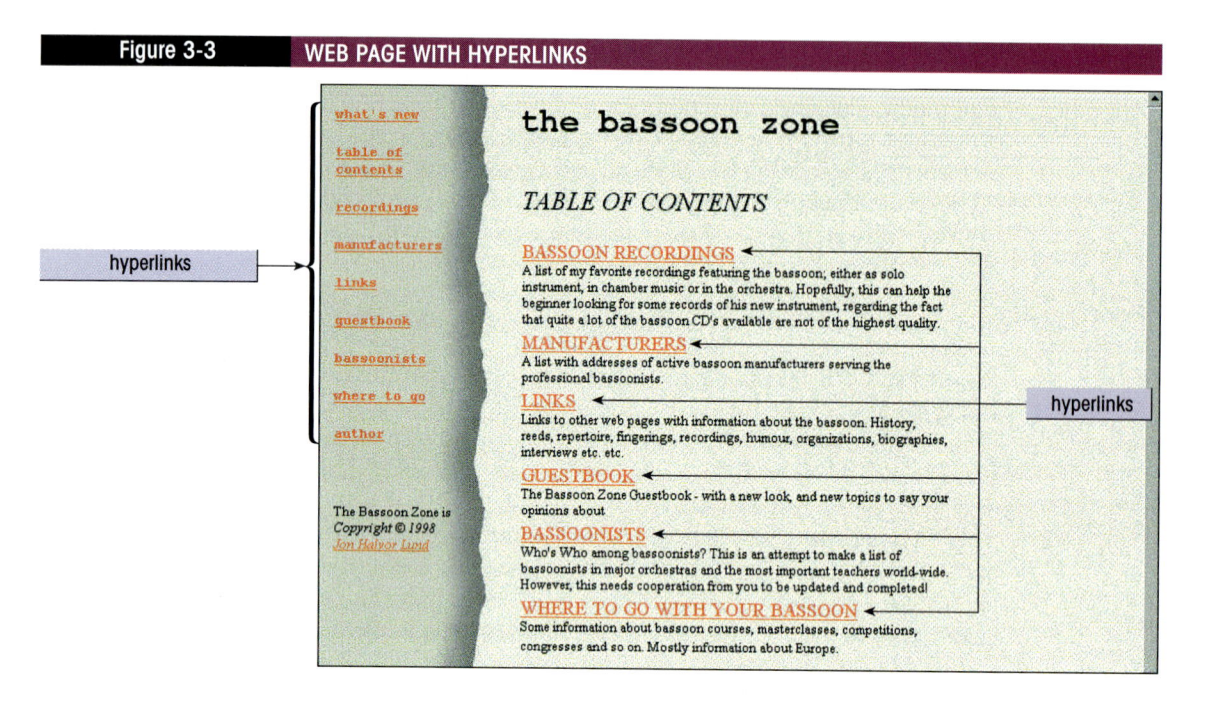

[Screenshot of "the bassoon zone" web page showing a left sidebar with hyperlinks (what's new, table of contents, recordings, manufacturers, links, guestbook, bassoonists, where to go, author) labeled "hyperlinks", and a Table of Contents with hyperlinked section headings (BASSOON RECORDINGS, MANUFACTURERS, LINKS, GUESTBOOK, BASSOONISTS, WHERE TO GO WITH YOUR BASSOON) also labeled "hyperlinks".]

Each of the hyperlinks on the Web page shown in Figure 3-3 allows the user to connect to another Web page. In turn, each of those Web pages contains hyperlinks to other pages, including one hyperlink that leads back to the Web page shown in Figure 3-3. Hyperlinks usually connect to other Web pages; however, they can lead to other media, including graphics image files, sound clips, and video files. Hyperlinks that connect to these types of files often are called **hypermedia links**. You are especially interested in learning more about these hypermedia links, but Maggie suggests you first need to understand a little more about how people organize the Web pages on their servers.

Maggie tells you that the easiest way to move from one Web page to another is to use the hyperlinks that the authors of Web pages have embedded in their HTML documents. Web page authors often use a graphic image as a hyperlink. Sometimes, it is difficult to identify which objects and text are hyperlinks just by looking at a Web page displayed on your computer. Fortunately, when you move the mouse pointer over a hyperlink in a Web browser, the pointer changes to 👆. For example, when you move the pointer over the Reservations hyperlink shown in Figure 3-4, it changes shape to indicate that if you click the Reservations text, the Web browser will open the Web page to which the hyperlink points.

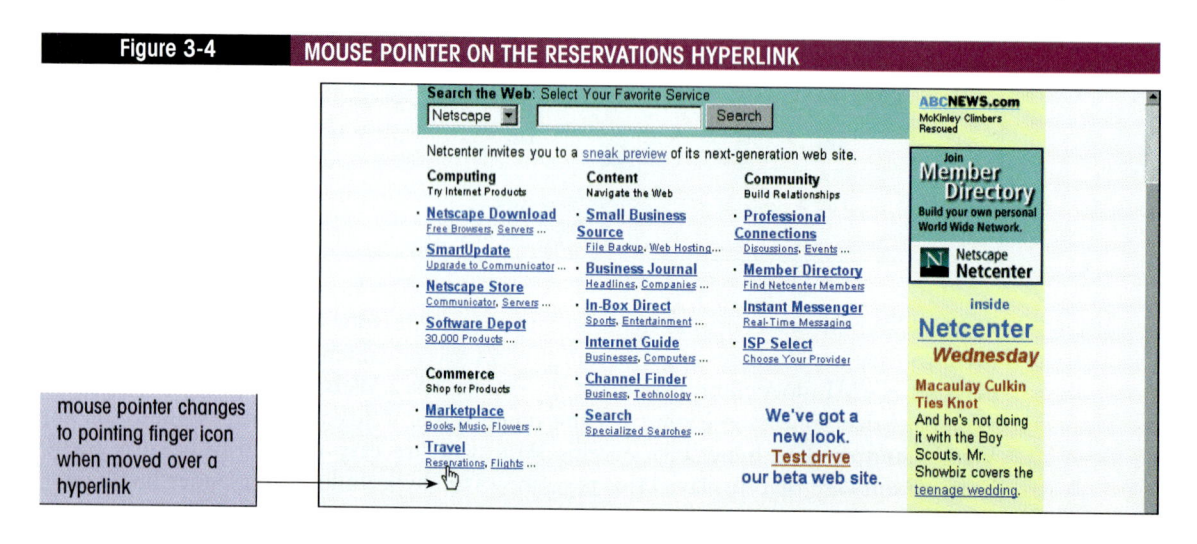

Figure 3-4   MOUSE POINTER ON THE RESERVATIONS HYPERLINK

[Screenshot of Netscape Netcenter page with categories including Computing, Content, Community, and Commerce. A pointing finger icon is shown over the "Reservations" hyperlink under Travel, with a callout labeled "mouse pointer changes to pointing finger icon when moved over a hyperlink".]

You might encounter an error message when you click one or more of the hyperlinks that appear on the search results page. Two common messages that appear in dialog boxes are the "server busy" and the "DNS entry not found" messages. Either of these messages means that your browser was unable to communicate successfully with the Web server that stores the page you requested. The cause for this inability might be temporary—in which case, you will be able to use the hyperlink later—or the cause might be permanent. The browser has no way of determining the cause of the connection failure, so it provides the same error messages in both cases. Another error message that you might receive displays as a Web page and includes the text "File not Found." This error message usually means that the Web page's location has changed permanently or that the Web page no longer exists.

Web Pages and Web Sites

Maggie explains that people who create Web pages usually have a collection of pages on one computer that they use as their Web server. A collection of linked Web pages that has a common theme or focus is called a **Web site**. The main page that all of the pages on a particular Web site are organized around and link back to is called the site's **home page**.

Home Pages

Maggie warns you that the term *home page* is used at least three different ways on the Web and that it is sometimes difficult to tell which meaning people intend when they use the term. The first definition of home page indicates the main page for a particular site: this home page is the first page that opens when you visit a particular Web site. The Bassoon Zone Table of Contents page shown in Figure 3-3 is a good example of this use. All of the hyperlinks on that page lead to pages in the Bassoon Zone site. Each page in the site links back to the Table of Contents page. The second definition of home page is the first page that opens when you start your Web browser. This type of home page might be an HTML document on your own computer. Some people create such home pages and include hyperlinks to Web sites that they frequently visit. If you are using a computer on your school's or employer's network, its Web browser might be configured to open the main page for the school or firm. The third definition of home page is the Web page that a particular Web browser loads the first time you use it. This page usually is stored at the Web site of the firm or other organization that created the Web browser software. Home pages that fall within the second or third definitions are sometimes called **start pages**.

Web Sites

Most people who create Web sites store all of the site's pages in one location, either on one computer or on one LAN. Some large Web sites, however, are distributed over a number of locations. In fact, it is sometimes difficult to determine where one Web site ends and another begins. Many people consider a Web site to be any group of Web pages that relates to one specific topic or organization, regardless of where the HTML documents are located.

Addresses on the Web

Maggie reminds you that there is no centralized control over the Internet. Therefore, no central starting point exists for the Web, which is a part of the Internet. However, each computer on the Internet does have a unique identification number, called an **IP (Internet Protocol) address**.

IP Addressing

The IP addressing system currently in use on the Internet uses a four-part number. Each part of the address is a number ranging from 0 to 255, and each part is separated from the previous part by a period, such as 106.29.242.17. You might hear a person pronounce this address as "one hundred six dot twenty-nine dot two four two dot seventeen." The combination of these four parts provides 4.2 billion possible addresses ($256 \times 256 \times 256 \times 256$). This number seemed adequate until 1998, when the accelerating growth of the Internet pushed the number of host computers from 5 to 30 million. Members of various Internet task forces are working to develop an alternative addressing system that will accommodate the projected growth; however, all of their working solutions require extensive hardware and software changes throughout the Internet.

Domain Name Addressing

Although each computer connected to the Internet has a unique IP address, most Web browsers do not use the IP address to locate Web sites and individual pages. Instead, they use domain name addressing. A **domain name** is a unique name associated with a specific IP address by a program that runs on an Internet host computer. This program, which coordinates the IP addresses and domain names for all computers attached to it, is called **DNS (domain name system) software**, and the host computer that runs this software is called a **domain name server**. Domain names can include any number of parts separated by periods; however, most domain names currently in use have only three or four parts. Domain names follow a hierarchical model that you can follow from top to bottom if you read the name from right to left. For example, the domain name gsb.uchicago.edu is the computer connected to the Internet at the Graduate School of Business (gsb), which is an academic unit of the University of Chicago (uchicago), which is an educational institution (edu). No other computer on the Internet has the same domain name.

The last part of a domain name is called its **top-level domain**. For example, DNS software on the Internet host computer that is responsible for the "edu" domain keeps track of the IP address for all of the educational institutions in its domain, including "uchicago." Similar DNS software on the "uchicago" Internet host computer would keep track of the academic units' computers in its domain, including the "gsb" computer. Figure 3-5 shows the seven currently used top-level domain names.

Figure 3-5 TOP-LEVEL INTERNET DOMAIN NAMES

DOMAIN NAME	DESCRIPTION
com	Businesses and other commercial enterprises
edu	Postsecondary educational institutions
gov	U.S. government agency, bureau, or department
int	International organizations
mil	U.S. military unit or agency
net	Network service provider or resource
org	Other organizations, usually charitable or not-for-profit

In addition to these top-level domain names, Internet host computers outside the United States often use two-letter country domain names. For example, the domain name uq.edu.au is the domain name for the University of Queensland (uq), which is an educational institution (edu) in Australia (au). Recently, state and local government organizations in the United States have started using an additional domain name, "us." The "us" domain is also being used by U.S. primary and secondary schools as they begin to create Web presences because the "edu" domain is reserved for postsecondary educational institutions. Figure 3-6 shows 10 of the most frequently accessed country domain names.

Figure 3-6 FREQUENTLY ACCESSED INTERNET COUNTRY DOMAIN NAMES

DOMAIN NAME	COUNTRY
au	Australia
ca	Canada
de	Germany
fi	Finland
fr	France
jp	Japan
nl	Netherlands
no	Norway
se	Sweden
uk	United Kingdom

The large increase in the number of host computers on the Internet has taxed the capacity of the existing top-level domain name structure, especially that of the "com" domain. A proposal to expand the available top-level domain names is currently under consideration by the Internet Policy Oversight Committee. The seven additional top-level domain names are shown in Figure 3-7.

Figure 3-7 PROPOSED ADDITIONAL TOP-LEVEL INTERNET DOMAIN NAMES

DOMAIN NAME	DESCRIPTION
firm	Business firms
shop	Businesses that offer goods for sale
web	Entities that engage in World Wide Web-related activities
arts	Entities that engage in cultural and entertainment activities
rec	Entities that engage in recreational and entertainment activities
info	Entities that provide information services
nom	Individuals

Uniform Resource Locators

The IP address and the domain name each identify a particular computer on the Internet, but they do not indicate where a Web page's HTML document resides on that computer. To identify a Web page's exact location, Web browsers rely on Uniform Resource Locators. A **Uniform Resource Locator (URL)** is a four-part addressing scheme that tells the Web browser:

- What transfer protocol to use when transporting the file
- The domain name of the computer on which the file resides
- The pathname of the folder or directory on the computer on which the file resides
- The name of the file

The **transfer protocol** is the set of rules that the computers use to move files from one computer to another on an internet. The most common transfer protocol used on the Internet is the hypertext transfer protocol (HTTP). You can indicate the use of this protocol by typing http:// as the first part of the URL. People do use other protocols to transfer files on the Internet, but most of these protocols were used more frequently before the Web became part of the Internet. Two protocols that you still might see on the Internet are the file transfer protocol (FTP), which is indicated in a URL as ftp:// and the Telnet protocol, which is indicated in a URL as telnet://. FTP is just another way to transfer files, and Telnet is a set of rules for establishing a remote terminal connection to another computer.

The domain name is the Internet address of the computer described in the preceding section. The pathname describes the hierarchical directory or folder structure on the computer that stores the file. Most people are familiar with the structure used on Windows and DOS PCs, which uses the backslash character (\) to separate the structure levels. URLs follow the conventions established in the UNIX operating system that use the forward slash character (/) to separate the structure levels. The forward slash character works properly in a URL, even when it is pointing to a file on a Windows or DOS computer.

The filename is the name that the computer uses to identify the Web page's HTML document. On most computers, the filename extension of an HTML document is either .html or .htm. Although many PC operating systems are not case-sensitive, computers that use the UNIX operating system *are* case-sensitive. Therefore, if you are entering a URL that includes mixed-case and you do not know the type of computer on which the file resides, it is safer to retain the mixed-case format of the URL.

Not all URLs include a filename. If a URL does not include a filename, most Web browsers will load the file named index.html. The **index.html** filename is the default name for a Web site's home page. Figure 3-8 shows an example of a URL annotated to show all four parts of the URL.

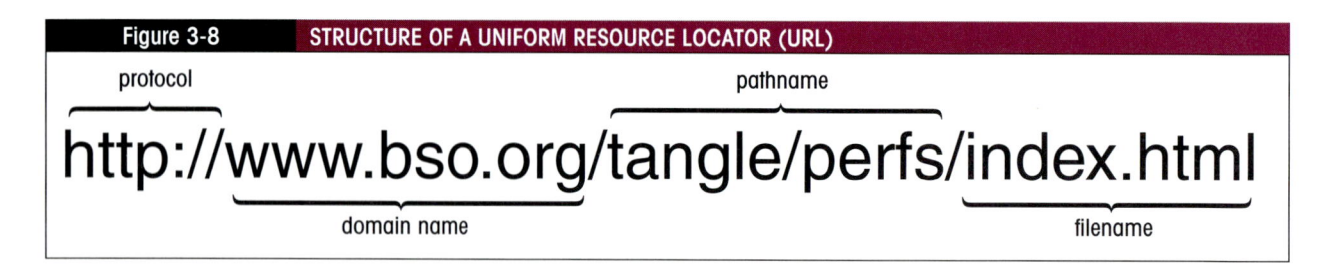

Figure 3-8 — STRUCTURE OF A UNIFORM RESOURCE LOCATOR (URL)

protocol | pathname

http://www.bso.org/tangle/perfs/index.html

domain name | filename

The URL shown in Figure 3-8 uses the HTTP protocol and points to a computer at the Boston Symphony Orchestra. The Boston Symphony's Web page contains many different kinds of information about the orchestra. The path shown in Figure 3-8 includes two levels. The first level indicates that the information is about the orchestra's summer home at

Tanglewood (tangle), and the second level indicates that the page will contain information about the orchestra's performances (perfs) at Tanglewood. The filename (index.html) indicates that this page is the home page in the Tanglewood performances folder or directory.

You tell Maggie how much you appreciate all of the help she has given you by explaining how you can use Internet addresses to find information on the Web. Now you understand that the real secret to finding good information on the Web is to know the right URLs. Maggie tells you that you can find URLs in many places; for example, newspapers and magazines often publish URLs of Web sites that might interest their readers. Friends who know about the subject area in which you are interested also are good sources. The best source, however, is the Web itself.

You are eager to begin learning how to use a Web browser, so Maggie explains some elements common to all Web browsers. Most Web browsers have similar functions, which makes it easy to use any Web browser after you have learned how to use one.

Main Elements of Web Browsers

Now that you know a little more about Web sites, you start to wonder how you can make your computer communicate with the Internet. Maggie tells you that there are many Web browsers that turn your computer into a Web client that communicates through an Internet service provider (ISP) or a network connection with the Web servers. Two popular browsers are **Netscape Navigator**, or simply **Navigator**, and **Microsoft Internet Explorer**, or simply **Internet Explorer**. Each browser has been released in different versions; however, the steps in this book should work for most browsers.

Maggie reminds you that most Windows programs use a standard graphical user interface (GUI) design that includes a number of common screen elements. As you can see in Figures 3-9 and 3-10, the Navigator and Internet Explorer program windows share common Windows elements: a title bar at the top of the window, a scroll bar on the right side of the window, and a status bar at the bottom of the window

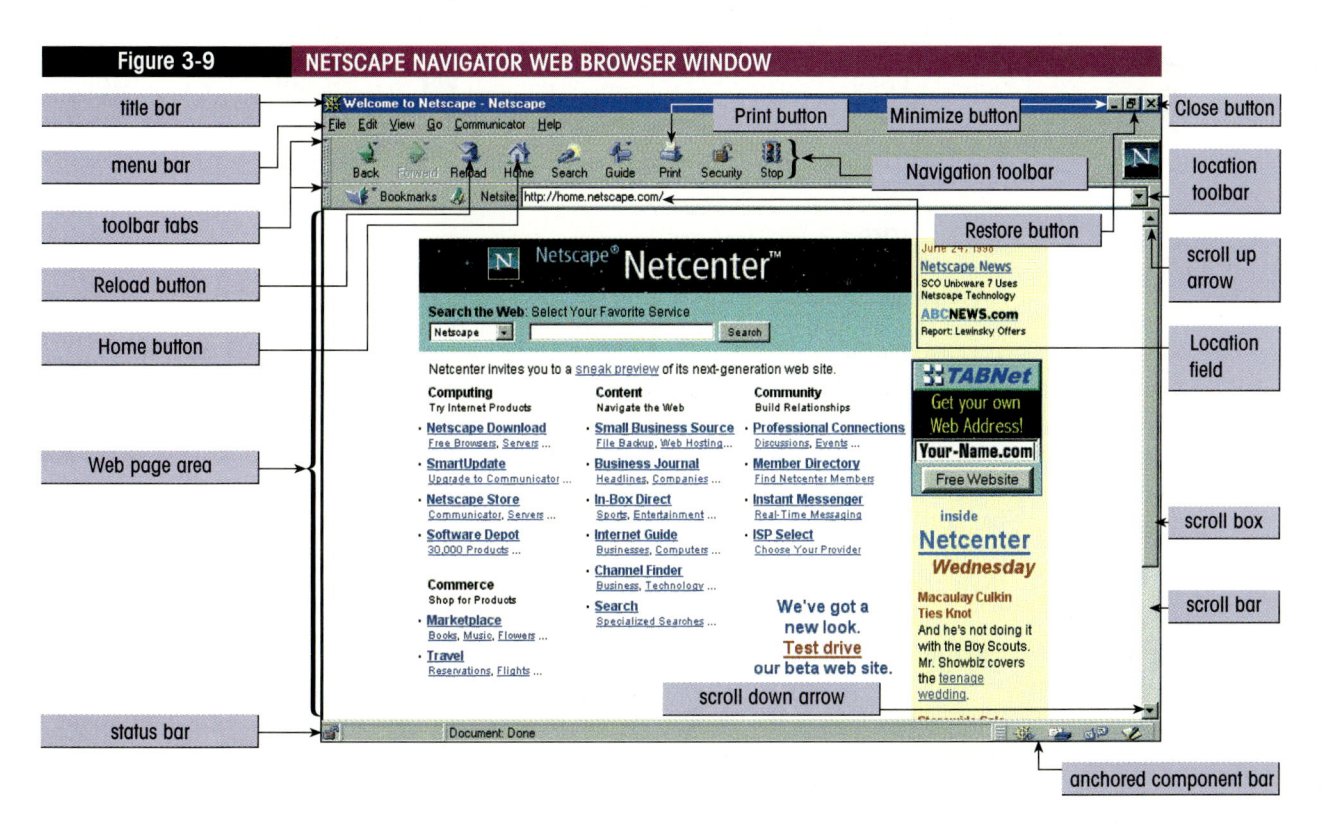

Figure 3-9   NETSCAPE NAVIGATOR WEB BROWSER WINDOW

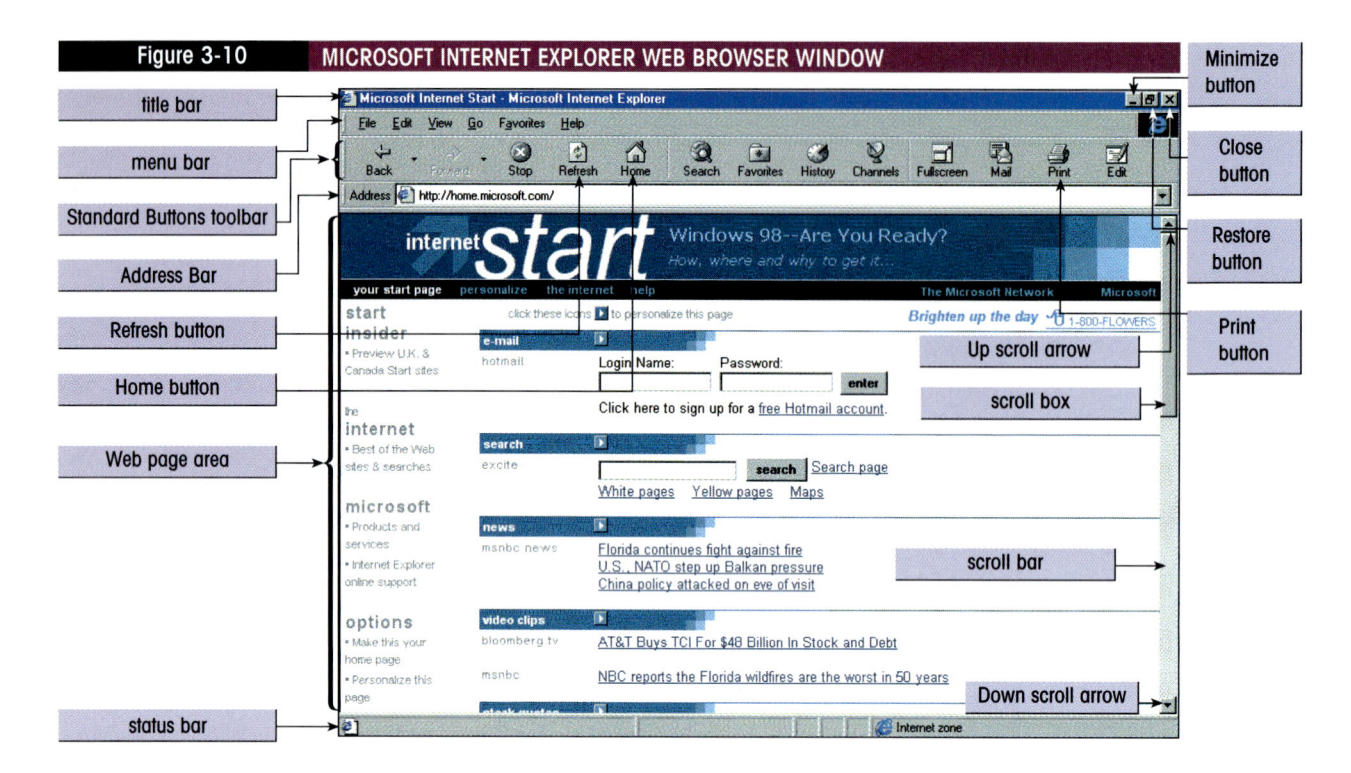

Figure 3-10: MICROSOFT INTERNET EXPLORER WEB BROWSER WINDOW

Labels: title bar, menu bar, Standard Buttons toolbar, Address Bar, Refresh button, Home button, Web page area, status bar, Minimize button, Close button, Restore button, Print button, Up scroll arrow, scroll box, scroll bar, Down scroll arrow

The menu bar appears below the title bar. Many of the toolbar button functions in Navigator and Internet Explorer are similar, too. Next, Maggie describes each of these elements.

Title Bar

A Web browser's **title bar** shows the name of the open Web page and the Web browser's program name. As in all Windows programs, you can double-click the title bar to resize the window quickly. The title bar contains the Minimize, Restore, and Close buttons when the window is maximized to fill the screen. To restore a resized window to its original size, click the Maximize button.

Scroll Bars

A Web page can be much longer or wider than a regular-sized document, so you usually need to use the **scroll bar** at the right side of the program window to move the page up, down, right, or left through the document window. You can use the mouse to click the **Up scroll** arrow or the **Down scroll** arrow to move the Web page up or down through the window's **Web page area**. Although most Web pages are designed to resize automatically when loaded into different browser windows with different display areas, some Web pages might be wider than your browser window. When this happens, the browser places another scroll bar at the bottom of the window and above the status bar, so you can move the page horizontally through the browser. You also can click and drag the scroll box in the scroll bar to move the Web page through the window.

Status Bar

The **status bar** at the bottom of the browser window includes information about the browser's operations. Each browser uses the status bar to deliver different information, but generally, the status bar indicates the name of the Web page that is loading, the load status (partial or complete), and important messages, such as "Document: Done." Some Web sites send messages as part of their Web pages that are displayed in the status bar, as well. You will learn more about the specific functions of the status bar in Navigator and Internet Explorer in Sessions 3.2 and 3.3, respectively.

Menu Bar

The browser's **menu bar** provides a convenient way for you to execute typical File, Edit, View, and Help commands. In addition to these common Windows command sets, the menu bar also provides specialized command sets for the browser that allow you to navigate the Web.

Home Button

Clicking the **Home** button in Navigator or the **Home** button in Internet Explorer displays the home (or start) page for your browser. Most Web browsers let you specify a page that loads automatically every time you start the program. You might not be able to do this if you are in your school's computer lab because schools often set the start page for all browsers on campus and then lock that setting. If you are using your own computer, you can use this program feature to choose your own start page. Some people like to use a Web page that someone else has created and made available for others to use. One example of a start page is the My Virtual Reference Desk page shown in Figure 3-11.

Figure 3-11   MY VIRTUAL REFERENCE DESK WEB PAGE

News		Magazines
7amWorldWires	**(1) First Things First** — Where Each Day Begins	Atlantic
ABC		Forbes
AP	**(2) Ask the Experts** — Answers to Questions from Experts	Life
Africa News		Money
BBC	**(3) Devices on the Net** — Cams: outdoor, traffic, live	Nat. Geograph.
C-SPAN Sched		People
CBS	**(4) Do-It-Yourself** — How-To's and Do-It-Yourself Resources	Pop. Mechanic
CNN		Pop. Science
Canada.com	**(5) Fast Facts 1998** — Over 375 Sources of Specific Facts	Reader's Dig
FOX		Rolling Stone
Latino News	**(6) Free Stuff** — Over 230 Free Stuff Sites	Salon
MSNBC		Slate
NPR	**(7) Front Page** — Main Gateway to MVRD	Time
ForeignWire		TV Guide
France-Presse	**(8) Fun Stuff** — Fun and Games on the Net	U.S. News
NewsHub		
Reuters		**Features I**
UPI		
WorldNetDaily		Books

| | (12) New Sites Added — New Links Added to MVRD During Week |
| (13) My Facts Page — 24 Facts / Reference Categories |
| (14) My Homework Helper — Research & Study Resources for K-College |
| (15) My Search Engines — 260 Search Engines - 19 Categories |
| (16) My Virt. Encyclopedia — 50 Subject Categories |
| (17) My Virt. Newspaper — USA / Worldwide Newspapers, Wire Services |
| (18) My Weather Sites — Over 150 Weather Related Sites |
| (19) Quick Ref. / Research — Over 300 Links to Essential Facts & Information |
| (20) Table of Contents — Listing of All MVRD Features |
| (21) What's New — New Features Added to MVRD |
| (22) Window 95 / NT — Links to Win 95 / NT Resources |

Papers
Age, The
Ariz. Republic
Ark.Dem.-Gaz
Asahi
AtlaJourConst
Bahrain Trib.
Balt. Sun
Bild
Boston Globe
Chi. Sun-Times
Chicago Trib.
China Daily

(9) Internet Help / FAQ — Tutorials and Guides, on Learning the Net

(10) Mission Statement — Ojectives of MVRD

(11) My Daily Almanac — A Diverse Blend of Daily Amusements

Calendar
Classifieds
Comics
Crosswords
Daily Almanac
Drudge Report
EarthCam
Editorials
Editorial Toons

Features II

Entertainment
Games

Pages such as the one shown in Figure 3-11 offer links to pages that many Web users frequently use. The people and organizations that create these pages often sell advertising space on their pages to pay the cost of maintaining their sites.

Quick Access to Web Page Directories and Guides

You are starting to understand how to use the Internet to gather information about wind quintets. Maggie explains that a **Web directory** is a Web page that contains a list of Web page categories, such as education or recreation. The hyperlinks on a Web directory page lead to other pages that contain lists of subcategories that lead to other category lists and Web pages that relate to the category topics. **Web search engines** are Web pages that conduct searches of the Web to find the words or expressions that you enter. The result of such a search is a Web page that contains hyperlinks to Web pages that contain matching text or expressions. These pages can give new users an easy way to find information on the Web.

Web addresses can be very long and hard to remember—even if you are using domain names instead of IP addresses. In Netscape, you use a **bookmark** to save the URL of a specific page so you can return to it. In Internet Explorer, you save the URL as a **favorite** in the Favorites folder. You realize that using the browser to remember important pages will be a terrific asset as you start collecting information for the quintet, so you ask Maggie to explain more about how to return to a Web page.

Using the History List

As you click the hyperlinks to go to new Web pages, the browser stores the locations of each page you visit during a single session in a **history list**. You click the **Back** button in Navigator or the **Back** button in Internet Explorer, and the **Forward** button in Navigator or the **Forward** button in Internet Explorer to move through the history list.

When you start your browser, both buttons are inactive (dimmed) because no history list for your new session exists yet. After you follow one or more hyperlinks, the Back button lets you retrace your path back through the hyperlinks you have followed. Once you use the Back button, the Forward button becomes active and lets you move forward through the session's history list.

In most Web browsers, if you click and hold the mouse button down on either the Back or Forward button (or if you right-click either button), a portion of the history list appears. You can reload any page on the list by clicking its name in the list. The Back and Forward buttons duplicate the functions of commands on the browser's menu commands. You will learn more about the history list in Sessions 3.2 and 3.3.

Reloading a Web Page

Clicking the **Reload** button in Navigator or the **Refresh** button in Internet Explorer loads the same Web page that appears in the browser window again. The browser stores a copy of every Web page it displays on your computer's hard drive in a **cache** folder, which increases the speed at which the browser can display pages as you navigate through the history list. The cache folder lets the browser load the pages from the client instead of from the remote Web server.

When you click the Reload button or the Refresh button, the browser contacts the Web server to see if the Web page has changed since it was stored in the cache folder. If it has changed, the browser gets the new page from the Web server; otherwise, it loads the cache folder copy.

Stopping a Web Page Transfer

Sometimes a Web page takes a long time to load. When this occurs, you can click the **Stop** button in Navigator or the **Stop** button in Internet Explorer to halt the Web page transfer from the server; then you can click the hyperlink again. A second attempt may connect and transfer the page more quickly. You also might want to use the Stop button to abort a transfer when you accidentally click a hyperlink that you do not want to follow.

Returning to a Web Page

You use a Navigator bookmark or Internet Explorer's Favorites feature to store and organize a list of Web pages that you have visited so you can return to them easily without having to remember the URL or search for the page again. Navigator bookmarks and Internet Explorer favorites each work very much like a paper bookmark that you would use in a printed book: they mark the page at which you stopped reading.

You can save as many Navigator bookmarks or Internet Explorer favorites as you want to mark all of your favorite Web pages, so you can return to pages that you frequently use or pages that are important to your research or tasks. You could even bookmark every Web page you visit!

Keeping track of many bookmarks and favorites requires an organizing system. You store bookmarks or favorites in a system folder. Netscape stores bookmarks in one file on your computer, and Internet Explorer stores *each* favorite as a separate file on your computer. Storing each favorite separately, instead of storing all bookmarks together, offers somewhat more flexibility but uses more disk space. You can organize your bookmarks or favorites in many different ways to meet your needs. For example, you might store all of the bookmarks or favorites for Web pages that include information about wind quintets in a folder named "Wind Quintet Information."

Printing and Saving Web Pages

You can use your browser to view Web pages, but sometimes you will want to store entire Web pages on disk; at other times, you will only want to store selected portions of Web page text or particular graphics from a Web page.

Printing a Web Page

The easiest way to print a Web page is to click the **Print** button in Navigator or the **Print** button in Internet Explorer. In either case, the current page (or frame) that appears in the Web page area is sent to the printer. If the page contains light colors or many graphics, you might want to consider changing the printing options so the page prints without the background, or with all black text. You will learn how to change the print settings for Navigator and Internet Explorer in Sessions 3.2 and 3.3, respectively.

Although printing an entire Web page is often useful, there are times when you need to save all or part of the page to disk, as you will see next.

Saving a Web Page

When you save a Web page to disk, you save only the text portion. If the Web page contains graphics, such as photos, drawings, or icons, you should note that these graphics will not be saved with the HTML document. To save the graphics, right-click them in the browser window, click Save Image As or Save Picture As on the shortcut menu, and then save the graphic to the same location as the Web's HTML document. The graphics file is specified to appear on the HTML document as a hyperlink, so you might have to change the HTML code in the Web page to identify the location of the graphic. Copying the graphics files to the same disk as the HTML document will *usually* work. You will learn more about saving a Web page and its graphics in Sessions 3.2 and 3.3.

Reproducing Web Pages and Copyright Law

Maggie explains that there might be significant restrictions on the way that you can use information or images that you copy from another entity's Web site. The United States and other countries have copyright laws that govern the use of photocopies, audio or video recordings, and other reproductions of authors' original work. A **copyright** is the legal right of the author or other owner of an original work to control the reproduction, distribution, and sale of that work. A copyright comes into existence as soon as the work is placed into a tangible form such as a printed copy, an electronic file, or a Web page. The copyright exists even if the work does not contain a copyright notice. If you do not know whether material that you find on the Web is copyrighted, the safest course of action is to assume that it is.

You can use limited amounts of copyrighted information in term papers and other reports that you prepare in an academic setting, but you must cite the source. Commercial use of copyrighted material is much more restricted. You should obtain permission from the copyright holder before using anything you copy from a Web page. It can be difficult to determine the owner of a source's copyright if no notice appears on the Web page; however, most Web pages provide a hyperlink to the e-mail address of the person responsible for maintaining the page. That person, often called a **webmaster**, usually can provide information about the copyright status of materials on the page.

QUICK CHECK

1. True or False: Web browser software runs on a Web server computer.

2. Name two things you can accomplish using HTML tags.

3. Briefly define the term *home page*.

4. Name two examples of hypermedia.

5. A local political candidate is creating a Web site to help in her campaign for office. Describe some of the things she might want to include in her Web site.

6. What is the difference between IP addressing and domain name addressing?

7. Identify and interpret the meaning of each part of the following URL:
   http://www.savethetrees.org/main.html

8. What is the difference between a Web directory and a Web search engine?

Now that you understand the basic function of a browser and how to find information on the Web, you are ready to start using your browser to find information for the quintet. If you are using Navigator, your instructor will assign Session 3.2; if you are using Internet Explorer, your instructor will assign Session 3.3. The authors recommend, however, that you read both sessions because you might encounter a different browser on a public or employer's computer in the future.

TUTORIAL 3 BROWSER BASICS   WEB   3.15   INTERNET

SESSION 3.2

In this session, you will learn how to configure the Netscape Navigator Web browser and use it to display Web pages and follow hyperlinks to other Web pages. You will learn how to copy text and images from Web pages and how to mark pages so you can return to them easily.

Starting Netscape Navigator

To be effective in searching the Web for the Sunset Wind Quintet, Maggie is sure that you will want to become familiar with Netscape Navigator from Netscape Communications Corporation, which is part of a suite of programs called Netscape Communicator. The other programs in the Communicator suite provide e-mail, discussion group, realtime collaboration, and Web page creation tools. This overview assumes that you have Navigator installed on your computer. You should have your computer turned on so you can see the Windows desktop.

To start Navigator:

1. Click the **Start** button on the taskbar, point to **Programs**, point to **Netscape Communicator**, and then click **Netscape Navigator**. After a moment, Navigator opens.

   TROUBLE? If you cannot find Netscape Communicator on the Programs menu, check to see if a Netscape Navigator shortcut icon appears on the desktop, and then double-click it. If you do not see the shortcut icon, ask your instructor or technical support person for help. The program might be installed in a different folder on the computer you are using.

2. If the program does not fill the screen entirely, click the **Maximize** button on the Navigator program's title bar. Your screen should look like Figure 3-12.

Figure 3-12   NETSCAPE HOME PAGE

if you do not have a complete installation of Netscape Communicator, then you will not see this menu item (the "Window" menu item will appear in its place)

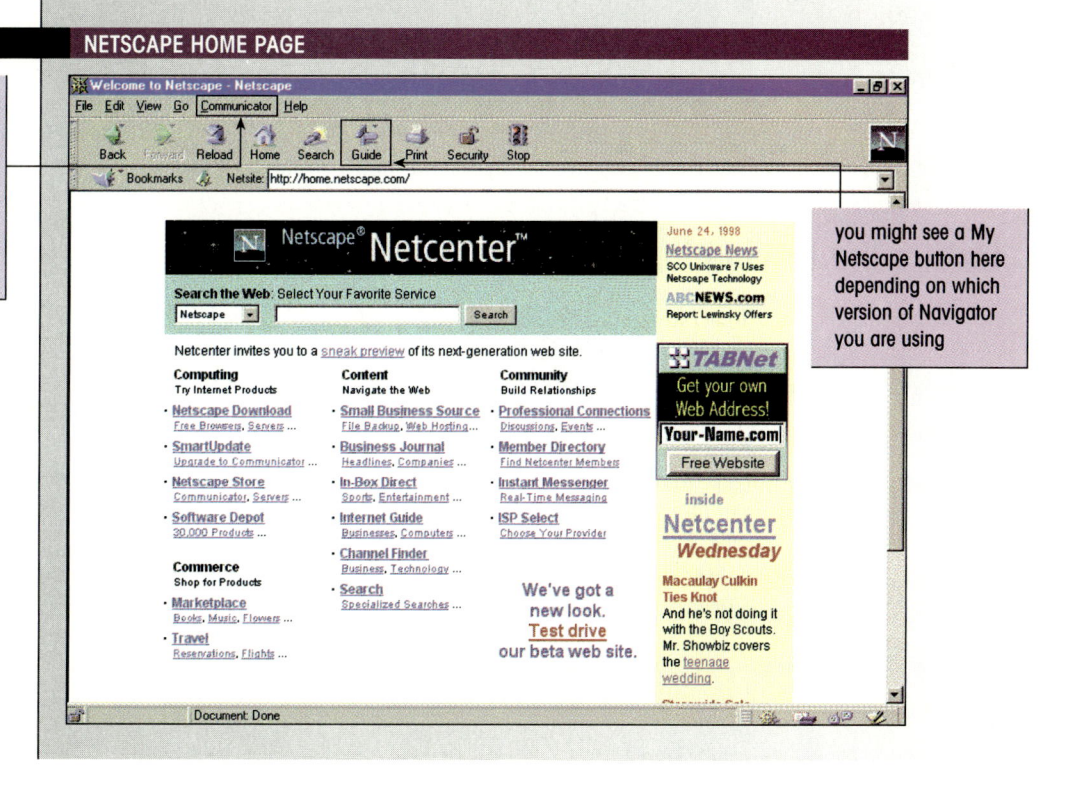

you might see a My Netscape button here depending on which version of Navigator you are using

TROUBLE? Figure 3-12 shows the Netscape Communications Corporation home page, which is the page that Netscape Navigator opens the first time it starts. Your computer might be configured to open to a different Web page, or no page at all.

TROUBLE? If necessary, click View on the menu bar, and then click Hide Personal Toolbar, so your screen looks like Figure 3-12.

TROUBLE? If a floating component bar like the one shown in Figure 3-13 appears anywhere in your window, click its Close button ⊠ to anchor it to the right edge of the status bar.

Figure 3-13   NETSCAPE COMMUNICATOR FLOATING COMPONENT BAR

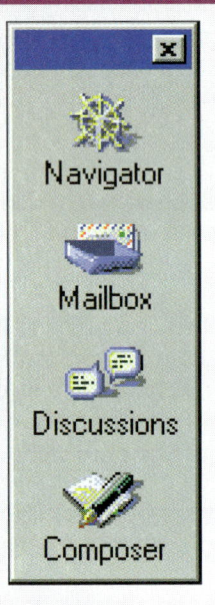

Now that you understand how to start Navigator, you tell Maggie that you are ready to start using it to find information on the Internet. To find information, you need to know how the Navigator toolbars and menu commands work.

Using the Navigation Toolbar and Menu Commands

The Navigation toolbar includes 10 buttons that execute frequently used commands for browsing the Web. Figure 3-14 shows the Navigation toolbar buttons and describes their functions. (Depending on which version of Navigator you are using, you might see different toolbar buttons. Use online Help to get more information about buttons not pictured in Figure 3-14.)

In addition to the toolbar buttons, the Navigation toolbar contains a toolbar tab that you can click to hide the toolbar so there is more room to display a Web page in the Web page area. You can hide both the Navigation and Location toolbars so that the toolbar tabs fold up and remain visible, or you can hide the toolbars completely by using the options on the View menu, as you will see next.

Figure 3-14 NAVIGATION TOOLBAR BUTTONS

BUTTON	BUTTON NAME	DESCRIPTION
	Back	Moves to the last previously visited Web page
	Forward	Moves to the next previously visited Web page
	Reload	Reloads the current page
	Home	Loads the program's defined home page
	Search	Opens a Web page that has hyperlinks to Web search engines and directories
or	Guide or My Netscape	Opens a Web page that contains Netscape's Guide, a hierarchical Web directory Loads your designated start page
	Print	Prints the current Web page
	Security	Shows security information about the Web page that is currently displayed
	Stop	Stops the transfer of a new Web page
	Netscape Home Page	Loads the Netscape home page

REFERENCE WINDOW   RW

Hiding or showing a toolbar using a toolbar tab
- To hide the toolbar, click the toolbar tab for the toolbar that you want to hide. The toolbar tab will appear under any remaining toolbars.

or
- Click View on the menu bar, and then click the Hide option to hide the desired toolbar.
- To show a hidden toolbar, click the toolbar tab for the toolbar you want to show.

or
- Click View on the menu bar, and then click the Show option to show the desired toolbar.

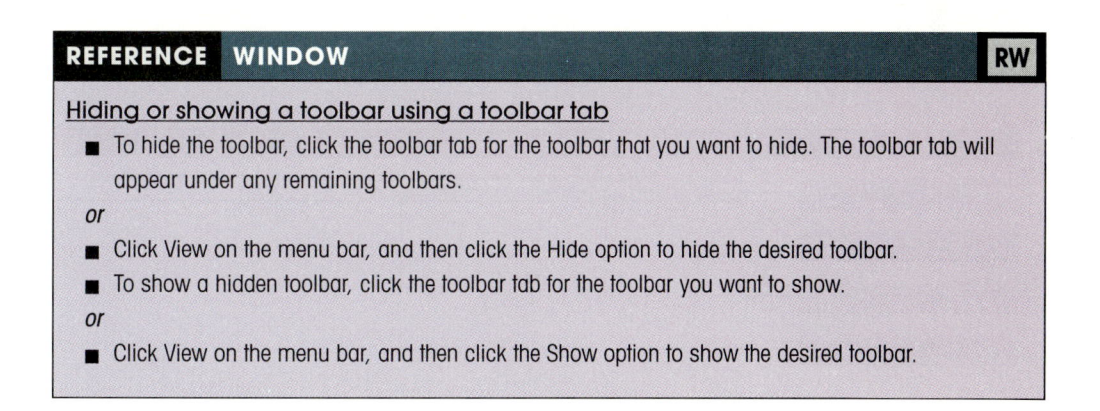

To hide the Navigation toolbar and then show it again:

1. Click the **Navigation toolbar** tab, which appears on the left edge of the Navigation toolbar. The toolbar will disappear and its toolbar tab appears under the Location toolbar.

2. Move the pointer to the Navigation toolbar tab below the Location toolbar and notice that the message indicates that you are pointing to the Navigation toolbar.

3. Click the **Navigation toolbar** tab. The Navigation toolbar appears above the Location toolbar.

You can use the toolbar tabs to hide or show the toolbars quickly. However, if you want to hide the toolbars and their tabs, you must use the View menu. The View menu commands are toggles. A **toggle** is like a pushbutton switch on a television set; you press the button once to turn on the television and press it a second time to turn it off.

> ### To hide the Navigation toolbar using the View menu:
>
> 1. Click **View** on the menu bar.
>
> 2. Click **Hide Navigation Toolbar** to hide the Navigation toolbar and its toolbar tab. To see the Navigation toolbar again, you use the Show Navigation Toolbar command on the View menu.
>
>   **TROUBLE?** If Hide Navigation Toolbar does not appear on the View menu, then the Navigation toolbar already is hidden. Go to Step 3.
>
> 3. Click **View** on the menu bar, and then click **Show Navigation Toolbar** to show the toolbar again.

Now you are ready to use the Navigation toolbar buttons and the menu commands to browse the Web.

Using the Location Toolbar Elements

Maggie explains that there are four elements in the Location toolbar: the **Location toolbar** tab, the **Location** field, **Page proxy** icon, and the **Bookmarks** button. Figure 3-15 shows these four elements.

Figure 3-15	LOCATION TOOLBAR BUTTONS

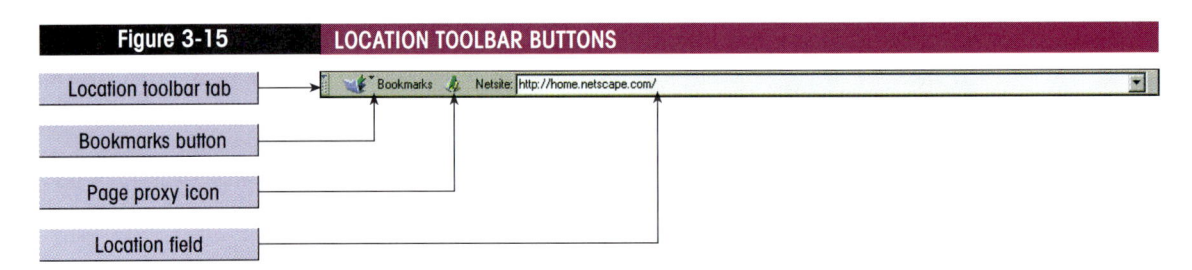

Labels: Location toolbar tab, Bookmarks button, Page proxy icon, Location field

Hiding and Showing the Location Toolbar

You can click the Location toolbar tab or use the View menu commands to hide and show the Location toolbar, just as when you used the Navigation toolbar tab and the View menu commands to hide and show the Navigation toolbar. Clicking the Location toolbar tab hides the toolbar but keeps the tab visible so it folds up under any visible toolbars.

Entering a URL into the Location Field

Maggie tells you to use the **Location field** to enter URLs directly into Netscape Navigator. Marianna gave you the URL for the Pennsylvania Quintet, so you can see its Web page.

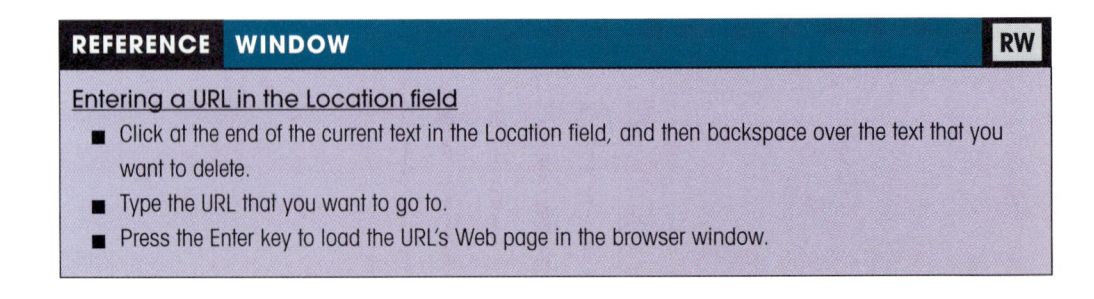

REFERENCE WINDOW — RW

Entering a URL in the Location field

- Click at the end of the current text in the Location field, and then backspace over the text that you want to delete.
- Type the URL that you want to go to.
- Press the Enter key to load the URL's Web page in the browser window.

To load the Pennsylvania Quintet's Web page:

1. Click in the Location field; if there is text in the Location field, click at the end of the text and then press the **Backspace** key to delete it.

   TROUBLE? Make sure that you delete *all* of the text in the Location field so the text you type in Step 2 will be correct.

2. Type **http://www.course.com/NewPerspectives/Internet** in the Location field to go to the Student Online Companion page on the Course Technology Web site. In this book, you will go to the Course Technology site and then click hyperlinks to go to individual Web pages.

3. Press the **Enter** key. The Location field's label changes from "Location" to "Go to" and the Student Online Companion Web page loads as shown in Figure 3-16. When the entire page has loaded, the Location field's label will change back to "Location."

   TROUBLE? If a Dial-Up Networking dialog box opens after you press the Enter key, click the Connect button. You must have an Internet connection to complete the steps in this tutorial.

Figure 3-16   STUDENT ONLINE COMPANION WEB PAGE

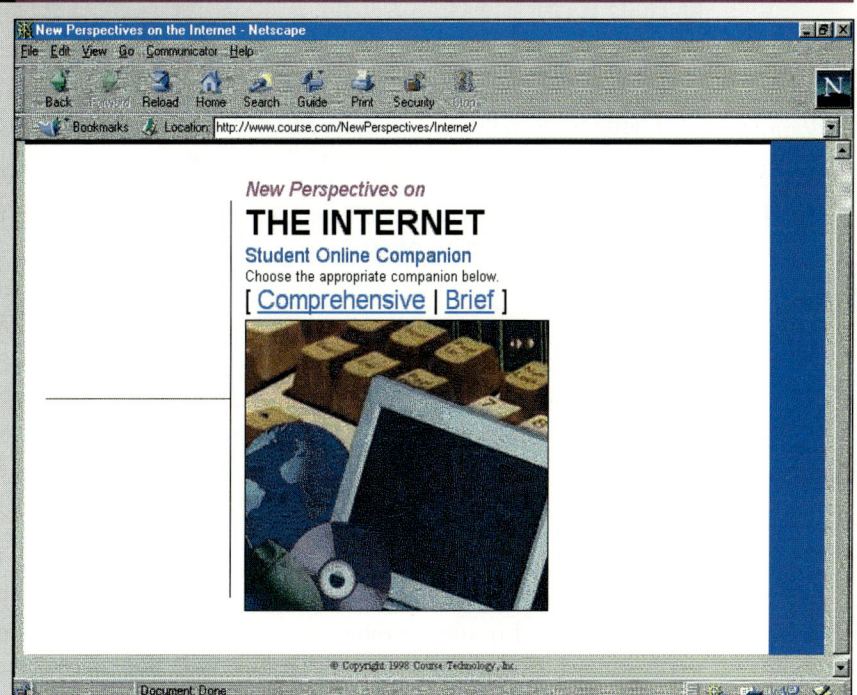

4. Click the link for the book you are using to open the main page, click the **Tutorial 3** link to open the page that contains the links for this tutorial, and then click the **Session 3.2** link in the left frame to see the links in the right frame.

5. Click the **Pennsylvania Quintet** link. The Web page opens, as shown in Figure 3-17.

INTERNET   WEB 3.20   TUTORIAL 3   BROWSER BASICS

Figure 3-17   PENNSYLVANIA QUINTET'S WEB PAGE

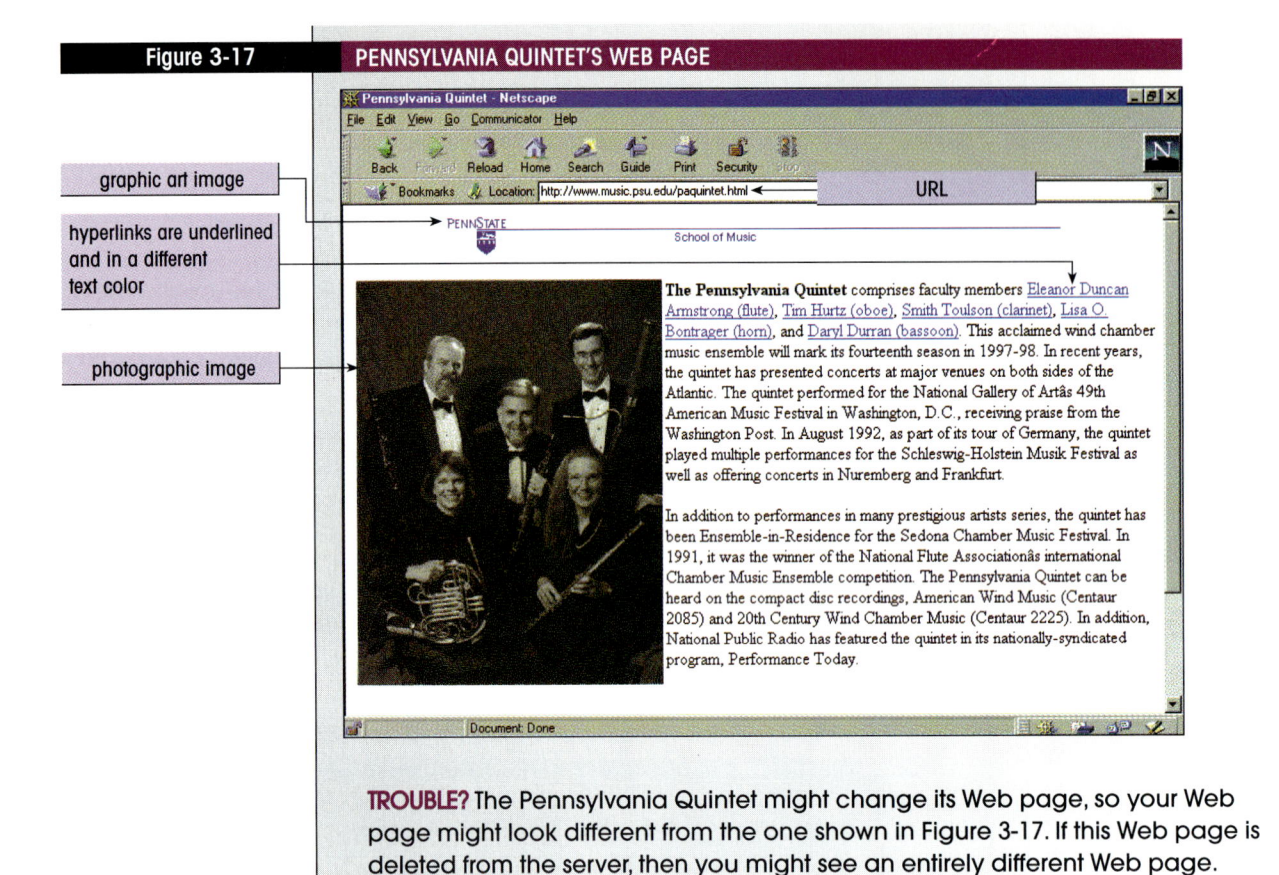

- graphic art image
- hyperlinks are underlined and in a different text color
- photographic image
- URL

TROUBLE? The Pennsylvania Quintet might change its Web page, so your Web page might look different from the one shown in Figure 3-17. If this Web page is deleted from the server, then you might see an entirely different Web page. However, the steps should work the same.

6. Read the Web page, and then click the **Back** button to return to the Student Online Companion page.

You like the format of the Pennsylvania Quintet's home page, so you want to make sure that you can go back to that page later if you need to review its contents. Maggie explains that you can write down the URL so you can refer to it later, but an easier way is to store the URL in a **bookmark file** to save in the Navigator program for future use.

Creating a Bookmark for a Web Site

You use a **bookmark** to store and organize a list of Web pages that you have visited so you can return to them easily. You use the **Bookmarks** button and the **Page proxy** icon on the Location toolbar to use the bookmarking system. You can use the Bookmarks button to add new bookmarks, to open the Bookmarks menu, or open the Bookmarks window. Figure 3-18 shows a Bookmarks menu that contains bookmarks that are sorted into categories according to the user's needs.

Figure 3-18 USING THE BOOKMARKS BUTTON TO OPEN THE BOOKMARKS MENU

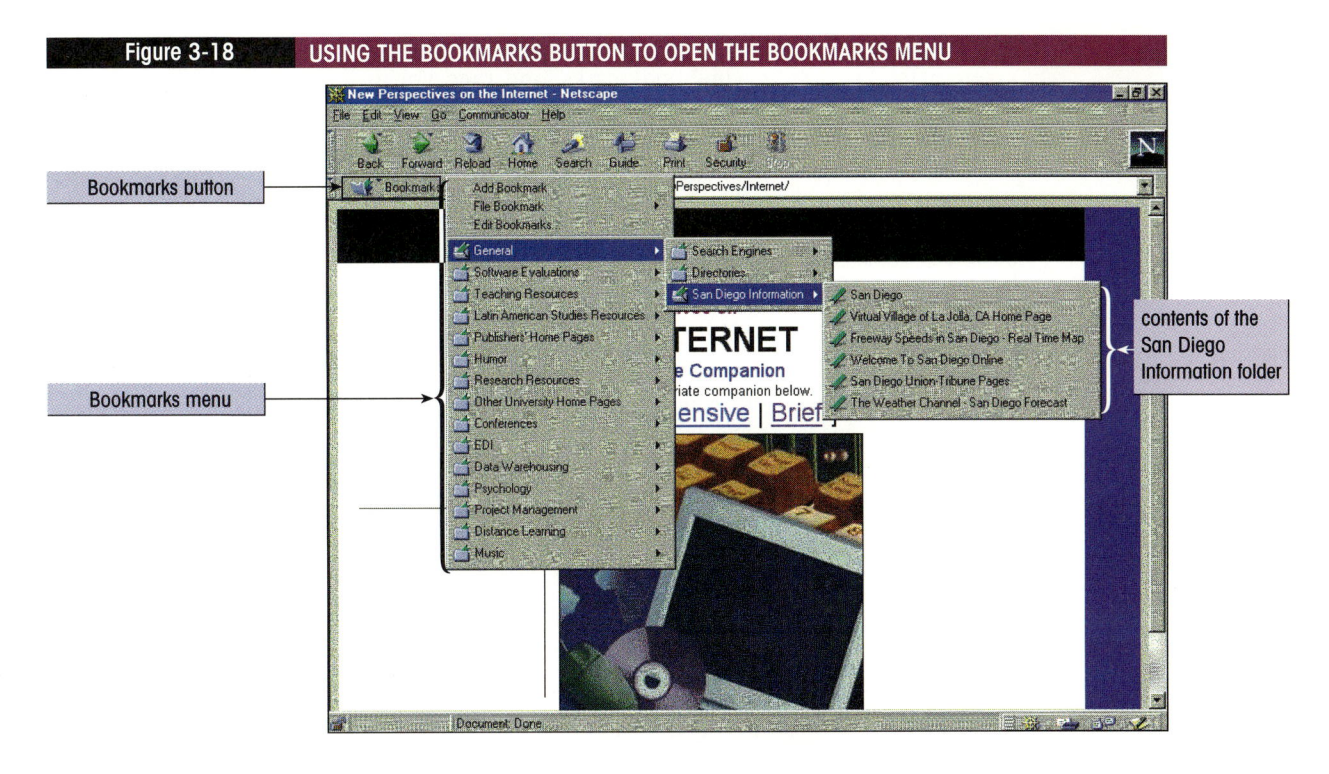

(Screenshot of Netscape browser showing cascading Bookmarks menu. Labels: "Bookmarks button", "Bookmarks menu", "contents of the San Diego Information folder" listing: San Diego; Virtual Village of La Jolla, CA Home Page; Freeway Speeds in San Diego - Real Time Map; Welcome To San Diego Online; San Diego Union-Tribune Pages; The Weather Channel - San Diego Forecast.)

The hierarchical structure of the bookmark file is easy to see in Figure 3-18. The six Web pages shown in the San Diego Information folder provide information about San Diego.

A **Bookmarks window** provides the same information as the cascading Bookmark menus, but it also includes tools for editing and rearranging the bookmarks. For example, you can use the Bookmarks window menu commands to create new folders, or you can use drag and drop to move Web pages to another folder or to move folders to new locations. Figure 3-19 shows the same set of bookmarks in the Bookmarks window, where you can see more detail about the user's bookmarks and their organization.

Figure 3-19 EXAMINING BOOKMARKS IN THE BOOKMARKS WINDOW

(Screenshot of the Bookmarks window. Labels: "header", "closed folders", "bookmarks", "open folders", "URL of selected bookmark". Contents shown: Main Bookmarks > General > Search Engines, Directories, San Diego Information (San Diego; Virtual Village of La Jolla, CA Home Page; Freeway Speeds in San Diego - Real Time Map [selected]; Welcome To San Diego Online; San Diego Union-Tribune Pages; The Weather Channel - San Diego Forecast), Software Evaluations, Teaching Resources, Latin American Studies Resources (WWW Virtual Library: Latin American Studies; Yahoo! - Social Science:Latin American Studies; Political Database of the Americas; Library of Congress/HLAS Online Home Page; Business & Finance in Latin America - LANIC), Publishers' Home Pages (The Atlantic Monthly; Course Technology). URL: http://www.scubed.com/caltrans/sd/big_map.shtml)

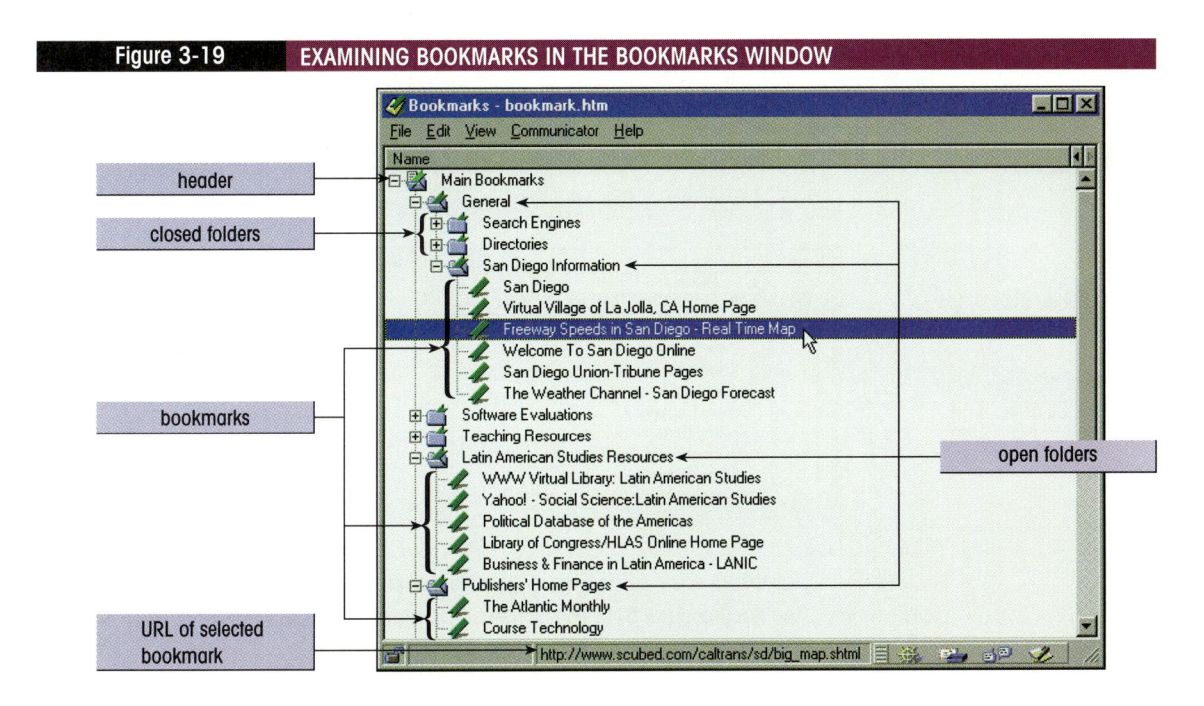

You decide to create a bookmark for the Pennsylvania Quintet Web page. First, you will create a folder to store your bookmarks, and then you will save your bookmark in that folder. You might not work on the same computer again, so you will save a copy of the bookmark file to your Student Disk for future use.

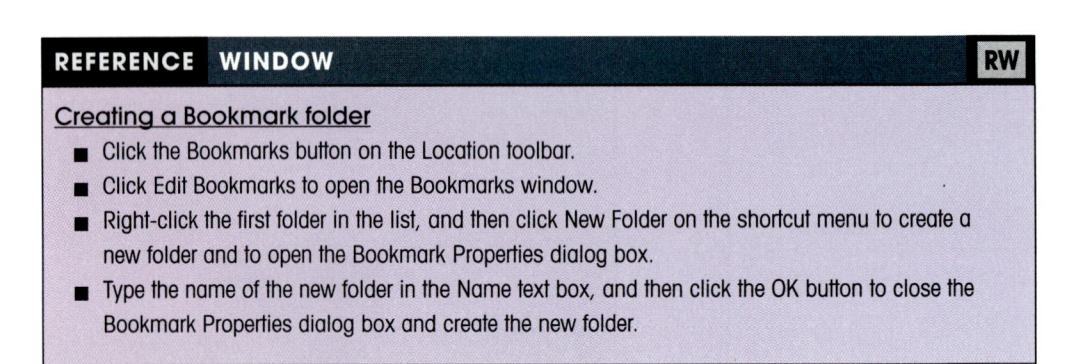

REFERENCE WINDOW

Creating a Bookmark folder
- Click the Bookmarks button on the Location toolbar.
- Click Edit Bookmarks to open the Bookmarks window.
- Right-click the first folder in the list, and then click New Folder on the shortcut menu to create a new folder and to open the Bookmark Properties dialog box.
- Type the name of the new folder in the Name text box, and then click the OK button to close the Bookmark Properties dialog box and create the new folder.

To create a new Bookmark folder:

1. Click the **Bookmarks** button on the Location toolbar to open the Bookmarks menu, and then click **Edit Bookmarks** to open the Bookmarks window.

2. Right-click the first item in the Bookmarks window; usually, this item is "Main Bookmarks" or "Bookmarks for <name>," but it might have another title on your computer. After you right-click the first item, a shortcut menu opens.

3. Click **New Folder** on the shortcut menu to open the Bookmark Properties dialog box. The text "New Folder" appears selected in the Name text box. To change the new folder's name, you just type the new name.

4. Type **Wind Quintet Information** in the Name text box, and then click the **OK** button to close the Bookmark Properties dialog box and create the new Wind Quintet Information folder in the bookmark file. The new folder should appear under the first item in the Bookmarks window, as shown in Figure 3-20.

Figure 3-20 **CREATING A BOOKMARK FOLDER**

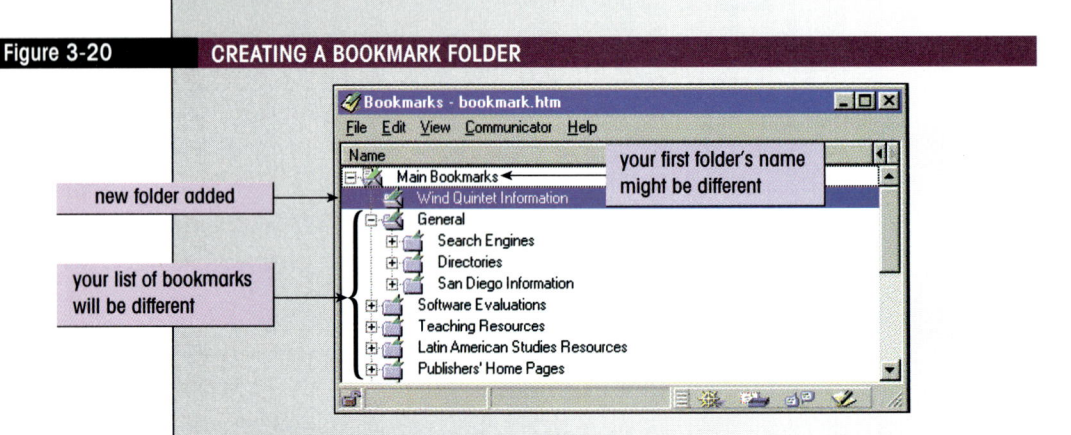

TROUBLE? If your Wind Quintet Information folder appears in a different location, don't worry. Just make sure that the folder appears in the Bookmarks window.

5. Click the **Close** button on the Bookmarks window title bar to close the Bookmarks window.

Now that you have created a folder, you can save your bookmark for the Pennsylvania Quintet's Web page in the new folder. However, first you must return to the Web page that you want to bookmark.

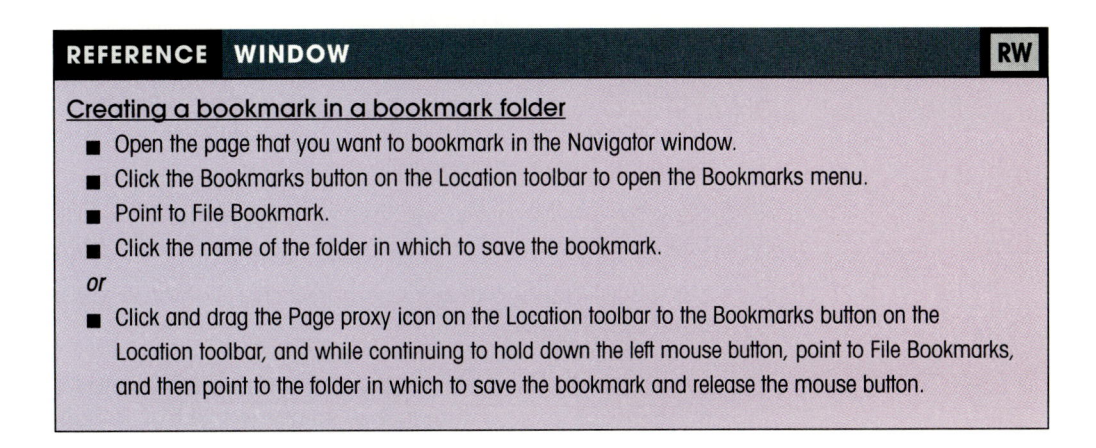

> **REFERENCE WINDOW** | **RW**
>
> **Creating a bookmark in a bookmark folder**
> - Open the page that you want to bookmark in the Navigator window.
> - Click the Bookmarks button on the Location toolbar to open the Bookmarks menu.
> - Point to File Bookmark.
> - Click the name of the folder in which to save the bookmark.
>
> or
> - Click and drag the Page proxy icon on the Location toolbar to the Bookmarks button on the Location toolbar, and while continuing to hold down the left mouse button, point to File Bookmarks, and then point to the folder in which to save the bookmark and release the mouse button.

To save a bookmark for a Web page in a folder:

1. Click the **Forward** button on the Navigation toolbar to return to the Pennsylvania Quintet Web page.

2. Click the **Bookmarks** button on the Location toolbar to open the Bookmarks menu.

3. Point to **File Bookmark**, and then click the **Wind Quintet Information** folder. Now, the bookmark is saved in the correct folder. You can test your bookmark by using the bookmark to visit the site.

4. Click the **Back** button on the Navigation toolbar to go to the previous Web page.

5. Click the **Bookmarks** button on the Location toolbar, point to **Wind Quintet Information**, and then click **Pennsylvania Quintet**. The Pennsylvania Quintet page opens in the browser, which means that you created the bookmark successfully.

   TROUBLE? If the Pennsylvania Quintet page does not open, click Edit Bookmarks on the Bookmarks menu and make sure that you have the correct URL for the page, and then repeat the steps. If you still have trouble, ask your instructor or technical support person for help.

Because you might need to visit the Pennsylvania Quintet page from another client, you can save your bookmark file on your Student Disk.

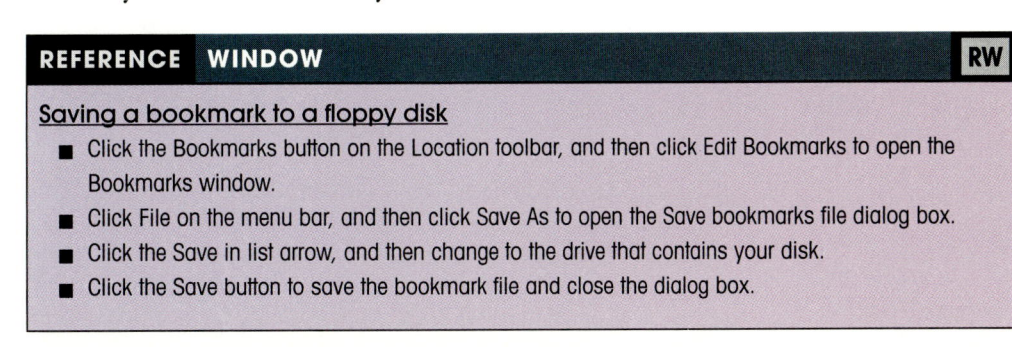

> **REFERENCE WINDOW** | **RW**
>
> **Saving a bookmark to a floppy disk**
> - Click the Bookmarks button on the Location toolbar, and then click Edit Bookmarks to open the Bookmarks window.
> - Click File on the menu bar, and then click Save As to open the Save bookmarks file dialog box.
> - Click the Save in list arrow, and then change to the drive that contains your disk.
> - Click the Save button to save the bookmark file and close the dialog box.

To store the revised bookmarks file to your floppy disk:

1. Click the **Bookmarks** button [Bookmarks] on the Location toolbar, and then click **Edit Bookmarks** to open the Bookmarks window. When you save your bookmarks, you save all of the bookmarks, and not just the one that you need: remember from Session 3.1 that Navigator stores *all* of your bookmarks in a single file.

2. Click **File** on the menu bar of the Bookmarks window, and then click **Save As** to open the Save bookmarks file dialog box.

3. Click **Save in** list arrow, and then change to the drive that contains your Student Disk (usually, this is 3½ Floppy (A:)).

4. Make sure that **bookmark** appears in the File name text box, and then click the **Save** button.

   TROUBLE? Your computer might be configured to display file extensions, so you might see bookmark.htm in the File name text box, which also is correct.

   TROUBLE? If bookmark or bookmark.htm does not appear in the File name text box, click in the File name text box and type bookmark.htm, and then click the Save button.

5. Close the Bookmarks window.

When you use another client, you can open the bookmark file from your Student Disk by starting Navigator, clicking the Bookmarks button on the Location toolbar, clicking File on the menu bar, and then clicking Open Bookmarks File. Change to the drive that contains your Student Disk, and then open the bookmark.htm file from the disk. Your bookmark file will open in the Bookmarks window, and then you can use it as you practiced.

Hyperlink Navigation with the Mouse

Now you know how to use Navigator to find information that will help you with the Sunset Wind Quintet. Maggie tells you that the easiest way to move from one Web page to another is to use the hyperlinks that the authors of Web pages embed in their HTML documents, as you will see next.

REFERENCE WINDOW   RW

Using hyperlinks on a Web page
- Click the hyperlink.
- After the new Web page has loaded, right-click anywhere on the Web page area.
- Click the Back button on the Navigation toolbar.

TUTORIAL 3 BROWSER BASICS WEB 3.25 INTERNET

To follow a hyperlink Web page and return:

1. Click the **Back** button on the Navigation toolbar to go back to the Student Online Companion page, click the **Lewis Music** link to open that page, and then point to the **Instrument Accessories** hyperlink shown in Figure 3-21 so your pointer changes to 👆.

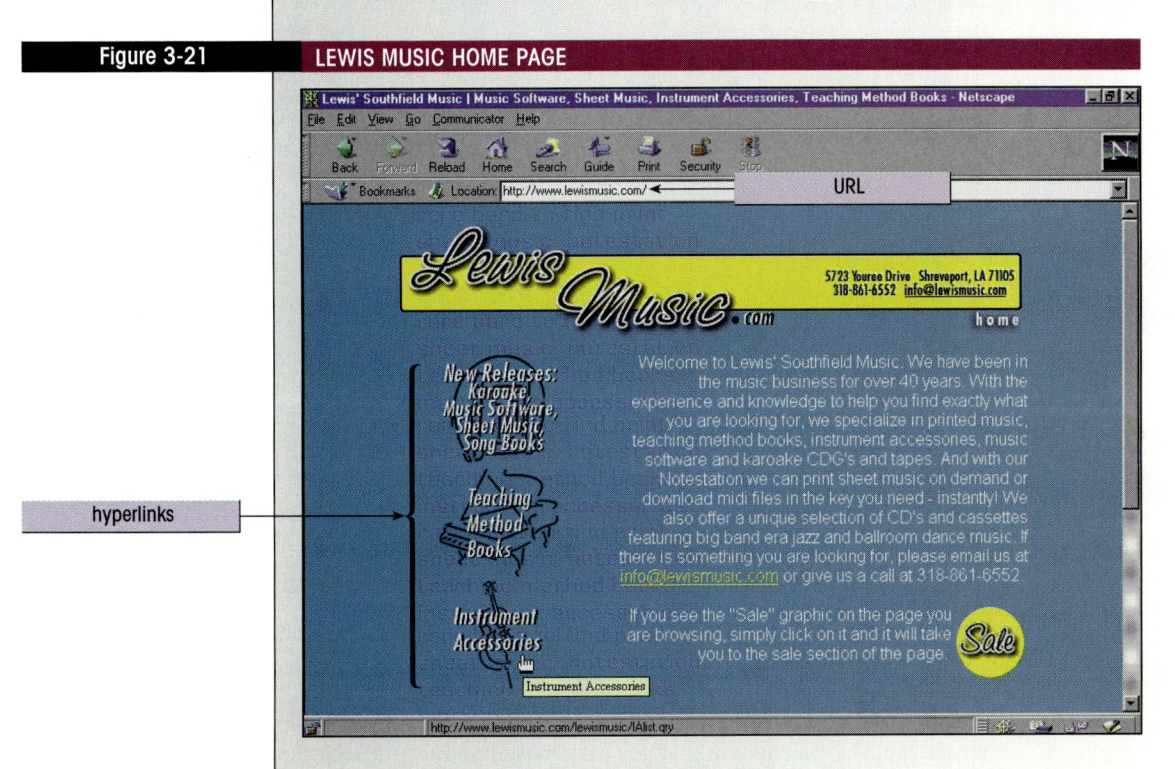

Figure 3-21   **LEWIS MUSIC HOME PAGE**

(screenshot of Lewis Music home page in Netscape browser, with callouts labeling "URL" and "hyperlinks")

2. Click the **Instrument Accessories** hyperlink to load the page. Watch the second panel in the status bar. When the shadow disappears, you know that Navigator has loaded the full page.

3. Right-click anywhere in the Web page area to open the shortcut menu, as shown in Figure 3-22.

    TROUBLE? If you right-click a hyperlink, your shortcut menu will display a longer list than the one shown in Figure 3-22, and the Back item will be third in the list, instead of first. If you don't see the shortcut menu shown in Figure 3-22, click anywhere outside of the shortcut menu to close it, and then repeat Step 3.

    TROUBLE? Web pages change frequently, so the Instrument Accessories page you see might look different from the one shown in Figure 3-22, but right-clicking anywhere on the Web page area will still work.

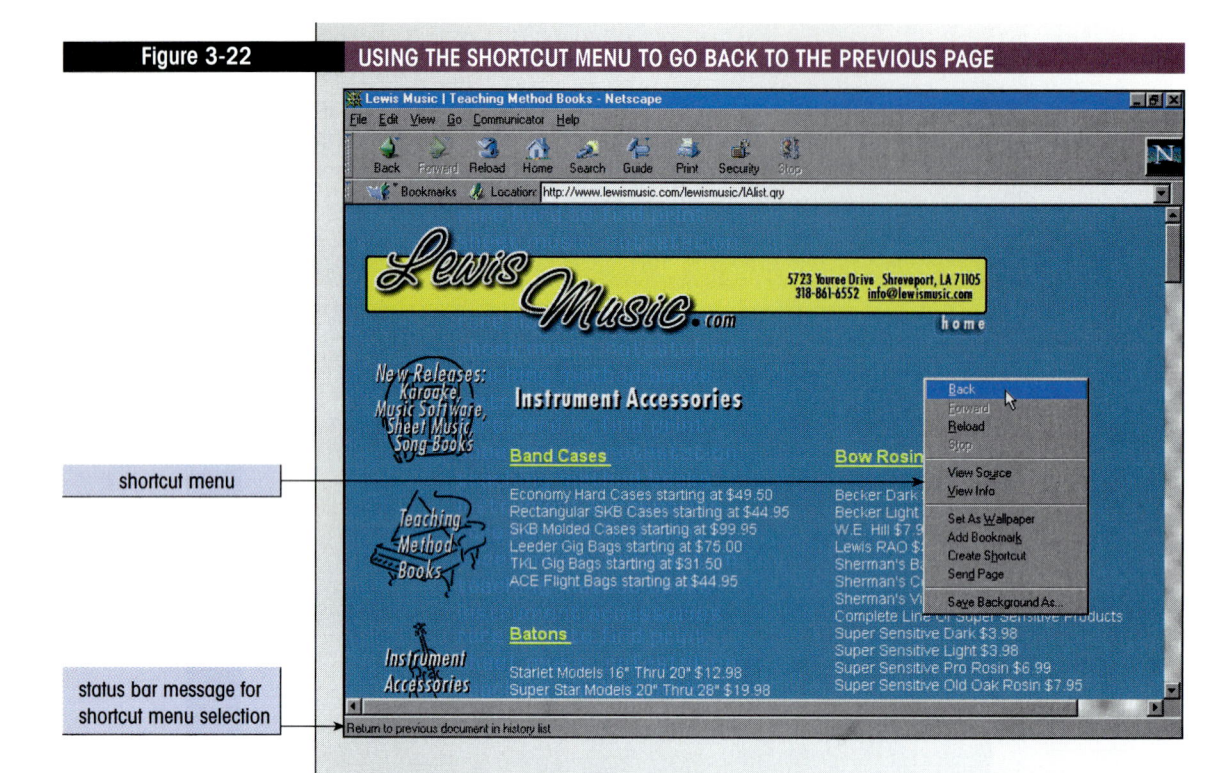

Figure 3-22 USING THE SHORTCUT MENU TO GO BACK TO THE PREVIOUS PAGE

shortcut menu

status bar message for shortcut menu selection

4. Click **Back** on the shortcut menu to go back to the Lewis Music home page.

5. Repeat Step 4 to return to the Student Online Companion page.

You are beginning to get a good sense of how to move from one Web page to another and back again, but Maggie tells you that you have mastered only one technique of many. She explains that the Navigation toolbar and the menu bar offer many tools for accessing and using Web sites.

Using the History List

In Session 3.1 you learned that the Back and Forward buttons let you move to and from previously visited pages. These buttons duplicate the functions of the menu bar's Go command. Clicking Go opens a menu that lets you move back and forward through a portion of the history list and allows you to choose a specific Web page from that list. You also can open a full copy of the history list.

To view the history list for this session:

1. Click **Communicator** on the menu bar, and then click **History** to open the History window, as shown in Figure 3-23.

   TROUBLE? If you don't see Communicator on the menu bar, click Window on the menu bar, and then click History.

| Figure 3-23 | **VIEWING THE HISTORY LIST** |

entries in your history list will be different

TROUBLE? The History window that appears on your computer might be a different size and contain different entries from the one that appears in Figure 3-23. You can resize the window by clicking and dragging its edges. You can resize the columns in the window by clicking and dragging on the edges of the column headers.

To return to a page, double-click the page in the list. You can change the way that pages are listed by using the commands on the View menu; for example, you can list the pages by title or in the order in which you visited them.

2. Click the **Close** button ⊠ on the History window title bar to close it.

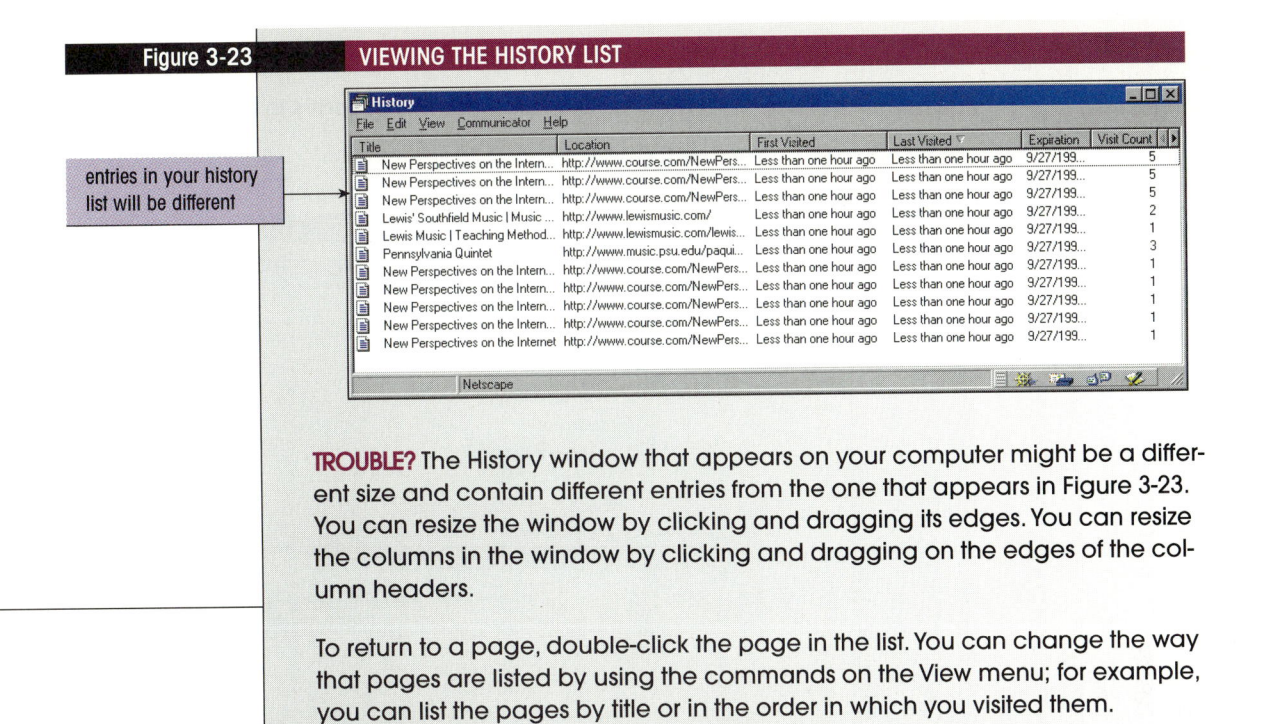

Reloading a Web Page

You learned in Session 3.1 that clicking the **Reload** button on the Navigator toolbar loads the same Web page that appears in the browser window again. You can force Navigator to get the page from the Web server by pressing the Shift key when you click the Reload button.

Going Home

The **Home** button displays the home (or start) page for your copy of Navigator. You can go to the Netscape home page, which is the software's default installation home page, by clicking the **Netscape Home Page** button on the Navigator toolbar. You cannot change the page that loads by clicking the Navigator Home Page button, but you can change the default URL that opens when you click the Home button by using the Preferences dialog box.

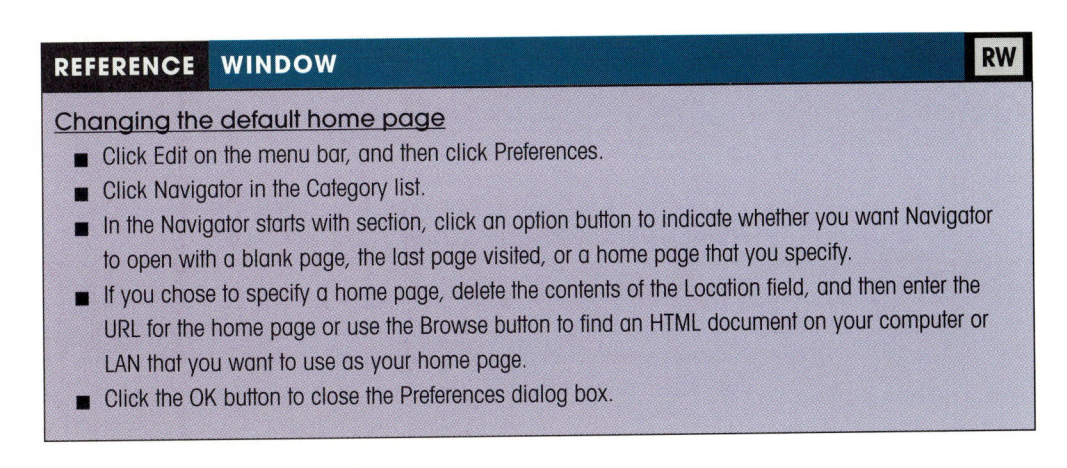

REFERENCE WINDOW RW

Changing the default home page
- Click Edit on the menu bar, and then click Preferences.
- Click Navigator in the Category list.
- In the Navigator starts with section, click an option button to indicate whether you want Navigator to open with a blank page, the last page visited, or a home page that you specify.
- If you chose to specify a home page, delete the contents of the Location field, and then enter the URL for the home page or use the Browse button to find an HTML document on your computer or LAN that you want to use as your home page.
- Click the OK button to close the Preferences dialog box.

To modify the Home navigation button settings:

1. Click **Edit** on the menu bar, and then click **Preferences** to open that dialog box.
2. Click **Navigator** in the Category list. See Figure 3-24.

Figure 3-24 | **CHANGING THE HOME PAGE**

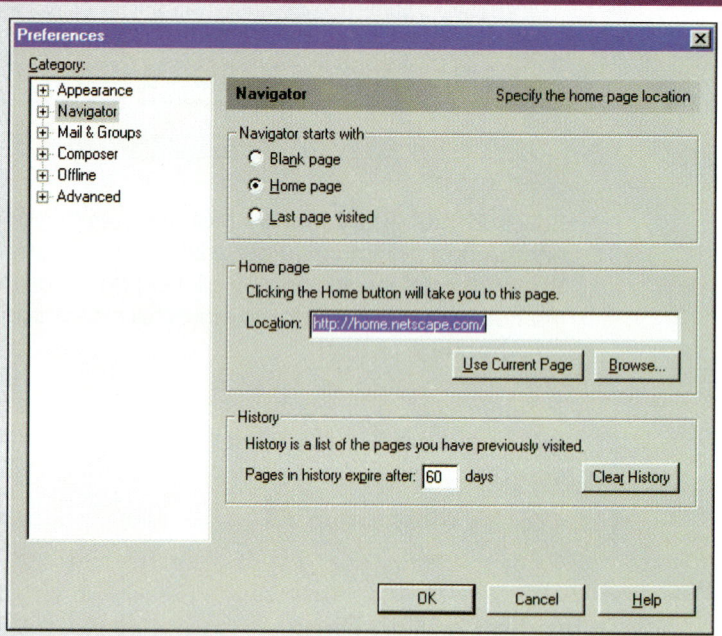

[Preferences dialog box showing Category list with Appearance, Navigator, Mail & Groups, Composer, Offline, Advanced. Navigator panel shows "Specify the home page location" with Navigator starts with options: Blank page, Home page (selected), Last page visited. Home page Location field contains http://home.netscape.com/ with Use Current Page and Browse buttons. History section shows "Pages in history expire after: 60 days" with Clear History button. OK, Cancel, Help buttons at bottom.]

3. To have Navigator open with a **Blank page**, the **Home page** you specify, or the **Last page visited**, click the corresponding option button in the Navigator starts with section of the Preferences dialog box.

   TROUBLE? You might not be able to change these and the following settings if you are using a computer in your school lab or at your office. Some organizations set the home page defaults on all of their computers and lock those settings.

   To specify a home page, select the text in the Location field in the Home page section of the Preferences dialog box as shown in Figure 3-24 and enter the URL of the Web page you would like to use. If you loaded the Web page that you would like to be your new home page into Navigator before beginning these steps, you can click the Use Current Page button to place its URL into the Location field. You also can specify an HTML document on your computer or LAN by clicking the Browse button and selecting the disk drive and folder location of that HTML document.

4. Click the **Cancel** button to close the dialog box without making any changes.

Netscape's Internet Guide

The **Guide** button leads Navigator to another page maintained by Netscape Communications Corporation that offers similar options for searching the Internet. In addition, right-clicking the Guide button displays a menu that offers quick access to hyperlinks that connect to Web resources such as Netscape's What's New! and What's Cool! Web pages. These hyperlinks lead to fun Web pages, such as David Letterman's Top Ten list and recent Dilbert comic strips.

Printing a Web Page

The **Print** button on the Navigation toolbar lets you print the current Web frame or page. You will learn more about saving and printing Web pages later in this session, but you can use the Print command to make a printed copy of most Web pages. (Some Web pages disable the Print command.)

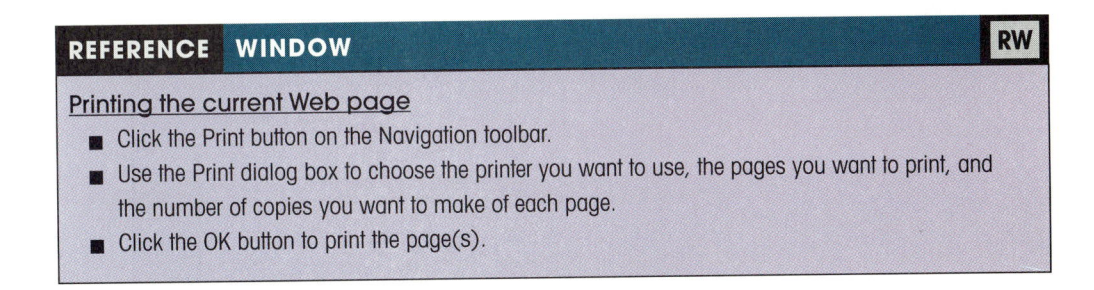

REFERENCE WINDOW

Printing the current Web page
- Click the Print button on the Navigation toolbar.
- Use the Print dialog box to choose the printer you want to use, the pages you want to print, and the number of copies you want to make of each page.
- Click the OK button to print the page(s).

To print a Web page:

1. Click in the main (right) frame of the Student Online Companion page to select it.
2. Click the Print button on the Navigation toolbar to open the Print dialog box shown in Figure 3-25.

Figure 3-25 PRINT DIALOG BOX

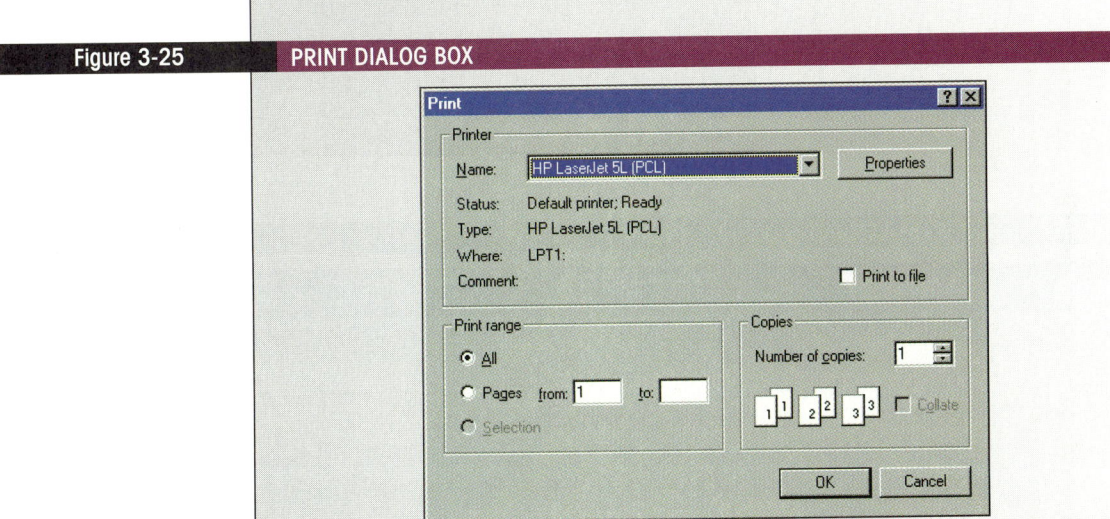

3. Make sure that the printer in the Name text box shows the printer you want to use; if necessary, click the Name list arrow to change the selection.
4. Click the **Pages** option button in the Print range section of the Print dialog box, type **1** in the **from** text box, press the **Tab** key, and then type **1** in the to text box to specify that you want to print only the first page.
5. Make sure that the Number of copies text box shows that you want to print one copy.
6. Click the **OK** button to print the Web page and close the Print dialog box.

Changing the Settings for Printing a Web Page

You already have seen how to print Web pages using the basic options available in the Print dialog box. Also you learned how to store a bookmark so you can return to a Web page later. Usually, the default settings in the Print dialog box are fine for printing a Web page, but you can use the Page Setup dialog box to change the way a Web page prints. Figure 3-26 shows the Page Setup dialog box, and Figure 3-27 describes its settings.

Figure 3-26   PAGE SETUP OPTIONS FOR PRINTING WEB PAGES

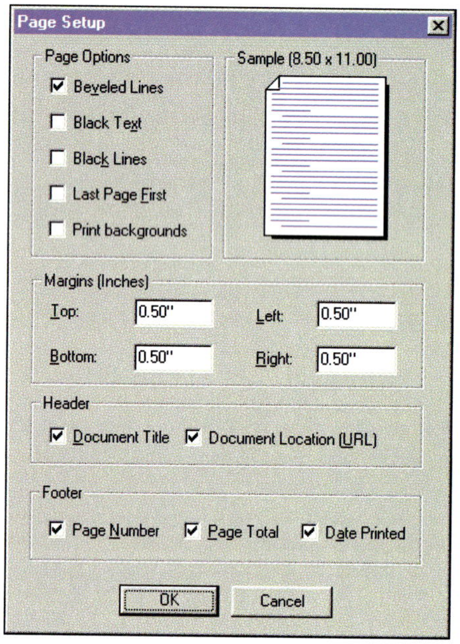

Figure 3-27   PAGE SETUP DIALOG BOX OPTIONS

OPTION	DESCRIPTION	USE
Black Text	Prints all of the text on a Web page as black.	Use when the Web page contains text set in light colors, so it will be legible when printed.
Black Lines	Prints all of the lines on a Web page as black.	Use when the Web page contains light-colored lines, so they will be legible when printed.
Last Page First	Reverses the normal order in which pages are printed.	Some printers eject pages face up. Using this setting will correctly collate the Web page printout.
Print backgrounds	Prints a Web page background, if there is one on the page.	You should leave this option off unless you are using a color printer. Backgrounds can render text and images illegible, and dark colors can waste your printer's toner or ink.
Margins	Use to change the margin of the printed page.	Normally, you should leave the default settings, but you can change the right, left, top, or bottom margins as needed.
Header	Prints the Web page's document title and/or document location (URL).	Selecting these options lets you print the name and location of the page for later reference.
Footer	Prints the Web page's page number, the total number of pages, or the date that the page is printed.	Selecting these options provides a record of the page number, total number of pages, and the date that you printed the page.

When printing Web pages, another print option that is extremely useful for saving paper when printing long Web pages is to reduce the font size of the Web pages before you print them.

To do this, click Edit on the menu bar, click Preferences, click the Fonts category, and then use the Size list arrow to decrease the size of the font used in the Web page. See Figure 3-28.

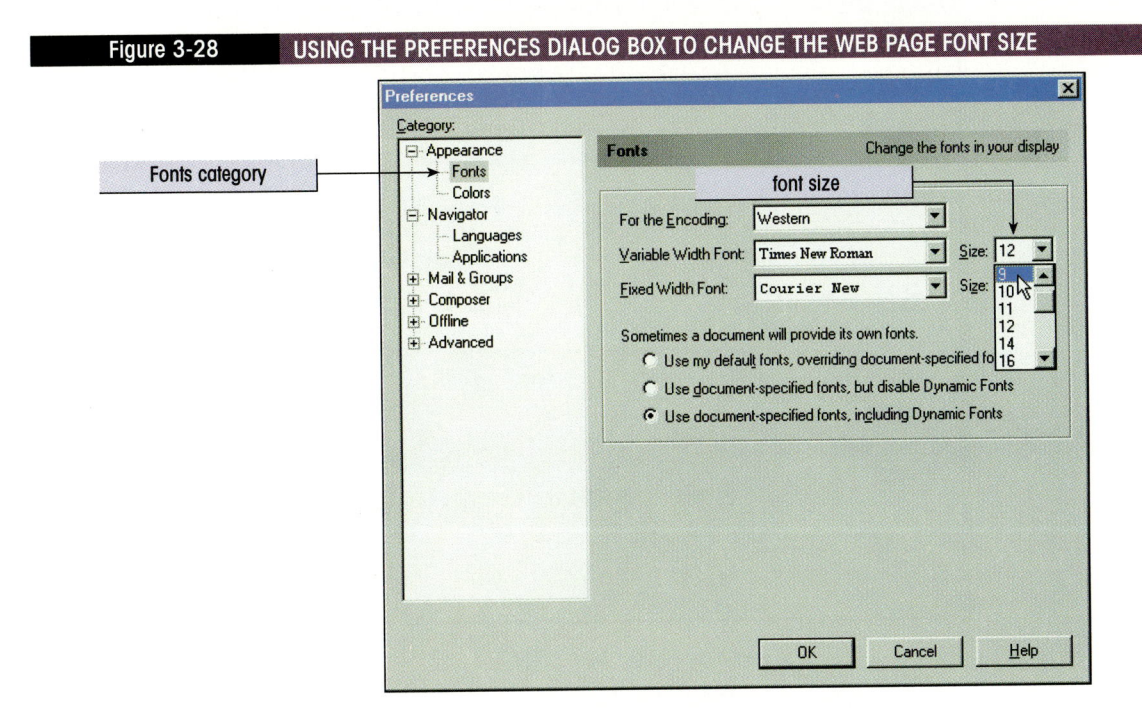

Figure 3-28	USING THE PREFERENCES DIALOG BOX TO CHANGE THE WEB PAGE FONT SIZE

Fonts category

Checking Web Page Security Features

The **Security** button on the Navigation toolbar lets you check some of the security elements of a Web page. This button displays either an open padlock icon or a closed padlock icon . The icon on the Security button will correspond to the icon displayed in the left section of the status bar at the bottom of the Web page to indicate whether the Web page was encrypted during transmission from the Web server. **Encryption** is a way of scrambling and encoding data transmissions that reduces the risk that a person who intercepted the Web page as it traveled across the Internet would be able to decode and read the page's contents. Web sites use encrypted transmission to send and receive information such as credit card numbers to ensure privacy. You can obtain more information about the details of the encryption used on a Web page by examining the Security Info dialog box that opens when you click the Security button on the Navigation toolbar. Figure 3-29 shows the Security Info dialog box for an encrypted Web page after the user clicked the Security button on the Navigation toolbar.

Figure 3-29 SECURITY INFO WINDOW FOR AN ENCRYPTED WEB PAGE

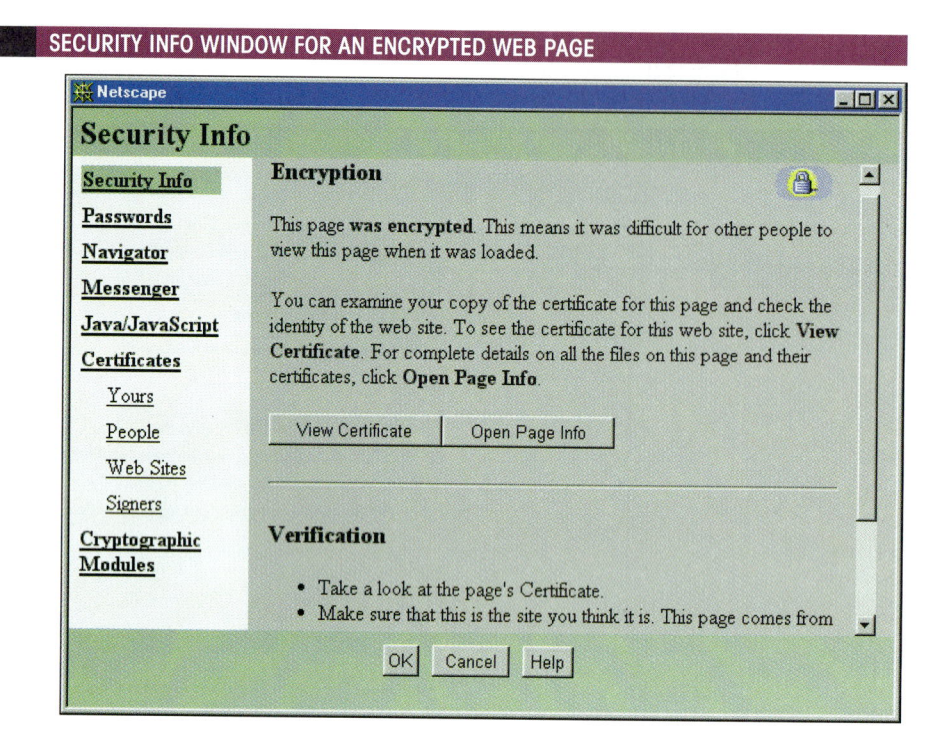

Getting Help in Netscape Navigator

The Netscape Communicator suite includes a comprehensive online Help facility for all of the programs in the suite, including Navigator. You open the Help Contents window to use Help.

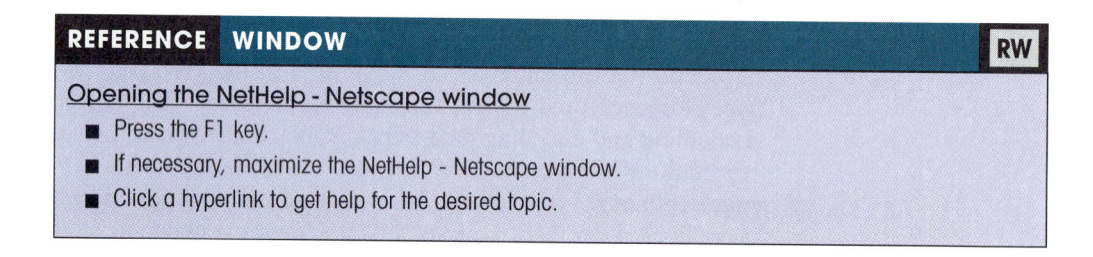

REFERENCE WINDOW

Opening the NetHelp - Netscape window
- Press the F1 key.
- If necessary, maximize the NetHelp - Netscape window.
- Click a hyperlink to get help for the desired topic.

To open the Navigator help window:

1. Press the **F1** key, and then click the **Maximize** button on the NetHelp - Netscape window, which provides help for all the programs in the Netscape Communicator Suite.

2. Click the **Browsing the Web** hyperlink to get help for the Navigator program. Read the page shown in Figure 3-30, and use the scroll box or scroll down button to move down the page.

TUTORIAL 3 BROWSER BASICS   WEB 3.33   INTERNET

| Figure 3-30 | OPENING THE NETHELP - NETSCAPE WINDOW |

Contents icon
Index icon
Find icon
hyperlinks to Help contents

Help text area
hyperlinks to Help pages for all of the Netscape Communicator suite components
Exit Help button
Print Help topic button
Forward button
Back button

You can click any of the Contents hyperlinks to obtain help on the topics listed. You also can click the Index icon to obtain an alphabetized, searchable list of hyperlinks to specific terms used in the Netscape Help pages, or you can click the Find icon, which opens the standard Windows Find dialog box, and enter search terms.

3. Click the **Close** button ❎ to close the NetHelp – Netscape window and return to Navigator.

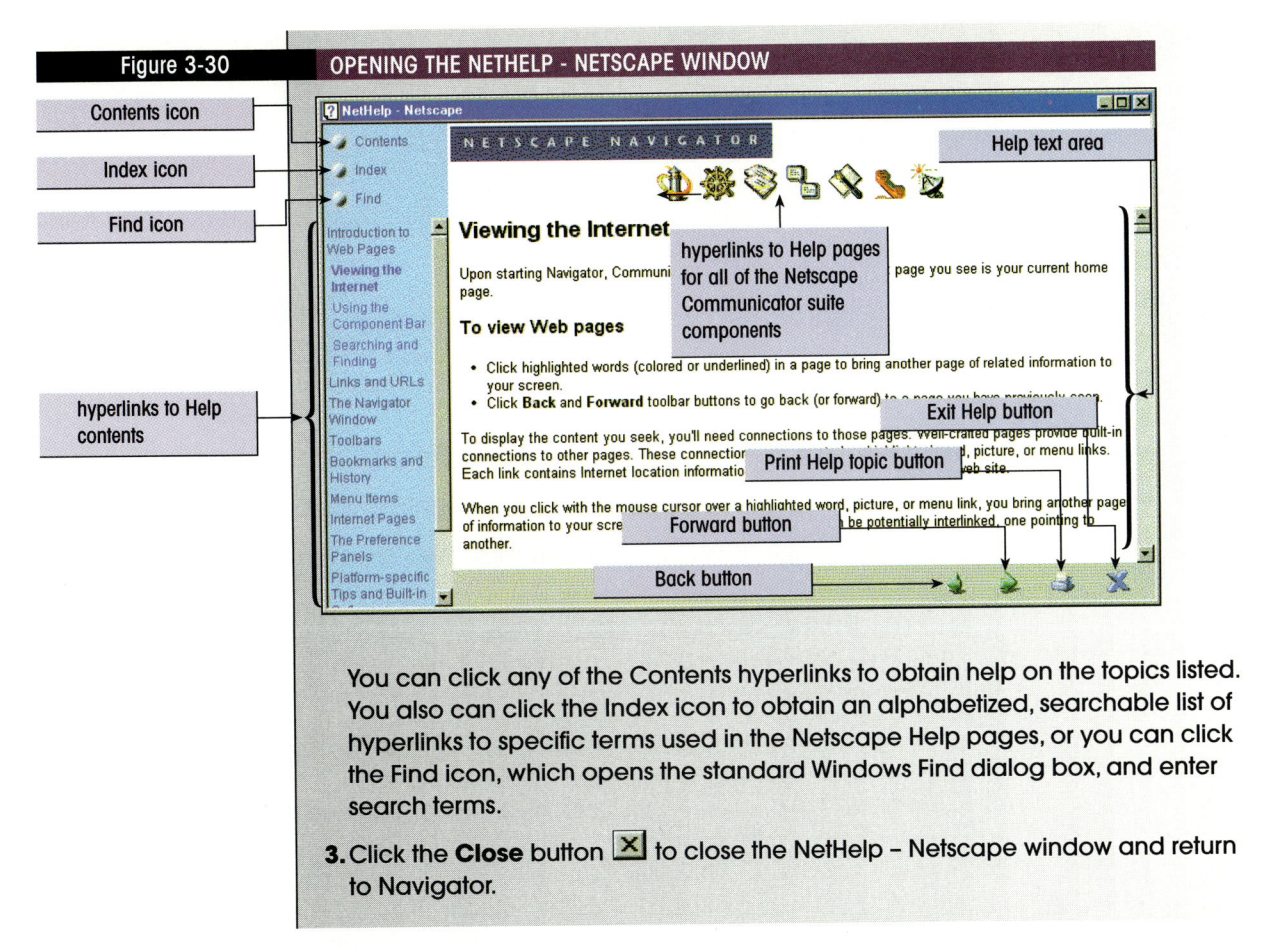

Now you are convinced that you have all of the tools you need to successfully find information on the Web. Marianna probably will be interested in seeing the Pennsylvania Quintet Web page, but you are not sure if she will have Internet access while she's touring. Maggie says that you can save the Web page on disk, so Marianna can open the page locally in her Web browser using the files that you save on a disk.

Using Navigator to Save a Web Page

You have learned how to use most of the Navigator tools for loading Web pages and saving bookmarks. Now, Maggie wants you to learn how to save a Web page. Sometimes, you will want to store entire Web pages on disk; at other times, you will only want to store selected portions of Web page text or particular graphics from a Web page.

Saving a Web Page

You like the Pennsylvania Quintet's Web site and want to save the page on disk so you can send it to Marianna. That way, she can review it without having an Internet connection. To save a Web page, you must have the page open in Navigator.

> **REFERENCE WINDOW**
>
> **Saving a Web page to a floppy disk**
> - Open the Web page in Navigator.
> - Click File on the menu bar, and then click Save As to open the Save As dialog box.
> - Click the Save in list arrow, and then change to the drive on which to save the Web page.
> - Accept the default filename, or change the filename, if you want; however, retain the file extension .htm or .html.
> - Click the Save button to save the Web page to the floppy disk.

To save the Web page on your Student Disk:

1. Use your bookmark to return to the Pennsylvania Quintet page.
2. Click **File** on the menu bar, and then click **Save As** to open the Save As dialog box.
3. Click the **Save in** list arrow, click the drive that contains your Student Disk (usually, this is 3½ Floppy (A:)), and then double-click the **Tutorial.03** folder to open it. You will accept the default filename of paquintet.htm.
4. Click the **Save** button. Now the HTML document for the Pennsylvania Quintet's home page is saved on your Student Disk in the Tutorial.03 folder. When you send it to Marianna, she can open her Web browser and then use the Open command on the File menu to open the Web page.

If the Web page contains graphics, such as photos, drawings, or icons, you should note that these items will not be saved with the HTML document. To save the graphics, right-click them in the browser window, click Save Image As, and then save the graphic to the same location as the Web's HTML document. The graphics file is specified to appear on the HTML document as a hyperlink, so you might have to change the HTML code in the Web page to identify its location. Copying the graphics files to the same disk as the HTML document will *usually* work.

Saving Web Page Text to a File

Maggie suggests that you might want to know how to save portions of Web page text to a file, so that you can save only the text from the Web page and use it in other programs. You will use WordPad to receive the text you will copy from a Web page, but any word processor or text editor will work.

Marianna just called to let you know that the quintet will play a concert in Cleveland on a Friday night, and she asks you to identify other opportunities for scheduling local concerts during the following weekend. Often, museums are willing to book small ensembles for weekend afternoon programs, and Marianna has given you the URL for the Cleveland Museum of Art. You will visit the site and then get the museum's address and telephone number so you can contact it about scheduling a concert.

TUTORIAL 3 BROWSER BASICS   WEB 3.35   INTERNET

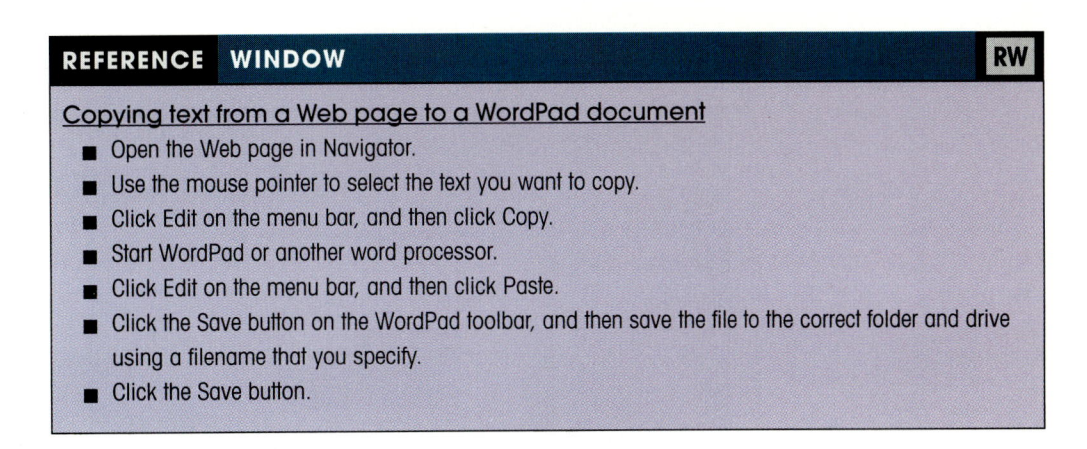

> **REFERENCE WINDOW**   RW
>
> **Copying text from a Web page to a WordPad document**
> - Open the Web page in Navigator.
> - Use the mouse pointer to select the text you want to copy.
> - Click Edit on the menu bar, and then click Copy.
> - Start WordPad or another word processor.
> - Click Edit on the menu bar, and then click Paste.
> - Click the Save button on the WordPad toolbar, and then save the file to the correct folder and drive using a filename that you specify.
> - Click the Save button.

To copy text from a Web page and save it to a file:

1. Use the **Back** button to return to the Student Online Companion page, and then click the **Cleveland Museum of Art** link to open that Web page in the browser window.

2. Click the **hours and address** hyperlink in the left frame on the Web page to open the museum information page in the main (right) frame.

3. Click and drag the mouse pointer over the address and telephone number to select it, as shown in Figure 3-31.

Figure 3-31   SELECTING TEXT ON A WEB PAGE

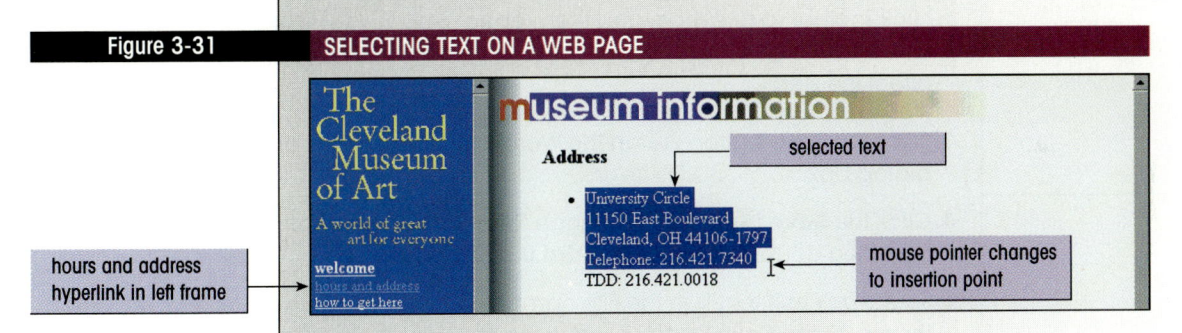

The Cleveland Museum of Art — A world of great art for everyone

welcome
hours and address ← hours and address hyperlink in left frame
how to get here

museum information

Address
- University Circle
  11150 East Boulevard
  Cleveland, OH 44106-1797
  Telephone: 216.421.7340   ← selected text
  TDD: 216.421.0018   ← mouse pointer changes to insertion point

4. Click **Edit** on the menu bar, and then click **Copy** to copy the selected text to the Windows Clipboard.

Now, you can start WordPad and paste the copied text into a new document.

To start and copy the text into WordPad:

1. Click the **Start** button on the taskbar, point to **Programs**, point to **Accessories**, and then click **WordPad** to start the program and open a new document.

2. Click the **Paste** button on the WordPad toolbar to paste the text into the WordPad document, as shown in Figure 3-32.

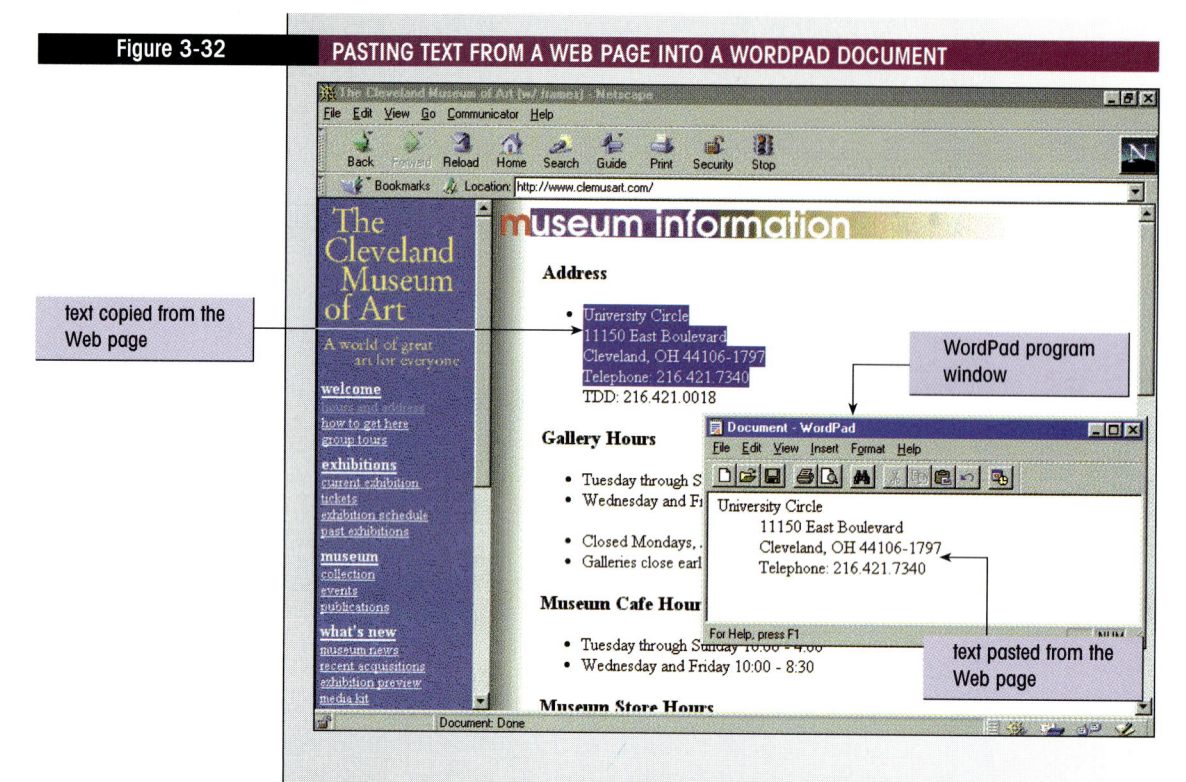

Figure 3-32 PASTING TEXT FROM A WEB PAGE INTO A WORDPAD DOCUMENT

text copied from the Web page

WordPad program window

text pasted from the Web page

TROUBLE? If the WordPad toolbar does not appear, click View on the menu bar, click Toolbar to turn it on, and then repeat Step 2. Your WordPad program window might be a different size from the one shown in Figure 3-32, which does not affect the steps.

3. Click the **Save** button on the WordPad toolbar to open the Save As dialog box.

4. Click the **Save in** list arrow, change to the drive that contains your Student Disk, and then double-click the **Tutorial.03** folder.

5. Select any text that is in the File name text box, type **CMoA-Address.txt**, and then click the **Save** button to save the file. Now, the address and phone number of the museum is saved in a file on your Student Disk for future reference.

6. Click the **Close** button on the WordPad title bar to close it.

Later, you will contact the museum. You notice that the left frame of the Cleveland Museum of Art Web page has a hyperlink titled "how to get here." This page might offer some helpful information that you could give to Marianna about where the museum is located, so you decide to save the graphic on your disk.

Saving a Web Page Graphic to Disk

Clicking the "how to get here" hyperlink loads a page that contains a hyperlink to a street map of the area surrounding the museum. You can save this map to your disk, as you will see next. Then you can send the file to Marianna so she has a resource for getting to the museum.

TUTORIAL 3   BROWSER BASICS   WEB **3.37**   INTERNET

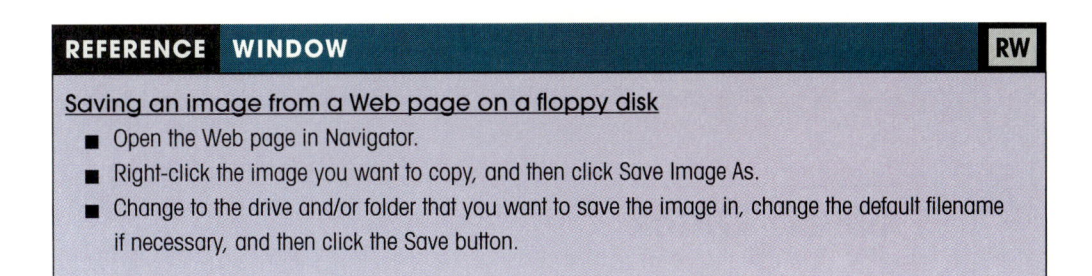

| REFERENCE WINDOW | RW |

Saving an image from a Web page on a floppy disk
- Open the Web page in Navigator.
- Right-click the image you want to copy, and then click Save Image As.
- Change to the drive and/or folder that you want to save the image in, change the default filename if necessary, and then click the Save button.

To save the street map image on a floppy disk:

1. Click the **how to get here** hyperlink in the left frame of the Cleveland Museum's home page, and then click the **street map** hyperlink on the Getting around: Directions and Transportation Web page in the main (right) frame.

2. Right-click the map image to open its shortcut menu, as shown in Figure 3-33.

Figure 3-33   SAVING THE MAP IMAGE TO DISK

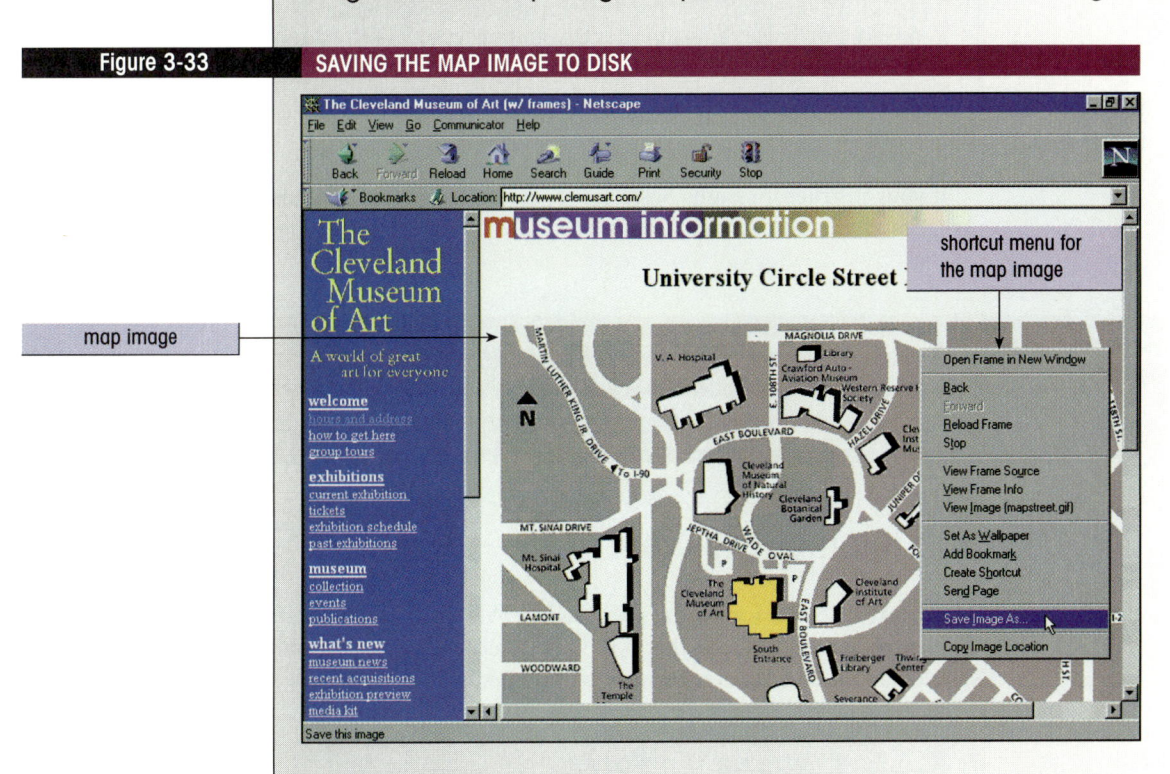

3. Click **Save Image As** on the shortcut menu to open the Save As dialog box.

4. Click the **Save in** list arrow, change to the drive that contains your Student Disk, and then double-click the **Tutorial.03** folder. You will accept the default filename, mapstreet, so click the **Save** button. Now the image is saved on your Student Disk, so you can send the file to Marianna. Marianna can use her Web browser to open the image file and print it.

5. Close your Web browser, and close your dial-up connection, if necessary.

Now you can send a disk to Marianna so she has the Pennsylvania Wind Quintet Web page and a map that shows her how to get to the museum. Marianna is pleased to hear of your progress in using the Web to find information for the quintet.

QUICK CHECK

1. Describe three ways to load a Web page in the Navigator browser.
2. You can use the _____ in Navigator to visit previously visited sites during your Web session.
3. When would you use the Reload command?
4. What happens when you click the Home button on the Navigation toolbar?
5. Some Web servers _____ Web pages before returning them to the client to prevent unauthorized access.
6. True or False: You can identify an encrypted Web page when viewing it in Navigator.
7. What is a Netscape Navigator bookmark?

If your instructor assigns Session 3.3, continue reading. Otherwise, complete the Tutorial Assignments at the end of this tutorial.

SESSION 3.3

In this session, you will learn how to configure the Microsoft Internet Explorer Web browser and use it to display Web pages. You will learn how to use Internet Explorer to follow hyperlinks from one Web page to another and how to record the URLs of sites to which you would like to return. Also, you will print and save Web pages.

Starting Microsoft Internet Explorer

Microsoft Internet Explorer is Microsoft's Web browser that installs with Windows 95 or 98. This introduction assumes that you have Internet Explorer installed on your computer. You should have your computer turned on and open to the Windows desktop to begin.

To start Internet Explorer:

1. Click the **Start** button on the taskbar, point to **Programs**, point to **Internet Explorer**, and then click **Internet Explorer**. After a moment, Internet Explorer opens.

   TROUBLE? If you cannot find Internet Explorer on the Programs menu, check to see if an Internet Explorer shortcut icon appears on the desktop, and then double-click it. If you do not see the shortcut icon, ask your instructor or technical support person for help. The program might be installed in a different folder on your computer.

TUTORIAL 3 BROWSER BASICS   WEB 3.39   INTERNET

2. If the program does not fill the screen entirely, click the **Maximize** button on the Internet Explorer program's title bar. Your screen should look like Figure 3-34.

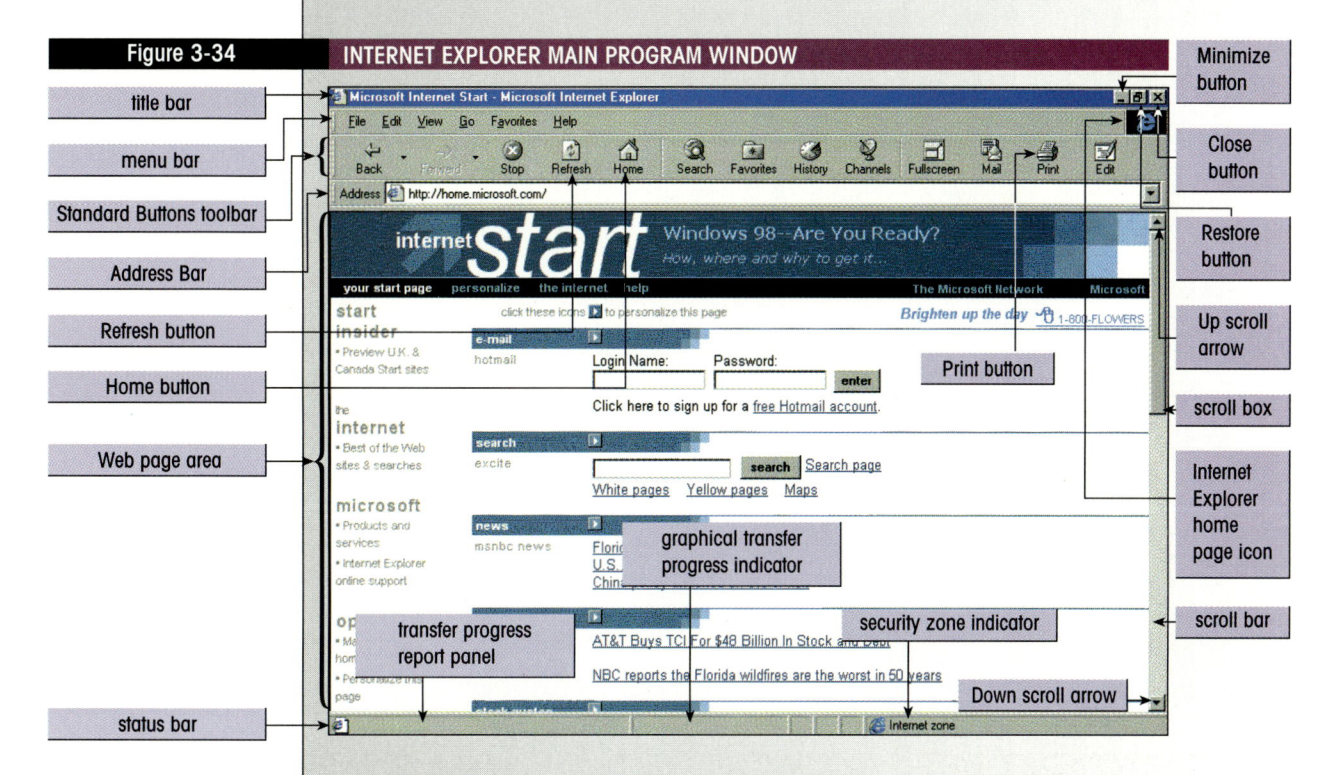

Figure 3-34   INTERNET EXPLORER MAIN PROGRAM WINDOW

Labels: title bar, menu bar, Standard Buttons toolbar, Address Bar, Refresh button, Home button, Web page area, status bar, Minimize button, Close button, Restore button, Up scroll arrow, scroll box, Internet Explorer home page icon, scroll bar, Down scroll arrow, Print button, graphical transfer progress indicator, transfer progress report panel, security zone indicator

TROUBLE? Figure 3-34 shows the Microsoft home page, which is the page that Internet Explorer opens the first time it starts. Your computer might be configured to open to a different Web page or no page at all.

TROUBLE? If you do not see the bars shown in Figure 3-34, click View on the menu bar, point to Toolbars, and then click the name of the bar that you want to turn on.

Internet Explorer includes a Standard Buttons toolbar with 13 buttons. Many of these buttons execute frequently used commands for browsing the Web. Figure 3-35 shows these buttons and describes their functions.

Figure 3-35 STANDARD BUTTONS TOOLBAR BUTTON FUNCTIONS

BUTTON	BUTTON NAME	DESCRIPTION
Back	Back	Moves to the last previously visited Web page.
Forward	Forward	Moves to the next previously visited Web page.
Stop	Stop	Stops the transfer of a new Web page.
Refresh	Refresh	Reloads the current page.
Home	Home	Loads the program's defined home page.
Search	Search	Opens a Search frame in the Internet Explorer window, which displays a Web search engine chosen by Microsoft.
Favorites	Favorites	Opens the Favorites frame in the Internet Explorer window, which allows you to return to Web pages that you have saved as favorites.
History	History	Opens the History frame in the Internet Explorer window, which allows you to choose from a list of Web pages that you have visited recently.
Channels	Channels	Opens the Channels frame in the Internet Explorer window (the Channels feature is beyond the scope of this tutorial).
Fullscreen	Fullscreen	Removes the browser frame and fills the screen with the current Web page image.
Mail	Mail	Opens the e-mail program specified in the Internet Options settings.
Print	Print	Prints the current Web page.
Edit	Edit	Opens the current Web page in an HTML editing program.

Now that you understand how to start Internet Explorer, you tell Maggie that you are ready to start using it to find information on the Internet. To find information, you need to know about the different Internet Explorer functions.

Status Bar

The **status bar** at the bottom of the window includes three panels that give you information about Internet Explorer's operations. The first panel—the **transfer progress report**—presents status messages that show, for example, the URL of a page while it is loading. When a page is completely loaded, this panel displays the text "Done" until you move the mouse or execute a command. This panel also displays the URL of any hyperlink on the page when you move the mouse pointer over it.

The second panel contains a blue **graphical transfer progress indicator** that moves from left to right in the panel to indicate how much of a Web page has loaded while Internet Explorer is loading it from a Web server. This indicator is especially useful for monitoring progress when you are loading large Web pages.

The third status bar panel reports to which **security zone** the page you are viewing has been assigned. As part of its security features, Internet Explorer lets you classify Web pages by the security risk they present. You can open the Internet Security Properties dialog box shown in Figure 3-36 by double-clicking the third status bar panel. This window lets you set four levels of security-enforcing procedures, including one that you can tailor to your specific needs.

| Figure 3-36 | INTERNET SECURITY PROPERTIES DIALOG BOX |

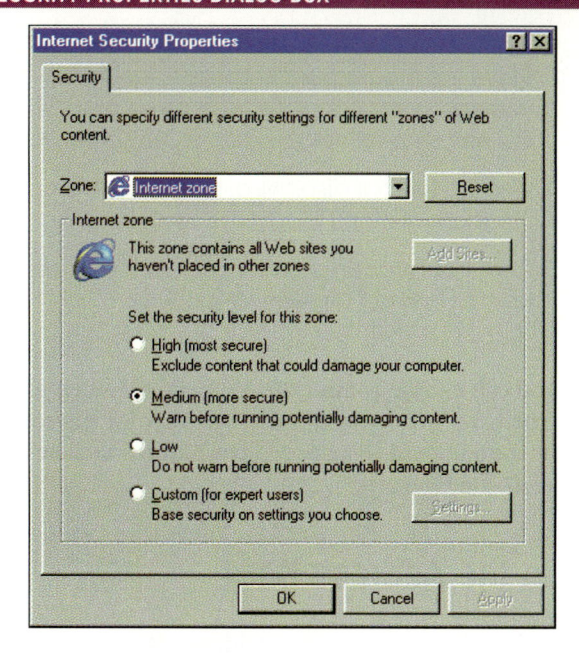

Menu Bar

In addition to the standard Windows commands, the menu bar also provides two specialized Internet Explorer command sets—Go and Favorites. The **Go** menu command lets you navigate or go to a Web site directly. The **Favorites** menu command lets you store and organize URLs of sites that you have visited.

Hiding and Showing the Internet Explorer Toolbars

Internet Explorer lets you hide its toolbars to show more of the Web page area. The easiest way to increase the display area for a Web page is to click the **Fullscreen** button.

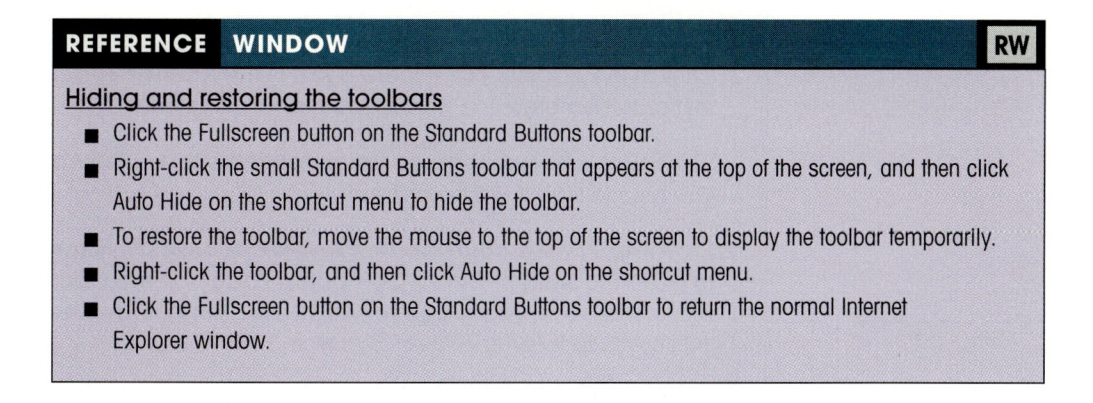

REFERENCE WINDOW   RW

<u>Hiding and restoring the toolbars</u>
- Click the Fullscreen button on the Standard Buttons toolbar.
- Right-click the small Standard Buttons toolbar that appears at the top of the screen, and then click Auto Hide on the shortcut menu to hide the toolbar.
- To restore the toolbar, move the mouse to the top of the screen to display the toolbar temporarily.
- Right-click the toolbar, and then click Auto Hide on the shortcut menu.
- Click the Fullscreen button on the Standard Buttons toolbar to return the normal Internet Explorer window.

To use the Fullscreen button and its Auto Hide feature:

1. Click the **Fullscreen** button on the Standard Buttons toolbar.

2. Right-click the small Standard Buttons toolbar that appears at the top of the screen to open the shortcut menu, and then click **Auto Hide** on the shortcut menu.

3. Move the mouse pointer away from the top of the screen for a moment. Now, you can see more of the Web page area. When the toolbar disappears, return the mouse pointer to the top of the screen to display it again.

4. With the toolbar displayed, right-click the toolbar and then click **Auto Hide** on the shortcut menu to turn the toolbar on again.

5. Click the **Fullscreen** button on the Standard Buttons toolbar to return to the normal Internet Explorer window.

You can use the commands on the View menu to **toggle**, or turn on and off, the individual toolbars. Also, you can use the Text Labels command on the View/Toolbars menu to show the Standard Buttons toolbar buttons with or without the text labels that describe each button's function.

Entering a URL in the Address Bar

Maggie tells you to use the **Address Bar** to enter URLs directly into Internet Explorer. Marianna gave you the URL for the Pennsylvania Quintet, so you can see its Web page.

REFERENCE WINDOW

Entering a URL in the Address Bar
- Click at the end of the current text in the Address Bar, and then backspace over the text that you want to delete.
- Type the URL of the location that you want.
- Press the Enter key to load the URL's Web page in the browser window.

To load the Pennsylvania Quintet's Web page:

1. Click in the Address Bar; if there is text in the Address Bar, click at the end of the text and then press the **Backspace** key to delete it.

   TROUBLE? Make sure that you delete *all* of the text in the Address Bar so the text you type in Step 2 will be correct.

2. Type **http://www.course.com/NewPerspectives/Internet** in the Address Bar to go to the Student Online Companion page on the Course Technology Web site. In this book, you will go to the Course Technology site and then click hyperlinks to go to individual Web pages.

3. Press the **Enter** key. After you press the Enter key, the Student Online Companion Web page loads as shown in Figure 3-37. When the entire page has loaded, the graphical transfer progress indicator in the status bar will stop moving and the transfer progress report panel will display the text "Done."

   TROUBLE? If a Dial-Up Networking dialog box opens after you press the Enter key, click the Connect button. You must have an Internet connection to complete the steps in this tutorial.

TUTORIAL 3   BROWSER BASICS   WEB 3.43   INTERNET

Figure 3-37   STUDENT ONLINE COMPANION WEB PAGE

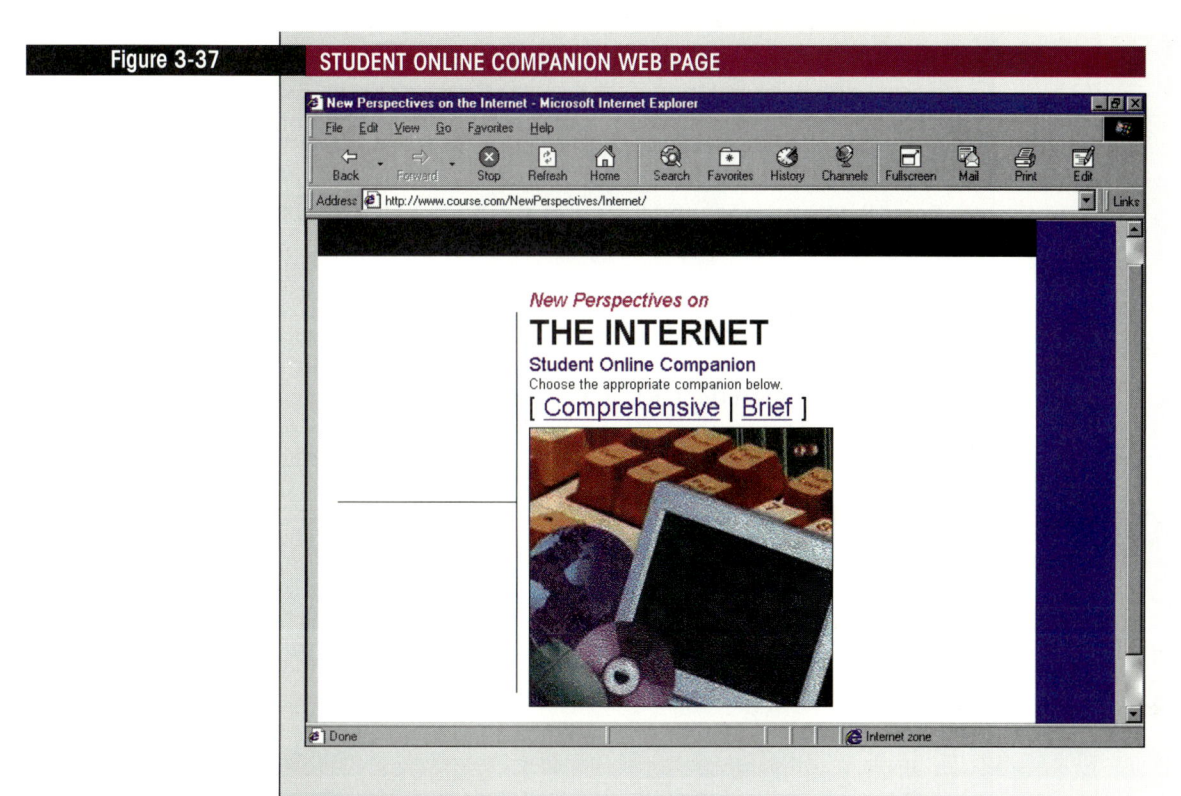

4. Click the link for the book you are using to open the main page, click the **Tutorial 3** link to open the page that contains the links for this tutorial, and then click the **Session 3.3** link in the left frame.

5. Click the link to the **Pennsylvania Quintet** in the right frame. The Web page opens, as shown in Figure 3-38.

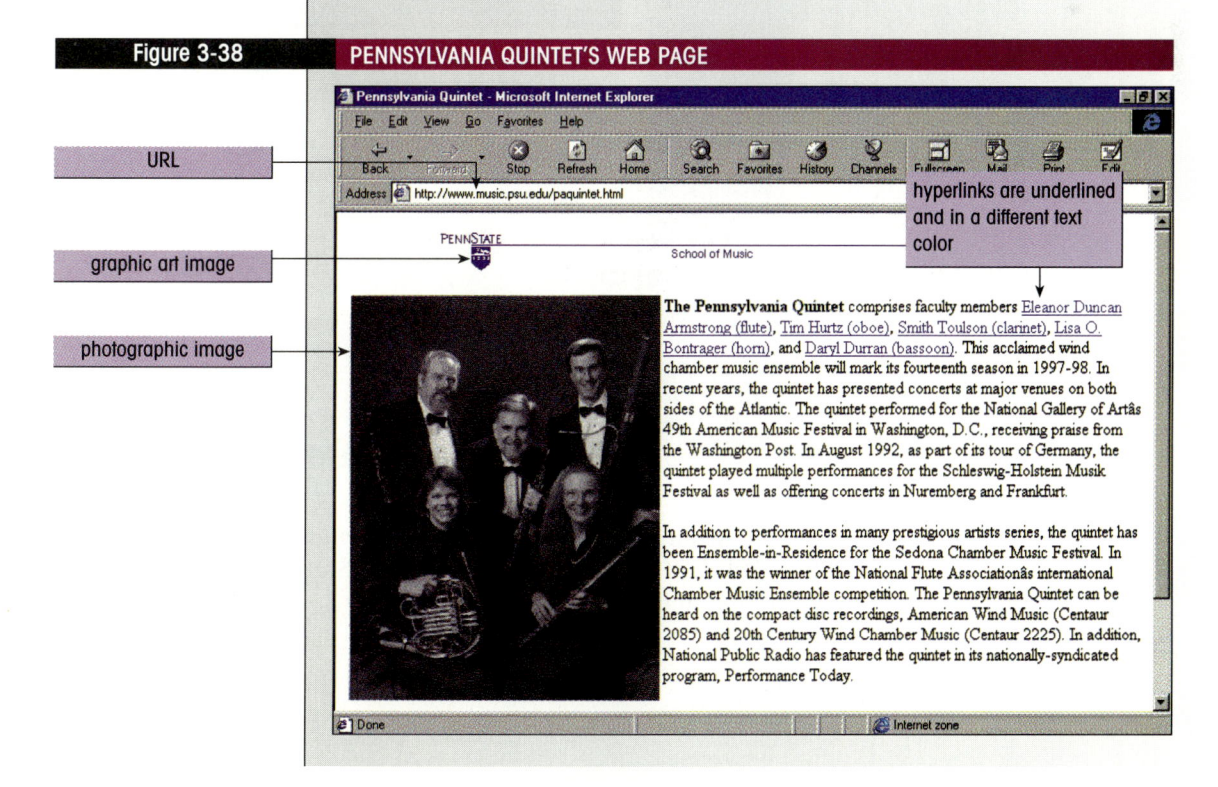

Figure 3-38   PENNSYLVANIA QUINTET'S WEB PAGE

URL

graphic art image

photographic image

hyperlinks are underlined and in a different text color

> **TROUBLE?** The Pennsylvania Quintet might change its Web page, so your Web page might look different from the one shown in Figure 3-38. If this Web page is deleted from the server, you might see an entirely different Web page. However, the steps should work the same.
>
> 6. Read the Web page, and then click the **Back** button to return to the Student Online Companion page.

You like the format of the Pennsylvania Quintet's home page, so you want to make sure that you can go back to that page later if you need to review its contents. Maggie explains that you can write down the URL so you can refer to it later, but an easier way is to use the Favorites feature to store the URL for future use.

Using the Favorites Feature

Internet Explorer's **Favorites feature** lets you store and organize a list of Web pages that you have visited so you can return to them easily. The **Favorites** button on the Standard Buttons toolbar opens the Favorites frame shown in Figure 3-39. You can use the Favorites frame to open URLs you have stored as Favorites.

Figure 3-39 **FAVORITES FRAME**

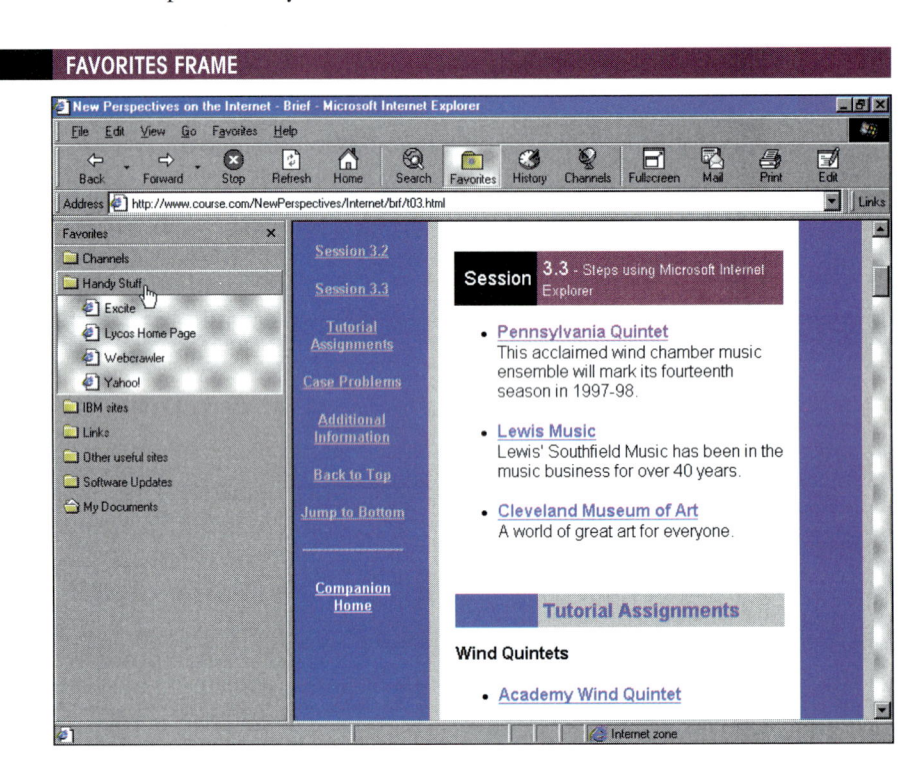

Figure 3-39 shows the hierarchical structure of the Favorites feature. This user stored the four search engine Web pages in a folder named "Handy Stuff". You can organize your favorites in the way that best suits your needs and working style.

You decide to save the Pennsylvania Quintet's Web page as a favorite in a Wind Quintet Information folder.

TUTORIAL 3 BROWSER BASICS   WEB   3.45   INTERNET

REFERENCE WINDOW

Creating a new Favorites folder
- Open the Web page in Internet Explorer.
- Click the Favorites button on the Standard Buttons toolbar to open the Favorites frame.
- Click Favorites on the menu bar, and then click Add to Favorites.
- Click the Create in button in the Add Favorite dialog box.
- Click the Favorites folder, and then click the New Folder button.
- Type the name of the new folder in the Folder name text box, and then click the OK button.
- Click the OK button in the Add Favorite dialog box.

To create a new Favorites folder:

1. Click the **Forward** button on the Standard Buttons toolbar to return to the Pennsylvania Quintet Web page.

2. Click the **Favorites** button on the Standard Buttons toolbar to open the Favorites frame.

3. Click **Favorites** on the menu bar, and then click **Add to Favorites** to open the Add Favorite dialog box.

4. Click the **Create in** button in the Add Favorite dialog box.

5. Click the **Favorites** folder in the Create in window, and then click the **New Folder** button to create a new folder in the Favorites folder.

6. Type **Wind Quintet Information** in the Folder name text box of the Create New Folder dialog box, and then click the **OK** button to close the Create New Folder dialog box. See Figure 3-40. Notice that the page name appears automatically in the Name text box in the Add Favorite dialog box. You can edit the page name, if necessary, by editing the suggested page name.

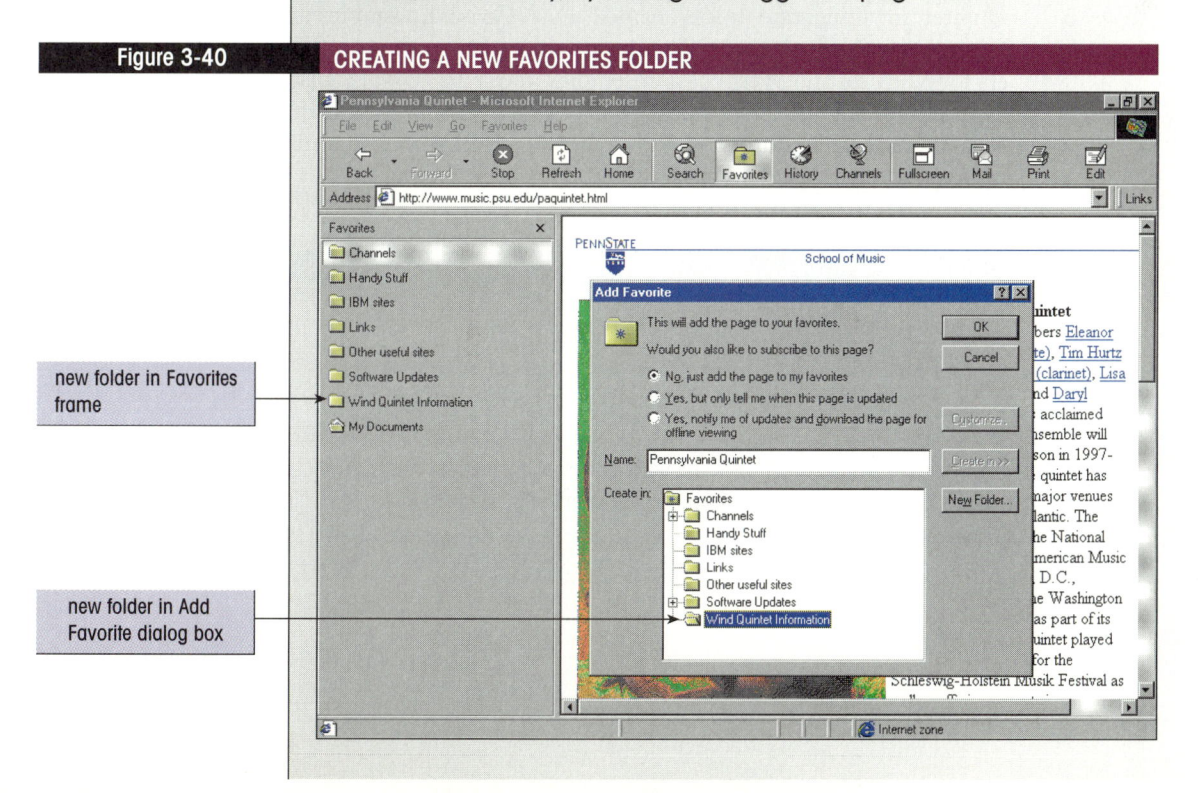

Figure 3-40   CREATING A NEW FAVORITES FOLDER

new folder in Favorites frame

new folder in Add Favorite dialog box

7. Click the **OK** button to close the Add Favorite dialog box. Now, the favorite is saved in Internet Explorer. You can test the favorite by opening it from the Favorites frame.

8. Click the **Back** button on the Standard Buttons toolbar to return to the previous page, click the **Wind Quintet Information** folder in the Favorites frame to open it, and then click **Pennsylvania Quintet**. The Pennsylvania Quintet page opens in the browser, which means that you created the favorite correctly.

TROUBLE? If the Pennsylvania Quintet page does not open, click Favorites on the menu bar, click the Wind Quintet Information folder, right-click the Pennsylvania Quintet favorite, and then click Properties. Click the Internet Shortcut tab and make sure that a URL appears in the Target URL text box. If there is no URL, then click the OK button to close the dialog box, click Favorites on the menu bar, click the Wind Quintet Information favorite, right-click the Pennsylvania Quintet folder, and then click Delete. Repeat the steps to re-create the favorite, and then try again. If you still have trouble, ask your instructor or technical support person for help.

As you use the Web to find information about wind quintets and other sites of interest for the group, you might find yourself creating many favorites so you can return to sites of interest. When you start accumulating favorites, it is important to keep them organized, as you will see next.

Organizing Favorites

You explain to Maggie that you have created a new folder for Wind Quintet Information in the Internet Explorer Favorites frame and stored the Pennsylvania Quintet's URL in that folder. Maggie suggests that you might not want to keep all of the wind quintet-related information you gather in one folder. She notes that you are just beginning your work for Marianna and the quintet and that you might be collecting all types of information for them. Maggie suggests that you might want to put information about the Pennsylvania Quintet in a separate folder named East Coast Ensembles under the Wind Quintet Information folder. As you collect information about other performers, you might add folders for Midwest and West coast ensembles, too.

Internet Explorer offers an easy way to organize your folders in a hierarchical structure—even after you have stored them. To rearrange URLs or even folders within folders, you use the Organize Favorites command on the Favorites menu.

REFERENCE WINDOW RW

Moving an existing favorite into a new folder
- Click Favorites on the menu bar, and then click Organize Favorites.
- Double-click the folder under which you would like to add the new folder.
- Click the Create New Folder button in the Organize Favorites dialog box.
- Type the name of the new folder, and then press the Enter key.
- Drag the favorite that you want to move into the new folder.
- Click the Close button.

TUTORIAL 3 BROWSER BASICS WEB 3.47 INTERNET

To move an existing favorite into a new folder:

1. Click **Favorites** on the menu bar, and then click **Organize Favorites**.
2. Double-click the **Wind Quintet Information** folder in the Organize Favorites dialog box.
3. Click the **Create New Folder** button in the Organize Favorites dialog box.
4. Type **East Coast Ensembles** to replace the "New Folder" selected text, and then press the **Enter** key to rename the folder.
5. Click and drag the Pennsylvania Quintet favorite to the new East Coast Ensembles folder as shown in Figure 3-41, and then release the mouse button. Now, the East Coast Ensembles folder contains the favorite.

Figure 3-41 REARRANGING FAVORITES IN FOLDERS

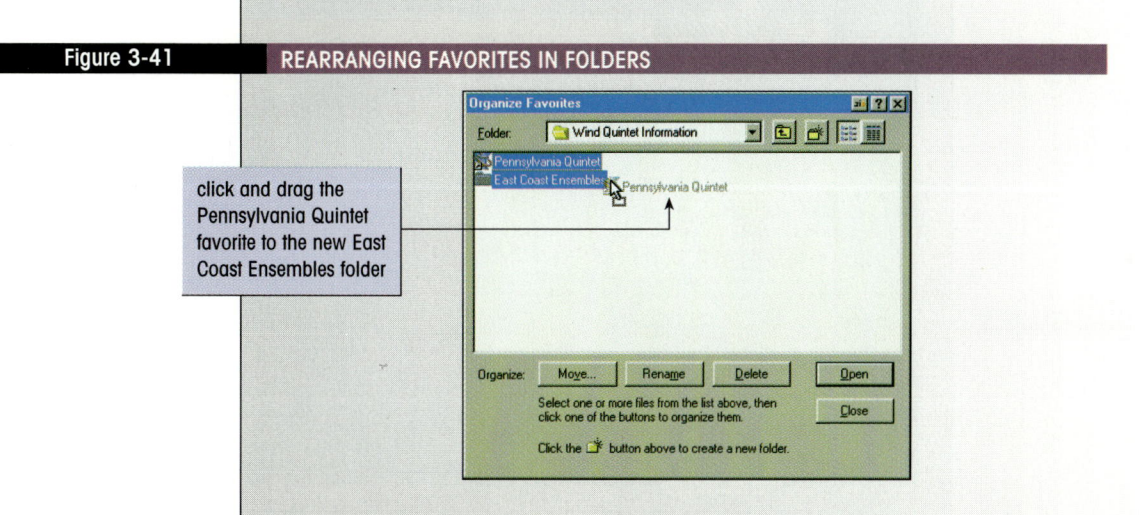

click and drag the Pennsylvania Quintet favorite to the new East Coast Ensembles folder

6. Click the **Close** button to close the Organize Favorites dialog box. The Favorites frame is updated automatically to reflect your changes.
7. Click the **Favorites** button on the Standard Buttons toolbar to close the Favorites list.

Hyperlink Navigation with the Mouse

Now you know how to use the Internet to find information that will help you with the Sunset Wind Quintet. Maggie tells you that the easiest way to move from one Web page to another is to use the hyperlinks that the authors of Web pages embed in their HTML documents, as you will see next.

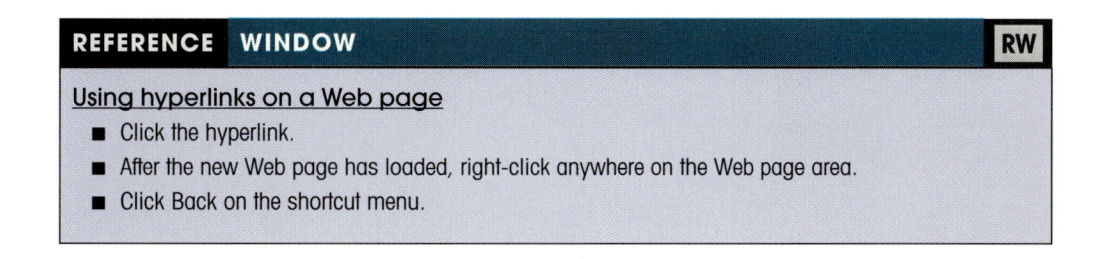

REFERENCE WINDOW

Using hyperlinks on a Web page
- Click the hyperlink.
- After the new Web page has loaded, right-click anywhere on the Web page area.
- Click Back on the shortcut menu.

To follow a hyperlink Web page and return:

1. Click the **Back** button on the Standard Buttons toolbar to go back to the Student Online Companion page, click the **Lewis Music** link to open that page, and then point to the **Instrument Accessories** hyperlink shown in Figure 3-42 so your pointer changes to .

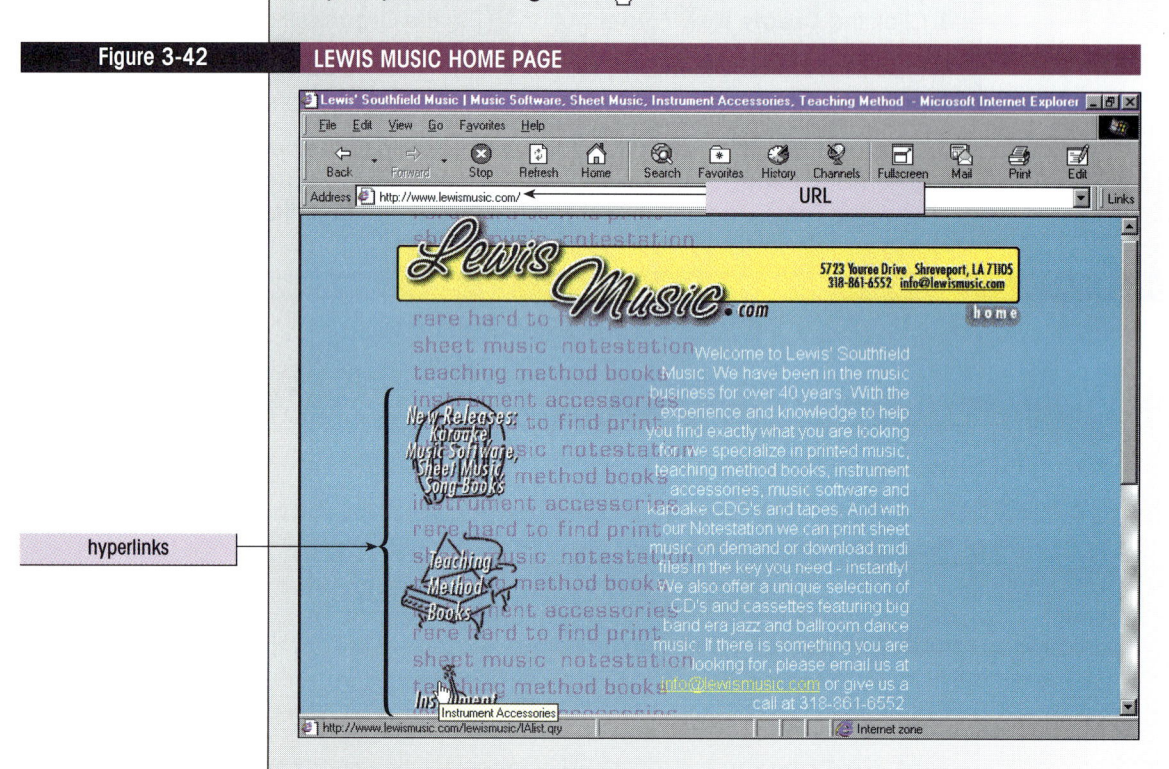

Figure 3-42   **LEWIS MUSIC HOME PAGE**

hyperlinks

2. Click the **Instrument Accessories** hyperlink to load the page. Watch the first panel in the status bar—when it displays the text "Done," you know that Internet Explorer has loaded the full page.

3. Right-click anywhere in the Web page area to display the shortcut menu, as shown in Figure 3-43.

   TROUBLE? If you right-click a hyperlink, your shortcut menu will display a shorter list than the one shown in Figure 3-43, and the Back item will not appear in the menu. If you don't see the shortcut menu shown in Figure 3-43, click anywhere outside of the shortcut menu to close it, and then repeat Step 3.

   TROUBLE? Web pages change frequently, so the Instrument Accessories page you see might look different from the one shown in Figure 3-43, but right-clicking anywhere on the Web page area will still work.

TUTORIAL 3 BROWSER BASICS WEB 3.49 INTERNET

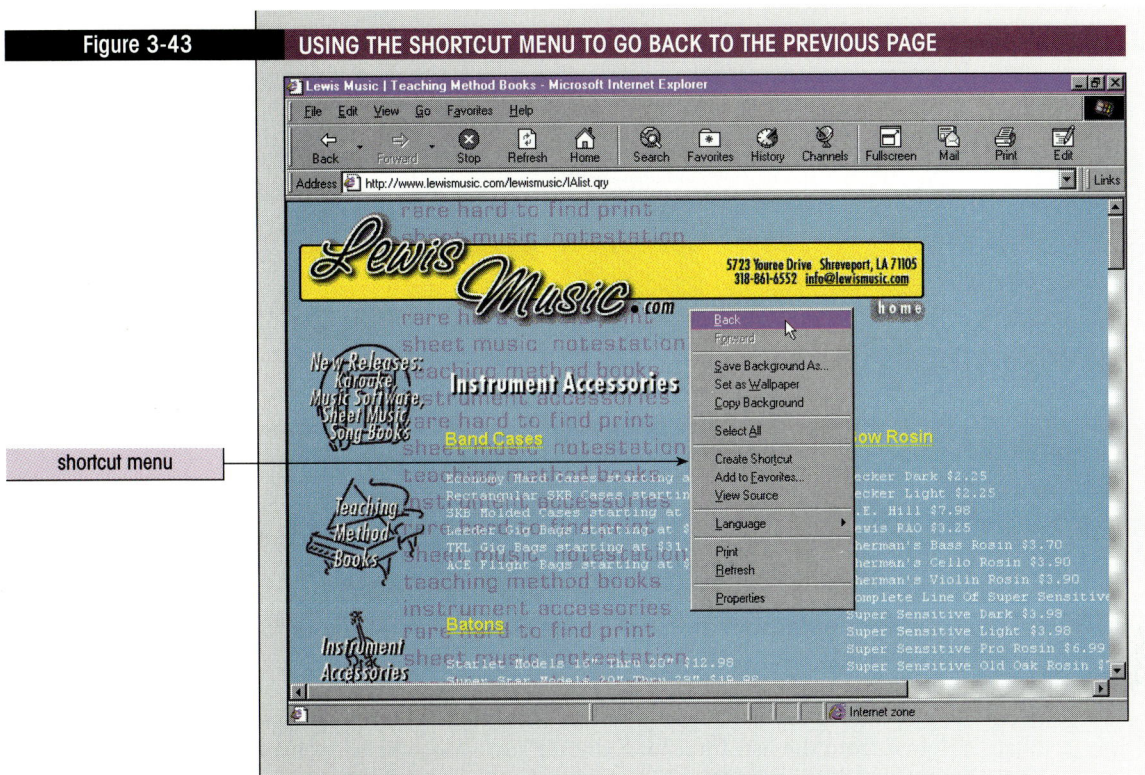

| Figure 3-43 | USING THE SHORTCUT MENU TO GO BACK TO THE PREVIOUS PAGE |

shortcut menu

4. Click **Back** on the shortcut menu to return to the Lewis Music home page.

5. Repeat Step 4 to return to the Student Online Companion page.

You are beginning to get a good sense of how to move from one Web page to another and back again, but Maggie tells you that you have mastered only one technique of many. She explains that the Standard Buttons toolbar and the menu bar offer many tools for accessing and using Web sites.

Using the History List

In Session 3.1 you learned that the Back and Forward buttons let you move to and from previously visited pages. These buttons duplicate the functions of the menu bar's Go command. Clicking Go opens a menu that lets you move back and forward through a portion of the history list and allows you to choose a specific Web page from that list. You also can open a full copy of the history list.

To view the history list for this session:

1. Click the **History** button on the Standard Buttons toolbar. The history list opens in a hierarchical structure in a separate window on the left side of the screen. The history list stores each URL you visited during the past week or during a specified time period. It also maintains the hierarchy of each Web site; that is, pages you visit at a particular Web site are stored in a separate folder for that site. To return to a particular page, click that page's entry in the list. You can see the full URL of any item in the History frame by moving the mouse pointer over the history list item, as shown in Figure 3-44.

Figure 3-44 **EXPLORING THE HISTORY LIST**

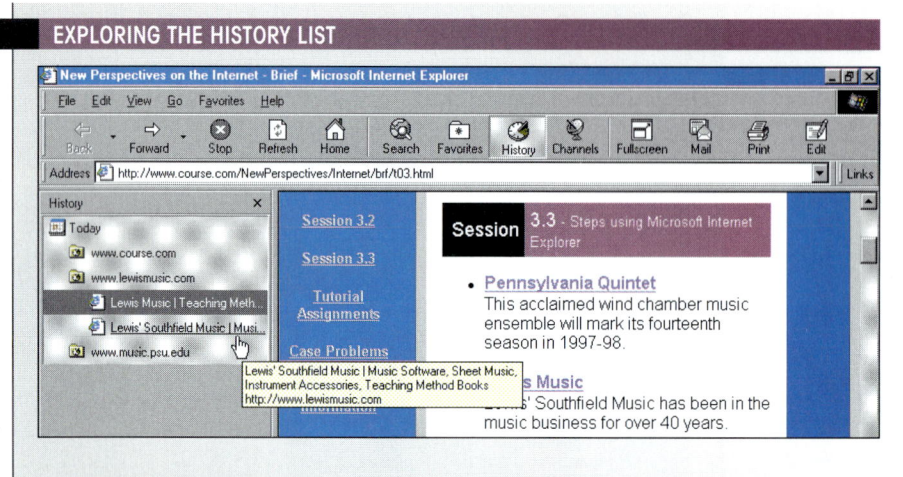

TROUBLE? Your History frame might be a different size from what appears in Figure 3-44. You can resize the window by clicking and dragging its left edge either right or left to make it narrower or wider.

2. Click the **Close** button ⊠ on the History frame title bar to close it.

You can right-click any entry in the Internet Explorer history list and copy the URL or delete it from the list. Internet Explorer stores each history entry as a shortcut in a History folder, which is in the Windows folder.

Refreshing a Web Page

The **Refresh** button makes Microsoft Internet Explorer load a new copy of the current Web page that appears in the browser window. Internet Explorer stores a copy of every Web page it displays on your computer's hard drive in a **Temporary Internet Files** folder in the Windows folder. This increases the speed at which Internet Explorer can display pages as you move back and forth through the history list because the browser can load the pages from a local disk drive instead of reloading the page from the remote Web server. When you click the Refresh button, Internet Explorer contacts the Web server to see if the Web page has changed since it was stored in the cache folder. If it has changed, Internet Explorer gets the new page from the Web server; otherwise, it loads the cache folder copy.

Returning to Your Start Page

The **Home** button displays the home (or start) page for your copy of Internet Explorer. You can go to the Microsoft Start Page, which is the software's default installation home page, by clicking the **Internet Explorer icon** button on the menu bar. Although you cannot change where the Microsoft Internet Explorer icon button takes your browser, you can change the setting for the Home toolbar button, as you will see next.

| REFERENCE WINDOW | RW |

Changing the Home toolbar button settings
- Click View on the menu bar, and then click Internet Options.
- Click the General tab.
- Select whether you want Internet Explorer to open with the current page, its default page, or a blank page by clicking the corresponding button in the Home page section of the Internet Options dialog box.
- If you want to specify a home page, type the URL of that Web page in the Address text box.

To modify your home page:

1. Click **View** on the menu bar, and then click **Internet Options** to open the dialog box shown in Figure 3-45.

Figure 3-45   CHANGING THE DEFAULT HOME PAGE

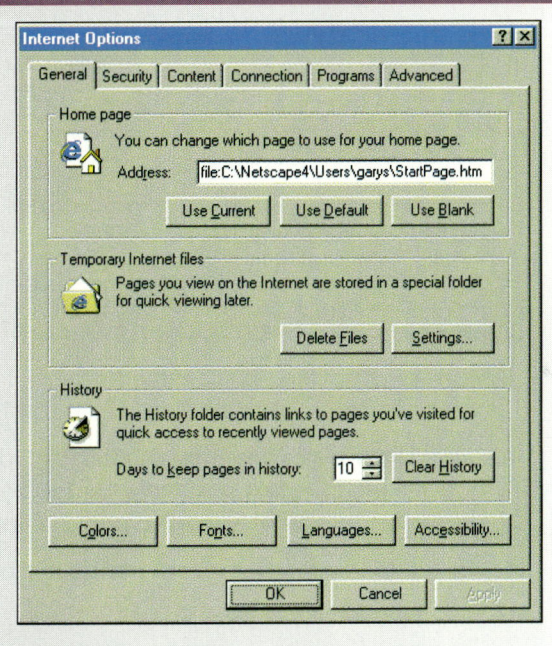

To use the currently loaded Web page as your home page, click the Use Current button. To use the default home page that was installed with your copy of Internet Explorer, click the Use Default button. If you don't want a page to open when you start your browser, click the Use Blank button. If you want to specify a home page other than the current, default, or blank page, type the URL for that page in the Address text box.

TROUBLE? You might not be able to change these settings if you are using a computer in your school lab or at your office. Some organizations set the home page defaults on all of their computers and then lock those settings.

2. Click the **Cancel** button to close the dialog box without making any changes.

In the next section, you will learn how to print the Web page so you have a permanent record of its contents.

Printing a Web Page

The **Print** button on the Standard Buttons toolbar lets you print the current Web frame or page. You will learn more about saving and printing Web pages later in this session, but you can use the Print command to make a printed copy of most Web pages. (Some Web pages disable the Print command.)

> **REFERENCE WINDOW** **RW**
>
> **Printing the current Web page**
> - Click the Print button on the Standard Buttons toolbar to print the current Web page with the default print settings.
>
> or
> - Click File on the menu bar, and then click Print.
> - Use the Print dialog box to choose the printer you want to use, the pages you want to print, and the number of copies you want to make of each page.
> - Click the OK button to print the page(s).

To print a Web page:

1. Click in the main (right) frame of the Student Online Companion page to select it.

2. Click **File** on the menu bar, and then click **Print** to open the Print dialog box.

3 Make sure that the printer in the Name text box shows the printer you want to use; if necessary, click the Name list arrow to change the selection.

4. Click the **Pages** option button in the Print range section of the Print dialog box, type **1** in the from text box, press the **Tab** key, and then type **1** in the to text box to specify that you only want to print the first page.

5. Make sure that the Number of copies text box shows that you want to print one copy.

6 Click the **OK** button to print the Web page and close the Print dialog box.

Changing the Settings for Printing a Web Page

You already have seen how to print Web pages using the basic options available in the Print dialog box. Also, you learned how to create a favorite in the Favorites list so you can return to a Web page later. Usually, the default settings in the Print dialog box are fine for printing a Web page, but you can use the Page Setup dialog box to change the way a Web page prints. Figure 3-46 shows the Page Setup dialog box, and Figure 3-47 describes its settings.

| Figure 3-46 | PAGE SETUP DIALOG BOX |

| Figure 3-47 | PAGE SETUP DIALOG BOX OPTIONS |

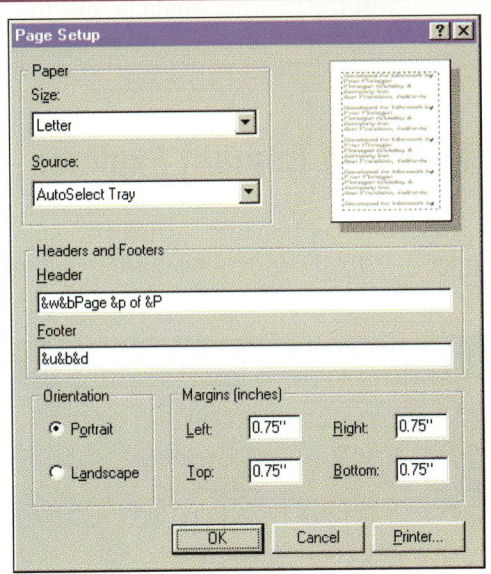

OPTION	DESCRIPTION	USE
Paper Size	Changes the size of the printed page.	Use the Letter size default unless you are printing to different paper stock, such as Legal or A4.
Paper Source	Changes the printer's paper source.	Use the default AutoSelect Tray unless you want to specify a different tray or manual feed for printing on heavy paper.
Header	Prints the Web page's title, URL, date/time printed, and page numbers at the top of each page.	To obtain details on how to specify exact header printing options, click the Header text box to select it, and then press the F1 key.
Footer	Prints the Web page's title, URL, date/time printed, and page numbers at the bottom of each page.	To obtain details on how to specify exact footer printing options, click the Footer text box to select it, and then press the F1 key.
Orientation	Selects the orientation of the printed output.	Portrait works best for most Web pages, but you can use landscape orientation to print the wide tables of numbers included on some Web pages.
Margins	Changes the margin of the printed page.	Normally, you should leave the default settings, but you can change the right, left, top, or bottom margins as needed.

When printing Web pages, another print option that is extremely useful for saving paper when printing long Web pages is to reduce the font size of the Web pages before you print them. To do this, click View on the menu bar, click Fonts, and then click either Smaller or Smallest on the Fonts menu.

Checking Web Page Security Features

You can check some of the security elements of a Web page by clicking File on the menu bar, clicking Properties, and then clicking the Certificates button. Internet Explorer will display security information for the page, if it is available, to advise you of the overall security of the page that appears in the browser window. When you click the Certificates button, you also can learn about how a page was encrypted. **Encryption** is a way of scrambling and encoding

INTERNET   WEB 3.54   TUTORIAL 3   BROWSER BASICS

data transmissions that reduces the risk that a person who intercepted the Web page as it traveled across the Internet would be able to decode and read the page's contents. Web sites use encrypted transmission to send and receive information such as credit card numbers to ensure privacy.

Getting Help in Microsoft Internet Explorer

Microsoft Internet Explorer includes a comprehensive online Help facility. You can obtain help by opening the Internet Explorer Help window.

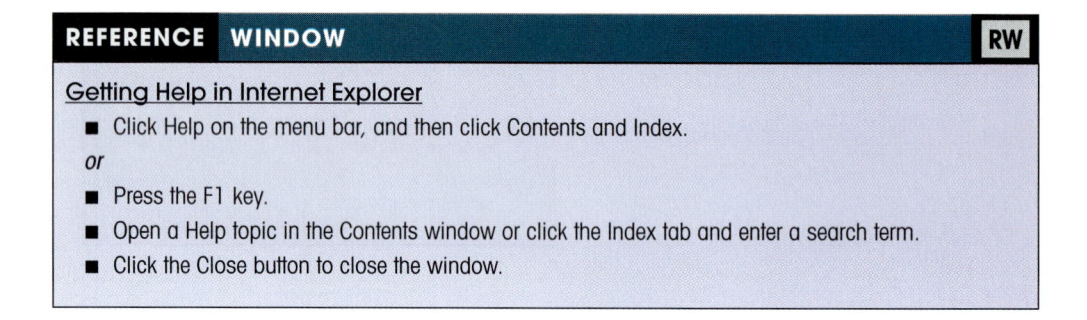

REFERENCE WINDOW

Getting Help in Internet Explorer
- Click Help on the menu bar, and then click Contents and Index.

or
- Press the F1 key.
- Open a Help topic in the Contents window or click the Index tab and enter a search term.
- Click the Close button to close the window.

To open the Internet Explorer Help window:

1. Click **Help** on the menu bar, and then click **Contents and Index** to open the Internet Explorer Help window.

2. If necessary, click the **Maximize** button on the Internet Explorer Help window so it fills the desktop.

3. Click the **Contents** tab in the Contents window, click **Tips and Tricks**, and then click **Organizing your links to Web pages for easier access** to open that help topic in the Help window. Notice that the page that opens contains other links to related categories that you can explore. See Figure 3-48.

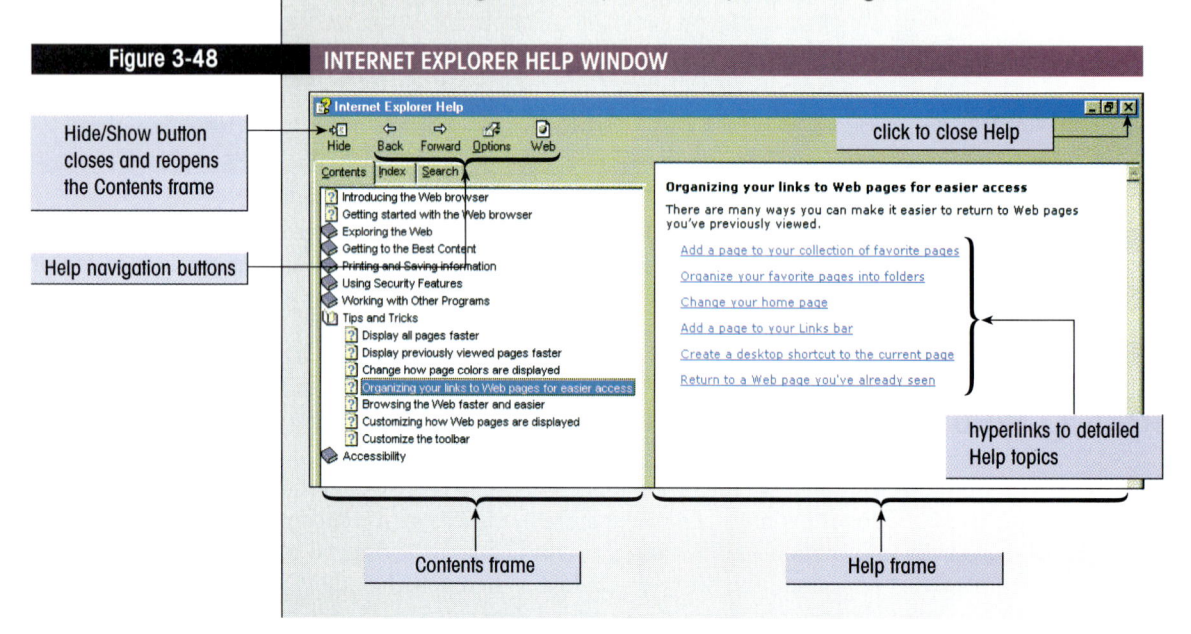

Figure 3-48   INTERNET EXPLORER HELP WINDOW

- Hide/Show button closes and reopens the Contents frame
- click to close Help
- Help navigation buttons
- hyperlinks to detailed Help topics
- Contents frame
- Help frame

> **4.** Click the **Close** button ⊠ to close the Internet Explorer Help window.

Now you are convinced that you have all of the tools you need to successfully find information on the Web. Marianna probably will be interested in seeing the Pennsylvania Quintet Web page, but you are not sure if she will have Internet access while she's touring. Maggie says that you can save the Web page on disk, so Marianna can open the page locally in her Web browser using the files that you save on a disk.

Using Internet Explorer to Save a Web Page

You have learned how to use most of the Internet Explorer tools for loading Web pages and saving bookmarks. Now, Maggie wants you to learn how to save a Web page. Sometimes, you will want to store entire Web pages on disk; other times, you will only want to store selected portions of Web page text or particular graphics from a Web page.

Saving a Web Page

You like the Pennsylvania Quintet's Web site and want to save the page on disk so you can send it to Marianna. That way, she can review it without having an Internet connection. To save a Web page, you must have the page open in Internet Explorer.

REFERENCE WINDOW

Saving a Web page to a floppy disk
- Open the Web page in Internet Explorer.
- Click File on the menu bar, and then click Save As to open the Save HTML Document dialog box.
- Click the Save in list arrow, and then change to the drive on which to save the Web page.
- Accept the default filename, or change the filename, if you want; however, retain the file extension .htm or .html.
- Click the Save button to save the Web page on the disk.

To save the Web page on your Student Disk:

1. Use the **Favorites** button to return to the Pennsylvania Quintet page. (You saved the favorite in the East Coast Ensembles folder, which is in the Wind Quintet Information folder.)

2. Click **File** on the menu bar, and then click **Save As** to open the Save HTML Document dialog box.

3. Click the **Save in** list arrow, click the drive that contains your Student Disk (usually this is 3½ Floppy (A:)), and then double-click the **Tutorial.03** folder to open it. You will accept the default filename of paquintet.htm.

4. Click the **Save** button. Now the HTML document for the Pennsylvania Quintet's home page is saved in the Tutorial.03 folder on your Student Disk. When you send it to Marianna, she can open her Web browser and then use the Open command on the File menu to open the Web page.

5. Close the Favorites frame.

If the Web page contains graphics, such as photos, drawings, or icons, you should note that these items will not be saved with the HTML document. To save a graphic, right-click it in the browser window, click Save Picture As, and then save the graphic to the same location as the Web's HTML document. The graphics file is specified to appear on the HTML document as a hyperlink, so you might have to change the HTML code in the Web page to identify its location. Copying the graphics files to the same disk as the HTML document will *usually* work.

Saving Web Page Text to a File

Maggie suggests that you might want to know how to save portions of Web page text to a file, so that you can save only the text from the Web page and use it in other programs. You will use WordPad to receive the text you will copy from a Web page, but any word processor or text editor will work.

Marianna just called to let you know that the quintet will play a concert in Cleveland on a Friday night, and she asks you to identify other opportunities for scheduling local concerts during the following weekend. Often, museums are willing to book small ensembles for weekend afternoon programs, and Marianna has given you the URL for the Cleveland Museum of Art. You will visit the site and then get the museum's address and telephone number so you can contact it about scheduling a concert.

REFERENCE WINDOW RW

Copying text from a Web page to a WordPad document
- Open the Web page in Internet Explorer.
- Use the mouse pointer to select the text you want to copy.
- Click Edit on the menu bar, and then click Copy.
- Start WordPad or another word processor.
- Click Edit on the menu bar, and then click Paste.
- Click the Save button on the WordPad toolbar, and then save the file to the correct folder and drive using a filename that you specify.
- Click the Save button.

To copy text from a Web page and save it to a file:

1. Use the **Back** button to return to the Student Online Companion page, and then click the **Cleveland Museum of Art** link to open that Web page in the browser window.

2. Click the **hours and address** hyperlink in the left frame on the Web page to open the museum information page in the main (right) frame.

3. Click and drag the mouse pointer over the address and telephone number to select it, as shown in Figure 3-49.

TUTORIAL 3 BROWSER BASICS   WEB   3.57   INTERNET

Figure 3-49 **SELECTING TEXT ON A WEB PAGE**

selected text

hours and address hyperlink in left frame

mouse pointer changes to insertion point

4. Click **Edit** on the menu bar, and then click **Copy** to copy the selected text to the Windows Clipboard.

Now, you can start WordPad and paste the copied text into a new document.

To start and copy the text into WordPad:

1. Click the **Start** button on the taskbar, point to **Programs**, point to **Accessories**, and then click **WordPad** to start the program and open a new document.

2. Click the **Paste** button on the WordPad toolbar to paste the text into the WordPad document, as shown in Figure 3-50.

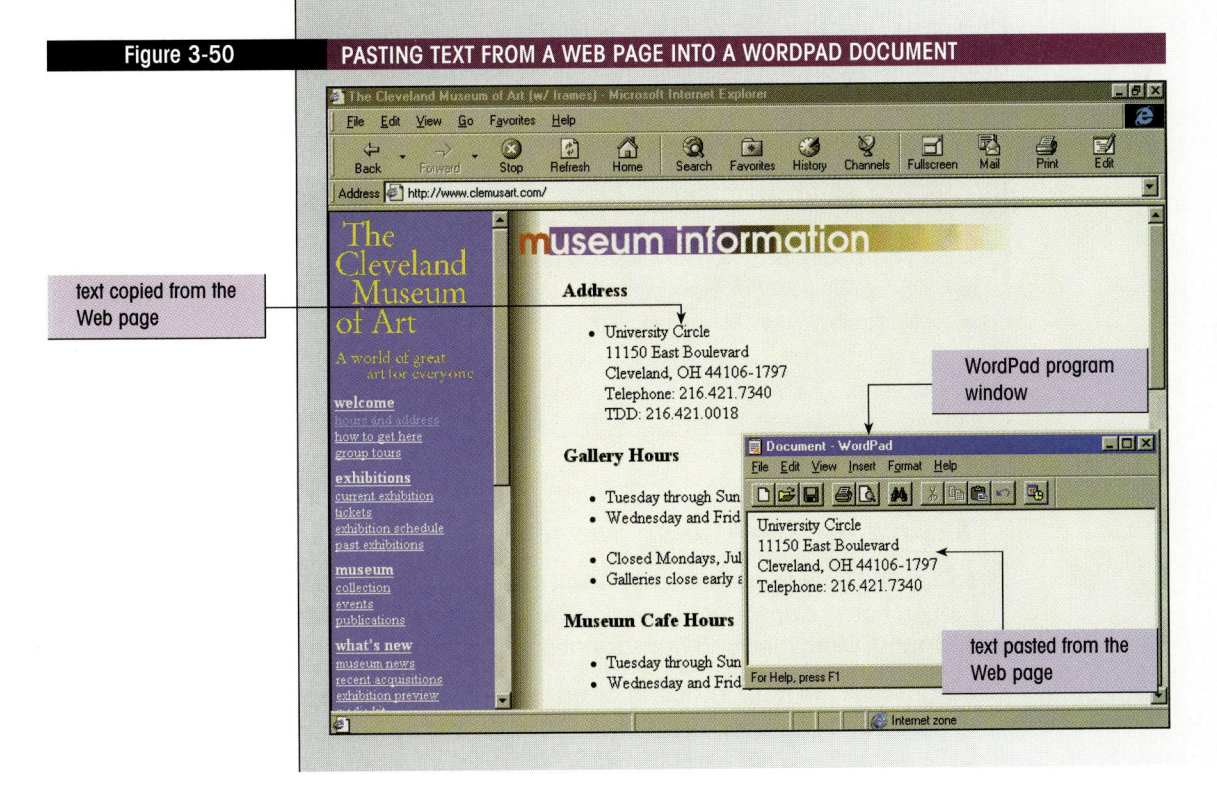

Figure 3-50 **PASTING TEXT FROM A WEB PAGE INTO A WORDPAD DOCUMENT**

text copied from the Web page

WordPad program window

text pasted from the Web page

TROUBLE? If the WordPad toolbar does not appear, click View on the menu bar, click Toolbar to turn it on, and then repeat Step 2. Your WordPad program window might be a different size from the one shown in Figure 3-50, which does not affect the steps.

3. Click the **Save** button on the WordPad toolbar to open the Save As dialog box.

4. Click the **Save in** list arrow, change to the drive that contains your Student Disk, and then double-click the **Tutorial.03** folder.

5. Select any text that is in the File name text box, type **CMoA-Address.txt**, and then click the **Save** button to save the file. Now, the address and phone number of the museum is saved in a file in the Tutorial.03 folder on your Student Disk for future reference.

TROUBLE? If you also completed the steps in Session 3.2, then a dialog box will open and ask if you want to replace the existing CmoA-Address.txt file on your Student Disk. Click the Yes button to replace it.

6. Click the **Close** button on the WordPad title bar to close it.

Later, you will contact the museum. You notice that the left frame of the Cleveland Museum of Art Web page has a hyperlink titled "how to get here." This page might offer some helpful information that you could give to Marianna about where the museum is located, so you decide to save the graphic on your disk.

Saving a Web Page Graphic to Disk

Clicking the "how to get here" hyperlink loads a page that contains a hyperlink to a street map of the area surrounding the museum. You can save this map to your disk, as you will see next. Then, you can send the file to Marianna so she has a resource for getting to the museum.

REFERENCE WINDOW | RW

Saving an image from a Web page on a floppy disk
- Open the Web page in Internet Explorer.
- Right-click the image you want to copy, and then click Save Picture As.
- Change to the drive and/or folder that you want to save the image in, change the default filename if necessary, and then click the Save button.

To save the street map image on a floppy disk:

1. Click the **how to get here** hyperlink in the left frame of the Cleveland Museum's of Art home page, and then click the **street map** hyperlink on the Getting around: Directions and Transportation Web page in the main (right) frame.

2. Right-click the map image to open its shortcut menu, as shown in Figure 3-51.

Figure 3-51 | **SAVING THE MAP IMAGE TO DISK**

map image

shortcut menu for the map image

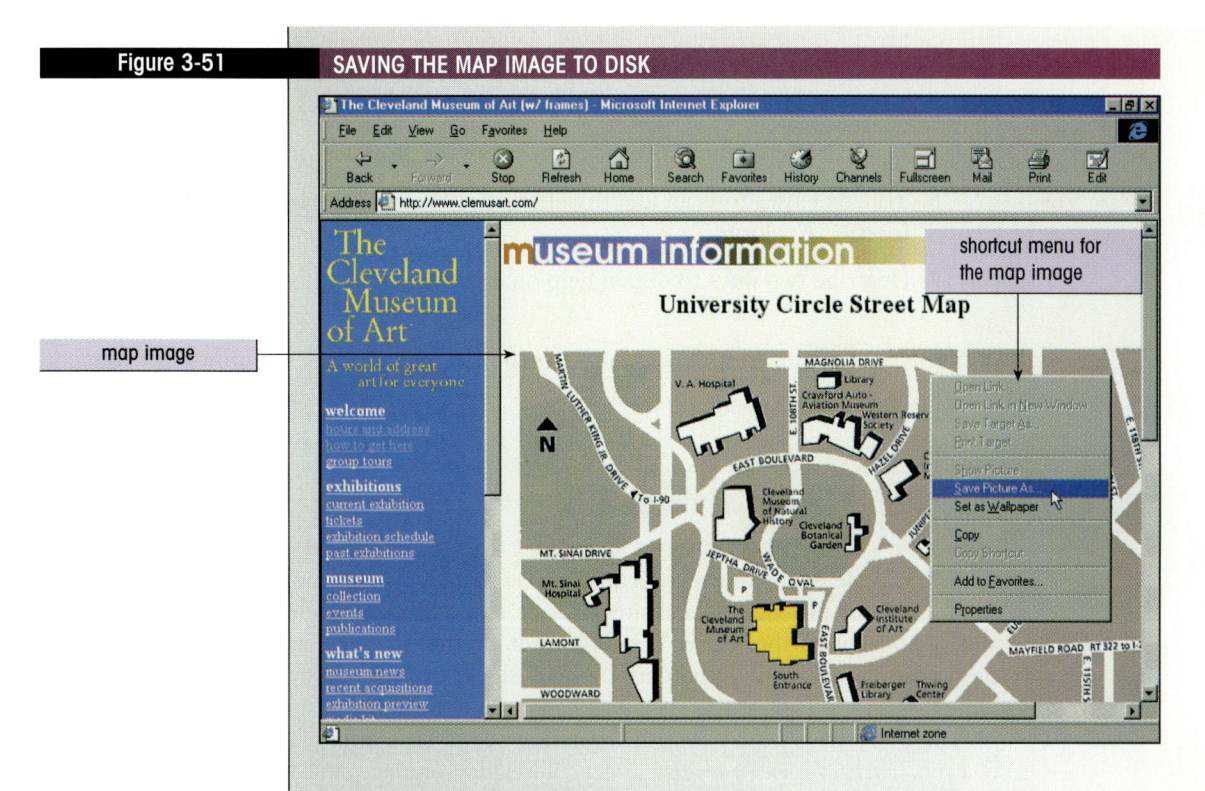

3. Click **Save Picture As** on the shortcut menu to open the Save Picture dialog box.

4. If necessary, click the **Save in** list arrow, change to the drive that contains your Student Disk, and then double-click the **Tutorial.03** folder. You will accept the default filename, mapstreet, so click the **Save** button. Now the image is saved on your Student Disk, so you can send the file to Marianna. Marianna can use her Web browser to open the image file and print it.

   TROUBLE? If you also completed the steps in Session 3.2, then a dialog box will open and ask if you want to replace the existing mapstreet.gif file on your Student Disk. Click the Yes button to replace it.

5. Close your Web browser and your dial-up connection, if necessary.

Now, you can send a disk to Marianna so she has the Pennsylvania Quintet Web page and a map to show how to get to the museum. Marianna is pleased to hear of your progress in using the Web to find information for the quintet.

QUICK CHECK

1. Describe two ways to increase the Web page area in Internet Explorer.

2. You can use the _____ button in Internet Explorer to visit previously visited sites during your Web session

3. Click the _____ button on the Standard Buttons toolbar to open a search engine quickly in Internet Explorer.

4. List the names of two additional Favorites folders you might want to add to the Wind Quintet Information folder as you continue to gather information for the Sunset Wind Quintet.

5. What happens when you click the Refresh button in Internet Explorer?

6. True or False: You can identify encrypted Web pages when viewing them in Internet Explorer.

7. Describe two ways to obtain help on a specific topic in Internet Explorer.

Now you are ready to complete the Tutorial Assignments using the browser of your choice.

TUTORIAL ASSIGNMENTS

Marianna is pleased with the information you gathered thus far about other wind quintet Web pages and potential recital sites. In fact, she is thinking about hiring someone to create a Web page for the Sunset Wind Quintet. So that she has some background information for her meetings with potential Web designers, Marianna would like you to compile some information about the Web pages that other small musical ensembles have created. Although you have searched for information about wind quintets, a large number of string quartets (two violinists, a violist, and a cellist) play similar venues.

Do the following:

1. Start your Web browser, go to the Student Online Companion (http://www.course.com/NewPerspectives/Internet), click the link for your book, click the Tutorial 3 link, and then click the Tutorial Assignments link in the left frame.

2. Click the hyperlinks listed under the category headings Wind Quintets, String Quartets, and Other Small Musical Ensembles to explore the Web pages for each entry.

3. Choose three interesting home pages, and print the first page of each. Create a bookmark or favorite for each of these sites, and then answer the following questions for these three sites.

4. Which sites include a photograph of the ensemble? Which photographs are in color and black and white? Which sites show the ensemble members dressed in formal concert dress?

5. Choose your favorite ensemble photograph and save it in the Tutorial.03 folder on your Student Disk.

6. Do any of the sites provide information about the ensemble's CDs? If so, which ones? Is this information on the home page, or did you click a hyperlink to find it?

7. Do any of the sites offer CDs or other products for sale? If so, which ones? Is this information on the home page, or did you click a hyperlink to find it?

8. Write a one-page report that summarizes your findings for Marianna. Include a recommendation regarding what the Sunset Wind Quintet should consider including in its Web site.

9. Close your Web browser, and your dial-up connection, if necessary.

CASE PROBLEMS

1. Businesses on the Web Business Web sites range from very simple informational sites to comprehensive sites that offer information about the firm's products or services, history, current employment openings, and financial information. An increasing number of business sites offer products or services for sale using their Web sites. You just started a position on the public relations staff of Value City Central, a large retail chain of television and appliance stores. Your first assignment is to research and report on the types of information that other large firms offer on their Web sites.

Do the following:

1. Start your Web browser, go to the Student Online Companion (http://www.course.com/NewPerspectives/Internet), click the link for your book, click the Tutorial 3 link, and then click the Case Problems link in the left frame.

2. Use the Case Problem 1 hyperlinks to open the business sites on that page.

3. Choose three of those business sites that you believe would be most relevant to your assignment.

4. Print the home page for each Web site that you have chosen.

5. Select one site that you feel does the best job in each of the following five categories: overall presentation of the corporate image, description of products or services offered, presentation of the firm's history, description of employment opportunities, and presentation of financial statements or other financial information about the company.

6. Prepare a report that includes one paragraph describing why you believe each of the sites you identified in the preceding step did the best job.

7. Close your Web browser, and log off the Internet, if necessary.

2. Browser Wars Your employer, Bristol Mills, is a medium-sized manufacturer of specialty steel products. The firm has increased its use of computers in all of its office operations and in many of its manufacturing operations. Many of the Bristol's computers currently run either the Netscape Navigator or Microsoft Internet Explorer; however, the chief financial officer (CFO) has decided the firm can support only one of these products. As the CFO's special assistant, you have been asked to recommend which Web browser the company should choose to support.

Do the following:

1. Start your Web browser, go to the Student Online Companion (http://www.course.com/NewPerspectives/Internet), click the link for your book, click the Tutorial 3 link, and then click the Case Problems link in the left frame.

2. Use the Case Problem 2 hyperlinks to learn more about these two widely used Web browser software packages.

3. Write a one-page memo to the CFO (your instructor) that outlines the strengths and weaknesses of each product. Recommend one program and support your decision using the information you collected.

4. Prepare a list of features that you would like to see in a new Web browser software package that would overcome important limitations in either Navigator or Internet Explorer. Do you think it would be feasible for a firm to develop and use such a product? Why or why not?

5. Close your Web browser, and log off the Internet, if necessary.

3. Citizens Fidelity Bank You are a new staff auditor at the Citizens Fidelity Bank. You have had more recent computer training than other audit staff members at Citizens, so Sally DeYoung, the audit manager, asks you to review the bank's policy on Web browser cookie settings. Some of the bank's board members expressed concerns to Sally about the security of the bank's computers. They understand that the bank has PCs on its networks that are connected to the Internet. One of the board members learned about browser cookies and was afraid that an innocent bank employee might connect to a site that would write a dangerous cookie file on the bank's computer network. A browser cookie is a small file that a Web server can write to the disk drive of the computer running a Web browser. Not all Web servers write cookies, but those that do can read the cookie file the next time the Web browser on that computer connects to the Web server. Then the Web server can retrieve information about the Web browser's last connection to the server. None of the bank's board members knows very much about computers, but all of them became concerned that a virus-laden cookie could significantly damage the bank's computer system. Sally asks you to help inform the board of directors about cookies and to establish a policy on using them.

Do the following:

1. Start your Web browser, go to the Student Online Companion (http://www.course.com/NewPerspectives/Internet), click the link for your book, click the Tutorial 3 link, and then click the Case Problems link in the left frame.

2. Use the Case Problem 3 hyperlinks to Cookie Information Resources to learn more about cookie files.

3. Prepare a brief outline of the content on each Web page you visit.

4. List the risks that Citizens Fidelity Bank might face by allowing cookie files to be written to their computers.

5. List the benefits that individual users obtain by allowing Web servers to write cookies to the computers that they are using at the bank to access the Web.

6. Close your Web browser, and log off the Internet, if necessary.

4. Columbus Suburban Area Council The Columbus Suburban Area Council is a charitable organization devoted to maintaining and improving the general welfare of people living in Columbus suburbs. As the director of the council, you are interested in encouraging donations and other support from area citizens and would like to stay informed of grant opportunities that might benefit the council. You are especially interested in developing an informative and attractive presence on the Web.

Do the following:

1. Start your Web browser, go to the Student Online Companion (http://www.course.com/NewPerspectives/Internet), click the link for your book, click the Tutorial 3 link, and then click the Case Problems link in the left frame.

2. Follow the Case Problem 4 hyperlinks to charitable organizations to find out more about what other organizations are doing with their Web sites.

3. Select three of the Web sites you visited and, for each, prepare a list of the site's contents. Note whether each site included financial information and whether the site disclosed how much the organization spent on administrative, or nonprogram activities.

4. Identify which site you believe would be a good model for the Council's new Web site. Explain why you think your chosen site would be the best example to follow.

5. Close your Web browser, and log off the Internet, if necessary.

LAB ASSIGNMENTS

The Internet: World Wide Web

One of the most popular services on the Internet is the World Wide Web. This Lab is a Web simulator that teaches you how to use Web browser software to find information. You can use this Lab whether or not your school provides you with Internet access.

1. Click the Steps button to learn how to use Web browser software. As you proceed through the Steps, answer all of the Quick Check questions that appear. After you complete the Steps, you will see a Quick Check Summary Report. Follow the instructions on the screen to print this report.

2. Click the Explore button on the Welcome screen. Use the Web browser to locate a weather map of the Caribbean Virgin Islands. What is its URL?

3. A SCUBA diver named Wadson Lachouffe has been searching for the fabled treasure of Greybeard the pirate. A link from the Adventure Travel Web site www.atour.com leads to Wadson's Web page called "Hidden Treasure." In Explore, locate the Hidden Treasure page and answer the following questions:
   a. What was the name of Greybeard's ship?
   b. What was Greybeard's favorite food?
   c. What does Wadson think happened to Greybeard's ship?

4. In the Steps, you found a graphic of Jupiter from the photo archives of the Jet Propulsion Laboratory. In the Explore section of the Lab, you can also find a graphic of Saturn. Suppose one of your friends wanted a picture of Saturn for an astronomy report. Make a list of the blue, underlined links your friend must click in the correct order to find the Saturn graphic. Assume that your friend will begin at the Web Trainer home page.

5. Enter the URL http://www.atour.com to jump to the Adventure Travel Web site. Write a one-page description of this site. In your paper include a description of the information at the site, the number of pages the site contains, and a diagram of the links it contains.

6. Chris Thomson is a student at UVI and has his own Web pages. In Explore, look at the information Chris has included on his pages. Suppose you could create your own Web page. What would you include? Use word-processing software to design your own Web pages. Make sure you indicate the graphics and links you would use.

Quick Check Answers

Session 3.1

1. False
2. Format text and create hyperlinks
3. The main page of a Web site, the first page that opens when you start your Web browser, or the page that opens the first time you start a particular Web browser
4. Any two: graphics image, sound clip, or video files
5. Candidate's name and party affiliation, list of qualifications, biography, position statements on campaign issues, list of endorsements with hyperlinks to the Web pages of individuals and organizations that support her candidacy, audio or video clips of speeches and interviews, address and telephone number of the campaign office, and other similar information
6. A computer's IP address is a unique identifying number; its domain name is a unique name associated with the IP address on the Internet host computer responsible for that computer's domain
7. "http://" indicates use of the hypertext transfer protocol, "www.savethetrees.org" is the domain name and suggests a charitable or not-for-profit organization that is probably devoted to forest ecology, "main.html" is the name of the HTML file on the Web server
8. A Web directory contains a hierarchical list of Web page categories; each category contains hyperlinks to individual Web pages. A Web search engine is a Web site that accepts words or expressions you enter and finds Web pages that include those words or expressions

Session 3.2

1. Any three of: type the URL in the Location field, click a hyperlink on a Web page, click the Back button, click the Forward button, click the Bookmarks button and select from the menu, or click Communicator on the menu bar then click History and double-click the History listing entry
2. history list
3. When you believe the Web page might have changed since you last visited it
4. Navigator loads the page that is specified in the Home page section of the Preferences dialog box (which you can open from the Edit menu)
5. encrypt
6. True
7. Navigator feature that lets you store and organize a list of Web pages that you have visited

Session 3.3

1. Hide its toolbars or click the Fullscreen button
2. History
3. Search
4. Midwest Ensembles, West Coast Ensembles
5. Internet Explorer contacts the Web server to see if the currently loaded Web page has changed since it was stored in its cache folder. If the Web page has changed, it obtains the new page; otherwise, it loads the cache folder copy.
6. True
7. Press F1, click Help on the menu bar

TUTORIAL 4

OBJECTIVES

In this tutorial you will:

- Determine whether a research question is specific or exploratory

- Learn how to develop an effective Web search strategy to answer research questions

- Learn about Web search tools and how they work

- Create different kinds of search expressions

- Find information using search engines, directories, and other Web research tools

SEARCHING THE WEB

Using Search Engines and Directories Effectively

CASE

Midland News Business Section

The *Midland News* is a top-rated daily newspaper that serves the Midland metropolitan area. The *News* is especially proud of its business section, which has won a number of awards for business reporting and analysis over the years. Anne Hill is the business editor at the *News* and has recruited an excellent staff of editors, reporters, and columnists, who each specialize in different areas of business. Anne has hired you to fill an intern position as her staff assistant. The writers in the business section offices use computers to write and edit the newspaper. Recently, each writer gained access to the Internet on his or her computer. Anne would like you to work with Dave Burton, who is the paper's international news reporter, and Ranjit Singh, who writes a syndicated column on current economic trends. Dave and Ranjit are busy and do not have time to learn how to use the Internet for the quick, reliable research that they need to create and support their writing.

Anne expects you to begin by doing most of the Web searching for Ranjit and Dave yourself; eventually, she wants you to train them to use the Web. You tell Anne that you are just learning to use the Web yourself, but she explains that this will be your full-time job during your internship and she is counting on you to become skilled in Web searching. Anne also reassures you by telling you that she has been working with the Web quite a bit herself and would be happy to help you with questions you might have as you find your way around the Web.

SESSION 4.1

In this session, you will learn about two types of search questions, how to create search expressions, and how to use Web search engines and directories. Also, you will use other Web resources to find answers to your questions or information related to topics in which you are interested.

Types of Search Questions

Anne is present at your first meeting with Dave and Ranjit. Dave asks about what kinds of Web information can help him do his job better. You reply that Dave's Internet connection provides him with information about every country in the world and on most major businesses and industries. No matter what type of story he is writing, you probably can find relevant facts that he can use. Dave mentions that his stories always can use more facts. Anne agrees and says that one of the most frequent editor comments on reporters' stories is to "get the facts."

Ranjit says that his columns do not rely as much on current events and facts—they are longer, more thought-provoking pieces about broad economic and business issues. Quick access to facts is not nearly as important to him as it is to a business news reporter like Dave. Ranjit hopes that the Web can provide him with new ideas that he could explore in his columns. So, instead of fast answers to specific questions, Ranjit explained that he wanted to use the Web as a resource for interesting concepts and ideas. He knows that the Web is a good way to find unusual and interesting views on the economy and general business practices. Ranjit is always looking for new angles on old ideas, so he is optimistic that you can find many useful Web resources for him.

Both writers were happy to have an eager assistant "working the Web" for them. Anne explained to you that each writer will need a different kind of help because of their different writing goals. Dave will need quick answers to specific questions. For example, he might need to know the population of Bolivia and perhaps some related information about demographic trends. Ranjit will need to find Web sites that contain, for example, collected research papers that discuss the causes of the Great Depression.

You can use the Web to obtain answers to both of these question types—specific and exploratory—but each question type requires a different search strategy. A **specific question** is a question that you can phrase easily and one for which you will recognize the answer when you find it. In other words, you will know when to end your search. The search process for a specific question is one of narrowing the field down to the answer you seek. An **exploratory question** is an open-ended question that can be harder to phrase; it also is difficult to determine when you find a good answer. The search process for an exploratory question requires you to fan out in a number of directions to find relevant information. You can use the Web to find answers to both kinds of questions, but each requires a different search strategy.

Specific questions require you to start with broad categories of information and gradually narrow the search until you find the answer to your question. Figure 4-1 shows this process of sequential, increasingly focused questions.

Figure 4-1 SPECIFIC RESEARCH QUESTION SEARCH PROCESS

Specific Question
What is the population of Bolivia?
World population statistics
↓
South America population statistics
↓
Population of Bolivia
↓
About 8 million

Increasing focus (left and right)

- Asia population statistics (blind alley)
- Population of Argentina (blind alley)
- Europe population statistics (blind alley)
- Population of Chile (blind alley)

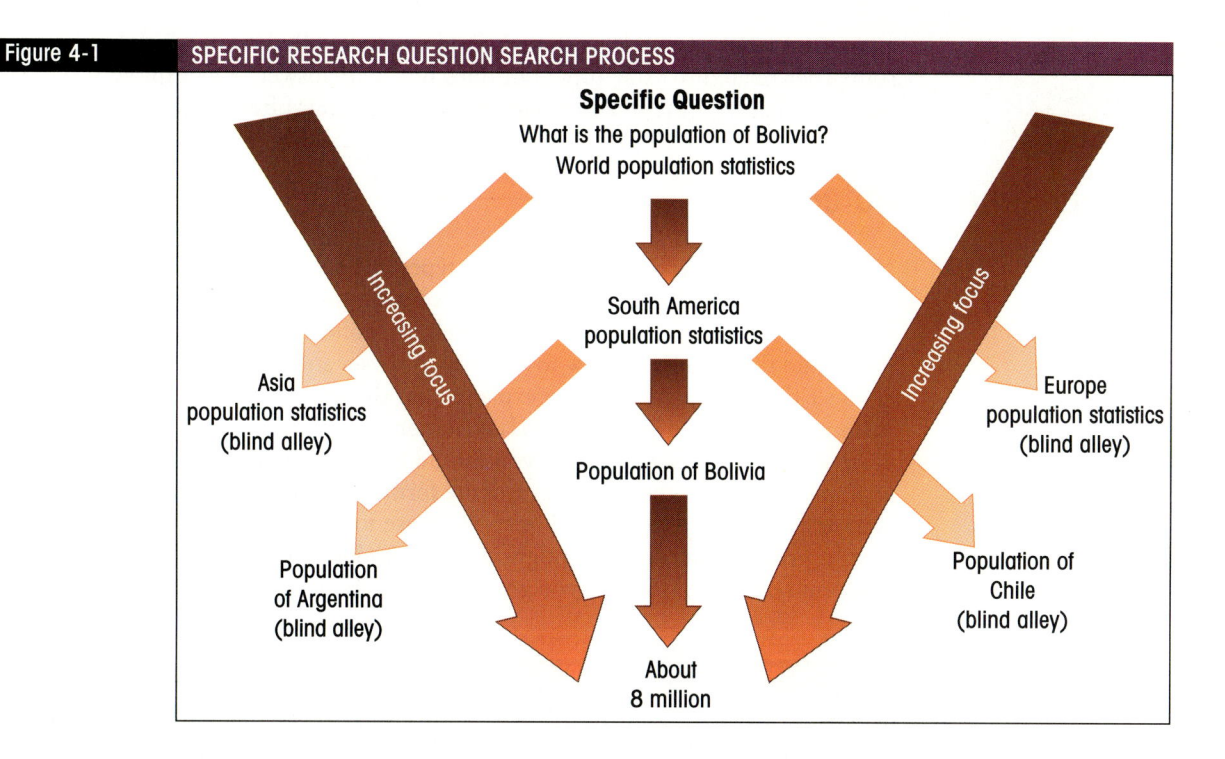

As you narrow your search, you might find that you are heading in the wrong direction, or down a blind alley. In that case, you need to move back up the funnel shown in Figure 4-1 and try another path.

Exploratory questions start with general questions that lead to other, less-general questions. The answers to the questions at each level should lead you to more information about the topic in which you are interested. This information then leads you to more questions. Figure 4-2 shows how this questioning process leads to a broadening scope as you gather information pertinent to the exploratory question.

Figure 4-2 EXPLORATORY RESEARCH QUESTION SEARCH PROCESS

Exploratory Question
What caused the Great Depression?
What events are associated with the Great Depression?
↓
1929 Stock Market crash   Deflation   Massive unemployment

What caused these events to occur?
↓
Business failures   Bank failures   Restrictive monetary policies

What conditions led to these causes?
↓
Reduced European-U.S. trade | Farmers' increased mortgage debt | Rapid economic growth of 1920s based on a few basic industries | Largely unregulated banking system | Banks invested heavily in stock market and European loans

Broadening scope (left and right)

- European war debts (tangential)
- World War I (tangential)
- Conservative political mood in U.S. during the 1920s (tangential)

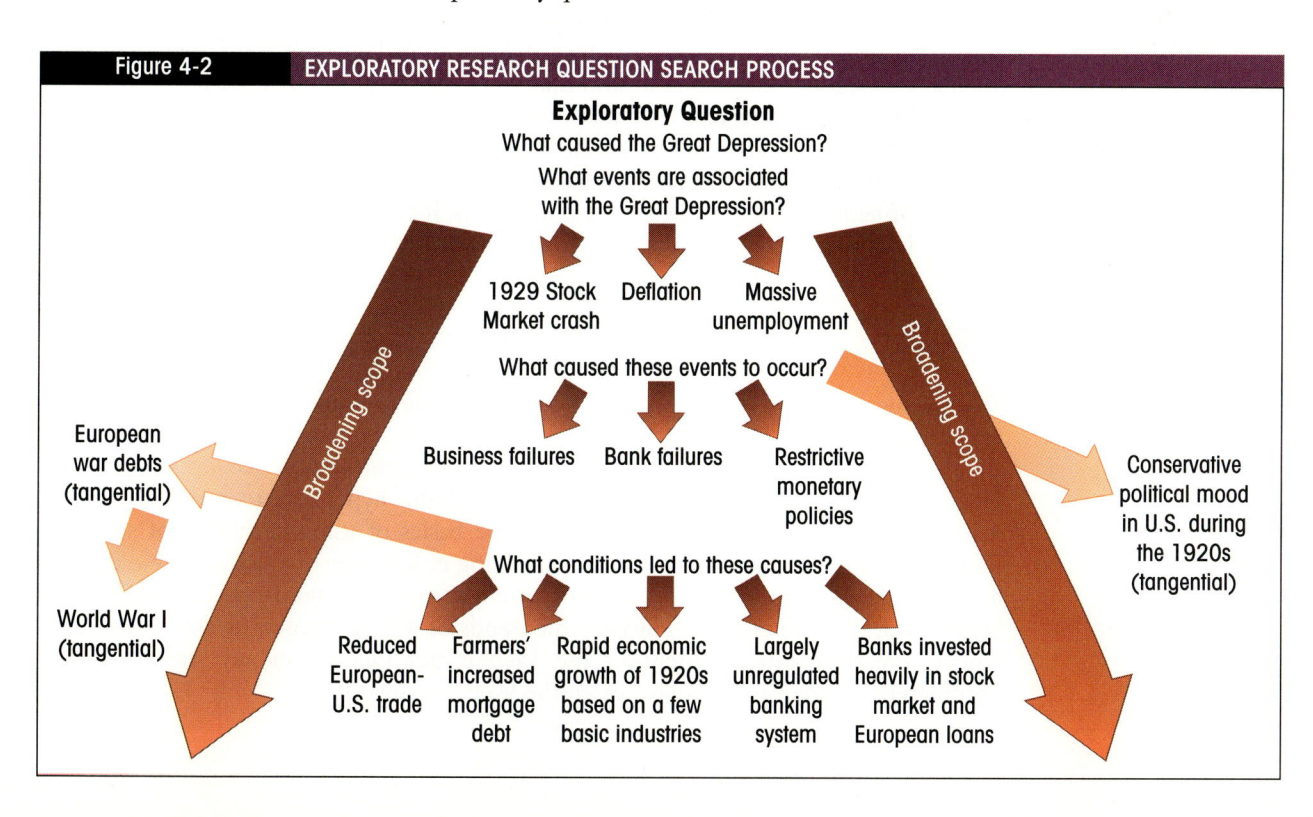

As your search expands, you might find yourself collecting tangential information that is somewhat related to your topic but does not help answer your exploratory question. The boundary between useful and tangential information is often difficult to identify precisely.

Web Search Strategy

Now that you understand the different types of questions that Ranjit and Dave will ask as you begin to work for them, Anne suggests that you learn something about searching the Web. You tell her that you know the Web is a collection of interconnected HTML documents and that you know how to use Web browser software to navigate the hyperlinks that connect these documents. Anne explains that the search tools available on the Web are an integral part of these linked HTML documents, or Web pages.

To search the Web effectively, you should first decide whether your question is specific or exploratory. Second, you should carefully formulate and state your question. The third step is to select the appropriate tool or tools to use in your search. After obtaining your results from a Web search tool, you might need to re-define or refine your question and select a different search tool to see if you get a different result. Figure 4-3 shows the search process.

Figure 4-3	WEB SEARCH PROCESS

1. Is the question specific or exploratory?
2. Formulate and state the question.
3. Select the appropriate Web search tool.
4. Evaluate the search results.
5. Repeat the previous steps until you find the answer.

You can repeat this process as many times as necessary until you obtain the specific answer or the range of information regarding your exploratory topic that you find satisfactory. Sometimes, you might find that the nature of your original question is different than you had originally thought. You also might find that you need to reformulate, or more clearly state, your question. As you restate your question, you should try to think of synonyms for each word. Unfortunately, many words in the English language have multiple meanings. If you use a word in your search that is common and has many meanings, you will be buried in irrelevant information or be led down many blind alleys. Identifying unique phrases that relate to your topic or question is a helpful way to avoid some of these problems.

Web Search Tools

To implement any Web search strategy, you will use one or more Web search tools. The four broad categories of Web search tools include search engines, directories, meta-search engines, and other Web resources. The Additional Information section of the Student Online Companion Web page for Tutorial 4 includes hyperlinks to many of these Web search tools. In this section, you will learn the basics of using each type of search tool. Remember that searching the Web is a challenging task for any of these tools. No one knows how many pages exist on the Web, but current estimates range from 100 to 600 million pages. Each of these pages might have thousands of words, images, or downloadable files. Unlike any library, the content of the Web is not indexed in any standardized way. Fortunately, the tools you have to search the Web are powerful.

Using Search Engines

A Web **search engine** is a special kind of Web page that finds other Web pages that match a word or phrase you enter into it. The word or phrase you enter, called a **search expression** or a **query**, might include instructions that tell the search engine how to search. A search engine does not examine every Web page to find a match; it only searches its *own* database of Web pages and Web page information. Therefore, if you enter the same search expression into different search engines, you will get different results. Most search engines report the number of hits they find. A **hit** is a Web page that is indexed in the search engine's database and contains text that matches your search expression. All search engines provide a series of **results pages**, which are Web pages that contain hyperlinks to the Web pages that contain text that matches your search expression.

Each search engine uses a Web robot to build its database. A **Web robot**, also called a **bot** or a **spider**, is a program that automatically searches the Web to find new Web sites and update information about old Web sites that already are in the database. One of a Web robot's more important tasks is to delete information in the database when a Web site no longer exists. The main advantage of using an automated searching tool is that it can examine far more Web sites than an army of people ever could.

Many search engines allow Web page creators to submit the URLs of their pages to search engine databases. Most search engine operators screen such Web page submissions to prevent a Web page creator from submitting a large number of duplicate or similar Web pages.

The business firms and other organizations that operate search engines often sell advertising space on the search engine Web page and on the results pages to sponsors. They use the advertising revenue to generate profit after covering the costs of maintaining the computer hardware and software required to search the Web and create and search the database. The only price you pay for access to these excellent tools is that you will see advertising banners on many of the pages; otherwise, your usage is free.

You just received an e-mail message from Dave with your first research assignment. He wants to mention the amount of average rainfall in Belize to make a point in a story that he is writing. First, you must determine what tasks to perform:

1. Decide that the question is specific: What is the average annual rainfall in Belize?

2. Next, identify key search terms in the question that you will use in your search expression: *Belize*, *rainfall*, and *annual*. You decide to use these terms because they should each appear on any Web page that includes the answer to Dave's question. None of these terms are articles, prepositions, or other common words. None of the words have multiple meanings. The term *Belize* should be especially useful in narrowing the search to relevant Web pages.

3. You will use a search engine to find the answer.

4. When you receive the results, you will examine them and decide whether a second search using a different tool, question, or search expression is necessary.

To find the average annual rainfall in Belize:

1. Start your Web browser, go to the **Student Online Companion** Web page (http://www.course.com/NewPerspectives/Internet), click the hyperlink for your book, click the **Tutorial 4** hyperlink, and then click the **Session 4.1** hyperlink.

2. Click the **AltaVista** link to open the AltaVista search engine page.

3. Type **Belize annual rainfall** in the AltaVista search text box, as shown in Figure 4-4.

Figure 4-4 — TYPING THE SEARCH EXPRESSION INTO THE ALTAVISTA SEARCH ENGINE

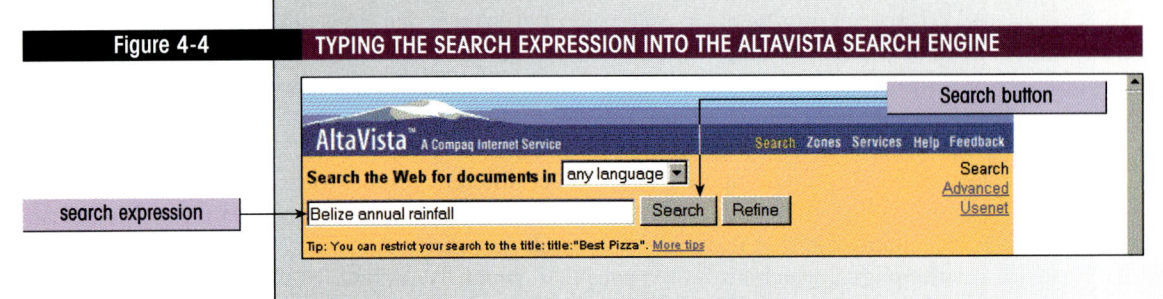

4. Click the AltaVista **Search** button (see Figure 4-4) to run the search. The search results appear on a new page—there are over 400,000 Web pages that match your search criteria!

5. Scroll down the results page and examine your search results. Click some of the links until you find a page that provides the average annual rainfall for Belize. Click the **Back** button on your Web browser to return to the results page after going to each hyperlink. You should find that Belize has several climate zones and that the annual rainfall ranges from 50 to 170 inches, or 130 to 430 centimeters.

Dave expected you to find one rainfall amount that would be representative for the entire country, which is not the case. Web searches often disclose information that helps you adjust the assumptions you made when you formulated the original research question. Remember that the Web changes constantly and information is updated continuously, so you might find different information. Dave wants you to check another source to confirm your results, so you decide to search for the same information in another search engine.

To conduct the same search using another search engine:

1. Use your browser's **Back** button to return to the Student Online Companion page, and then click the **HotBot** search engine link to open the HotBot search engine page.

2. Type **Belize annual rainfall** in the Search the Web text box, as shown in Figure 4-5.

Figure 4-5 — TYPING THE SEARCH EXPRESSION INTO THE HOTBOT SEARCH ENGINE

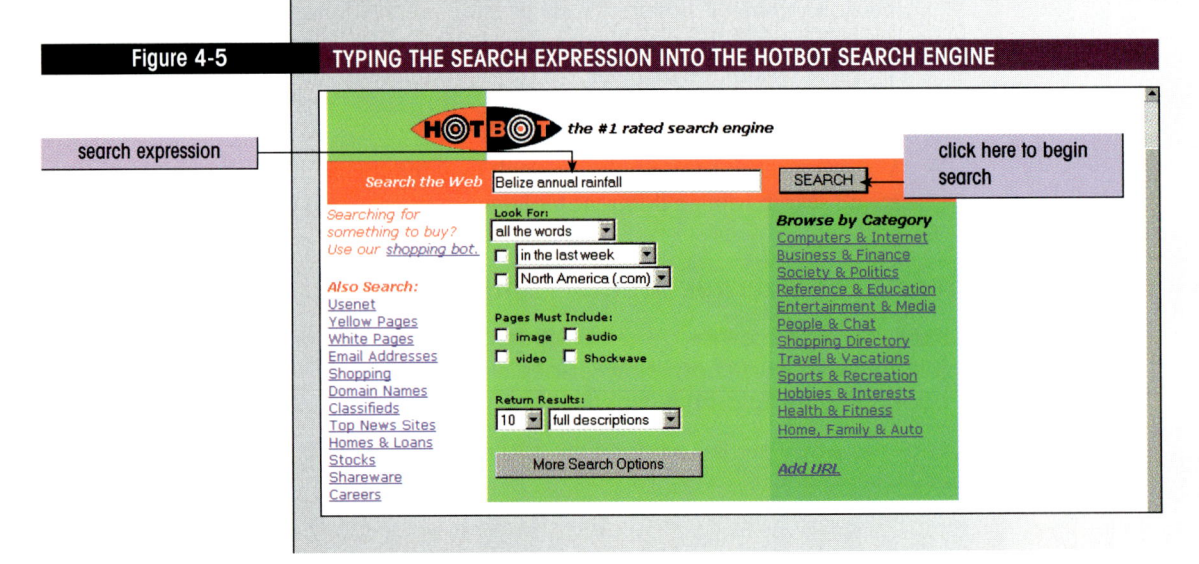

3. Click the HotBot **SEARCH** button to run the search. The search results appear on a new page, and this time, your search returns about 500 hits.

4. Scroll down the results page and examine your search results, and then click some of the links until you find a page that provides the average annual rainfall for Belize. Click the **Back** button on your Web browser to return to the results page after going to each hyperlink. Once again, you should find that Belize has several climate zones and that the annual rainfall ranges from 50 to 170 inches, or 130 to 430 centimeters.

HotBot returned a substantially different number of Web pages than the AltaVista search engine for two reasons: First, each search engine includes different Web pages in its database; second, the HotBot search engine, by default, only returns hits for pages that include *all* of the words you enter in a search expression. The AltaVista search engine's default is to return hits for pages that include *any* of the words. You found the same information after running both searches, so you can give Dave an answer with the second confirmation he requested.

As you can see, different search engine databases store different collections of information about the pages that exist on the Web at any given time. Many search engine robots do not search all of the Web pages at a particular site. Further, each search engine database indexes the information it has collected from the Web differently. Some search engine robots only collect information from a Web page's title, description, keywords, or HTML tags; others only read a certain amount of the HTML code in each Web page. Figure 4-6 shows the HTML code from a Web page that contains information about electronic commerce.

Figure 4-6	META TAGS FOR A WEB PAGE

```
<HEAD>

<TITLE>
Current Developments in Electronic Commerce
</TITLE>

<META NAME ="description" CONTENT="Current
news and reports about electronic commerce
developments.">

<META NAME ="keywords" CONTENT ="electronic
commerce, electronic data interchange,
value added reseller, EDI, VAR, secure
socket layer, business on the internet">

</HEAD>
```

The description and keywords tags are examples of HTML META tags. A **META tag** is HTML code that a Web page creator places in the page header for the specific purpose of informing Web robots about the content of the page. META tags do not cause any text to appear on the page when a Web browser loads it; rather, they exist solely for the use of search engine robots.

The information contained in META tags can become a key part of a search engine's database. For example, the keywords META tag shown in Figure 4-6 includes the phrase "electronic data interchange." These keywords could be a very important phrase in a search engine's database because the three individual words *electronic*, *data*, and *interchange*, are common terms that often are used in search expressions that have nothing to do with electronic commerce. The word *data* is so common that many search engines might be programmed to ignore it. A search engine that includes the full phrase "electronic data interchange" in its database will greatly increase the chances that a user interested in that topic will find this particular page.

If the terms you use in your search expression are not in the part of the Web page that a search engine stores in its database, the search engine will not return a hit for that page. Some search engines store the entire content of every Web page they place in their databases. This practice is called **full text indexing**. All search engines, even those that are full text indexed search engines, omit common words such as *and*, *the*, *it*, and *by* from their databases. Many search engine operators include information about their search engines, robots, and databases on their Web sites. You will learn more about several of the major search engines in Session 4.2.

Using Directories and Hybrid Search Engine Directories

Search engines provide a powerful tool for executing keyword searches of the Web. However, because most search engine URL databases are built by computers running programs that perform the search automatically, they can miss important classification details that you would notice instantly. For example, if a search engine's robot found a Web page with the title "Test Data: Do Not Use," it would probably include content from the page in the search engine database. If you were to read such a warning in a Web page title, *you* would know not to include the page's contents. However, keep in mind that with 100 to 600 million Web pages on the Web, the volume of data that a search engine robot obtains as it travels the Web precludes screening by people.

Web directories use a completely different approach from search engines to build useful indexes of information on the Web. A **Web directory** is a listing of hyperlinks to Web pages that is organized into hierarchical categories. The difference between a search engine and a Web directory is that *people* select the Web pages to include in a Web directory. These people, who are knowledgeable experts in one or more subject areas and skilled in various classification techniques, review candidate Web pages for inclusion in the directory. When the experts decide that a Web page is worth listing in the directory, they determine the appropriate category in which to store the hyperlink to that page. Many directories allow a Web page to be indexed in several different categories. The main weakness of a directory is that you must know which category is likely to yield the information you desire. If you begin searching in the wrong category, you might follow many hyperlinks before you realize that the information you seek is not in that category. Some directories overcome this limitation by including hyperlinks in category levels that link to lower levels in other categories.

One of the oldest and most respected directories on the Web is **Yahoo!**. Two Stanford doctoral students, David Filo and Jerry Yang, who wanted a way to keep track of interesting sites they found on the Internet, started Yahoo! in 1994. Since 1994, Yahoo! has grown to become one of the most widely used resources on the Web. Yahoo! currently lists over 500,000 Web pages in its categories—a sizable number, but only a small portion of the hundreds of millions of pages on the Web. Although Yahoo! does use some automated programs for checking and classifying its entries, it relies on human experts to do most of the selection and classification work. You can open the Yahoo! directory by clicking the Yahoo! link on the Session 4.1 Student Online Companion page. The Yahoo! home page appears in Figure 4-7.

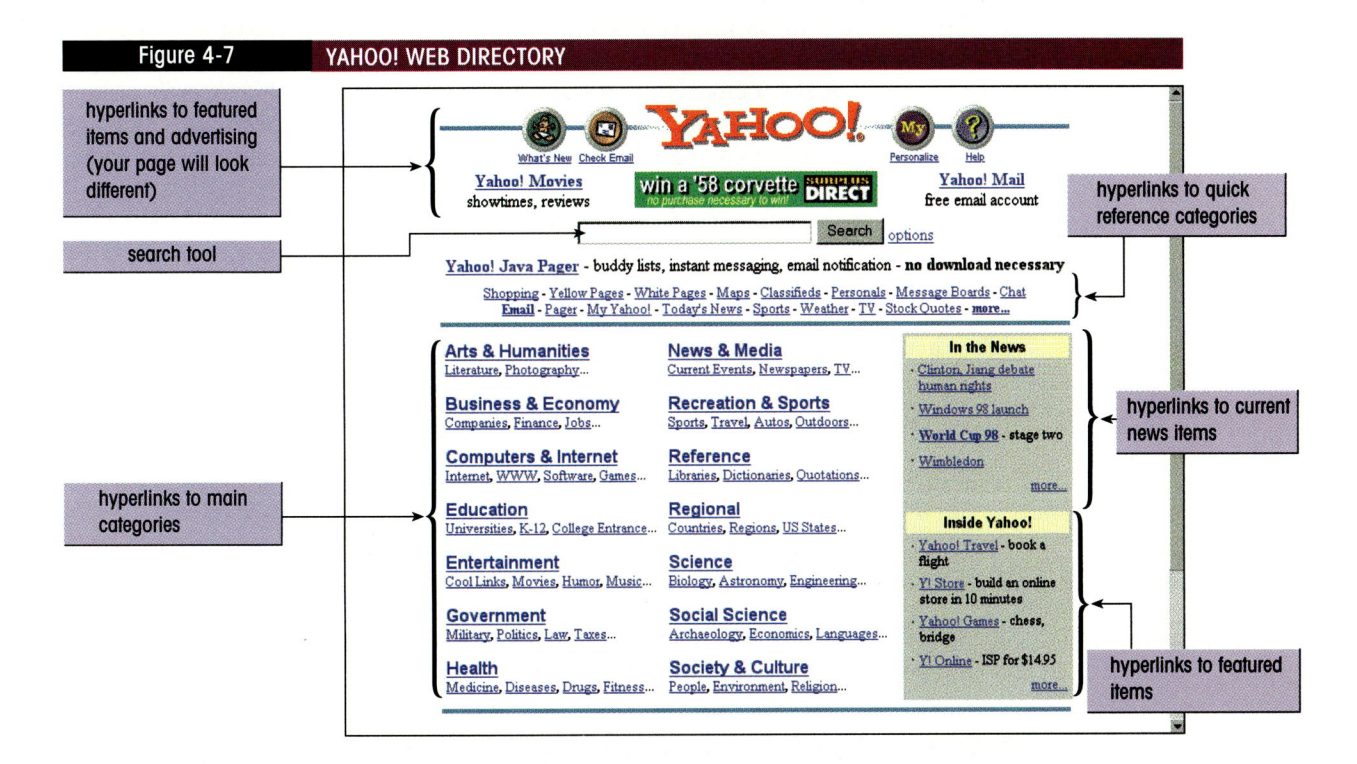

Figure 4-7 YAHOO! WEB DIRECTORY

- hyperlinks to featured items and advertising (your page will look different)
- search tool
- hyperlinks to main categories
- hyperlinks to quick reference categories
- hyperlinks to current news items
- hyperlinks to featured items

The top section of the Yahoo! page includes featured items and advertising. The featured items change regularly and usually highlight timely topics that the Yahoo! editors believe will interest many of the site's visitors.

The search tool that appears below the advertising banner is a search engine within the Yahoo! directory. You can enter search terms into this tool, and Yahoo! will search its listings to find a match. Although many directories allow you to search within the directory using a search engine, the Yahoo! search function automatically sends your search query to the AltaVista search engine if it does not find matching entries in its hierarchical category database. Then, the AltaVista search engine examines its database to find any matches for your search expression. This combination of search engine and directory, called a **hybrid search engine directory**, can provide a powerful and effective tool for searching the Web. Using a hybrid search engine directory can help you identify which category in the directory is likely to contain the information you need. After you enter a category, the search engine is useful for narrowing a search even further; you can enter a search expression and limit the search to that category.

The next section of the Yahoo! page includes quick reference categories, which are commonly used categories that might otherwise be hard to find because they would be buried several layers under a main category heading. Also, users might find it difficult to guess which main categories might include these items. For example, "weather" might be classified under the main category headings "News and Media" or "Science." The quick reference section makes often sought information categories easier to find.

The main categories section of the Yahoo! page is the primary tool for searching the directory's listings. Under each of the 14 main categories, Yahoo! lists several subcategories. These are not the only subcategories; they are just a sample of those that are the largest or most used. You can click a main category hyperlink to see all of the subcategories under that category. The hyperlinks marked "[Xtra!]" lead to collections of recent stories from the Reuters news wire service that pertain to the main category topic under which they appear.

The bottom of the Yahoo! main page, which is not visible in Figure 4-7, includes a collection of hyperlinks to other parts of the directory that contain specialized categories of hyperlinks, such as the Yahoo! Seniors' Guide. The bottom section also has hyperlinks to Yahoo! directories for other countries and large U.S. cities.

Just as you are becoming familiar with the layout of the Yahoo! directory, Dave calls you. He is up against a deadline and needs some information from Intel Corporation's financial statements for a story he is writing. Not all firms publish financial statements on the Internet, but Dave wants you to see what you can find. You tell Dave that you will call him back as quickly as possible. Following your guidelines for searching on the Web, you:

1. Decide that the question is specific: Where can I find the Intel Corporation's Web site?

2. Identify a key search term—Intel—in the question that you will use in your search expression.

3. Use a Web directory to find the answer, so you can search in the business directory, instead of searching the entire Web.

4. Examine the results and decide whether a second search using a different category, question, or search expression is necessary.

To find Intel Corporation's financial statements on the Web:

1. Use your browser's **Back** button to return to the Student Online Companion page, and then click the **Yahoo!** link to open the Yahoo! page.

   You consider the main categories on the Yahoo! page and determine that you could probably find your information in either the Business and Economy category or the Computers and Internet category because you know that Intel manufactures computer chips. You decide to look in the Business and Economy category first. You make a note that if this search does not work, you will try the Computers and Internet category next.

2. Click the **Business & Economy** category hyperlink, which opens the page shown in Figure 4-8. The page shown in Figure 4-8 includes hyperlinks to lower levels in the hierarchy and to other points in the hierarchies of other categories. The hyperlinks to lower-level numbers in parentheses that indicate the number of Web pages included in each category. The hyperlinks that include the "@" symbol are links to other points in the hierarchies of other categories. New categories and categories that include new Web pages are indicated by a "new!" icon.

3. Click the **Companies** subcategory hyperlink (see Figure 4-8) to open the Companies page.

TUTORIAL 4 SEARCHING THE WEB WEB 4.11 INTERNET

Figure 4-8 YAHOO! BUSINESS AND ECONOMY CATEGORIES PAGE

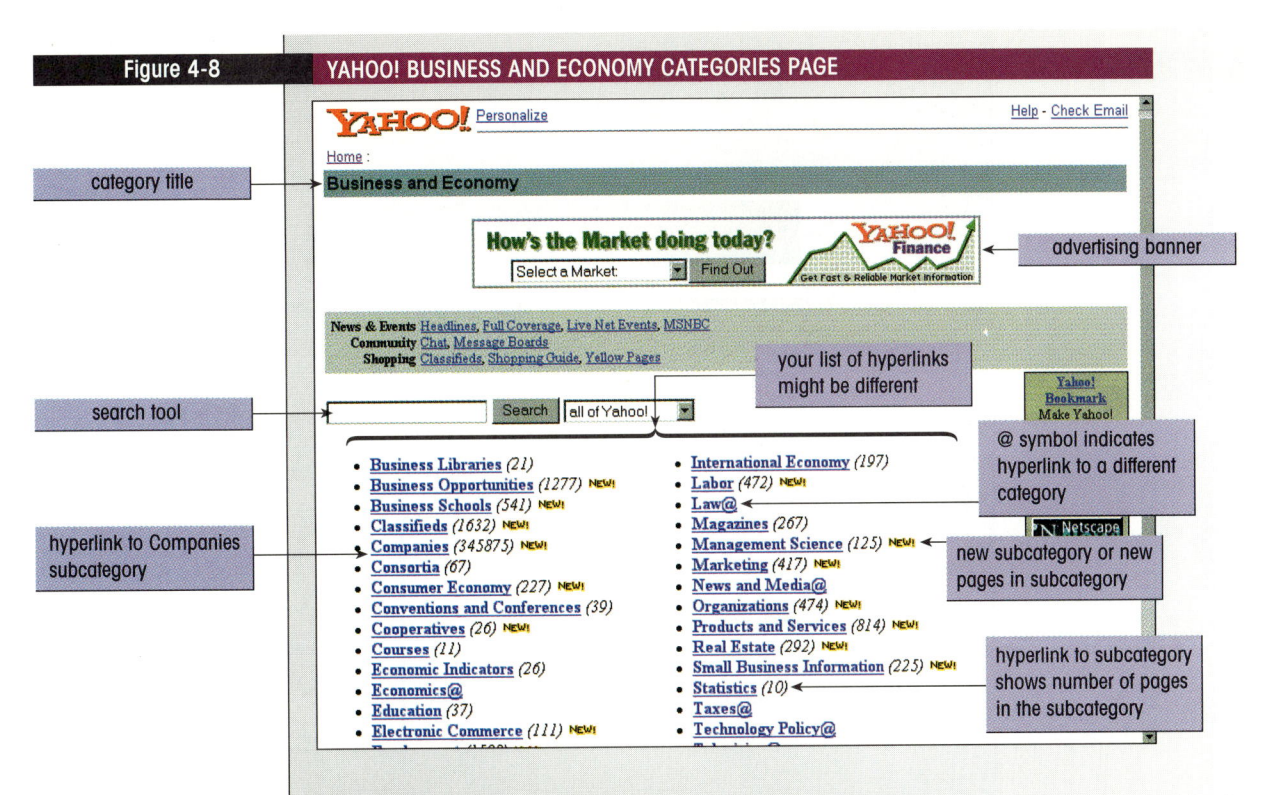

- category title → Business and Economy
- advertising banner
- search tool
- your list of hyperlinks might be different
- hyperlink to Companies subcategory → Companies
- @ symbol indicates hyperlink to a different category
- new subcategory or new pages in subcategory
- hyperlink to subcategory shows number of pages in the subcategory

4. Type **Intel** in the search text box, and then click the down arrow in the next text box to select **just this category**, as shown in Figure 4-9.

Figure 4-9 CHOOSING TO SEARCH WITHIN THE COMPANIES SUBCATEGORY

- page header shows category and subcategory hierarchy → Companies
- advertising banner
- search expression → Intel
- limit search to the Companies subcategory

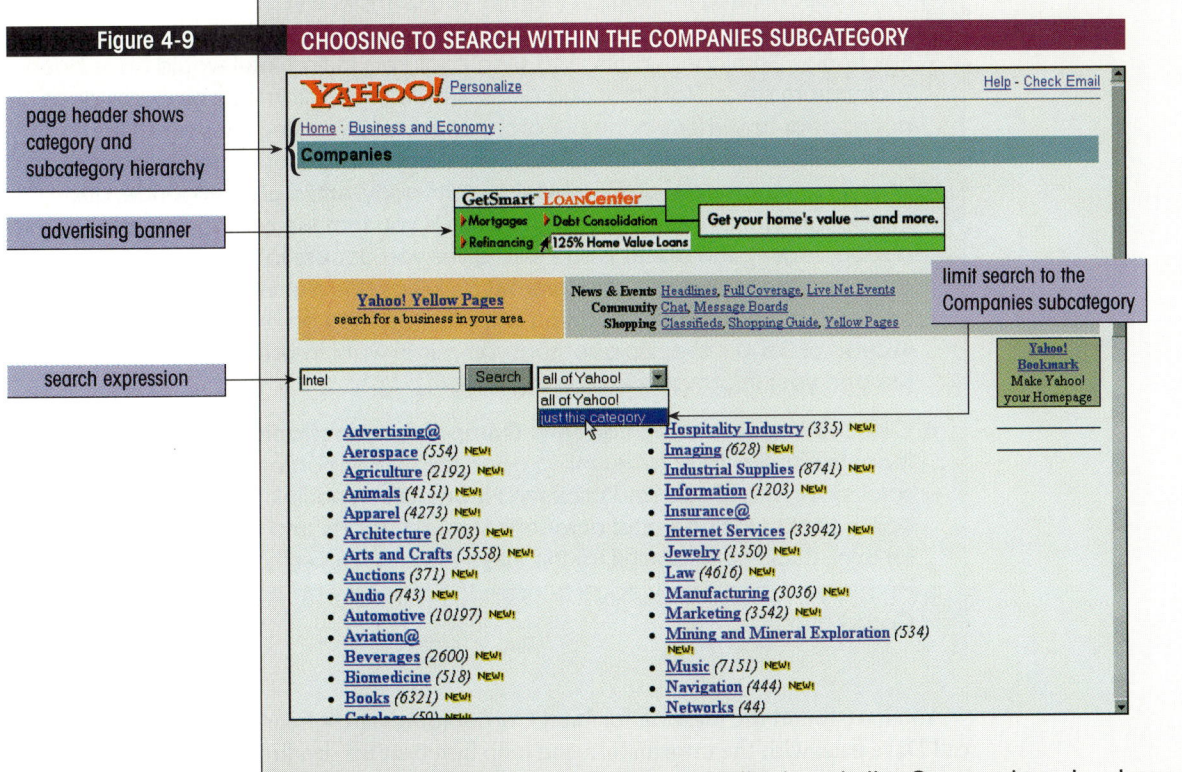

5. Click the **Search** button to search for the term in the Companies subcategory. The results page shown in Figure 4-10 opens and lists the hits.

INTERNET   WEB 4.12   TUTORIAL 4   SEARCHING THE WEB

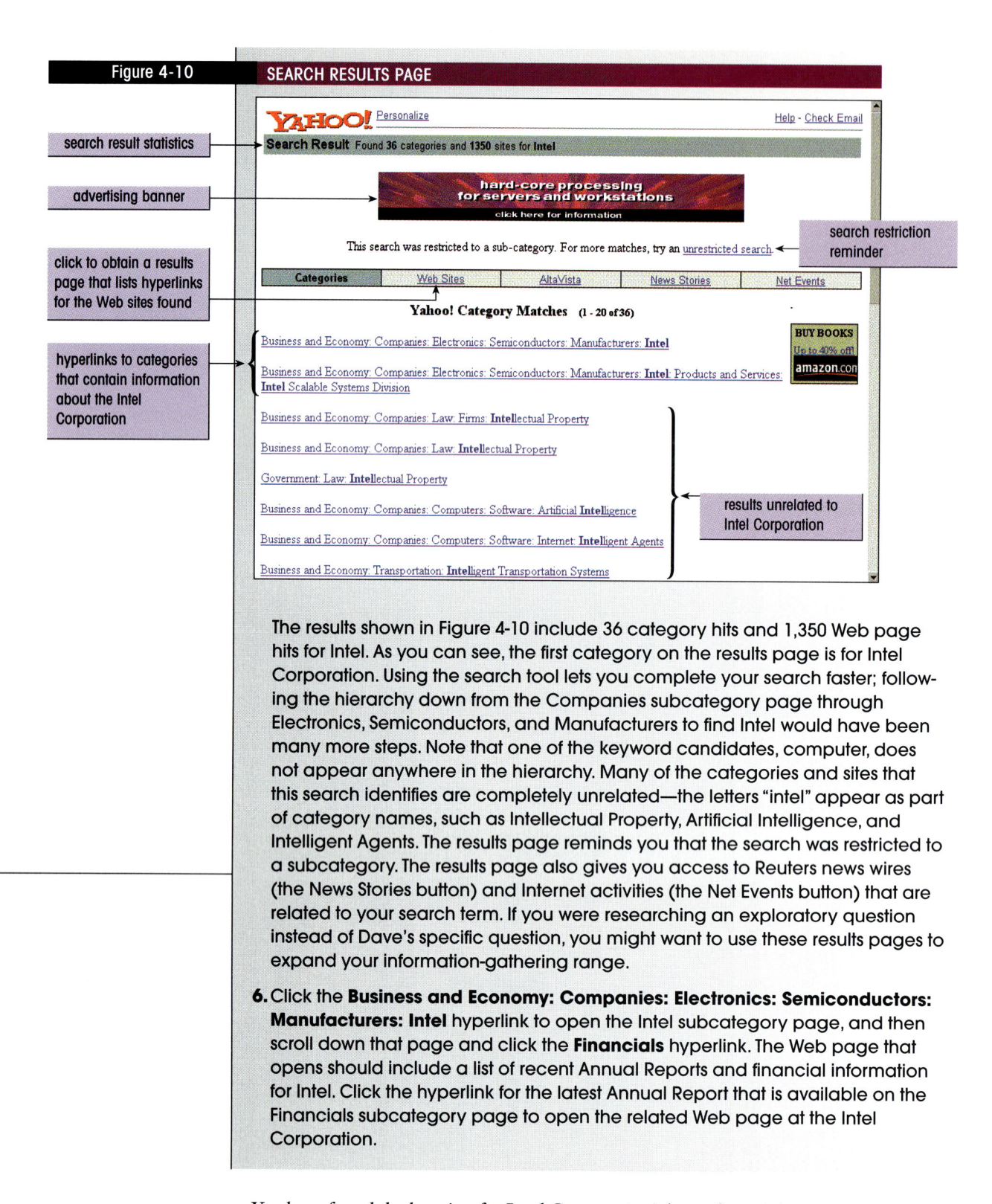

Figure 4-10   SEARCH RESULTS PAGE

- search result statistics
- advertising banner
- click to obtain a results page that lists hyperlinks for the Web sites found
- hyperlinks to categories that contain information about the Intel Corporation
- search restriction reminder
- results unrelated to Intel Corporation

YAHOO! Personalize   Help - Check Email

Search Result Found 36 categories and 1350 sites for Intel

[hard-core processing for servers and workstations — click here for information]

This search was restricted to a sub-category. For more matches, try an unrestricted search.

Categories | Web Sites | AltaVista | News Stories | Net Events

Yahoo! Category Matches   (1 - 20 of 36)

BUY BOOKS
Up to 40% off
amazon.com

Business and Economy: Companies: Electronics: Semiconductors: Manufacturers: Intel

Business and Economy: Companies: Electronics: Semiconductors: Manufacturers: Intel: Products and Services: Intel Scalable Systems Division

Business and Economy: Companies: Law: Firms: Intellectual Property

Business and Economy: Companies: Law: Intellectual Property

Government: Law: Intellectual Property

Business and Economy: Companies: Computers: Software: Artificial Intelligence

Business and Economy: Companies: Computers: Software: Internet: Intelligent Agents

Business and Economy: Transportation: Intelligent Transportation Systems

The results shown in Figure 4-10 include 36 category hits and 1,350 Web page hits for Intel. As you can see, the first category on the results page is for Intel Corporation. Using the search tool lets you complete your search faster; following the hierarchy down from the Companies subcategory page through Electronics, Semiconductors, and Manufacturers to find Intel would have been many more steps. Note that one of the keyword candidates, computer, does not appear anywhere in the hierarchy. Many of the categories and sites that this search identifies are completely unrelated—the letters "intel" appear as part of category names, such as Intellectual Property, Artificial Intelligence, and Intelligent Agents. The results page reminds you that the search was restricted to a subcategory. The results page also gives you access to Reuters news wires (the News Stories button) and Internet activities (the Net Events button) that are related to your search term. If you were researching an exploratory question instead of Dave's specific question, you might want to use these results pages to expand your information-gathering range.

6. Click the **Business and Economy: Companies: Electronics: Semiconductors: Manufacturers: Intel** hyperlink to open the Intel subcategory page, and then scroll down that page and click the **Financials** hyperlink. The Web page that opens should include a list of recent Annual Reports and financial information for Intel. Click the hyperlink for the latest Annual Report that is available on the Financials subcategory page to open the related Web page at the Intel Corporation.

You have found the location for Intel Corporation's latest financial statements, so you can call Dave back with the information and help him beat his deadline. Now that you have seen how to use a search engine and a hybrid search engine directory, you are ready to use an even more powerful combination of Web research tools: the meta-search engine.

Using Meta-Search Engines

A **meta-search engine** is a tool that combines the power of multiple search engines. Some meta-search tools also include directories. The idea behind meta-search tools is simple. Each search engine on the Web has different strengths and weaknesses because each search engine:

- Uses a different Web robot to gather information about Web pages.
- Stores a different amount of Web page text in its database.
- Selects different Web pages to index.
- Has different storage resources.
- Interprets search expressions somewhat differently.

You saw how these differences cause different search engines to return vastly different results for the same search expression. To perform a complete search for a particular question, you might need to use several individual search engines. Using a meta-search engine lets you search several engines at the same time, so you don't have to conduct the same search many times. A meta-search engine accepts your search expression and transmits it to several search engines, such as the AltaVista and HotBot search tools you used earlier in this session. These search engines run the search expression against their databases of Web page information and return results to the meta-search engine. The meta-search engine reports consolidated results from all of the search engines it queried. Meta-search engines use the same kinds of programs to run their queries, but they do not have their own databases of Web information.

You want to learn how to use meta-search engines so you can access information faster. So, you decide to test a meta-search engine using Dave's Belize rainfall question. **Dogpile** is one of the more comprehensive meta-search engines available; it forwards your queries to a number of major search engines and directories, including AltaVista, Excite, GoTo.com, InfoSeek, Lycos, Magellan, WebCrawler, Yahoo!, and several others. The list of search engines and directories might be different when you use this tool because newer and better search tools become available and old favorites disappear over time. Dogpile allows you to set the amount of time, from 10 to 60 seconds, to wait for its queries to return results. Longer waiting times generally yield more results. Dogpile reports results from each search engine or directory separately and does not eliminate duplicate hits. The list of hyperlinks returned by each search engine remains in the order that the search engine reports them to Dogpile.

REFERENCE WINDOW

Using the Dogpile meta-search engine
- Formulate your search question.
- Open the Dogpile home page in your Web browser.
- Enter the search terms into the Dogpile search text box.
- Set the wait time.
- Evaluate the results and decide whether to revise the question or your choice of search tools.

To use the Dogpile meta-search engine:

1. Click the **Back** button on your Web browser until you return to the Student Online Companion page for Session 4.1, and then click the **Dogpile** link to open the Dogpile meta-search engine page.

2. Type **Belize annual rainfall** in the Dogpile search text box, click the **Wait a maximum of** list arrow, and then click **Thirty** to change the wait time to 30 seconds. See Figure 4-11.

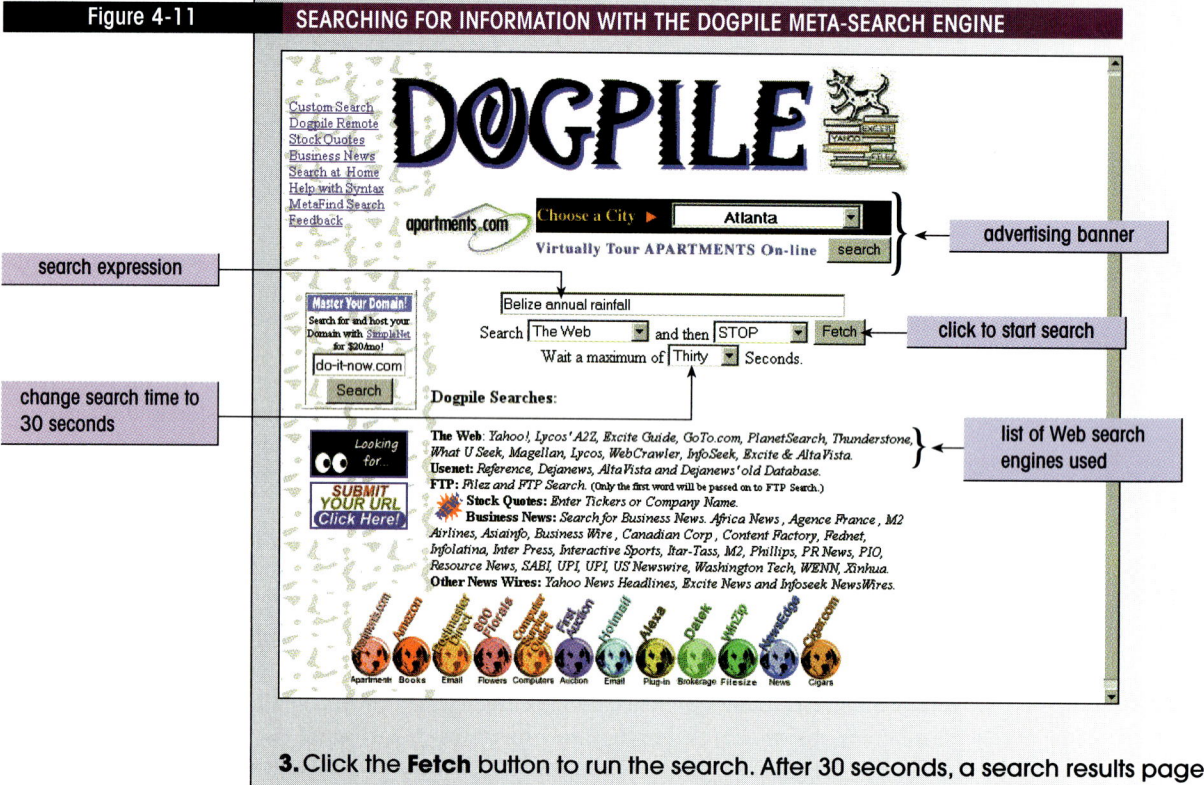

Figure 4-11 SEARCHING FOR INFORMATION WITH THE DOGPILE META-SEARCH ENGINE

3. Click the **Fetch** button to run the search. After 30 seconds, a search results page opens and shows the hits for each search engine.

4. Examine your search results.

As you scroll through the search results pages, you can see that there is a wide variation in the number and quality of the results provided by each search engine and directory. You might see many hits, but no hyperlinks. You also might notice a number of duplicate hits; however, most of the Web pages returned by one search tool are not returned by any other. You can click the Next Set of Search Engines button at the bottom of the results page to see the hits returned by other search engines.

You might notice that the search results that Dogpile reports from the AltaVista search engine are dramatically lower than what you obtained when using AltaVista for the same search earlier. When you entered the search expression "Belize annual rainfall" into AltaVista directly, you are indicating that you want to find Web pages that include *any* of these three words. When you enter the same expression into Dogpile, it interprets your expression the same way HotBot did—that you want to find Web pages that include *all* of these three words—and sends the query in that form to AltaVista. You will learn more about how you can refine search expressions in Session 4.2.

Using Other Web Resources

A variety of other resources are available for searching the Web that do not fit exactly into the three preceding categories. These search resources are similar to bibliographies, but instead of listing books or journal articles, they contain lists of hyperlinks to Web pages. Just as some bibliographies are annotated, many of these resources include summaries or reviews of Web pages.

These other resources can be very useful when you want to obtain a broad overview or a basic understanding of a complex subject area. A search for such resources that uses a search engine or directory is likely to turn up a narrow list of references that are too detailed and that assume a great deal of prior knowledge. For example, using a search engine or directory to find information about quantum physics will probably give you many references to technical papers and Web pages devoted to current research issues in quantum physics. However, your search probably will yield very few Web pages that provide an introduction to the topic. A Web bibliography page can offer hyperlinks to information regarding a particular subject that is presented at various levels. Many of these resources include annotations and reviews of the sites they list. This information can help you identify Web pages that fit your level of interest.

Some of the names used to identify these Web bibliographies include **resource lists**, **guides**, **clearinghouses**, and **virtual libraries**. Many of these bibliographies are general references, such as the Librarian's Index to the Internet the Free Internet Encyclopedia, the Scout Report Signpost, and the Argus Clearinghouse. Others are more focused, such as the Martindale Reference Desk, which emphasizes science-related links. You can visit any of these Web sites by clicking their links on the Tutorial 4 page of the Student Online Companion. The hyperlinks for these resources appear in the Additional Information section of the page under the Other Search Tools and Resources heading.

Ranjit stops by your office and asks for your help. He is planning to write a series of columns on the business and economic effects of current trends in biotechnology. The potential effects of genetic engineering research particularly intrigue him, but he admits that he does not know much about any of these topics. Ranjit wants you to find some Web sites that he could explore to learn more about biotechnology trends in general and genetic engineering research in particular. He mentions that it would be nice, but not essential, to find some recent news summaries about biotechnology and business. You decide to use the Argus Clearinghouse site as a resource to work on the exploratory question that Ranjit has given you. The **Argus Clearinghouse** reviews and provides hyperlinks to subject guides. You determine that Ranjit's request is an exploratory search. You know that biotechnology is a branch of the biological sciences, so you identify three category terms: *biotechnology*, *genetic engineering*, and *biology* to use as your search categories.

REFERENCE WINDOW

Using the Argus Clearinghouse Web site
- Identify categories and search terms that might lead you to the desired information resources.
- Open the Argus home page in your Web browser.
- Explore the Argus categories that are related to the categories and search terms you identified.
- Follow the category hyperlinks to subcategories and Web pages.
- Evaluate the results and decide whether to revise your categories or choice of Web resources.

To use Argus to conduct an exploratory search:

1. Return to the Student Online Companion page for Session 4.1, and then click the **Argus Clearinghouse** link to open that page.

2. As you scan the main categories on the Argus Clearinghouse home page, you do not see any of your search categories listed; however, you know that biology is a science, so click the **Science & Mathematics** hyperlink.

3. Click the **biology** link that appears on the Science & Mathematics subcategory page. You see two of your search terms in the keywords list on the biology page and decide to follow both of them.

4. Click the **biotechnology** keyword hyperlink to open the Web page shown in Figure 4-12.

INTERNET   WEB 4.16   TUTORIAL 4 SEARCHING THE WEB

Figure 4-12   **BIOTECHNOLOGY SUBCATEGORY IN ARGUS CLEARINGHOUSE**

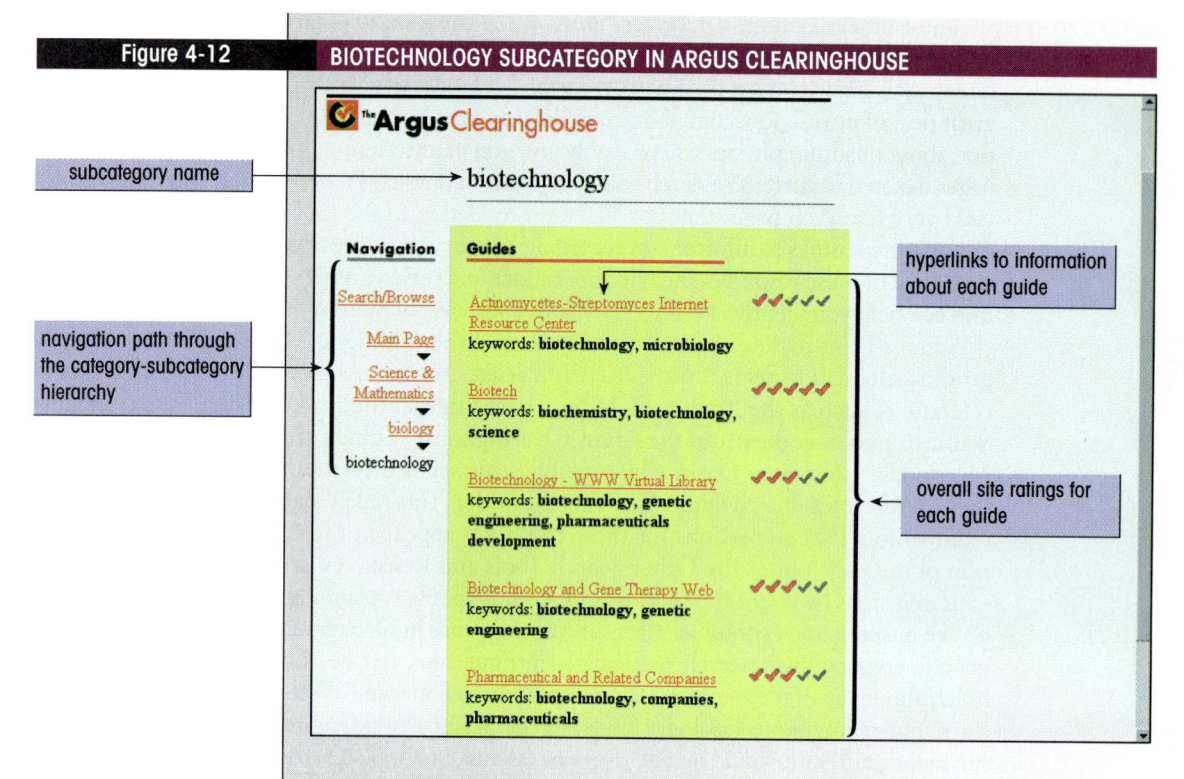

The Argus Clearinghouse

→ biotechnology

Navigation — subcategory name

Guides

Search/Browse

Main Page

Science & Mathematics

biology

biotechnology

Actinomycetes-Streptomyces Internet Resource Center
keywords: **biotechnology, microbiology** ✓✓✓✓

Biotech
keywords: **biochemistry, biotechnology, science** ✓✓✓✓✓

Biotechnology - WWW Virtual Library
keywords: **biotechnology, genetic engineering, pharmaceuticals development** ✓✓✓✓

Biotechnology and Gene Therapy Web
keywords: **biotechnology, genetic engineering** ✓✓✓✓

Pharmaceutical and Related Companies
keywords: **biotechnology, companies, pharmaceuticals** ✓✓✓✓

— navigation path through the category-subcategory hierarchy

— hyperlinks to information about each guide

— overall site ratings for each guide

The Biotech hyperlink is the most highly rated site, as indicated by its five dark check marks, so you decide to open the page.

5. Click the **Biotech** hyperlink to open the Guide Information page for that site shown in Figure 4-13. The Guide Information page includes a hyperlink to the Web site, indexing keywords, information about the author of the site, and detailed ratings on several dimensions. You can follow this site to gather specific information for Ranjit or give him the site's URL and let him explore the site. You might want to gather the URLs of this and other sites that you find and send them all to Ranjit in one e-mail message. You have explored the biotechnology subcategory; next, you will explore the genetic engineering subcategory.

Figure 4-13   **INFORMATION ABOUT THE BIOTECH GUIDE WEB SITE**

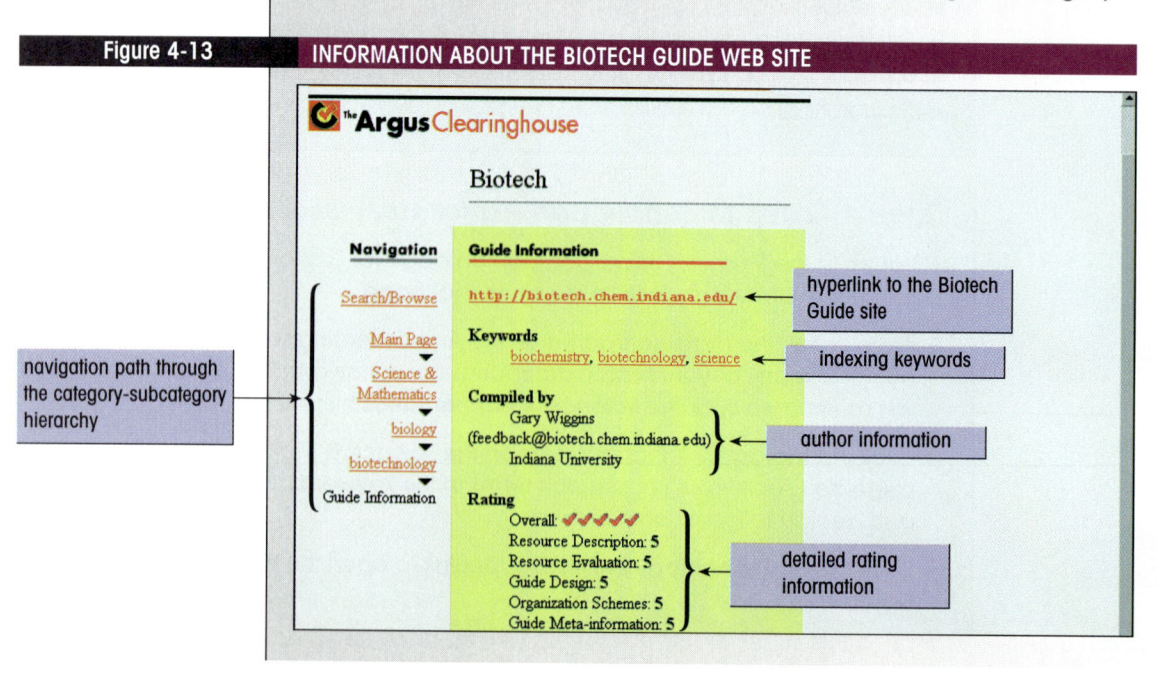

The Argus Clearinghouse

Biotech

Navigation

Search/Browse

Main Page

Science & Mathematics

biology

biotechnology

Guide Information

Guide Information

http://biotech.chem.indiana.edu/ ← hyperlink to the Biotech Guide site

Keywords
biochemistry, biotechnology, science ← indexing keywords

Compiled by
Gary Wiggins
(feedback@biotech.chem.indiana.edu) ← author information
Indiana University

Rating
Overall: ✓✓✓✓✓
Resource Description: 5
Resource Evaluation: 5
Guide Design: 5
Organization Schemes: 5
Guide Meta-information: 5

— navigation path through the category-subcategory hierarchy

— detailed rating information

6. Click the **biology** hyperlink that appears in the Navigation path on the left side of the Web page to return to the list of biology keywords.

7. Click the **genetic engineering** hyperlink to open the Argus list of Guides to that topic. The genetic engineering Guide lists three entries. One of these entries is the WWW Virtual Library Biotechnology page that also appeared on the biotechnology Guide page shown in Figure 4-13.

8. Click the **Biotechnology and Gene Therapy Web** hyperlink to explore the resources at that site. Remember that Ranjit does not expect you to understand the contents of the Web pages you find; he just wants you to identify resources to help him learn more about trends in this area of scientific research.

9. Examine your search results and determine whether you have gathered sufficient useful information to respond to Ranjit's request.

10. Close your browser, and log off the Internet, if necessary.

You have completed your search for Web sites that might help Ranjit. Many of these sites contain hyperlinks to other useful sites that Ranjit might want to explore. You can deliver information from these pages to Ranjit by printing copies of the Web pages, sending the URLs by e-mail, or saving the Web pages and attaching them to an e-mail message. Because your answer to Ranjit's question involves so many pages at different sites, your best approach would be to send an e-mail message with a list of relevant URLs.

Quick Check

1. What are the key characteristics of an exploratory search question?
2. What steps do you take to use the Web to find the answer to a specific type question?
3. What is a Web robot, and how does it work?
4. True or False: Web search engine operators use advertising revenue to cover their expenses and earn a profit.
5. True or False: Search engines consider all words in their database; words such as *and* or *the* are included in their databases.
6. What is one advantage and one disadvantage of using a Web directory instead of a Web search engine to locate information?
7. How does a hybrid search engine-directory overcome the disadvantages of using either a search engine or a directory alone?
8. How does a meta-search engine process the search expression you enter into it?
9. What are the key features offered by Web bibliographies?

In this session, you learned how to identify the two basic types of search questions and formulate a search process for each type. You also used Web search engines, directories, meta-search engines, and other information-finding resources on the Web to find information. In the next session, you will use these Web search tools to conduct more complex searches so you can filter out irrelevant hits and narrow your search more quickly.

SESSION 4.2

Although you can find the answers to many research questions on the Web with a simple search using one of the tools described in Session 4.1, some questions are more complex. In this session, you will learn how to use the advanced features of Web search engines, directories, and other Web resources to answer complex questions. Many of these Web search tools use Boolean logic and other filtering mechanisms to select and sort search results; however, many of these search tools implement these mechanisms differently. After learning the basics of Boolean logic and filtering techniques, you will use those techniques in a variety of Web search tools.

Boolean Logic and Filtering Techniques

The most important factor in getting good results from a search engine, a meta-search engine, or a search tool within a hybrid search engine-directory is to select the search terms you use carefully. When the object of your search is straightforward, you can choose one or two words that will work well. More complex search questions require more complex queries, which you can use along with Boolean logic, search expression operators, or filtering techniques, to broaden or narrow your search expression. In the next three sections, you will learn how to use each of these techniques.

Boolean Operators

When you enter a single word into a Web search tool, it searches for matches to that word. When you enter a search expression into a Web search tool that includes more than one word, the search tool makes assumptions about the words that you enter. You learned in Session 4.1 that the AltaVista search engine assumes that you want to match any of the keywords in your search expression, and HotBot assumes that you want to match all of the keywords. These different assumptions can make dramatic differences in the number and quality of hits returned. Many search engine operators, realizing that users might want to match all of the keywords on one search and any of the keywords on a different search, have designed their search engines to offer these options. The most common way of implementing these options is to offer Boolean operators as part of their search engines.

George Boole was a Nineteenth Century British mathematician who developed a branch of mathematics and logic that bears his name, **Boolean algebra**. In Boole's algebra, all values are reduced to one of two values. In most practical applications of Boole's work, these two values are *true* and *false*. Although Boole did his work many years before practical electrically powered computers became commonplace, his algebra was useful to computer engineers and programmers. At the very lowest level of analysis, all computing is a manipulation of a single computer circuit's on and off states.

Some parts of Boolean algebra are also useful in search expressions. **Boolean operators**, also called **logical operators**, are a key part of Boolean algebra. **Boolean operators** specify the logical relationship between the elements they join, just as the mathematical plus sign arithmetic operator specifies the mathematical relationship between the two elements it joins. Three basic Boolean operators—AND, OR, and NOT—are recognized by most search engines. You can use these operators in many search engines by simply including them with search terms. For example, the search expression "exports AND France" returns hits for pages that contain both words, the expression "exports OR France" returns hits for pages that contain either word, and "exports NOT France" returns hits for pages that contain the word *export* but not the word *France*. Some search engines use "AND NOT" to indicate the Boolean NOT operator.

Figure 4-14 shows several ways to use Boolean operators in more complex search expressions that contain the words *exports*, *France*, and *Japan*. The figure shows the matches that a search engine will return if it interprets the Boolean operators correctly. Figure 4-14 also describes information-gathering tasks in which you might use these expressions.

Figure 4-14	USING BOOLEAN OPERATORS IN SEARCH EXPRESSIONS	
SEARCH EXPRESSION	SEARCH RETURNS PAGES THAT INCLUDE	USE TO FIND INFORMATION ABOUT
exports AND France AND Japan	All of the three search terms.	Exports from France to Japan or from Japan to France.
exports OR France OR Japan	Any of the three search terms.	Exports from anywhere, including France and Japan, and all kinds of information about France and Japan.
exports NOT France NOT Japan	Exports, but not if the page also includes the terms *France* or *Japan*.	Exports to and from any countries other than France or Japan.
exports AND France NOT Japan	Exports and France, but not Japan.	Exports to and from France to anywhere else, except exports shipped to Japan.

Other Search Expression Operators

When you join three or more search terms with Boolean operators, it is easy to become confused by the expression's complexity. To reduce the confusion, you can use precedence operators, a tool you probably learned in basic algebra, along with the Boolean operators. A **precedence operator**, also called an **inclusion operator** or a **grouping operator**, clarifies the grouping within a complex expression and is usually indicated by the parentheses symbols. Some search engines use double quotation marks to indicate precedence grouping; however, other search engines use double quotation marks to indicate search terms that must be matched exactly as they appear (that is, search for the exact search phrase) within the double quotation marks. Figure 4-15 shows several ways to use precedence operators with Boolean operators in search expressions.

Figure 4-15	USING BOOLEAN AND PRECEDENCE OPERATORS IN SEARCH EXPRESSIONS	
SEARCH EXPRESSION	SEARCH RETURNS PAGES THAT INCLUDE	USE TO FIND INFORMATION ABOUT
exports AND (France OR Japan)	Exports and either France or Japan.	Exports from or to either France or Japan.
exports OR (France AND Japan)	Exports or both France or Japan.	Exports from anywhere, including France and Japan, and all kinds of other information about France and Japan.
exports AND (France NOT Japan)	Exports and France, but not if the page also includes Japan.	Exports to and from France, except those going to or from Japan.

Some search engines recognize variants of the Boolean operators, such as "must include" and "must exclude" operators. For example, a search engine that uses the plus sign to indicate "must include" and the minus sign to indicate "must exclude" would respond to the expression "exports + France - Japan" with hits that included anything about exports and France, but only if those pages did not include anything about Japan.

Another useful search expression tool is the location operator. A **location operator**, or **proximity operator**, lets you search for terms that appear close to each other in the text of a Web page. The most common location operator offered in Web search engines is the NEAR operator. If you are interested in French exports, you might want to find only Web pages in which the terms *exports* and *France* are close to each other. Unfortunately, each search engine that implements this operator uses its own definition of how close "NEAR" is. One search engine might define NEAR to mean "within 10 words," whereas another search engine might define NEAR to mean "within 20 words." To use the NEAR operator effectively, you must read the search engine's help file carefully.

Wildcard Characters and Search Filters

Most search engines support some use of a wildcard character in their search expressions. A **wildcard character** allows you to omit part of the search term or terms. Many search engines recognize the asterisk (*) as the wildcard character. For example, the search expression "export*" would return pages containing the terms *exports*, *exporter*, *exporters*, and *exporting* in many search engines.

Many search engines allow you to restrict your search by using search filters. A **search filter** eliminates Web pages from a search. The filter criteria can include such Web page attributes as language, date, domain, host, or page component (URL, hyperlink, image tag, or title tag). For example, many search engines provide a way to search for the term *exports* in Web page titles and ignore pages in which the term appears in other parts of the page.

Advanced Searches

Most search engines implement many of the operators and techniques you have learned about, but search engine syntax varies. Some search engines provide separate advanced search pages for these techniques; others allow you to use advanced techniques such as Boolean operators on their simple search pages. Next, you will learn how to conduct complex searches using the advanced search features of several different search engines.

Advanced Search in AltaVista

Ranjit is working on a series of columns about the role that trade agreements play in limiting the flow of agricultural commodities between countries. This week's column concerns the German economy. He wants you to find some Web page references for him that might provide useful background information for his column. Ranjit is especially interested in learning more about the German perspective on trade issues, but he cannot read German.

You recognize this as an exploratory question and decide to use the advanced query capabilities of the AltaVista search engine to conduct a complex search for Web pages that Ranjit might use for his research. You want to provide Ranjit with a reasonable number of hyperlinks to Web pages, but you do not want to inundate him with thousands of URLs, so you decide to use Boolean and precedence operators to create a search expression that will focus on useful sites. To create a useful search expression, you must identify search terms that might lead you to appropriate Web pages. Some terms you might use are *Germany*, *trade*, *treaty*, and *agriculture*. You decide to use Boolean and precedence operators to combine your search terms. You also decide to use the wildcard character to allow the search to find plural and extended forms of the terms *treaty* (such as *treaties*) and *agriculture* (such as *agricultures*, *agricultural*, and *agriculturally*). Ranjit's primary interest is in trade issues, so you decide to rank the hits returned by *trade*.

TUTORIAL 4 SEARCHING THE WEB   WEB 4.21

REFERENCE WINDOW

Conducting a complex search using AltaVista
- Open the AltaVista search engine in your Web browser.
- Select the Advanced Search option.
- Choose a language filter.
- Devise and enter a suitable search expression.
- Click the Search button.
- Evaluate the results and revise your search expression as necessary.

To perform an advanced search using AltaVista:

1. If necessary, start your Web browser, go to the **Student Online Companion** (http://www.course.com/NewPerspectives/Internet), click the link for your book, click the **Tutorial 4** link, and then click the **Session 4.2** link.

2. Click the **AltaVista** link to open that page.

3. Click the **Advanced** hyperlink on the AltaVista page. Ranjit only reads English, so you need to filter the language.

4. Click the list arrow that says "any language," and then click **English**.

5. Click in the Boolean expression text box, and then type **Germany AND (trade OR treat*) AND agricult***.

6. Click the **Search** button to start the search. The search settings and results appear in Figure 4-16.

   The search returns over 30,000 hits, so you need to refine your search expression. You examine some of the descriptions provided for the first search results listed and find that many of them include information about fertilizer treatments. You decide that narrowing the search to exclude those sites would make the search results more useful to Ranjit.

Figure 4-16 COMPLEX SEARCH USING ALTAVISTA

Callouts on figure:
- language filter set to English
- search field for Boolean expressions
- number of Web pages found
- search results list
- hyperlink to AltaVista Help pages
- Advanced search indicator
- advertising banner

Boolean expression shown: Germany AND (trade OR treat*) AND agricult*

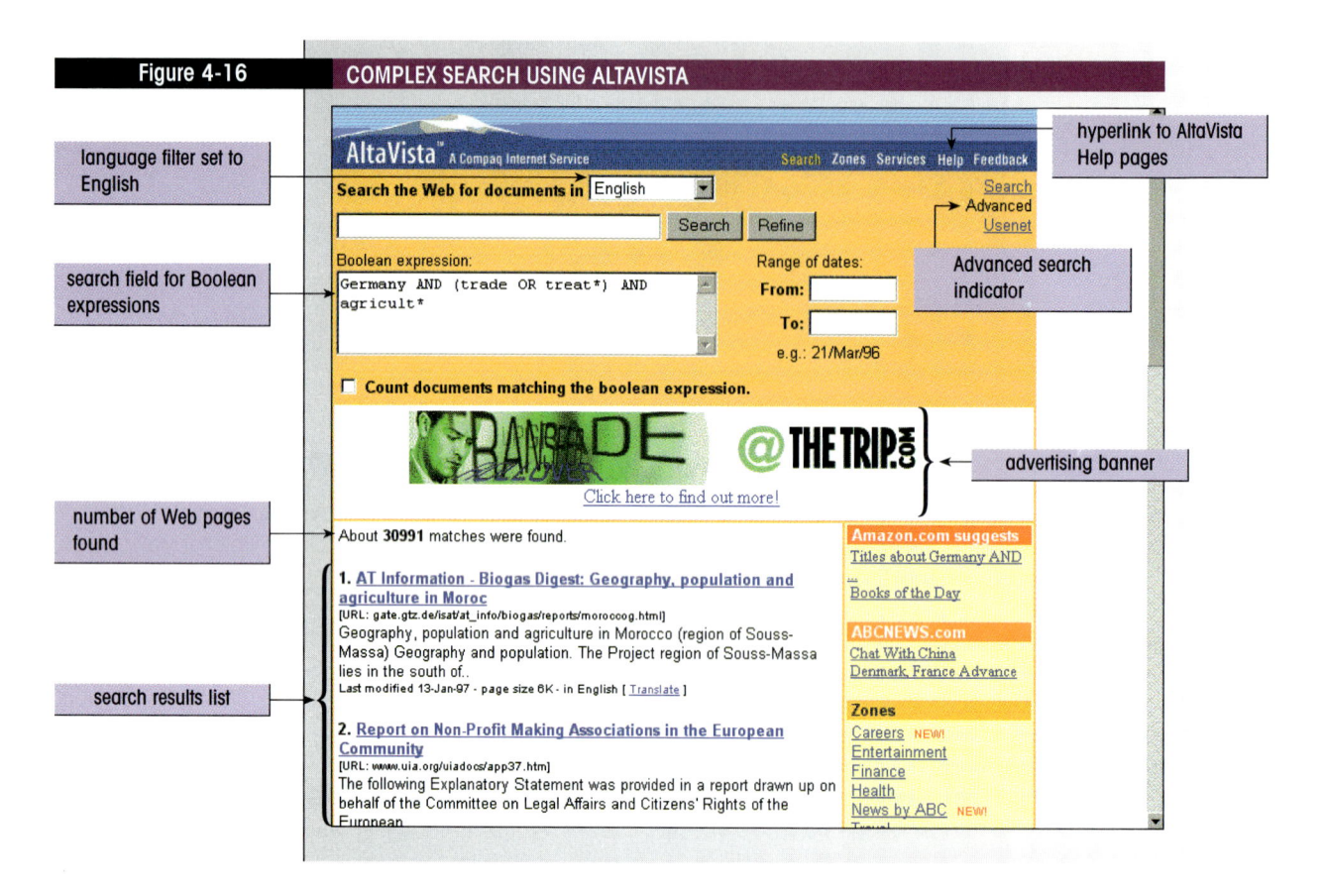

About 30991 matches were found.

1. AT Information - Biogas Digest: Geography, population and agriculture in Moroc
   [URL: gate.gtz.de/isat/at_info/biogas/reports/morocoog.html]
   Geography, population and agriculture in Morocco (region of Souss-Massa) Geography and population. The Project region of Souss-Massa lies in the south of..
   Last modified 13-Jan-97 - page size 6K - in English [Translate]

2. Report on Non-Profit Making Associations in the European Community
   [URL: www.uia.org/uiadocs/app37.htm]
   The following Explanatory Statement was provided in a report drawn up on behalf of the Committee on Legal Affairs and Citizens' Rights of the European

Getting Help and Refining an Advanced Search in AltaVista

Each search engine follows different rules and offers different features. To obtain help for a particular search engine, examine its home page and look for a hyperlink to help pages for that search engine. The AltaVista Advanced Search page includes a hyperlink titled "Help." You decide to exclude the word *treatment* from your Boolean search expression and, to obtain a narrower search that focuses better on the German viewpoint, you decide to restrict the domain to German Web sites.

To obtain help and refine an advanced search in AltaVista:

1. Scroll to the bottom of the results page, and then click the **Help** hyperlink on the AltaVista Advanced Search page to open that page.

2. Scroll down the Web page and look for the section that describes how to specify keywords in searches. You will find that, in AltaVista, the domain filter is "domain:" followed by the name of the domain to which you want to limit your search. Ranjit tells you that the domain name for Germany is "de."

3. Click your browser's **Back** button to return to the Advanced Search page.

4. Change your Boolean search expression (at the top of the page) to **Germany AND (trade OR treat*) AND agricult* AND NOT treatment AND domain:de**, and then click the **Search** button. AltaVista returns a much smaller number of hits this time. If you wanted to revise the search further, you could click the **Refine** button and try again.

TUTORIAL 4 SEARCHING THE WEB   WEB 4.23   INTERNET

5. Examine your search results and determine whether you have gathered sufficient useful information to respond to Ranjit's request. There are many sites to explore. You could give Ranjit this list or define the search expression further to reduce the number of hits.

Advanced Search in HotBot

Dave stops by your office to tell you he is working on a story for tomorrow's edition about the effect of unusual weather patterns and recent rainstorms on Southeast Asian rice crops during the past six months. You decide to use the HotBot search engine to run a complex query for Dave. Although HotBot offers a SuperSearch page with a wide array of search options (to use SuperSearch, click the More Search Options button on the HotBot main page), you can perform Boolean and filtered searches from HotBot's main search page.

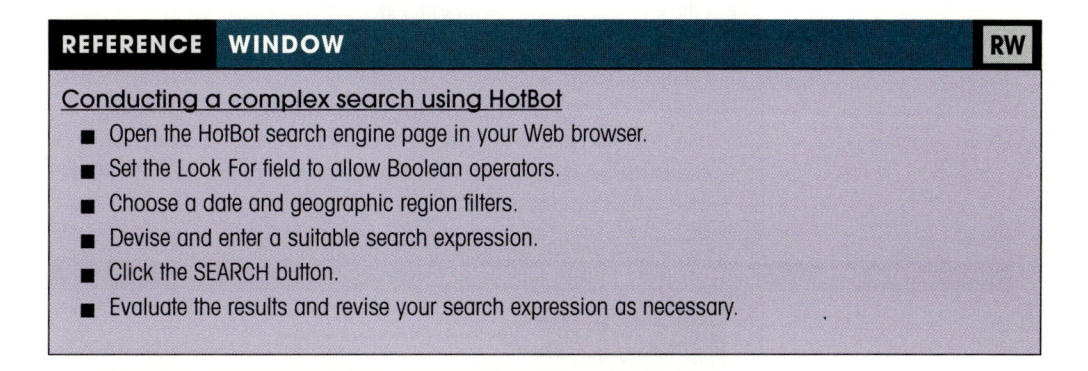

REFERENCE WINDOW

Conducting a complex search using HotBot
- Open the HotBot search engine page in your Web browser.
- Set the Look For field to allow Boolean operators.
- Choose a date and geographic region filters.
- Devise and enter a suitable search expression.
- Click the SEARCH button.
- Evaluate the results and revise your search expression as necessary.

To perform a complex search using HotBot:

1. Use your browser's **Back** button to return to the Student Online Companion page for Session 4.2, and then click the **HotBot** link to open that page. See Figure 4-17.

Figure 4-17   ADVANCED SEARCH FEATURES OF THE HOTBOT MAIN SEARCH ENGINE PAGE

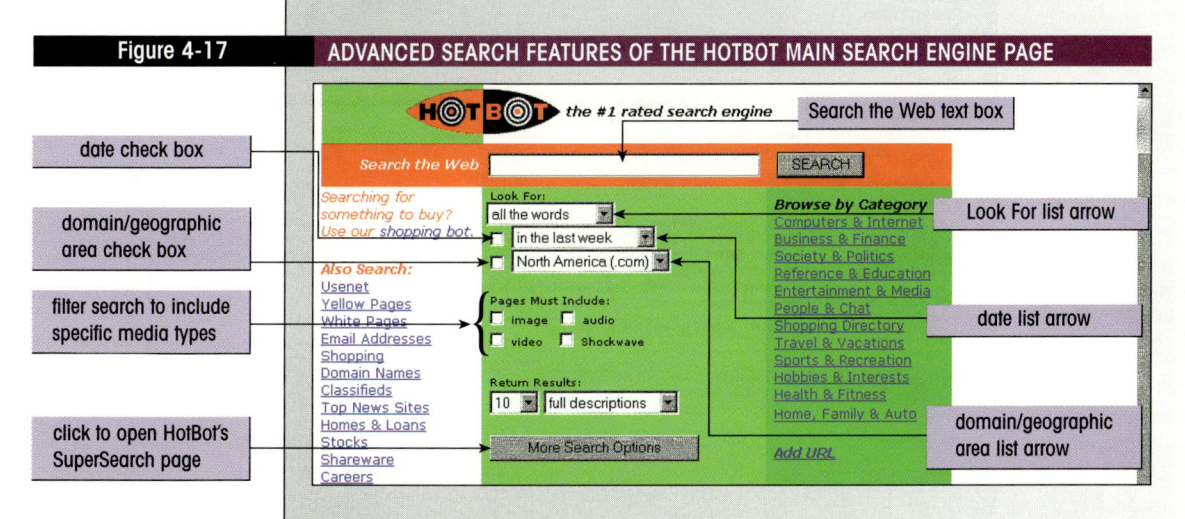

- date check box
- domain/geographic area check box
- filter search to include specific media types
- click to open HotBot's SuperSearch page
- Search the Web text box
- Look For list arrow
- date list arrow
- domain/geographic area list arrow

2. Click the **Look For** list arrow on the HotBot page (see Figure 4-17), and then click **Boolean phrase**.

3. Click the date **check box** (see Figure 4-17), click the date field **list arrow**, and then click **in the last 6 months**.

4. Click the domain/geographic area **check box** (see Figure 4-17), click the **list arrow**, and then click **Southeast Asia**.

To create a useful search expression, you must identify search terms that might lead you to appropriate Web pages. Some terms you might use are *rice*, *weather*, and *production*. Dave told you that Southeast Asia has a rainy season, so the term *season* might appear instead of *weather* on Web pages that contain information that Dave could use. You decide to use Boolean and precedence operators to combine your search terms. HotBot does not recognize wildcard characters, but it does allow you to set precedence operators.

5. Click in the Search the Web text box (see Figure 4-17), and then type **rice AND (weather OR season) AND production**.

6. Click the **SEARCH** button to start the search. Figure 4-18 shows the search results page, where you can see part of the search expression, the filter settings, information about the search, and a partial list of hyperlinks to related Web pages. Note that the description for each hit includes a rating (in percent) of how well the terms in the Web page match the search description you entered. The description also includes the size of each page's HTML document and the date it was last updated.

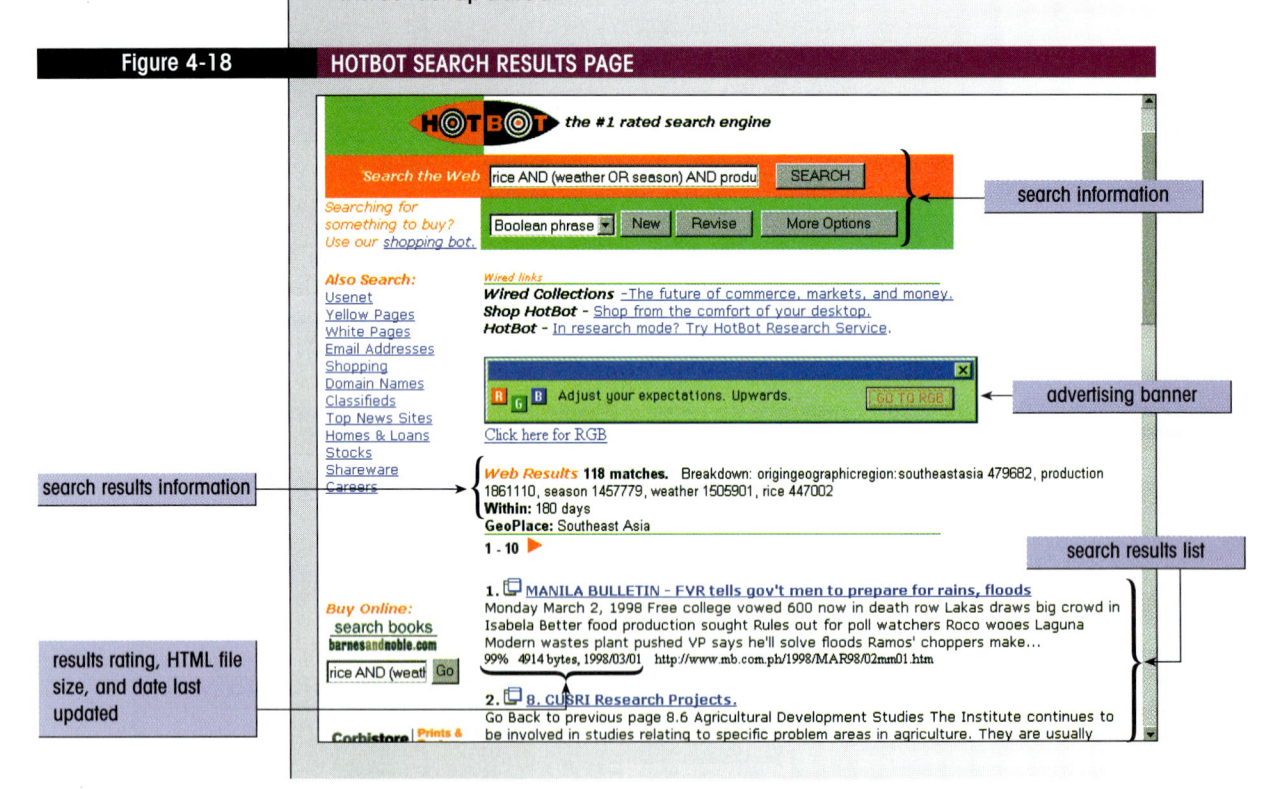

Figure 4-18 HOTBOT SEARCH RESULTS PAGE

7. Examine your search results and determine whether you have gathered sufficient useful information to respond to Dave's request. Since the search returned a small number of links that contained information relevant to Dave's query, you can conclude your work by forwarding the URLs to Dave.

Complex Search in Excite

Dave calls and has a quick request for your research help. He is working on a story about Finland and remembers that he met a professor who taught graduate business students there. He does not remember the professor's name or the name of the university at which the professor teaches. Dave is confident that he would recognize the university's name if he saw it again. He would like to interview the professor for his story. Dave asks if you can find some Finnish university names on the Web. After evaluating Dave's request, you decide to use the Excite search engine for this task. To create a useful search expression, you must identify search terms that might lead you to appropriate Web pages. Some terms you might use include *Finland*, *university*, and *business*. You consider that a university with a graduate business program might have an academic unit, "school," so you add that to your search expression as an alternative to "university." Hopeful that someone might have placed a list of universities on the Web, you decide to include *list* as a search term, too. The Excite search engine permits Boolean operators in its main page, so you decide to use that page for your query.

REFERENCE WINDOW

Conducting a complex search using Excite
- Open the Excite search engine page in your Web browser.
- Devise and enter a suitable search expression.
- Click the Search button.
- Evaluate the results and revise your search expression as necessary.

To perform an advanced search using Excite:

1. Use your browser's **Back** button to return to the Student Online Companion page for Session 4.2, and then click the **Excite** link to open that page.

2. Click in the Search text box at the top of the page, and then type **Finland AND list AND (university OR school) AND business**.

3. Click the **Search** button to start the search. Figure 4-19 shows the results page after scrolling it down to the first hit. Note that Excite provides a rating for each hyperlink that it returns. It also provides a hyperlink to a page that automatically performs a search using terms that Excite extracts from the Web page shown in the hyperlink reference.

Figure 4-19   **EXCITE SEARCH RESULTS**

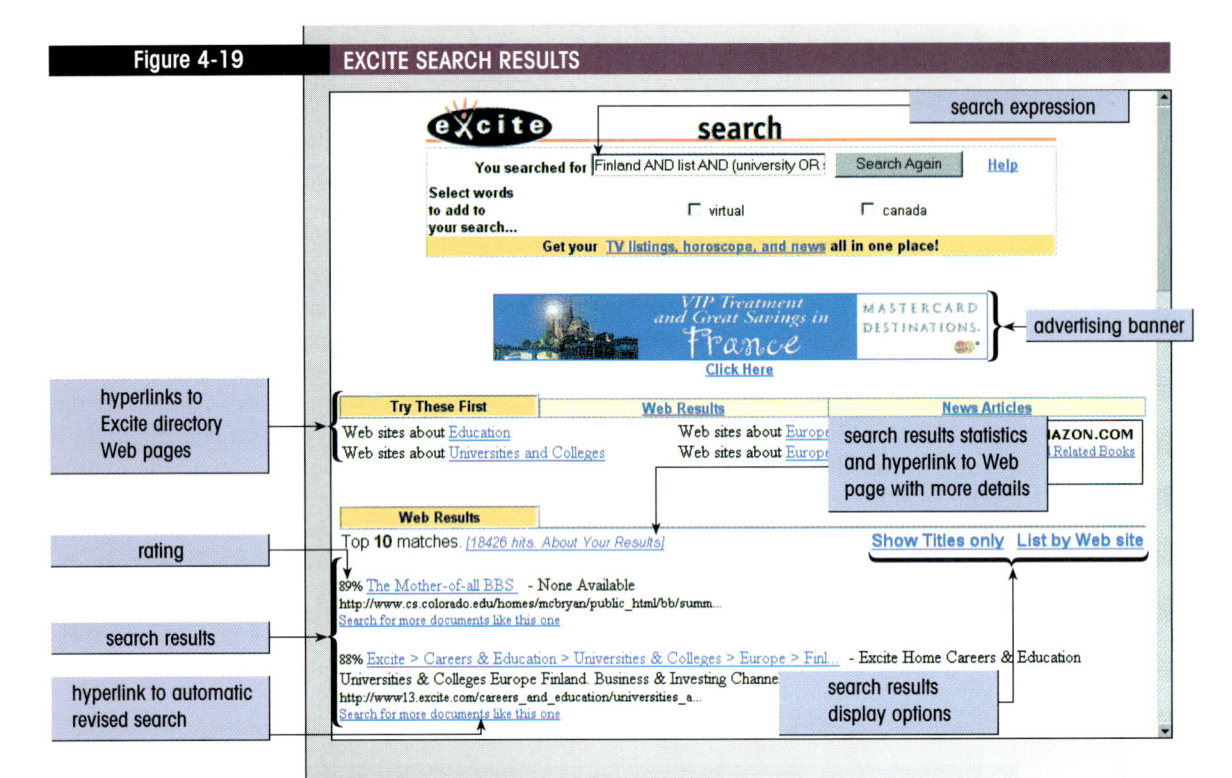

(Screenshot of Excite search results page with callouts: search expression; advertising banner; hyperlinks to Excite directory Web pages; search results statistics and hyperlink to Web page with more details; rating; search results; hyperlink to automatic revised search; search results display options)

4. Examine your search results and determine whether one or more of the hyperlinks in the search results leads you to a list of Finnish universities that you can give to Dave.

Complex Search in Northern Light

Ranjit is working on a series about fast-food franchises in various developing countries around the world. He would like to feature this industry's experience in Indonesia in his next column and asks you for help. He mentions that he would like to use industry publications in addition to Web sites for his research on this column. You know that the Northern Light search engine indexes not only the Web, but it also indexes a collection of periodicals, too. Therefore, you decide to run this search for Ranjit on the Northern Light search engine. To create a useful search expression, you must identify search terms that might lead you to appropriate Web pages. Some terms you might use include *fast*, *food*, *franchise*, and *Indonesia*. You decide that you are not interested in Web pages that have the individual terms *fast* and *food* as much as you are interested in Web pages that contain the phrase "fast food." The Northern Light search engine does not support full Boolean logic, so you decide to enter a simple expression and use Northern Light's folders feature to filter your results.

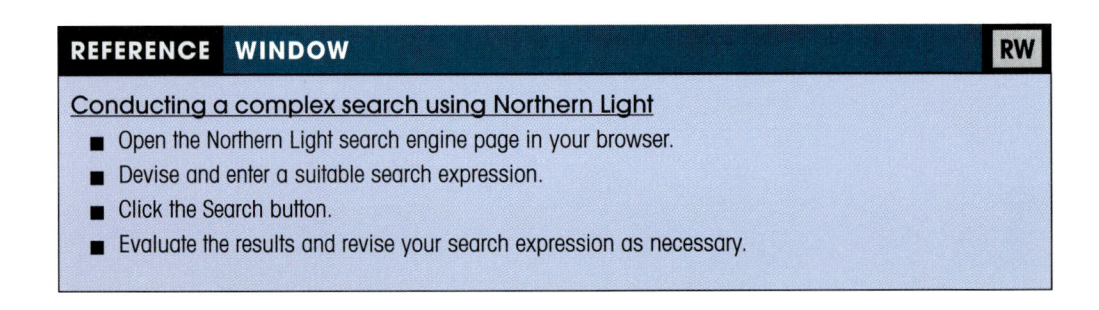

REFERENCE WINDOW

Conducting a complex search using Northern Light
- Open the Northern Light search engine page in your browser.
- Devise and enter a suitable search expression.
- Click the Search button.
- Evaluate the results and revise your search expression as necessary.

To perform a complex search using Northern Light:

1. Use your browser's **Back** button to return to the Student Online Companion page for Session 4.2, and then click the **Northern Light** link to open that page.

2. Click in the Search For text box, and then type **"fast food" franchise Indonesia**. Make sure that you type the quotation marks, so you find the phrase "fast food," instead of the individual terms.

3. Click the **Search** button to start the search. Figure 4-20 shows the search results page; these hyperlinks look promising.

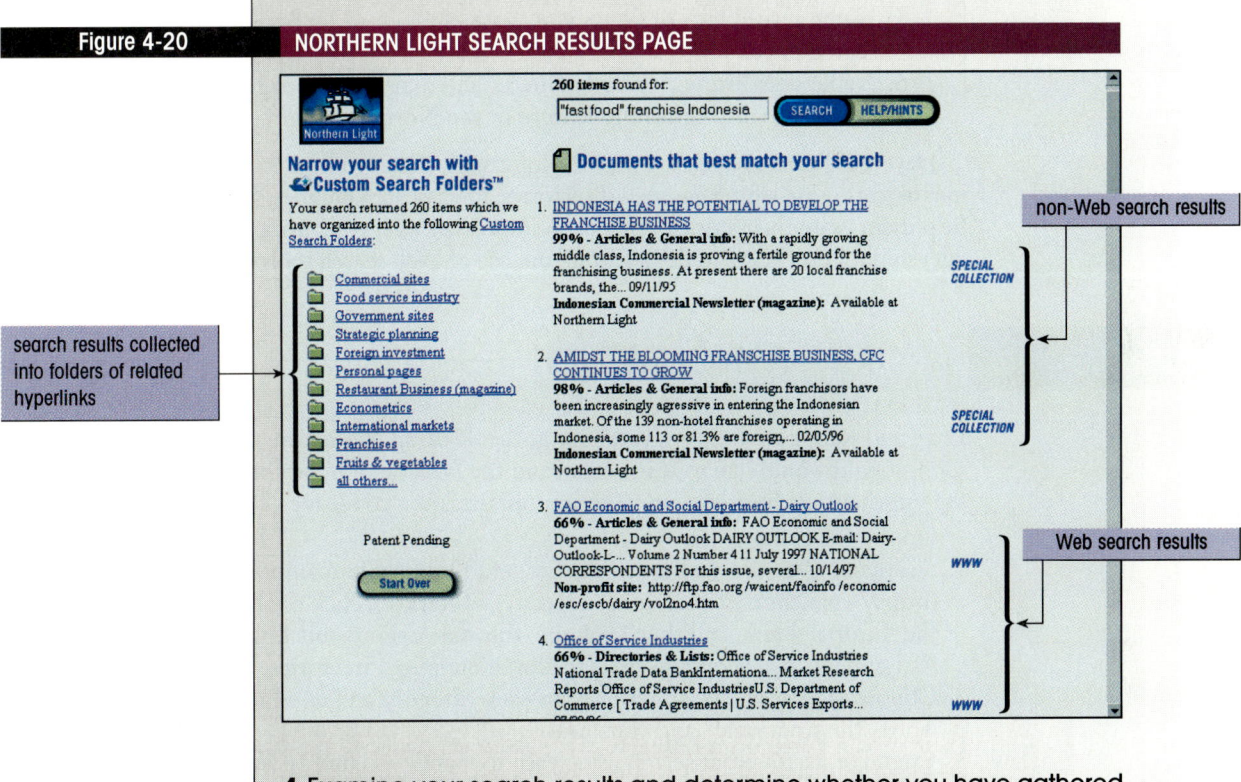

Figure 4-20 NORTHERN LIGHT SEARCH RESULTS PAGE

search results collected into folders of related hyperlinks

non-Web search results

Web search results

4. Examine your search results and determine whether you have gathered enough information about the fast-food industry in Indonesia for Dave.

5. Close your Web browser, and your dial-up connection, if necessary.

Northern Light provides hyperlinks to Web pages and to its own collection of several thousand journals, books, and other print resources. It provides a hyperlink to Web pages it finds and provides a summary of the print resources in its collection. For a fee, you can purchase the right to download and print an item from its collection. However, you usually can find the original source in your school or company library if you do not want to purchase the item from Northern Light. Downloading the item would be a nice convenience if you used this search engine frequently. Another unique feature of Northern Light is that it collects search results into folders as shown in Figure 4-20. These folders are organized collections of related hyperlinks found in the search. Clicking one of these folders—for example "Commercial sites"—will narrow your results page to include only those hits that fit the category of commercial sites. Your search provides Dave with the information he needs and congratulates you on a job well done.

QUICK CHECK

1. The three basic Boolean operators are _____, _____, and _____.
2. Write a search expression using Boolean and precedence operators that returns Web pages that contain information about wild mustang horses in Wyoming but not information about the Ford Mustang automobile.
3. True or False: The NEAR location operator always returns phrases that contain all keywords within 10 words of each other in a search expression.
4. True or False: In most search engines, the wildcard character is a * symbol.
5. Name three kinds of filters you can include in a HotBot search run from its main search page.
6. Name one distinguishing feature of an Excite results page.
7. Name one distinguishing feature of the Northern Light search engine.

Dave and Ranjit are pleased with the information that you collected for them. They are anxious to start using search engines, directories, meta-search engines, and other Web resources to help them write their stories. Anne is so impressed with your work that she wants you to conduct some short classes to demonstrate the use of Web search tools to all staff members.

TUTORIAL ASSIGNMENTS

Dave and Ranjit are keeping you busy at the *Midland News*. Your internship will be over soon, so you would like to leave Anne and the *News* with hyperlinks to some resources that the international business news section can use after you leave.

Do the following:
1. Start your Web browser, go to the Student Online Companion (http://www.course.com/NewPerspectives/Internet), click the link for your book, click the Tutorial 4 link, and then click the Tutorial Assignments link. The Tutorial Assignments page contains links to search engines, directories, and meta-search engines.
2. Choose at least one search tool from each category and conduct a search using the keywords "international" and "business."
3. Extend or narrow your search using each tool until you find 10 Web sites that you believe are comprehensive guides or directories that Anne, Dave, and Ranjit should include in their bookmark or favorites lists to help them get information about international business stories.
4. For each Web site, record the URL and write a paragraph that explains why you believe the site would be useful to an international business news writer. Identify each site as a guide, directory, or other resource.
5. When you are finished, close your Web browser and your dial-up connection, if necessary.

CASE PROBLEMS

1. Key Consulting Group You are a manager at Key Consulting Group, a firm of geological and engineering consultants who specialize in earthquake-damage assessment. When an earthquake strikes, Key Group sends a team of geologists and structural engineers to the quake's site to examine the damage in buildings and determine what kinds of reconstruction will be needed. In some cases, the buildings must be demolished. An earthquake can occur without warning in many parts of the world, so Key Group needs quick access to information about local conditions in various parts of the world, including the temperature, rainfall, money exchange rates, demographics, and local customs. It is early July when you receive a call that an earthquake has just occurred in Northern Chile. You decide to use the Web to obtain information about local mid-winter conditions there.

Do the following:

1. Start your Web browser, go to the Student Online Companion (http://www.course.com/NewPerspectives/Internet), click the link for your book, click the Tutorial 4 link, and then click the Case Problems link. The Case Problems section contains links to search engines, directories, and meta-search engines.
2. Use one of the search tools to conduct searches for information on local conditions in Northern Chile in July.
3. Prepare a short report that includes the daily temperature range, average rainfall, the current exchange rate for U.S. dollars to Chilean pesos, and any information you can obtain about the characteristics of the local population.
4. When you are finished, close your Web browser and your dial-up connection, if necessary.

2. Lightning Electrical Generators, Inc. You work as a marketing manager for Lightning Electrical Generators, Inc., a firm that has built generators for over 50 years. The generator business is not as profitable as it once was, and John Delaney, the firm's president, has asked you to investigate new markets for the company. One market that John would like to consider is the uninterruptible power supply (UPS) business. A UPS supplies continuing power to a single computer or to an entire computer system if the regular source of power to the computer fails. Most UPSs provide power only long enough to allow an orderly shutdown of the computer. John would like you to study the market for UPSs in the United States. He would like to know which firms currently make and sell these products and he would like some idea of what the power ratings and prices are of individual units.

Do the following:

1. Start your Web browser, go to the Student Online Companion (http://www.course.com/NewPerspectives/Internet), click the link for your book, click the Tutorial 4 link, and then click the Case Problems link. The Case Problems section contains links to search engines, directories, and meta-search engines.
2. Use one of the search tools to conduct searches for information about UPSs for John. You should design your searches to find the manufacturers' names and information about the products that they offer.
3. Prepare a short report that includes the information you have gathered, including the manufacturer's name, model number, product features, and suggested price for at least five UPSs.
4. When you are finished, close your Web browser and your dial-up connection, if necessary.

3. Dunwoody Cams, Inc. Gunther Dunwoody is the founder of Dunwoody Cams, Inc., a manufacturer of automobile parts. Buyers for the major auto companies frequently visit Dunwoody's factory Web page to obtain quotes on parts. Gunther would like you to find Web pages that contain information about the history of the automobile so he can place hyperlinks to those pages on the Dunwoody Web page, so the site is more interesting to use. He is especially interested in having links to Web sites that have photographs of old autos.

Do the following:

1. Start your Web browser, go to the Student Online Companion (http://www.course.com/NewPerspectives/Internet), click the link for your book, click the Tutorial 4 link, and then click the Case Problems link. The Case Problems section contains links to search engines, directories, and meta-search engines.
2. Use one of the search tools to find Web sites that contain historical information about automobiles and automobile manufacturing.
3. Prepare a list of at least five URLs that Gunther might want to include on the Dunwoody Web page. Be sure that at least one of the URLs is for a Web site that includes photographs of old automobiles.
4. When you are finished, close your Web browser and your dial-up connection, if necessary.

4. Glenwood Employment Agency You work as a staff assistant at the Glenwood Employment Agency. Eric Steinberg, the agency's owner, wants you to find Web resources for finding open positions in your geographic area. Eric would like this information to gauge whether his own efforts are keeping pace with the competition. He would like to monitor a few good pages but does not want to conduct exhaustive searches of the Web every week.

Do the following:
1. Start your Web browser, go to the Student Online Companion (http://www.course.com/NewPerspectives/Internet), click the link for your book, click the Tutorial 4 link, and then click the Case Problems link. The Case Problems section contains links to search engines, directories, and meta-search engines.
2. Use one of the search tools to find Web sites that contain information about job openings in your geographic area. You can use search expressions that include Boolean and precedence operators to limit your searches.
3. Prepare a list of at least five URLs of pages that you believe would be good candidates for Eric's monitoring program.
4. For each URL that you find, write a paragraph that explains why you selected it and then identify any particular strengths or weaknesses of the Web site based on Eric's intended use.
5. When you are finished, close your Web browser and your dial-up connection, if necessary.

Quick Check Answers

Session 4.1

1. Open-ended, hard to phrase, difficult to determine when you have found a good answer
2. Start with broad categories of information and ask increasingly narrow questions, trying to avoid blind alleys
3. A program that automatically searches the Web to find new Web sites and update information about old Web sites that already are in a search engine's database of URLs.
4. True
5. False
6. Advantage: Experts have selected, examined, and classified the entries in a Web directory. Disadvantage: You must know which category to search to find information.
7. The power of the search engine operates on the expert-selected and classified entries in the directory.
8. It forwards the expression to a number of other search engines, and then presents and organizes the search results it receives from them.
9. They offer lists of hyperlinks to other Web pages, frequently including summaries or reviews of the Web sites, organized by subject.

Session 4.2

1. AND, OR, NOT
2. One possibility is: (mustang OR horse) AND Wyoming NOT (Ford OR automobile OR auto OR car)
3. False
4. True
5. Time period, domain name or geographic location, pages that include a specific type of media
6. It provides a hyperlink to an automatic revised search for each search result and then rates each search result.
7. It includes non-Web search results from its special collection and then organizes search results into folders of related hyperlinks.

TUTORIAL 5

OBJECTIVES

In this tutorial you will:

- Learn how to assess the quality and credibility of Web sites
- Find and document research resources on the Web
- Find news and current information on the Web
- Learn to use FTP to download a program
- Learn the difference between freeware and shareware
- Identify several important sources of programs on the Web
- Decompress a downloaded file
- Check your disk for computer viruses

EVALUATING AND DOWNLOADING WEB RESOURCES

Assessing Web Site Quality and Obtaining Programs and Data

CASE

DigiComm Wireless Communication

DigiComm Wireless Communication is a rapidly growing company that produces and installs digital wireless communications products and technologies worldwide. It creates, assembles, and distributes communications systems for a wide range of markets and applications. Founded in 1989, DigiComm employs over 5,000 people in 16 offices around the world.

Among its major products is the UniTrack system, which is the one of the world's leading two-way mobile satellite tracking systems. The UniTrack system keeps tabs on commercial trucks and provides continuous position information so supervisors at the truck fleet headquarters know the precise location of each truck in the fleet at all times. Another of DigiComm's enormously successful products is its digital wireless telephone, the D-phone. The D-phone (for digital phone) provides communications services using a special encoding scheme that makes conversations impervious to eavesdropping and reduces background noise and static.

You have been assigned to work as an assistant to Nancy Moore, DigiComm's director of international sales and installations. Nancy is glad to have you on board because her office has needed a person who has Web search skills. She has used the Web but is concerned that she has not had the time to evaluate many of the Web pages on which she would like to rely for marketing and other research information. Your general responsibilities also will include helping the sales team find current information on the Web about sales prospects.

Once you have become familiar with DigiComm's sales operation, Nancy would like you to help her equip all of the members of her communications ground-station installation team with software they need. Besides the usual productivity software packages, such as e-mail and spreadsheet software, you will be responsible for providing each team member with a specially configured notebook computer that includes programs and data not normally included on DigiComm computers.

In particular, you will ensure that each person's computer has the latest version of a software compression/decompression program, a Web browser, an Internet file transfer program, a special document reader and decoder, and an antivirus program. The team will require access to data and statistics files maintained on the Web at various sites. You will make sure that they either know where those data are located or already have the data loaded on their notebook computers.

SESSION 5.1

In this session, you will find, document, and evaluate the quality of Web research resources, and you will find news and current information about specific topics on the Web.

Evaluating the Quality of Web Research Resources

In your first meeting with Nancy, you reviewed DigiComm's standards and practices for information that the firm collects using the Internet. One of the most important issues in doing Web research is determining the quality of the information provided on individual sites. Because the Web has made publishing so easy and inexpensive, it allows virtually anyone to create a Web page on almost any subject. Research published in scientific or literary journals is subjected to peer review. Books and research monographs often are reviewed by peers or edited by experts in the appropriate subject area. Information on the Web is seldom subjected to this review and editing process that has become a standard practice in print publishing.

When you are searching the Web for entertainment or general information, you are not likely to encounter a site that someone has created intentionally to misinform you. Even if you did, the potential damage you might experience usually is not great. When you are searching the Web for an answer to a serious research question, however, the risks are greater on both counts.

You can reduce your risks by carefully evaluating the quality of any Web resource on which you plan to rely to supply you with information related to an important judgment or decision. To develop an opinion about the quality of the resource, you can evaluate three major components of any Web page. These three components are the Web page's authorship, content, and appearance.

Author Identity and Objectivity

The first thing you should try to do when evaluating a Web research resource is to determine who authored the page. If you cannot easily find authorship information on the Web site, you should question the site's credibility. A Web site that does not identify its author has no credibility as a research resource. Any Web page that presents empirical research results, logical arguments, theories, or other information that purports to be the result of a research process should identify *and* present background information and credentials about the author. This information should be sufficient to establish the author's professional qualifications. You also should check secondary sources for corroborating information. For example, if the author of a Web page indicates that he or she is a member of a university faculty, you can find the university's Web site and see if the author is listed as a faculty member. The Website author should provide contact information, such as a street or an e-mail address or a telephone number, so you can contact the author or consult information directories to verify the author's identity.

It can be difficult to determine who owns a specific Web server or provides the space for the Web page. You can make a rough assessment by examining the domain identifier in the URL. If the site claims affiliation with an educational or research institution, then the domain should be .edu for educational institution. A not-for-profit organization would most likely have the .org domain, and a government unit or agency would have the .gov domain.

You also should consider whether the qualifications presented by the author pertain to the material that appears on the Web site. For example, the author of a Web site concerned with gene-splicing technology might list a Ph.D. degree as a credential. If the author's Ph.D. is in history or sociology, it would not support the credibility of the gene-splicing technology Web site. If you cannot determine the specific areas of the author's educational background, you can look for other examples of the author's work on the Web. By searching for the author's name and terms related to the subject area, you should be able to find other sites that include the author's work. If a Web site author has written extensively on a subject, that adds some evidence—though not necessarily conclusive—that the author has expertise in the field.

In addition to identifying the author's identity and qualifications, the author information should include details of the author's affiliations—either as an employee, owner, or consultant—with organizations that might have an interest in the research results or other information included in the Web site. Information about the author's affiliations will help you determine the level of independence and objectivity that the author can bring to bear on the research questions or topics. For example, research results supporting the contention that cigarette smoke is not harmful that are presented in a site authored by a researcher with excellent scientific credentials might be less compelling if you learn that the researcher is the chief scientist at a major tobacco company. By reading the page content carefully, you might be able to identify any bias in the results that is not justified by the evidence presented.

Content

Content is a criterion that is much more difficult to judge than the author's identity and objectivity; after all, you are searching for Web sites so you can learn more about your search topic, which implies that you probably are not an expert in that content area. However, there are some things you can look for in the Web site's presentation to help determine the quality of information. If the Web page has a clearly stated publication date, you can determine the timeliness of the content. You can read the content critically and evaluate whether the included topics are relevant to the research question. Possibly, you can determine whether important topics or considerations were omitted. You also might be able to assess the depth of treatment the author gives to the subject.

Form and Appearance

The Web does contain pages full of outright lies and misinformation that are nicely laid out, include tasteful graphics, and have grammatically correct and properly spelled text. However, many pages that contain low-quality information or actual misinformation are poorly designed and not well-edited. For example, a Web page devoted to an analysis of Shakespeare's plays that contains spelling errors indicates a low-quality resource. Loud colors, graphics that serve no purpose, and flashing text are all Web page design elements that often suggest a low-quality resource.

Having explained how these principles of assessing Web page quality are applied to the research team's work at DigiComm, Nancy asks you to evaluate a Web page. One of the firm's prospective new customers is Geo-Research, a scientific foundation that is studying global-warming and its potential effects on communications equipment. Geo-Research has observation stations all over the world and could become a large purchaser of DigiComm products and services. The sales team that will make the presentation to Geo-Research asked Nancy to give them some reliable background information on the global-warming issue. Nancy has been gathering a list of URLs from which she plans to take information to include in a briefing report for the sales team. She would like you to evaluate the quality of a URL titled "environmental health update" that is on her list.

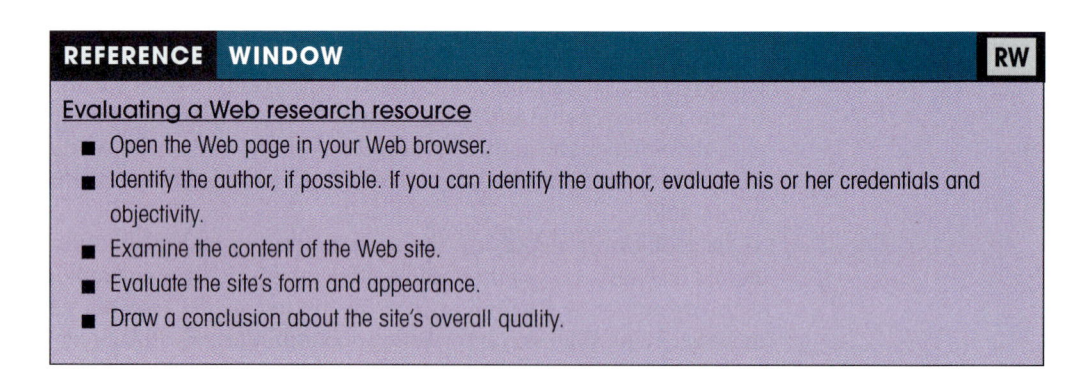

REFERENCE WINDOW

Evaluating a Web research resource
- Open the Web page in your Web browser.
- Identify the author, if possible. If you can identify the author, evaluate his or her credentials and objectivity.
- Examine the content of the Web site.
- Evaluate the site's form and appearance.
- Draw a conclusion about the site's overall quality.

To evaluate the quality of the environmental health update Web page:

1. Start your Web browser, if necessary, and then go to the Student Online Companion page by entering the URL **http://www.course.com/NewPerspectives/Internet** in the appropriate location in your Web browser. Click the hyperlink for your book, click the **Tutorial 5** link, and then click the **Session 5.1** link. Click the **PSR Program Update** link and wait while the browser loads the Web page that appears in Figure 5-1. Examine the content of the Web page: read the text, examine the titles and headings, and consider the page's appearance.

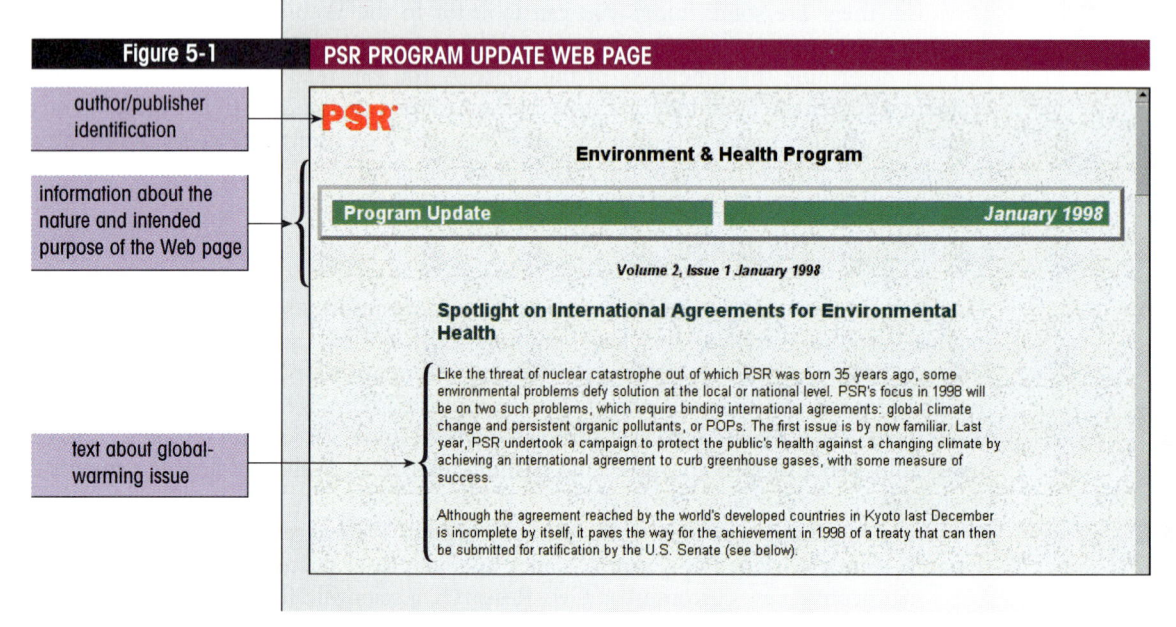

Figure 5-1 PSR PROGRAM UPDATE WEB PAGE

- author/publisher identification
- information about the nature and intended purpose of the Web page
- text about global-warming issue

PSR

Environment & Health Program

Program Update   January 1998

Volume 2, Issue 1 January 1998

Spotlight on International Agreements for Environmental Health

Like the threat of nuclear catastrophe out of which PSR was born 35 years ago, some environmental problems defy solution at the local or national level. PSR's focus in 1998 will be on two such problems, which require binding international agreements: global climate change and persistent organic pollutants, or POPs. The first issue is by now familiar. Last year, PSR undertook a campaign to protect the public's health against a changing climate by achieving an international agreement to curb greenhouse gases, with some measure of success.

Although the agreement reached by the world's developed countries in Kyoto last December is incomplete by itself, it paves the way for the achievement in 1998 of a treaty that can then be submitted for ratification by the U.S. Senate (see below).

TUTORIAL 5 EVALUATING AND DOWNLOADING WEB RESOURCES   WEB   5.5   INTERNET

You can see in Figure 5-1 that the author or publisher of the page is identified only as "PSR" and the page has a simple, clear design. The .org domain in the URL tells you that the publisher is a not-for-profit organization. You note that the grammar and spelling are correct, and that the content—although it clearly reflects a strong specific viewpoint on the issue—is not inflammatory or overly argumentative. As you read more of the page, you see that this style of layout and content is consistent in passages related to global warming and other issues discussed on the page. You note that the text cites such authorities as the U.S. National Oceanic and Atmospheric Administration and the *New England Journal of Medicine*. The reputable references and the consistent style of the page suggest that this might be a good-quality site.

2. Use your browser's scroll bar to scroll to the bottom of the page, which looks like Figure 5-2.

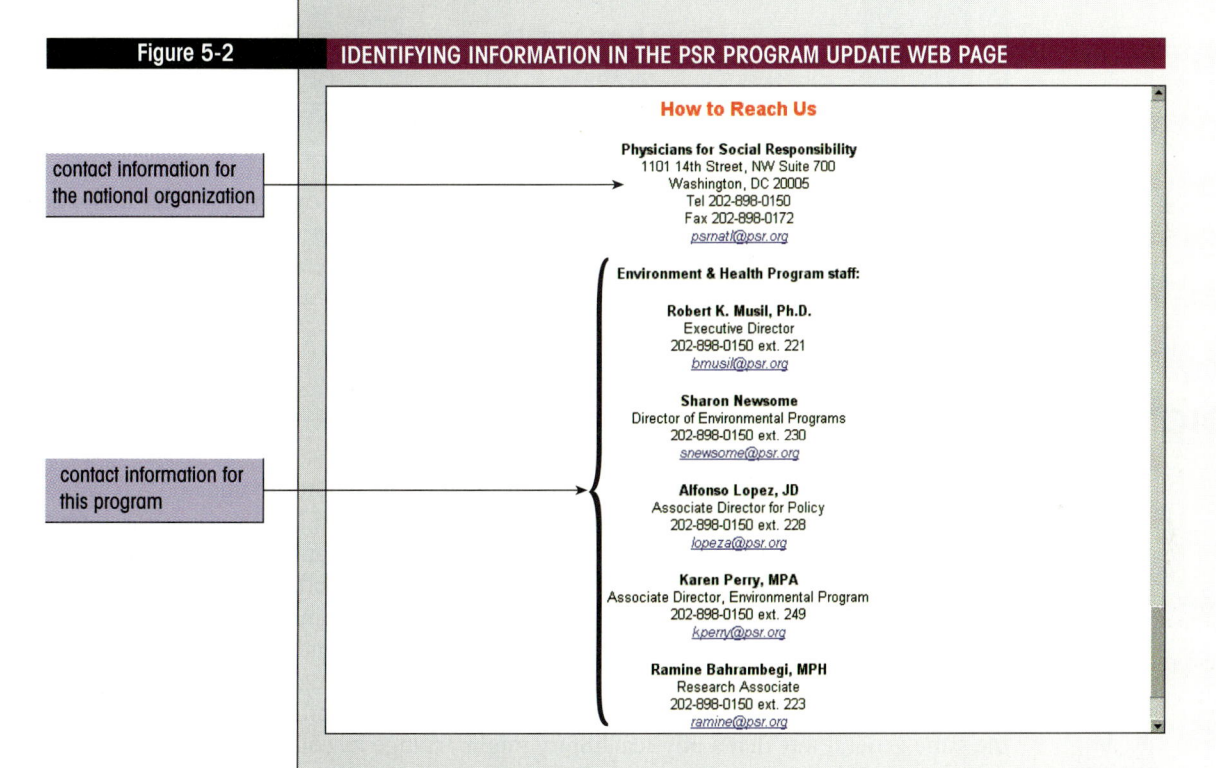

Figure 5-2   IDENTIFYING INFORMATION IN THE PSR PROGRAM UPDATE WEB PAGE

contact information for the national organization →

How to Reach Us

Physicians for Social Responsibility
1101 14th Street, NW Suite 700
Washington, DC 20005
Tel 202-898-0150
Fax 202-898-0172
psrnatl@psr.org

Environment & Health Program staff:

Robert K. Musil, Ph.D.
Executive Director
202-898-0150 ext. 221
bmusil@psr.org

contact information for this program →

Sharon Newsome
Director of Environmental Programs
202-898-0150 ext. 230
snewsome@psr.org

Alfonso Lopez, JD
Associate Director for Policy
202-898-0150 ext. 228
lopeza@psr.org

Karen Perry, MPA
Associate Director, Environmental Program
202-898-0150 ext. 249
kperry@psr.org

Ramine Bahrambegi, MPH
Research Associate
202-898-0150 ext. 223
ramine@psr.org

Now you can see that "PSR" is an acronym for the Physicians for Social Responsibility organization. Further, you can see that the organization's address, telephone number, and e-mail address are listed along with contact information for key individuals in the PSR's Environment & Health Program. To find more information about PSR, you might want to visit the organization's home page. The Web page shown in Figure 5-2 does not include a home page hyperlink, but you can guess that it might be the first part of the URL for this page.

3. Click in your browser's Location field or Address Bar, and then delete all of the text to the *right* of the .org/ domain name portion of the URL. Press the **Enter** key to load the Web page shown in Figure 5-3 with the shortened URL.

Figure 5-3 PSR HOME PAGE

hyperlinks to more information about PSR

contact information for PSR main offices

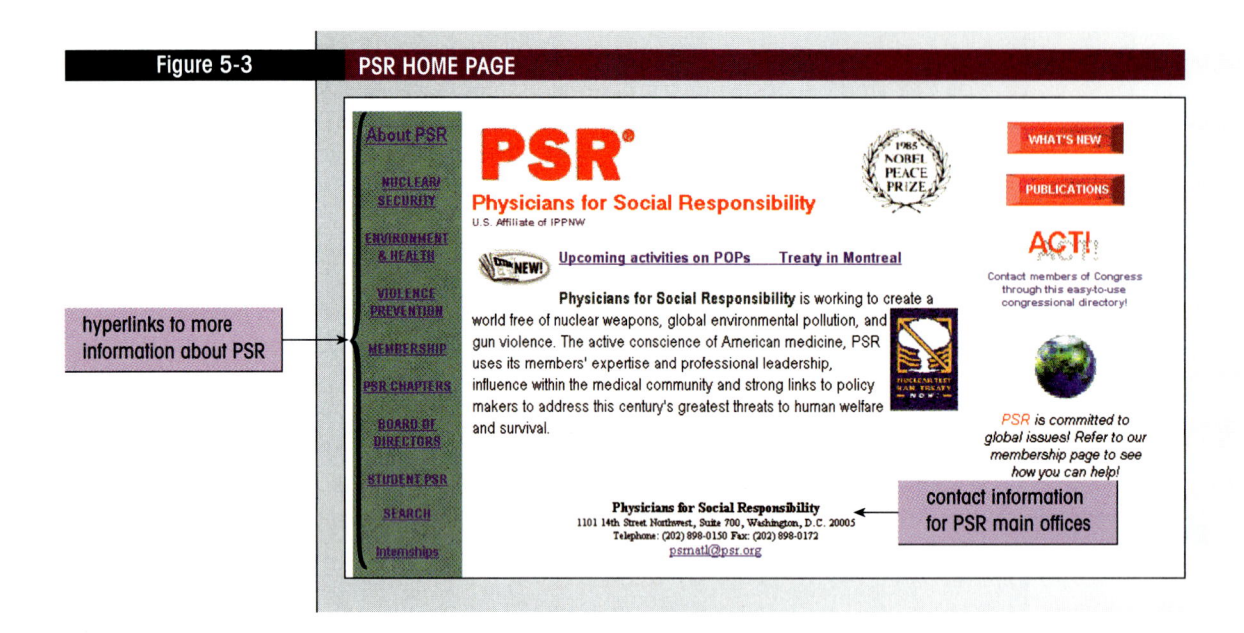

The Web page shown in Figure 5-3 is, in fact, the U.S. National PSR Office home page that includes hyperlinks to information about the organization, its goals, activities, directors, and membership. This information will allow you to make a worthwhile evaluation of the site and help Nancy determine how she can use its contents as she prepares her briefing for the DigiComm sales team.

Library Resources

Nancy is very happy with your evaluation of the environmental health update Web page and needs you do more work for the research department. You ask Nancy about the future of traditional libraries, given that so much information is available on the Web. She says that libraries will likely be around for a long time. In fact, the Web has made existing libraries more accessible to more people. As traditional libraries and online collections of works that have serious research value begin to recognize each other as complementary rather than as competing, library users should see many new and interesting research resources. One example of this is the **LibrarySpot** Web site, which is a collection of hyperlinks organized in the same general way that a physical library might arrange its collections.

To explore the LibrarySpot Web site:

1. Return to the Student Online Companion Web page for Session 5.1, and then click the **LibrarySpot** hyperlink and wait while your Web browser loads the Web page shown in Figure 5-4.

TUTORIAL 5 EVALUATING AND DOWNLOADING WEB RESOURCES   WEB 5.7   INTERNET

Figure 5-4   LIBRARYSPOT WEB SITE

- hyperlinks to lists and directories of libraries
- hyperlinks to commonly used reference materials
- hyperlinks to electronic text collections

Figure 5-4 shows that the LibrarySpot site includes many of the same things you would expect to find in a public or school library. However, this library is open 24 hours a day and seven days a week. The LibrarySpot site lets you access reference materials, electronic texts, and other library Web sites from one central Web page.

The Student Online Companion page for Tutorial 5 contains many other hyperlinks to useful library and library-related Web sites in the Additional Information section under the "Library Resources" heading. Feel free to explore the libraries of the Web the next time you need to complete a research assignment for school or your job.

Many libraries have made their collection catalogs available on the Web. The St. Joseph County Public Library's List of Public Libraries with Gopher/WWW Servers includes a list of over 500 libraries with online catalogs and other information. The Student Online Companion for Tutorial 5 contains hyperlinks to these library Web sites in the Additional Information section under the "Library Resources" heading.

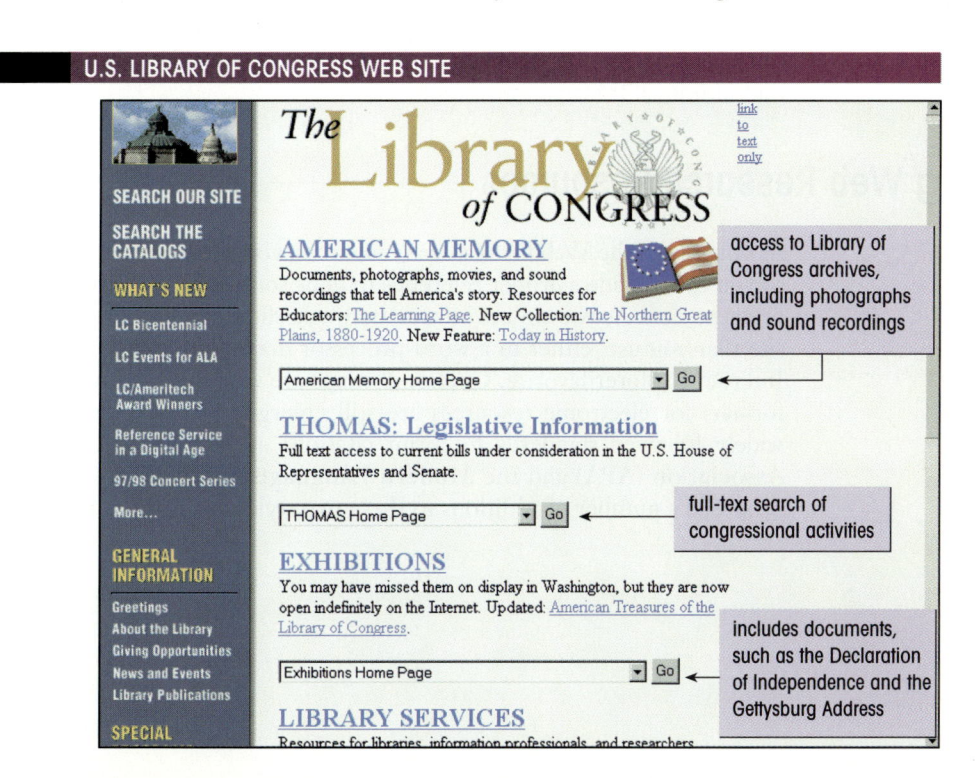

Figure 5-5   U.S. LIBRARY OF CONGRESS WEB SITE

- access to Library of Congress archives, including photographs and sound recordings
- full-text search of congressional activities
- includes documents, such as the Declaration of Independence and the Gettysburg Address

Figure 5-5 shows the U.S. Library of Congress Web site, which includes links to a huge array of research resources, ranging from the Thomas legislative information site to the Library of Congress archives.

The **Thomas** Web site provides you with search access to the full text of bills that are before Congress, the *Congressional Record*, and Congressional Committee Reports. Other hyperlinks on this page lead you to archived photographs, sound and video recordings, maps, and collections of everything from Seventeenth Century dance instruction manuals to baseball cards. The Exhibitions hyperlink leads you to information about and graphic images of historical documents, such as the Declaration of Independence and the Gettysburg Address.

Text on the Web

In addition to library catalogs and indexes to other information, the Web contains a number of text resources, including dictionaries, thesauri, encyclopedias, glossaries, and other reference works. Many people find reference works easier to use when they have a computerized search interface. For example, when you open a dictionary to find the definition of a specific word, the structure of the bound book actually interferes with your ability to find the answer you seek. A computer interface allows you to enter a search term—in this case, the word to be defined—and saves you the trouble of scanning several pages of text to find the correct entry.

Of course, publishers sell dictionaries and encyclopedias on CD-ROMs, but there are many alternatives on the Web. These alternatives range in quality from very low to very high. Many of the very best resources offered on the Web require you to pay a subscription fee. The free reference works on the Web are worth investigating, however. They are good enough to provide acceptable service for many users. In addition to dictionaries and encyclopedias, the Web includes grammar checkers, thesauri, rhyming dictionaries, and language-translation pages. The Student Online Companion page for Tutorial 5 includes a collection of hyperlinks to these resources in the Additional Information section.

The Web also offers a number of full-text copies of works that are no longer protected by copyright. Two of the most popular Web sites for full text storage are the **Project Gutenberg** and **Project Bartleby** Web sites. These volunteer efforts have collected the contributions of many people throughout the world who have spent enormous amounts of time entering or converting printed text into electronic form. The Student Online Companion page for Tutorial 5 includes hyperlinks to these and several other Web sites that offer electronic texts in the Additional Information section.

Citing Web Research Resources

As you search the Web for research resources, you should collect information about the sites so you can include a proper reference to your sources in any research report you write based on these sites. As you collect information, you should record the URL and name of any Web site that you use, either in a word-processor document, as a Navigator bookmark, or as an Internet Explorer favorite. Citation formats are very well-defined for print publications, but formats for electronic resources are still emerging. For academic research, the two most widely followed standards for print citations are those of the **American Psychological Association (APA)** and the **Modern Language Association (MLA)**. Various parties have proposed a number of additions to these two styles but without reaching a consensus.

One of the problems that both standards face is the difficulty of typesetting long URLs in print documents. No clear standards that specify where or how to break long URLs at the end of a print line have emerged. Another typesetting problem is how to distinguish between punctuation that is included in the URL and punctuation that is part of the sentence in which the URL appears. One solution used by some publishers is to enclose the URL with chevron symbols (< >); however, this solution is not generally accepted. The Additional Information section of the Student Online Companion page for Tutorial 5 includes hyperlinks to several citation style and formatting resources on the Web. You can check these Web pages periodically for updates to these changing standards. You also can request specific guidance from your instructor, if your research report is for a course requirement, or from the editor of the publication to which you plan to submit your work.

All Web citation methods face one serious, yet unsolved, problem—moving and disappearing URLs. The Web is a dynamic medium that changes constantly. The citation systems that academics and librarians use for published books and journals work well because the printed page has a physical existence. A Web page only exists in an HTML document on a Web server computer. If that file's name or location changes, or the Web server is disconnected from the Internet, the page is no longer accessible. Perhaps future innovations in Internet addressing technologies will solve this problem.

Future of Electronic Publishing

Nancy mentions that one of the key changes that the Internet and the Web have inspired is that information can now be disseminated more rapidly than ever in large quantities with a very low investment. The ease of publishing electronically on the Web might help reduce the concentration of media control that has been occurring over the past two or three decades as newspapers merged with each other and, along with radio and television stations, were purchased by large media interests.

To be successful in publishing in the print media—such as a monthly magazine—a publisher must have a large subscription market. The fixed costs of composing and creating the magazine are spread over enough units so that the publisher can earn a profit. The costs of publishing a Web page are low compared to printing magazines or newspapers. Therefore, the subscription market required for a Web publication to be successful can be very small or even nonexistent. If a Web-based magazine, or an **e-zine**, can attract advertisers, it can be financially successful with no subscribers and a small number of readers. As a result, e-zines are appearing on the Web in increasing numbers. An e-zine does not require a large readership to be successful, so these electronic publications can focus on very specialized, narrow interests. E-zines have become very popular places for publishing new fiction and poetry, for example. The Additional Information section of the Student Online Companion page for Tutorial 5 includes hyperlinks to several e-zine Web sites that you might want to explore.

Current Information

Nancy thanks you for the excellent job you did in evaluating the global-warming page. She explains that she would also like you to use the Web to find recent news and information about potential clients and client industries for the sales team.

To help you find current news and information, many search engines and directories include a hyperlink to a "What's new" page. The Yahoo! directory, for example, includes hyperlinks titled "New" and "Today's News" at the top of its home page. The Excite search engine's main page includes a hyperlink collection to current events, as shown in Figure 5-6.

You can see Excite's stock market summary and current news hyperlinks in Figure 5-6. The page also includes hyperlinks for sports, weather, and even horoscopes. If you are willing to register with Excite, you can follow the Personalize this page hyperlink to specify the kind of information that appears on this page when you log on.

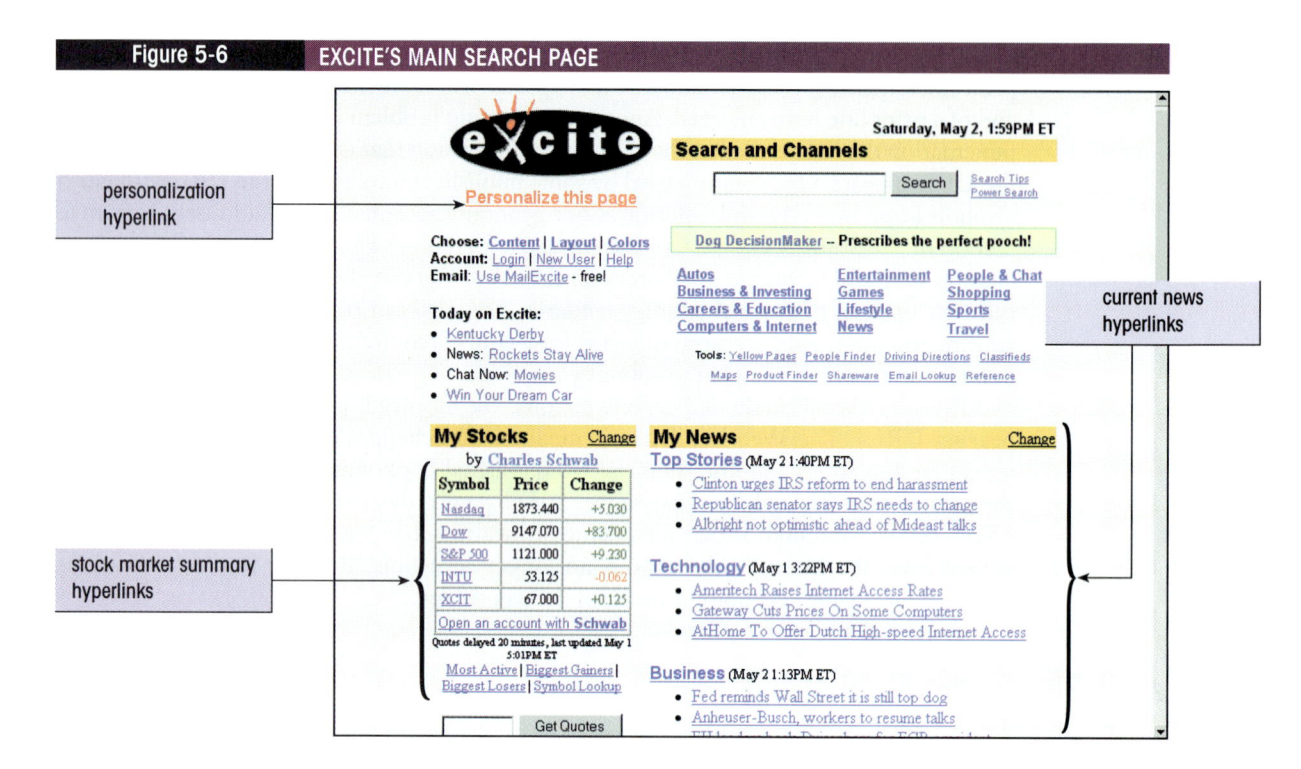

INTERNET   WEB 5.10   TUTORIAL 5 EVALUATING AND DOWNLOADING WEB RESOURCES

Figure 5-6   EXCITE'S MAIN SEARCH PAGE

(screenshot of Excite's main search page with the following annotations: "personalization hyperlink" pointing to Personalize this page; "current news hyperlinks" pointing to the My News section; "stock market summary hyperlinks" pointing to the My Stocks section)

Many search engines, including HotBot and AltaVista, allow you to specify a date range when you enter a search expression. HotBot provides two ways to do this. On its main page, you can specify one of a range of time options such as "in the last week" or "in the last 3 months" to limit your search to sites that were last modified within your selected time period. HotBot's SuperSearch page includes the same range of time options. To open the HotBot SuperSearch page shown in Figure 5-7, click the More Search Options button that appears on the HotBot search engine's main page.

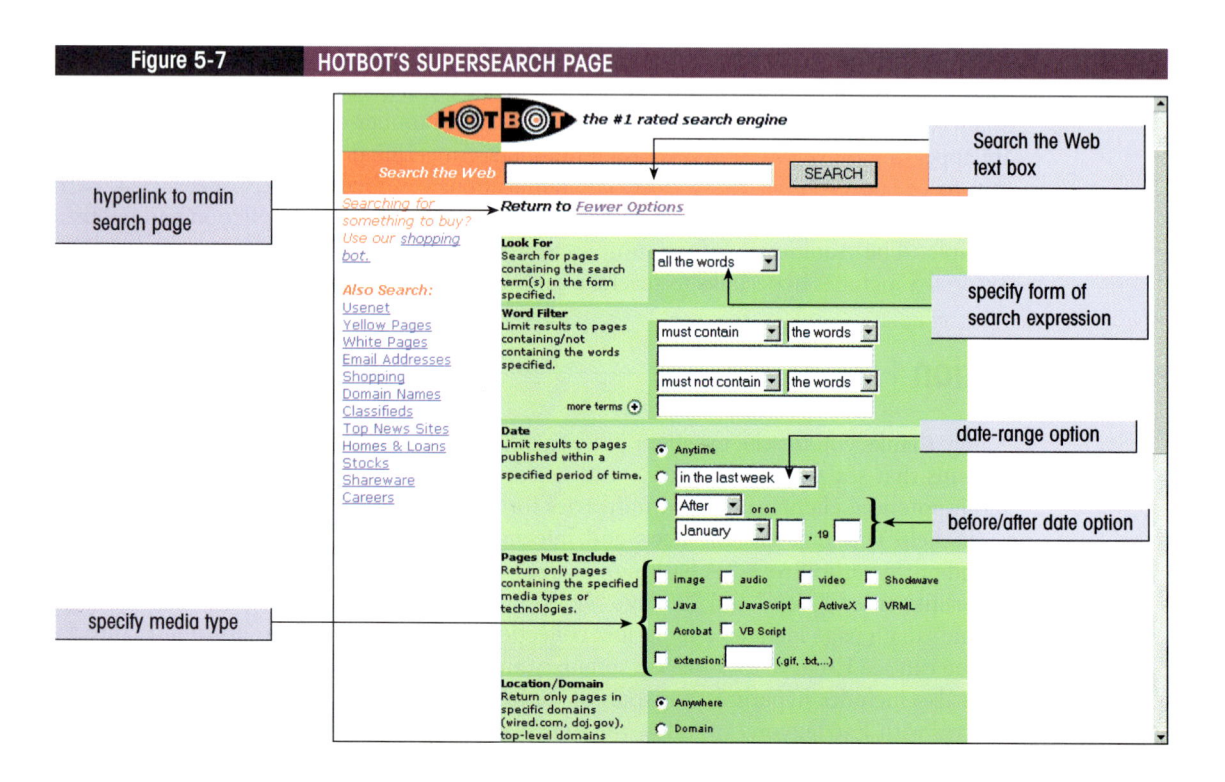

Figure 5-7   HOTBOT'S SUPERSEARCH PAGE

(screenshot of HotBot's SuperSearch page with the following annotations: "hyperlink to main search page"; "Search the Web text box"; "specify form of search expression"; "date-range option"; "before/after date option"; "specify media type")

Alternatively, you can limit a SuperSearch page search to include only sites last modified before or after a specific date by using the date controls that appear below the range of time options. HotBot, even on its SuperSearch page, does not provide a way to search for sites *within* a specific date range. For example, you could not limit a HotBot search to sites modified between April 24, 1999 and November 11, 1999. The AltaVista search engine does not have the pre-set range of time options that HotBot offers, but it does allow you to set an exact date range on its advanced search page. Figure 5-8 shows the AltaVista advanced search page with an exact date-range set.

Figure 5-8   **DATE-RANGE SETTINGS IN AN ALTAVISTA ADVANCED SEARCH**

language set to English

date-range settings

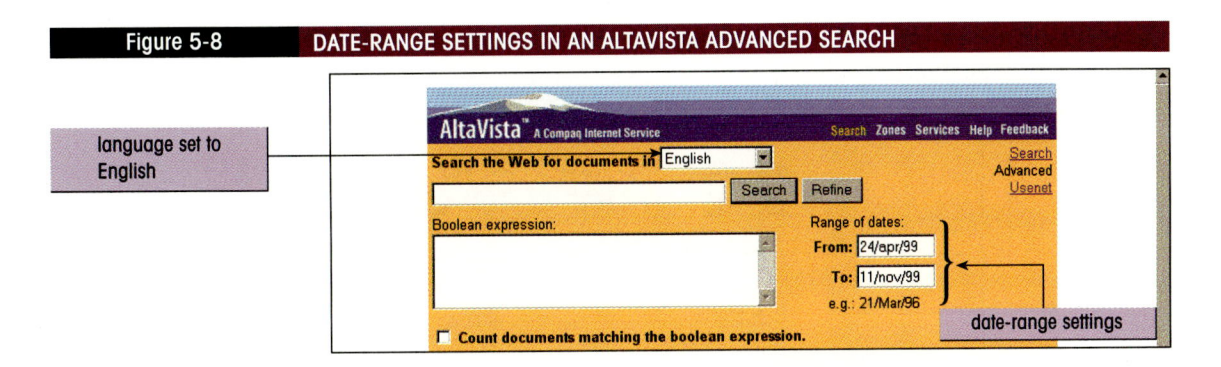

Nancy calls to tell you that she spoke with one of the firm's customers about future expansion plans. This customer manufactures and distributes industrial paint-spraying equipment and is a major supplier to several auto companies. The customer told her that his salespersons reported rumors that Honda, one of his largest customers, is considering a major expansion to its North American manufacturing facilities. If this information is true, he would like to buy a global UniTrack system from DigiComm so he can provide high-quality service to Honda and obtain all of its expansion business. Nancy would like you to search the Web and collect the URLs of any sites that mention Honda. You need the most recent information, so you will search for sites that have been modified within the last three months.

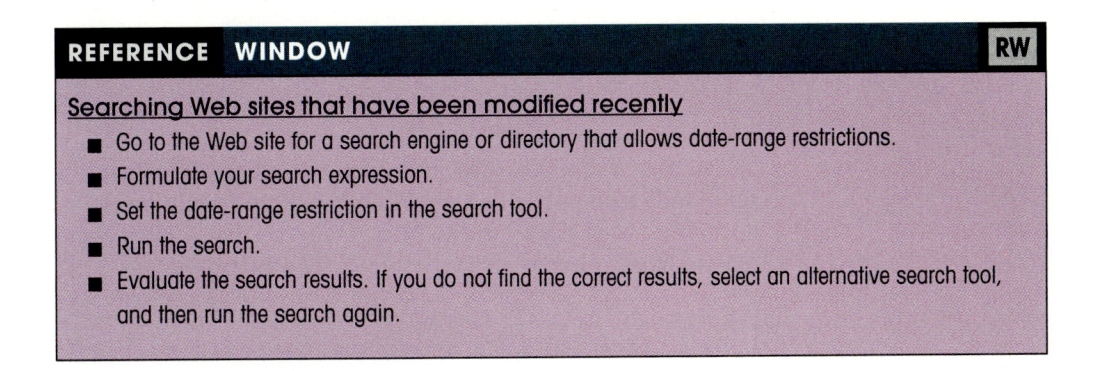

REFERENCE WINDOW

Searching Web sites that have been modified recently
- Go to the Web site for a search engine or directory that allows date-range restrictions.
- Formulate your search expression.
- Set the date-range restriction in the search tool.
- Run the search.
- Evaluate the search results. If you do not find the correct results, select an alternative search tool, and then run the search again.

Consider the search tools available. Your search term—Honda—is a brand name, so it is likely that directory builders will collect many useful sites that include that term in their databases. Yahoo! is a directory that includes a date-range restriction option, so you decide to use it for your first search. If you do not find what you are looking for with one search tool, you can try your search again using different tools until you are satisfied with your results.

To find specific Web pages based on last modified dates:

1. Return to the Student Online Companion page for Session 5.1, and then click the **Yahoo!** link and wait while the browser loads the Yahoo! home page.

2. Click the **options** hyperlink to the right of the Search button to open the Yahoo! search Options page.

3. Type **Honda** in the search text box.

4. Click the **Find only new listings added during the past** list arrow, click **3 months** (see Figure 5-9), and then click the **Search** button to start the search.

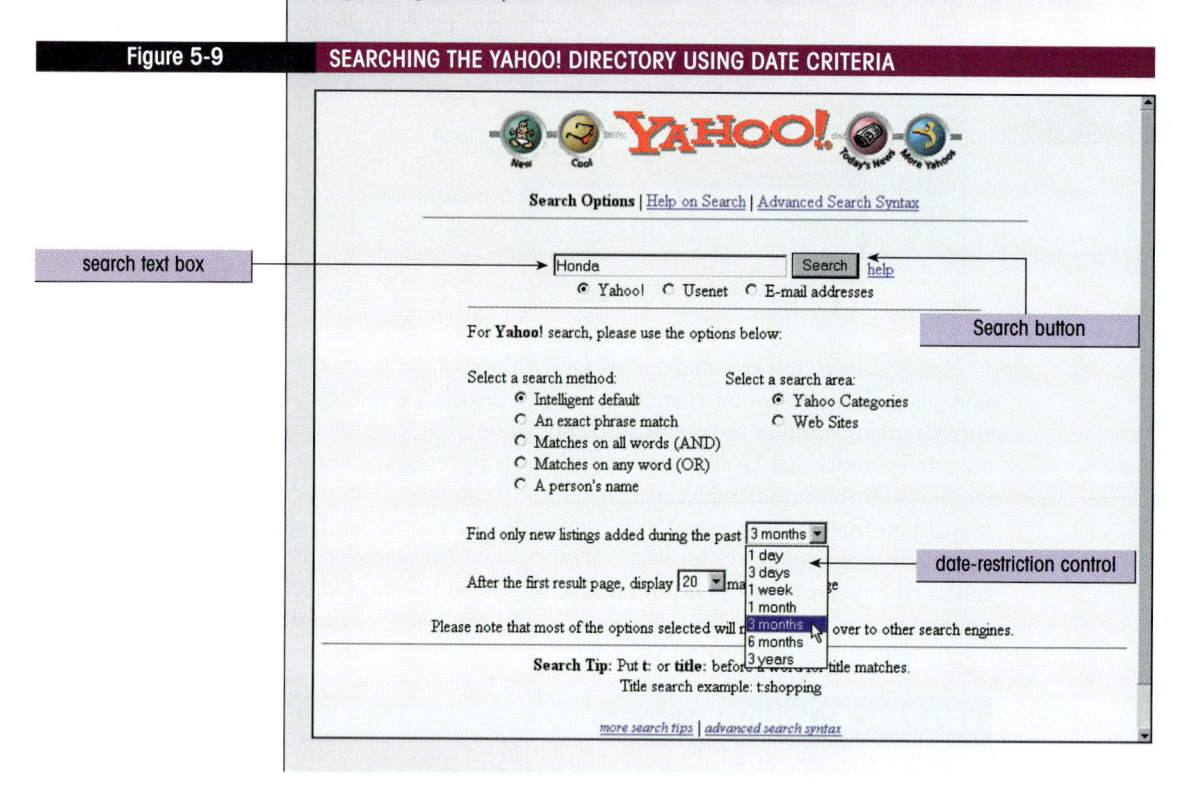

Figure 5-9 SEARCHING THE YAHOO! DIRECTORY USING DATE CRITERIA

Your search should return approximately 100 to 200 hits for Honda motorcycle products and Honda automobile dealers. However, after examining the results, you decide that you did not find what Nancy needs. Nancy suggests that you try your search again using HotBot because HotBot has more date controls than Yahoo!

To search for last modified dates using HotBot:

1. Use your browser's **Back** button or the history list to return to the Student Online Companion page for Session 5.1, and then click the **HotBot** hyperlink and wait for the HotBot home page to load in your Web browser.

2. Type **Honda AND (auto OR automobile) AND (manufacture OR manufacturing)** in the Search the Web text box to search for URLs of Web pages that relate to Honda's auto manufacturing operations.

3. Click the **Look for** list arrow, and then click **Boolean phrase**.

4. Click the second **Look for** list arrow (below the list arrow that now displays "Boolean phrase"), and then click **in the last 3 months** to search for URLs that have been modified in the last three months.

5. Click the **SEARCH** button to start the search. Once again, your search returned many more pages than Yahoo!—over 2,000 more—based on the specified criteria. You are certain that Nancy can find the information she is looking for from your list of URLs.

You can send the URLs to Nancy in an e-mail message, or you can tell her how to obtain the same search results. For now, you decide to cut and paste the URLs that look promising and then send them to her in an e-mail message.

Getting the News

Nancy stops by to see you the day after you send her the URLs she requested. She is pleased with many of the recently modified Web pages you found. Now, she asks you to find any recent news stories about Honda that might not appear as part of a recently modified Web page.

Finding current news stories on the Web is an easy task. Almost every search engine and directory includes a list of current news hyperlinks to broadcast networks, wire services, and newspapers. All of the major U.S. broadcasters, including ABC, CBS, CNN, Fox, MSNBC (the Microsoft-NBC joint venture), and National Public Radio (NPR) have Web sites that carry news features. Broadcasters in other countries, such as the BBC, also provide news reports on their Web pages. The Reuters Web page includes current news stories in addition to the news services that it sells. Major newspapers, such as *The New York Times*, the *Washington Post*, and the *London Times*, have Web sites that include current news and many other features from their print editions. Many of these broadcast news, wire service, and newspaper Web sites include search features that allow you to search the site for specific news stories. However, there are not many search tools available on the Web to search multiple news sources at the same time. As you begin to think about the time it will take to do a comprehensive search of just the major news sites for Nancy, you start to worry.

Nancy tells you that the **Internet Public Library** site includes hyperlinks to hundreds of international and domestic newspapers. Figure 5-10 shows a portion of the Internet Public Library Web site.

Figure 5-10   **INTERNET PUBLIC LIBRARY WEB SITE**

hyperlinks to non-U.S. newspapers, listed alphabetically by country

hyperlinks to U.S. newspapers, listed alphabetically by state

Search Terms text box

As you can see in Figure 5-10, this site has a search field; but it only searches the title and the main entry for each newspaper and does not search the newspaper sites' contents. Therefore, you could use it to identify all of the newspapers that were in New Jersey or all of the newspapers that had the word *Tribune* in their titles; but you could not use it to find news stories that include the word *Honda*.

Fortunately, at least two Web sites provide you with the ability to search the content of current news stories in multiple publications—these Web sites are Excite's NewsTracker and VPOP Technologies' NewsHub. **NewsTracker** searches the contents of over 300 newspapers, magazines, and wire services. **NewsHub** updates its news database with information from several major wire services every 15 minutes. Therefore, NewsTracker offers a broad range of coverage and NewsHub offers timely coverage of news events. To obtain both breadth and currency of coverage, you might want to run the same query using both search tools.

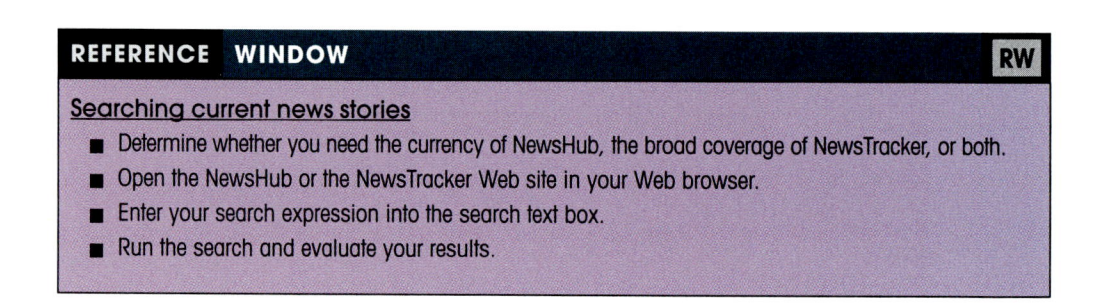

REFERENCE WINDOW   **RW**

Searching current news stories
- Determine whether you need the currency of NewsHub, the broad coverage of NewsTracker, or both.
- Open the NewsHub or the NewsTracker Web site in your Web browser.
- Enter your search expression into the search text box.
- Run the search and evaluate your results.

TUTORIAL 5 EVALUATING AND DOWNLOADING WEB RESOURCES   WEB 5.15   INTERNET

You would like search coverage that is both current and broad, so you decide to use both the NewsHub and the NewsTracker search tools.

To find Web pages that include recent news stories that mention Honda:

1. Return to the Student Online Companion Web page for Session 5.1, and then click the **NewsHub** hyperlink and wait while your Web browser loads the NewsHub page.

2. Type **Honda** in the search text box, and then click the **Search** button. Examine the hits returned by the search and note the URLs of any that might interest Nancy. You probably will find fewer than 100 hits, with even fewer of those hits related to Honda's expansion plans. Your search results might be different because the business world—and news reported about the business world—changes daily. You do not see many relevant hits, so you decide to try the NewsTracker search tool.

3. Return to the Student Online Companion Web page for Session 5.1, and then click the **NewsTracker** hyperlink to load that page in your Web browser.

4. Type **Honda** in the search text box (you might need to scroll down the page to see the search text box), and then click the **News Search** button to start your search. Your results page should look like Figure 5-11. Examine the hits returned by the search and see if any of the listed pages relate to Honda's expansion plans.

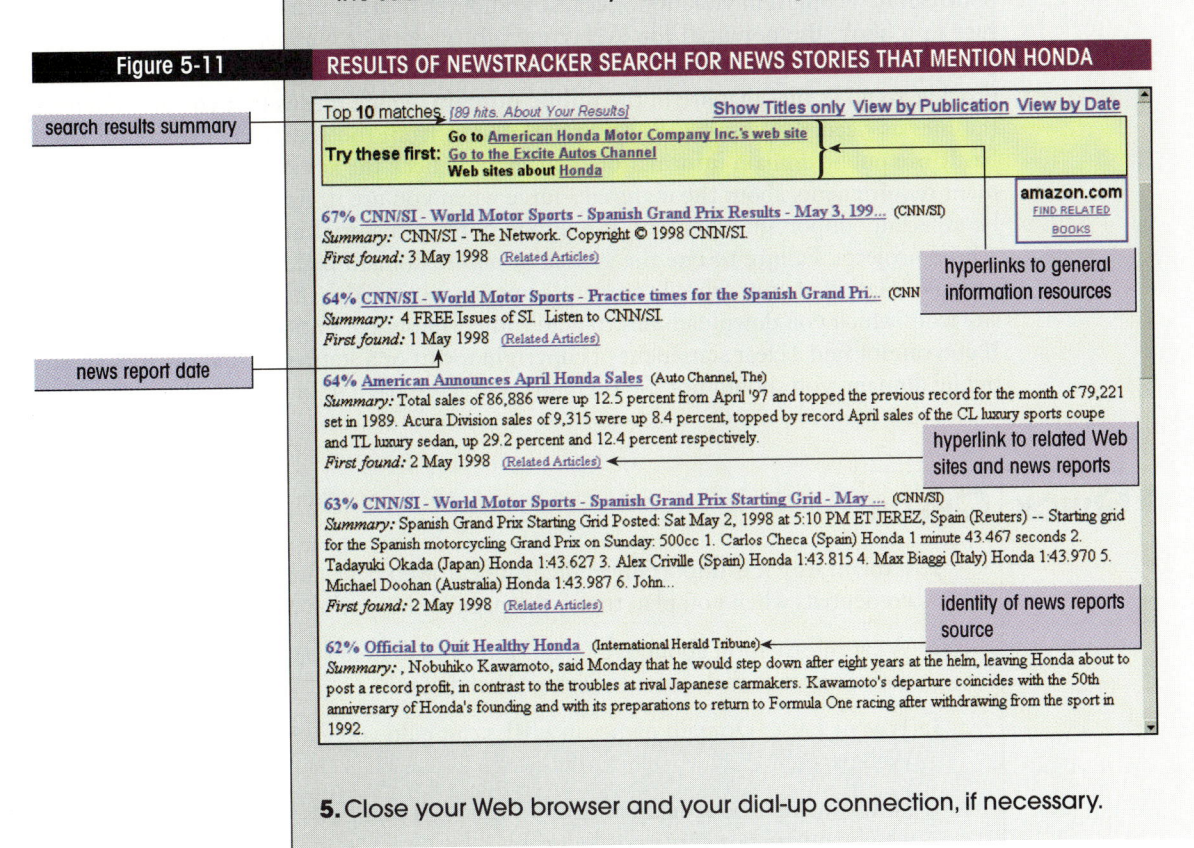

Figure 5-11 RESULTS OF NEWSTRACKER SEARCH FOR NEWS STORIES THAT MENTION HONDA

- search results summary
- news report date
- hyperlinks to general information resources
- hyperlink to related Web sites and news reports
- identity of news reports source

Top 10 matches. [89 hits. About Your Results]   Show Titles only   View by Publication   View by Date

Try these first:
Go to American Honda Motor Company Inc.'s web site
Go to the Excite Autos Channel
Web sites about Honda

amazon.com FIND RELATED BOOKS

67% CNN/SI - World Motor Sports - Spanish Grand Prix Results - May 3, 199... (CNN/SI)
Summary: CNN/SI - The Network. Copyright © 1998 CNN/SI.
First found: 3 May 1998 (Related Articles)

64% CNN/SI - World Motor Sports - Practice times for the Spanish Grand Pri... (CNN/SI)
Summary: 4 FREE Issues of SI. Listen to CNN/SI.
First found: 1 May 1998 (Related Articles)

64% American Announces April Honda Sales (Auto Channel, The)
Summary: Total sales of 86,886 were up 12.5 percent from April '97 and topped the previous record for the month of 79,221 set in 1989. Acura Division sales of 9,315 were up 8.4 percent, topped by record April sales of the CL luxury sports coupe and TL luxury sedan, up 29.2 percent and 12.4 percent respectively.
First found: 2 May 1998 (Related Articles)

63% CNN/SI - World Motor Sports - Spanish Grand Prix Starting Grid - May ... (CNN/SI)
Summary: Spanish Grand Prix Starting Grid Posted: Sat May 2, 1998 at 5:10 PM ET JEREZ, Spain (Reuters) -- Starting grid for the Spanish motorcycling Grand Prix on Sunday: 500cc 1. Carlos Checa (Spain) Honda 1 minute 43.467 seconds 2. Tadayuki Okada (Japan) Honda 1:43.627 3. Alex Criville (Spain) Honda 1:43.815 4. Max Biaggi (Italy) Honda 1:43.970 5. Michael Doohan (Australia) Honda 1:43.987 6. John...
First found: 2 May 1998 (Related Articles)

62% Official to Quit Healthy Honda (International Herald Tribune)
Summary: , Nobuhiko Kawamoto, said Monday that he would step down after eight years at the helm, leaving Honda about to post a record profit, in contrast to the troubles at rival Japanese carmakers. Kawamoto's departure coincides with the 50th anniversary of Honda's founding and with its preparations to return to Formula One racing after withdrawing from the sport in 1992.

5. Close your Web browser and your dial-up connection, if necessary.

The search results page returned by the NewsTracker tool provides some useful information. Search statistics appear at the top of the page, along with hyperlinks to sites that provide general information about your search term. Each news report entry includes a hyperlink to the Web site that contains the item, the news report's source, a brief summary, the date that NewsTracker's spider first found the item on the Web, and a hyperlink to a list of related news stories. After you have identified a useful item on the search results page, the Related Articles hyperlink for that item provides a useful way to narrow your search.

Now, you have accumulated a respectable list of URLs about Honda's expansion plans for Nancy. You have gained experience in searching for current topics by examining Web pages that have been modified recently and by using two tools that search the Web specifically for news reports. Before you use the information that you find on the Web, however, Nancy asks you to consider some important copyright issues.

Copyright Issues

When you use your Web browser to display text or a graphic image, or to play a sound or a video clip, your Web browser downloads the text or multimedia element from the Web server and stores it in a temporary file on your computer's hard drive. This process creates a new, intermediate level of ownership that did not exist before the emergence of the Web. For example, when you go to an art gallery and view a picture, you do not take possession of the picture in any way; in fact, if you went around touching all of the pictures in the gallery, someone would ask you to leave. When you visit an art gallery on the Web, however, your Web browser takes temporary possession of an electronic copy of the image. As you have learned in earlier tutorials, it is easy to make a permanent copy of Web page images, even though your copy might violate the image owner's rights.

Many people do not know this, but making a photocopy of a picture that appears in a book can be a copyright violation. Because computer files are even easier to copy than a picture in a book, the potential for Web copyright violations is much greater. Some uses of multimedia elements do not present a copyright violation, though. For example, some sites provide graphics files that are in the **public domain**, which means that you are free to copy the files as needed without requesting permission from the source. Even though you can freely use public domain information, you should check the site carefully for acknowledgement requirements about the material source when you use it. Acknowledging a source can be especially important when you use public domain material in papers, reports, or other school projects. Failure to cite the source of public domain material that you use can be a serious violation of your school's academic honesty policy. You should carefully examine any site from which you download files to determine what usage limitations apply to those files. If you cannot find a clear statement of copyright terms or a statement that the files are in the public domain, you should not use them on your Web page or anywhere else.

Quick Check

1. Explain why it is important to determine a Web page author's identity and credentials when you plan to use the page's information as a research resource.

2. What information about Web page authors can help you assess their objectivity with respect to the contents of their Web pages?

3. True or False: Domain names in URLs can help you assess the quality of Web pages.

4. How can you assess the quality of a Web page that deals with a subject area in which you are not very knowledgeable?

5. Briefly describe two ways that libraries use the Web.

6. True or False: The U.S. Library of Congress Web site includes hyperlinks to the full text of all U.S. Federal Court decisions.

7. What are the advantages of using online reference works such as dictionaries or encyclopedias instead of print editions?

8. The Reuters News Wire Service sells information to newspapers, broadcasters, and other firms. Why do you think they would provide some of this information on their Web page for free public access?

9. Compare the news-story indexing and retrieval capabilities of NewsHub and NewsTracker.

10. True or False: An image on a Web page that does not carry a copyright notice is in the public domain.

In the next session, you will learn how to use FTP to search a site and download data and programs.

SESSION 5.2

In this session you will learn what FTP is and how to use it to search a site and download a program. Then, you will learn how to upload information from your computer to another computer that is connected to the Internet.

What Is FTP and Why Do You Need It?

FTP, or **file transfer protocol**, is one of several services built into and supported by the Internet suite of protocols. FTP is the program for transferring files from one computer that is connected to the Internet to another computer that is connected to the Internet. When a file is transferred over the Internet—whether you are viewing it with a Web browser or not—FTP is responsible for sending the file between computers. Examples of files that you can send include spreadsheets, pictures, movies, sounds, programs, or documents. For example, if you want to send your résumé to a company, you can use FTP to upload the file to the company's computer. To **upload** a file means to send it from your computer to another computer. To **download** a file means to receive on your computer one or more files from another computer. Downloading is more common because people usually receive more files than they send to other computers. Whether files are uploaded or downloaded, FTP is the program that accomplishes the transfer. FTP can run from a Web browser, with an FTP client program, or through a command-line interface. A **command-line interface** is one in which you enter a command, press the Enter key, and then the receiving computer acts on the command you sent to it. This process continues until you have typed enough single-line commands to complete a task. An **FTP client** program is a Windows program that resides on your PC and transfers files between your computer and another computer connected to the Internet. Like any Windows client program, an FTP client program has a menu bar and, usually, one or more toolbars. Figure 5-12 shows a popular FTP client program, WS_FTP95 LE from Ipswitch, Inc., that is communicating with a remote computer.

Figure 5-12   **FTP CLIENT PROGRAM**

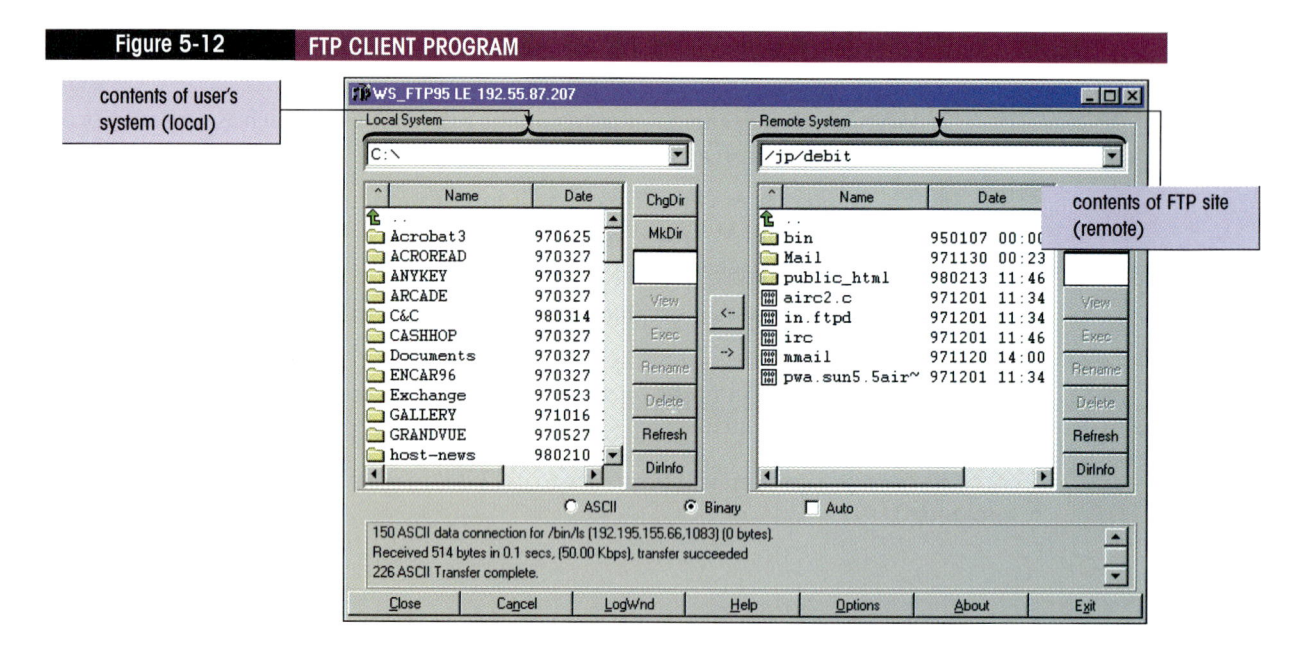

[Screenshot of WS_FTP95 LE showing Local System (C:\) with folders Acrobat3, ACROREAD, ANYKEY, ARCADE, C&C, CASHHOP, Documents, ENCAR96, Exchange, GALLERY, GRANDVUE, host-news, and Remote System (/jp/debit) with bin, Mail, public_html, airc2.c, in.ftpd, irc, mmail, pwa.sun5.5air~. Labels: "contents of user's system (local)" and "contents of FTP site (remote)".]

FTP programs that you execute using a command-line interface do not require Windows, but they are trickier to understand because you have to know a few commands to transfer files: commands such as *get*, *put*, *cd*, and others. Figure 5-13 shows an FTP session using a Telnet command-line FTP interface.

Figure 5-13   **FTP COMMAND-LINE INTERFACE USING TELNET**

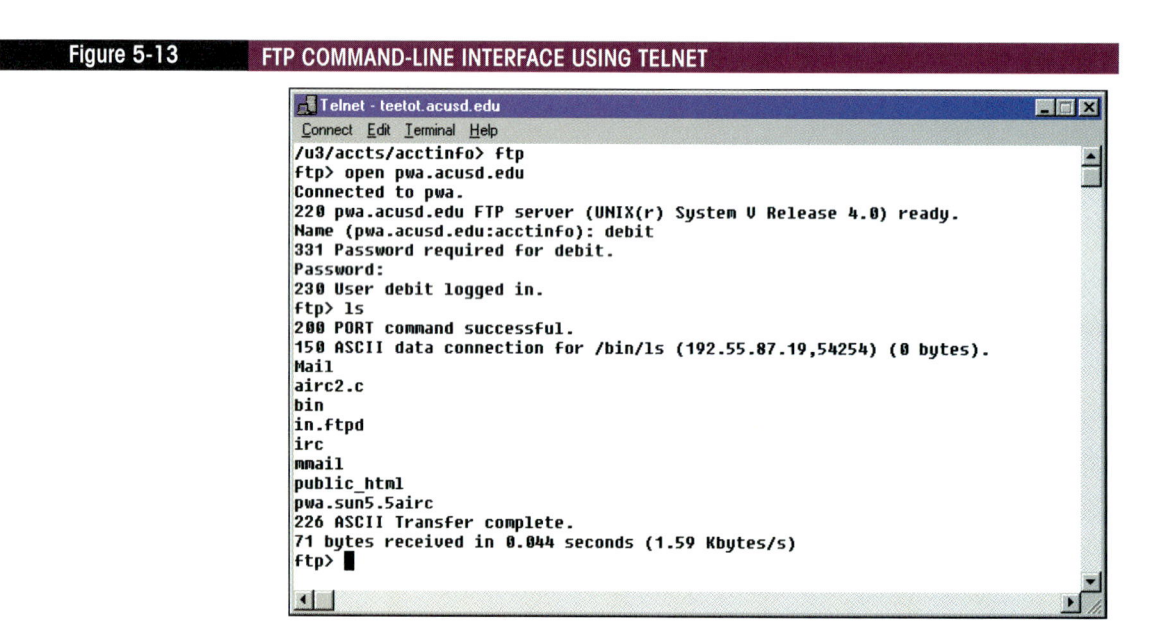

```
Telnet - teetot.acusd.edu
Connect  Edit  Terminal  Help
/u3/accts/acctinfo> ftp
ftp> open pwa.acusd.edu
Connected to pwa.
220 pwa.acusd.edu FTP server (UNIX(r) System V Release 4.0) ready.
Name (pwa.acusd.edu:acctinfo): debit
331 Password required for debit.
Password:
230 User debit logged in.
ftp> ls
200 PORT command successful.
150 ASCII data connection for /bin/ls (192.55.87.19,54254) (0 bytes).
Mail
airc2.c
bin
in.ftpd
irc
mmail
public_html
pwa.sun5.5airc
226 ASCII Transfer complete.
71 bytes received in 0.044 seconds (1.59 Kbytes/s)
ftp>
```

Like other Internet protocols, FTP follows the standard client/server model. The client FTP program resides on your computer. When you want to download or upload a file, you connect to a remote computer and request that the FTP server either receive files from you or transfer files from the remote computer to yours. An **FTP server** program receives file transfer requests from your FTP client program and then acts on those commands.

The FTP program manages the details of transferring files between your computer and the FTP server. FTP is operating-system neutral. For example, your PC might use FTP on a Windows 98 system while it is communicating with a large minicomputer running the FTP server on a UNIX operating system. It makes no difference that the operating systems are different on each computer; FTP seamlessly transfers files between them. If you know how to use a Web browser, then you already know how to use FTP. Web browsers support FTP and provide a simple and familiar interface for you to locate and download files. In this tutorial, you will learn how to transfer files using a standalone FTP program and a Web browser.

Accessing an FTP Server

To transfer files between your PC and another computer, first you must connect to the remote computer, which you can do by logging on to it directly or from your Web browser. (The Netscape Navigator and Microsoft Internet Explorer Web browsers both recognize the FTP protocol.) But you must identify yourself (or log on) to a remote computer in order to use it by supplying your user name and a password. Some computer systems provide public access to their computers, which means anyone can connect to the FTP site. When you connect to a publicly accessible site, you are restricted to particular files and directories on the public computer. Other systems allow restricted access to their computers. To access these computers, you must have an account on the computer.

Anonymous FTP

Logging on to one of the many publicly accessible, remote computers is known as an **anonymous login** because you enter the user name **anonymous**. You do not need a password to access public computers. However, it is both customary and polite to enter your full e-mail address when you are prompted for your password. That way, the organization hosting your access can identify which groups are accessing the public areas of their computer. When you transfer files—either by downloading or uploading—using an anonymous connection, you are participating in an **anonymous FTP session**. Figure 5-14 shows an example of an anonymous login.

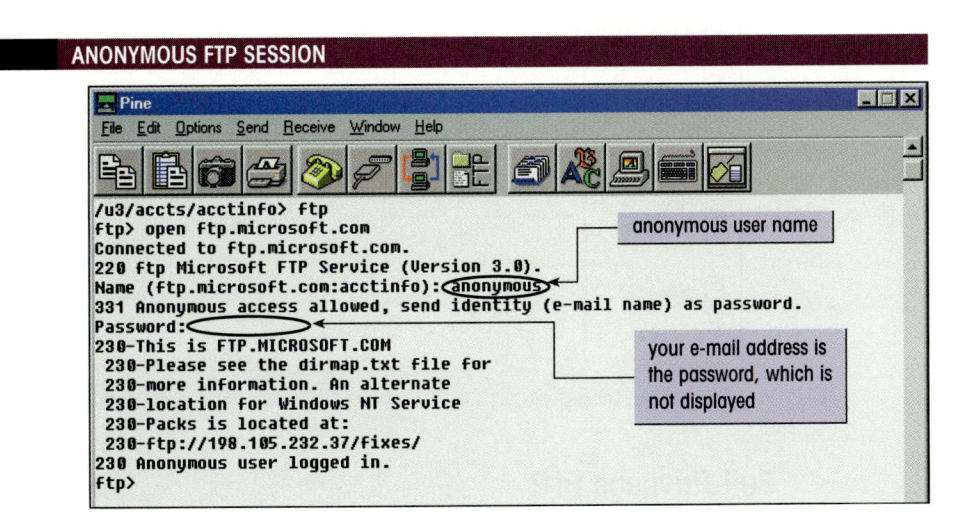

| Figure 5-14 | ANONYMOUS FTP SESSION |

```
/u3/accts/acctinfo> ftp
ftp> open ftp.microsoft.com
Connected to ftp.microsoft.com.
220 ftp Microsoft FTP Service (Version 3.0).
Name (ftp.microsoft.com:acctinfo): anonymous     ← anonymous user name
331 Anonymous access allowed, send identity (e-mail name) as password.
Password:                                         ← your e-mail address is
230-This is FTP.MICROSOFT.COM                       the password, which is
 230-Please see the dirmap.txt file for             not displayed
 230-more information. An alternate
 230-location for Windows NT Service
 230-Packs is located at:
 230-ftp://198.105.232.37/fixes/
230 Anonymous user logged in.
ftp>
```

There are many anonymous FTP computers connected to the Internet. You can use these anonymous computers to download many valuable and interesting files. Usually, you will use anonymous FTP to transfer files from another computer to your PC. Very infrequently, if ever, will you use full-privilege FTP. You rarely will need to subscribe to an FTP computer where you are given full access because most FTP computers allow anonymous logins. However, anonymous FTP computer sites impose limits on what you can do. Most publicly accessible computers prevent you from uploading files or provide only one publicly accessible directory to which you can upload files. Usually, anonymous FTP computers limit your access to selected directories and files on their systems. Anyone who logs on anonymously cannot open and view all the directories and files on the system. You can store uploaded files in a special directory accessible to all anonymous users called *pub* (short for *public*), if it exists. Other directories on the computer might not be accessible. You can determine which directories you can access by experimenting. If you attempt to open other directories or examine files in other directories that are not accessible, you will receive an error or warning message indicating that you do not have access to a particular area when the system enforces access restrictions. It is unlikely that the "security police" will cite you for a violation, but you should obey all rules and regulations regarding anonymous access. Remember that you are using another person's or organization's computer at no cost to download files for your use.

You can connect to an anonymous FTP site using a Web browser, such as Navigator or Internet Explorer. When you connect to an FTP site using a Web browser, the browser automatically supplies the user name *anonymous* and an appropriate password to access the computer. Figure 5-15 shows the Navigator browser with a connection to the FTP address for the Microsoft FTP site. Web browsers automatically understand how to handle FTP communications: you simply type **ftp://** instead of **http://** and the site's full URL to indicate that you want to use the FTP protocol and access an FTP site.

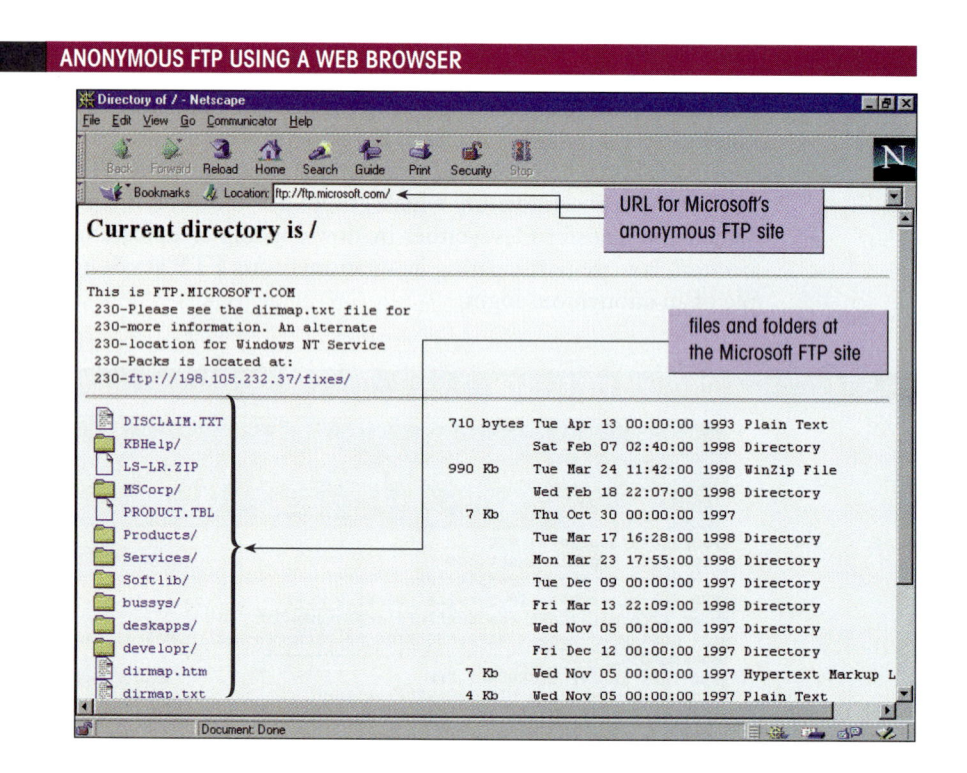

Figure 5-15 ANONYMOUS FTP USING A WEB BROWSER

Full-Privilege FTP

Logging on to a computer on which you have an account (with a user name and password) and using it to send and receive files is called **named FTP**, or **full-privilege FTP**. Even though you might have an account on a particular machine, if such as your school's computer, you probably are limited to reading and writing files from and to a particular selection of directories. When you log on to a computer with your user name and password, the system automatically directs you to a particular directory on that computer. Usually, you have full read and write access rights within that directory. Having named FTP access is convenient when you want to send a file to your company branch office or your account on the school's computer from another computer connected to the Internet. Anyone who develops Web pages will enjoy the convenience of full-privilege FTP. You can develop Web pages on your PC using any of several full-featured Web page-design programs, such as Microsoft's FrontPage or Adobe's Page Mill. When your Web pages are complete, you can upload them to your own directory on the Internet available through your Internet service provider (ISP) or your school. That Web space can be altered only if you use the correct user name and corresponding password. Of course, anyone can read your Web pages, but no one can change them without full-privilege FTP access. When you have an account on a computer that is connected to the Internet, typically you can store larger files for longer periods than you could on an anonymous FTP computer.

FTP Software

You learned that there are two general classes of FTP programs available: Windows-based (GUI) and command-line FTP clients. GUI FTP client programs are commonly used on Windows PCs. Command-line FTP programs are used on nongraphical interfaces, such as UNIX computer systems. You can use either an FTP client program or your Web browser to access FTP sites. If you use a graphical FTP client, be aware that the FTP client programs have two distinct advantages over Web browsers. First, FTP client programs usually transfer files faster than a Web browser. Second, when you use a Web browser to transfer files, it automatically determines if a file is ASCII or binary and then transfers the file in that mode. (ASCII and binary files and transfer modes are described later in this session.) If the browser makes a bad determination, it can corrupt the transferred files. FTP clients do not make this file type determination, so *you* are able to determine a file's type and set it properly with an FTP client program.

The choice of FTP program depends on your situation. If you are traveling and have dial-up access to your school's or company's computer with a UNIX operating system, then the best (or only) choice is to use command-line FTP. Then, you start an FTP program by typing *ftp* on the system prompt line and enter a series of one-word commands, one at a time, to establish your FTP session and upload or download files.

Fortunately, there are many FTP clients available, and all of them provide basic file transfer service. FTP client programs allow you to log on anonymously or log on with a user name and password for full-privilege FTP service. There are dozens, if not hundreds, of FTP clients from which you can choose, and most are either free or inexpensive. FTP clients provide many features that vary from one product to another. An FTP client program provides the following desirable features, although no single FTP program supports *all* of these features:

- Provides multipane displays so you can see both the local and remote computer directories simultaneously.
- Allows you to transfer many files in one FTP session.
- Permits drag and drop file transfer so you can drag a file from one pane (the remote computer) and drop it on the other pane (the local computer).
- Simplifies deleting directories and files on remote and local computers.
- Displays a familiar and comfortable Windows Explorer style appearance for both the local and remote computers.
- Allows you to set up scheduled file transfers so selected files can be transmitted automatically at a designated future date and time.

- Gracefully recovers from interrupted file transfers by continuing from the point where the transfer was interrupted.
- Automatically reconnects to sites that disconnect you when your connection exceeds the maximum connect time.

Many GUI FTP clients are easy to use because they have menus, toolbars, and help files to simplify the process of connecting and transferring files. However, an FTP client has one major advantage over a Web browser when transferring files: Whereas Web browsers and FTP clients both allow you to download files from the Internet, you can use only an FTP client program to upload a file using a full-privilege FTP connection. So, if you are traveling and want to send a file from a branch office back to your account in another city, then you must use an FTP client, and not a Web browser, to transfer the file. On the other hand, you will be downloading files most of the time using anonymous FTP, so a Web browser is all you need to download files from a remote computer to your PC. Figure 5-16 shows an FTP client program before it logs on to a remote computer.

Figure 5-16   LOGGING ON TO A REMOTE COMPUTER WITH AN FTP CLIENT

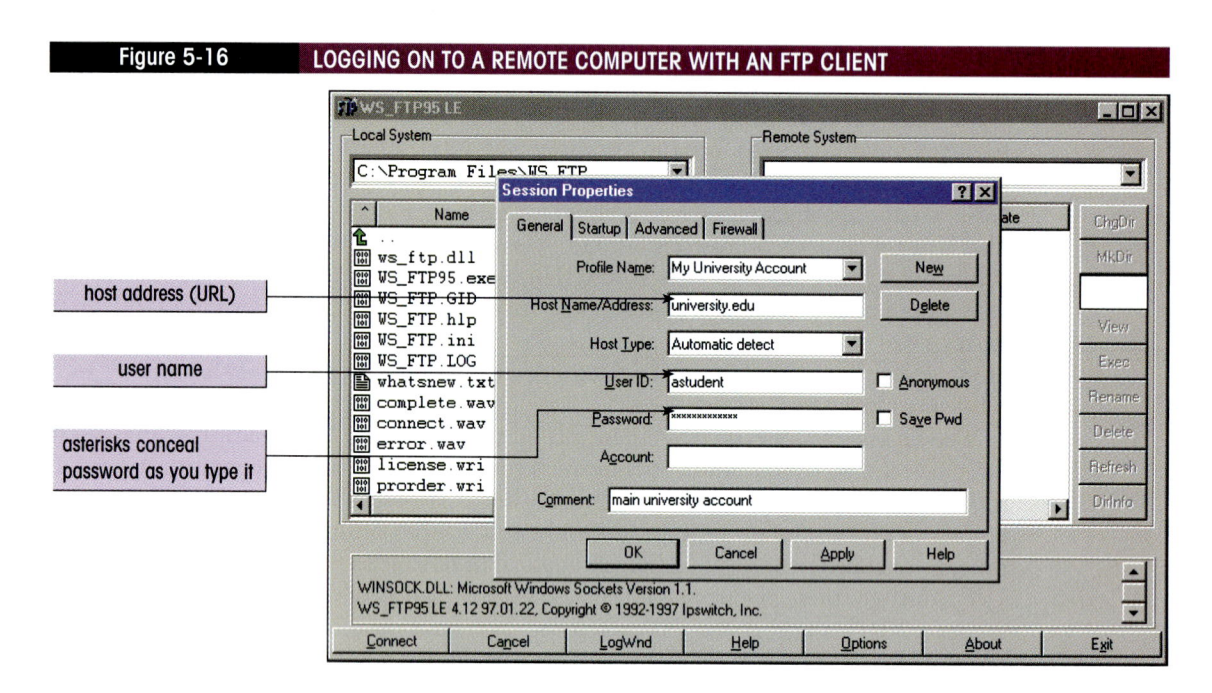

- host address (URL)
- user name
- asterisks conceal password as you type it

Figure 5-16 illustrates the login screen for the WS_FTP95 LE FTP client. (The Student Online Companion page for Session 5.2 contains a link to this and other Web sites that you can use to download FTP clients.) The user enters the remote computer's Internet address in the Host Name/Address text box, a user name in the User ID text box, and a password in the Password text box. This information establishes a full-privilege FTP connection. You can establish an anonymous FTP connection by entering the computer's Internet address, the user ID *anonymous* in the User ID text box, and your full e-mail address in the Password text box. If you click the Anonymous check box, the software will automatically enter *anonymous* in the User ID text box. In either case—full-privilege or anonymous—you click the OK button to transmit the login information to the remote computer and start the FTP session. Other FTP clients use a similar process to start the FTP session.

Locating Files and Exploring Directories

Because you are familiar with one or more Web browsers and know how hyperlinks work, you will have no difficulty navigating an FTP site in search of files. Using FTP is especially easy when you use a Web browser to log on to an FTP site anonymously. When you need to upload files to a site requiring full-privilege FTP access rights, then you will want to use an FTP client. FTP clients are simple to master.

FTP Hyperlinks

When you visit an FTP site, your first goal should be to become familiar with its organization. FTP sites are organized hierarchically. A **hierarchical structure** is organized like an upside-down tree. When you access an FTP site, you are at the site's **root directory**, or the **home directory** or **top-level directory**. Beneath the root directory are several "branches" corresponding to other directories that contain files and other directories, as shown in Figure 5-17. Most sites prevent you from moving to a directory that is above the FTP root directory, which is restricted for anonymous FTP users. When you visit a root directory for the first time, a brief message indicates which file contains important information about the site. To search an FTP site for files you want to download, you need to understand how to interpret FTP screens and how to navigate directory hyperlinks to other directories.

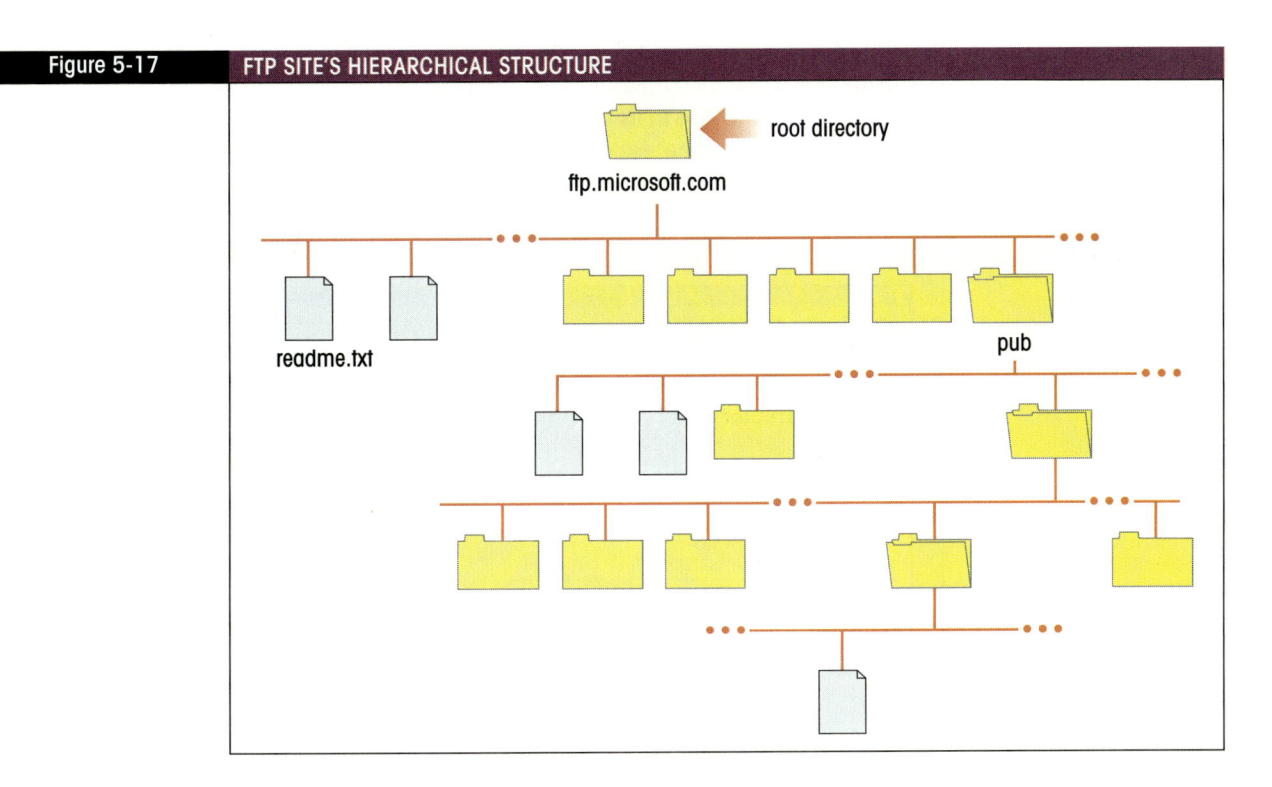

Figure 5-17 | FTP SITE'S HIERARCHICAL STRUCTURE

Regardless of what software you use to access an FTP site, the FTP site will look about the same and include two types of hyperlinks. A directory hyperlink will take you to another level in the hierarchical structure—to a page with more links. The other type of hyperlink represents a file. Clicking this hyperlink will either open the file so you can view it or will begin downloading the file to your computer. FTP client software displays different icons to distinguish between the two types of hyperlinks.

Of course, the two types of hyperlinks behave differently when you click them. If you are using a Web browser as your FTP program, clicking a file hyperlink might open the file or download the file to your computer after you respond to a dialog box requesting permission to download. Clicking a directory hyperlink opens the directory and reveals the directories and files within it—at the next level down the hierarchy. Whether you use a browser, FTP client, or command-line FTP program, the FTP server provides a special return link that takes you up one level in the directory hierarchy when you are not at the root directory. In some browsers and FTP client programs, the return link is a special icon that is a right angle arrow that points up. Usually, this link contains the text "Up to higher level directory" and appears at the top of a page.

Because Nancy has asked you to supply a standard inventory of Internet programs, you want to visit an FTP site using a Web browser to see exactly what the DigiComm staff will see. Besides, you know that Nancy expects you to aid the DigiComm training staff when they instruct the installation teams. Therefore, you want to view several FTP sites and try to predict if the installation team members might encounter problems as they use the Internet software you will install on their computers.

To open an FTP site using any Web browser:

1. Start your Web browser, and then go to the Student Online Companion page by entering the URL **http://www.course.com/NewPerspectives/Internet** in the appropriate location in your Web browser. Click the hyperlink for your book, click the **Tutorial 5** link, and then click the **Session 5.2** link. Click the **Microsoft FTP** link and wait while the browser loads the page. Microsoft's FTP server displays the directories and files in its root directory, as shown in Figure 5-18, which accesses the site using Internet Explorer. Your screen might be different because the site's contents change regularly.

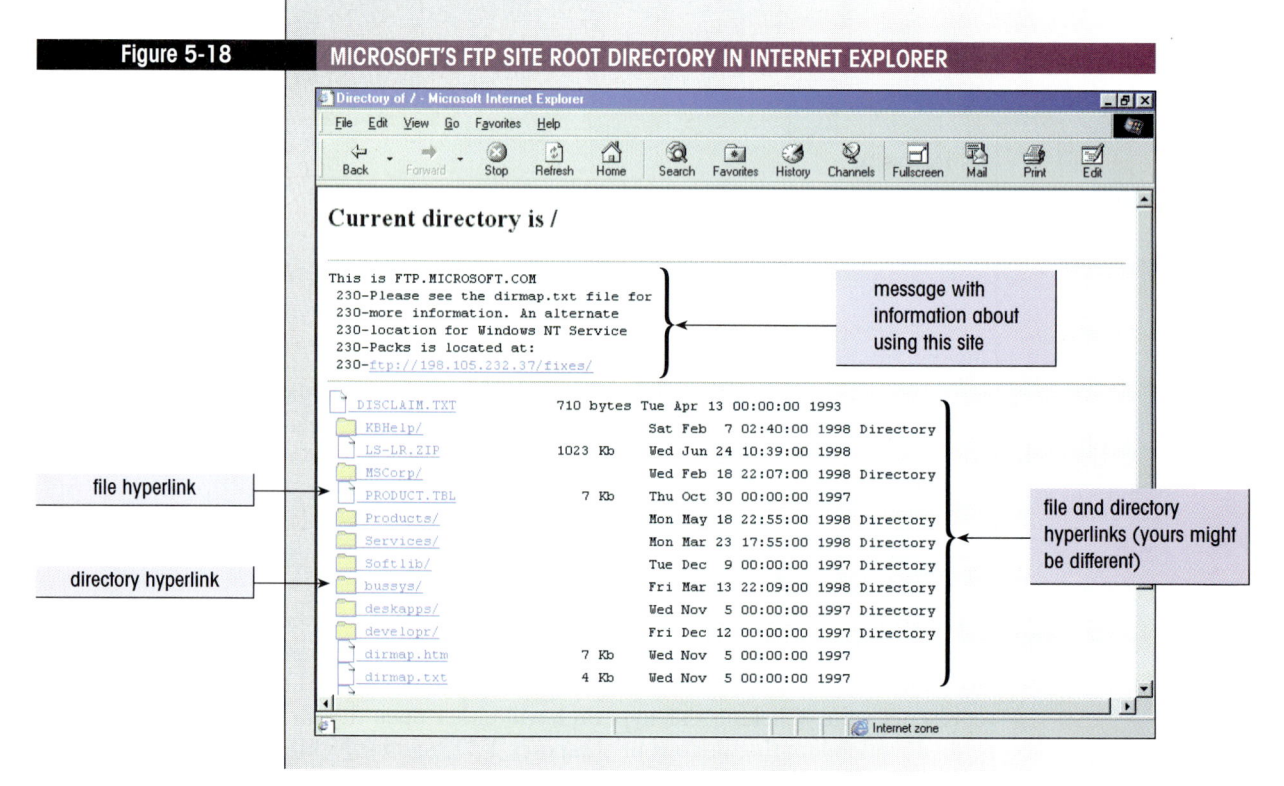

Figure 5-18   MICROSOFT'S FTP SITE ROOT DIRECTORY IN INTERNET EXPLORER

Regardless of which browser you are using, you notice that directories are labeled as such next to the hyperlink. File hyperlinks display the file size to the left of the filename hyperlink. Unlike Internet Explorer, Navigator shows folder icons for directories and page icons for files (see Figure 5-19).

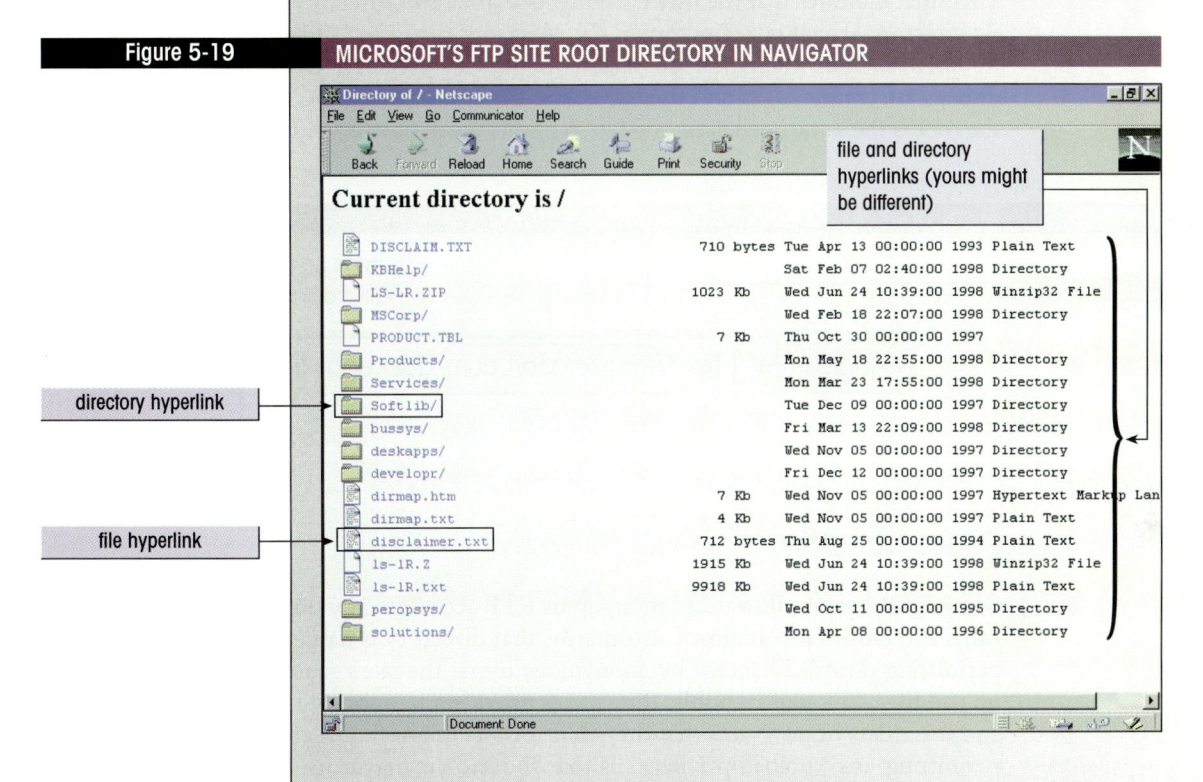

Figure 5-19 **MICROSOFT'S FTP SITE ROOT DIRECTORY IN NAVIGATOR**

```
Current directory is /

  DISCLAIM.TXT            710 bytes   Tue Apr 13 00:00:00 1993  Plain Text
  KBHelp/                             Sat Feb 07 02:40:00 1998  Directory
  LS-LR.ZIP              1023 Kb      Wed Jun 24 10:39:00 1998  Winzip32 File
  MSCorp/                             Wed Feb 18 22:07:00 1998  Directory
  PRODUCT.TBL               7 Kb      Thu Oct 30 00:00:00 1997
  Products/                           Mon May 18 22:55:00 1998  Directory
  Services/                           Mon Mar 23 17:55:00 1998  Directory
  Softlib/                            Tue Dec 09 00:00:00 1997  Directory
  bussys/                             Fri Mar 13 22:09:00 1998  Directory
  deskapps/                           Wed Nov 05 00:00:00 1997  Directory
  developr/                           Fri Dec 12 00:00:00 1997  Directory
  dirmap.htm                7 Kb      Wed Nov 05 00:00:00 1997  Hypertext Markup Lan
  dirmap.txt                4 Kb      Wed Nov 05 00:00:00 1997  Plain Text
  disclaimer.txt          712 bytes   Thu Aug 25 00:00:00 1994  Plain Text
  ls-lR.Z                1915 Kb      Wed Jun 24 10:39:00 1998  Winzip32 File
  ls-lR.txt              9918 Kb      Wed Jun 24 10:39:00 1998  Plain Text
  peropsys/                           Wed Oct 11 00:00:00 1995  Directory
  solutions/                          Mon Apr 08 00:00:00 1996  Directory
```

file and directory hyperlinks (yours might be different)

directory hyperlink

file hyperlink

2. Locate and then click the **deskapps** (or **deskapps/**) directory link to move down one level in the directory hierarchy. The new page that opens lists a set of directories with familiar names, such as access, excel, and word. Notice at the top of the page is an "Up to higher level directory" link that leads back to the root directory where you started. The hyperlink might be an icon or a text hyperlink, depending on your browser.

3. Click the **Up to higher level directory** link to return to the previous page. You also could use your browser's Back button to return to the previous Web page.

4. Click the **dirmap.txt** file hyperlink to open the page that lists files and directories available on the entire Microsoft FTP site. Sometimes, you might find site information in the readme.txt or about.txt files. You might encounter other names, but they all serve the same function—that is, to provide an overview of the site's structure and file locations.

5. Use your browser's **Print** button to print the site map so you can use it as a reference while you are visiting the site.

6. Close your Web browser, and close your dial-up connection, if necessary.

If you get lost in an FTP directory structure, there is a simple way to determine your location and get back to the root directory. (Remember the inverted-tree analogy: "up" a tree means moving toward the root of the tree from one of its branches, or directories, in this analogy.) Look at the URL in your browser's address field, which lists all the directories that lead to your current location. As you move deeper down the directory hierarchy, a forward slash (/) separates the individual directory names. To move back toward the root directory, click at the end of the URL and press the Backspace key to delete the rightmost (or current) directory name. Then press the Enter key to move up to the previous directory. Figure 5-20 shows a URL that indicates that the user currently is in the /unix directory, which is a directory in the /ie directory, which is a directory in the /deskapps directory, which is a directory in the root ftp.microsoft.com directory. To return to the /ie directory, you can delete the "/unix/" directory from the URL and then press the Enter key. Using the URL to move back toward the root is the same as clicking the Up to higher level directory link.

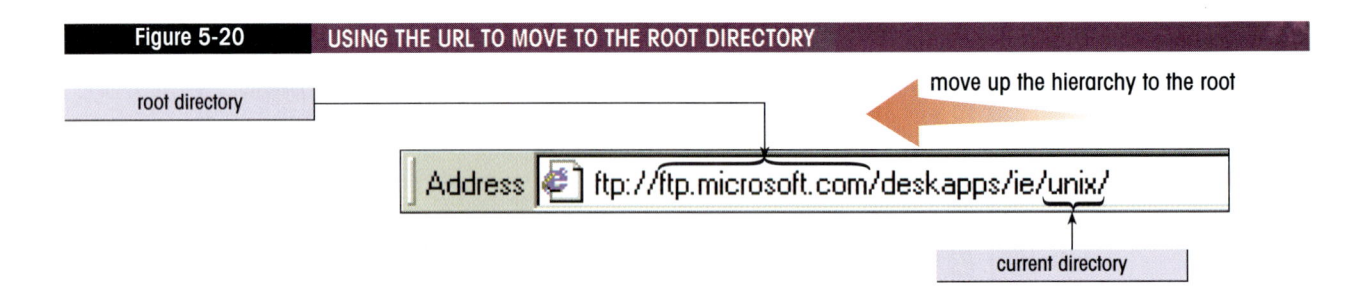

Figure 5-20 USING THE URL TO MOVE TO THE ROOT DIRECTORY

root directory

move up the hierarchy to the root

Address: ftp://ftp.microsoft.com/deskapps/ie/unix/

current directory

Public Directory

Some FTP servers allow users anonymous FTP access to only one directory and any files or other directories it contains. Customarily, that directory is named pub (for public). Besides permitting download access by anonymous users, the site's manager might allow users to upload files. Frequently, public directories provide a temporary location for users to upload and share data or programs that they think others might find useful. One problem with sites permitting users upload privileges is that the site's manager (or webmaster) must monitor the files uploaded to a public directory on a regular basis. In addition to worrying about harmful programs that might be hidden in uploaded programs, the site manager must find and delete any copyrighted programs that were uploaded to the site illegally for public use. For example, uploading a program such as Microsoft Word to a public directory is a clear copyright violation because Microsoft's license agreement prohibits you from sharing your program with other users. Many FTP sites have specific policies that force you to acknowledge, before you upload files, that you are the owner of the material or that its transfer to the FTP site will not violate any copyright or intellectual property restrictions. There are many legitimate uses for public directories, such as sharing data or results that you have accumulated with others. Just be sure that someone else does not hold the copyright to the data or results you are sharing.

Most sites have extensive rules about acceptable use of both the anonymous FTP in general and any public directory in particular. Be sure to read the site's "readme" files to learn about any rules about acceptable use when you enter an FTP site.

Downloading Files

Frequently, you use FTP to download free programs, data files, and software patches (programs that correct known problems in a particular application) from many different sites. Many software vendors use the Internet to distribute and sell new software releases. When you want the latest version of a particular program, you can browse the vendor's Web site, submit your address and credit card information, and then download a program. Software is delivered directly to your computer, and you avoid having to go to a store to purchase the software in person. You can download software and data using a command-line FTP program, a Windows FTP client program, or your Web browser. To download files using a command-line FTP program, you must first log on to an FTP site using a Telnet session. A **Telnet session** occurs when you establish a connection on the Internet with another computer and log on to it with a user name and password. Telnet is one of the several protocols that the Internet supports. Once you are connected, you can navigate the directories and locate files and programs you want to download.

Using either an FTP client or a Web browser simplifies locating and downloading files. To download a file using a command-line FTP program, you must understand and use commands such as *cd* and *mget* to download files. With an FTP client or a Web browser, you click the mouse to download files.

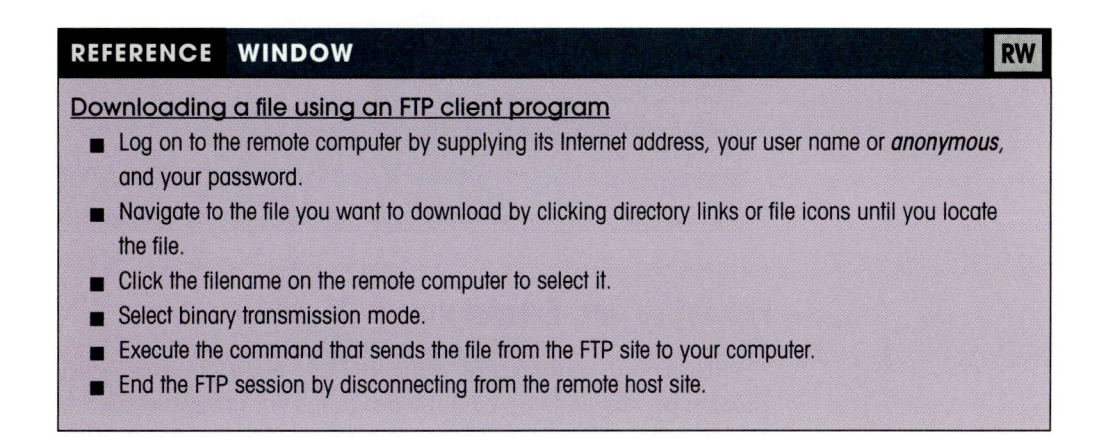

REFERENCE WINDOW

Downloading a file using an FTP client program
- Log on to the remote computer by supplying its Internet address, your user name or *anonymous*, and your password.
- Navigate to the file you want to download by clicking directory links or file icons until you locate the file.
- Click the filename on the remote computer to select it.
- Select binary transmission mode.
- Execute the command that sends the file from the FTP site to your computer.
- End the FTP session by disconnecting from the remote host site.

Why do you need to know about the transmission mode mentioned earlier? The next section describes the two FTP transmission modes.

File Transfer Modes

Many files, including Web pages and e-mail messages, consist of ASCII, or plain text. **ASCII text** contains symbols typed from the keyboard and does not include any nonprintable, binary codes. Besides ASCII, many files, such as pictures, movies, sound clips, and graphics, are **binary**. Any file created by a word-processing program or a file containing character formatting, such as bold or italicized text, is binary. FTP can handle both ASCII and binary files easily. You select which of the two **file transfer modes**—ASCII or binary—that you want to use before transferring the file. Choose **ASCII mode** to transfer plain-text files; select **binary mode** for transferring everything else. People usually read plain-text files, whereas computer programs, such as Word or Excel, read binary files. Although it is important to distinguish between the two types of files, they are related. ASCII characters or codes are actually a subset of the larger binary code set. That is, all ASCII characters also are binary characters. The opposite is not true; not all binary representations or codes are ASCII characters. People cannot read many binary codes— only computer programs can make sense of them. If you open a file and it contains gibberish—a lot of codes—then you have chosen the wrong transfer mode. Simply execute the FTP operation again using the correct transfer mode.

If you download a program, be sure to select binary mode. Programs contain binary data that will be destroyed if you transfer it as ASCII text. You should transfer ASCII files in ASCII mode. Figure 5-21 shows an FTP client with the binary mode option selected.

Figure 5-21 FTP SESSION USING BINARY FILE TRANSFER MODE

[Screenshot of WS_FTP95 LE ftp.qualcomm.com window showing Local System (c:\) with folders Acrobat3, ACROREAD, ANYKEY, ARCADE, C&C, CASHHOP, Documents, ENCAR96, Exchange, GALLERY, GRANDVUE, host-news and Remote System (/eudora) with folders central, developers, eims1, eims2, elight_kit, eudoralight, eudorapro, migration_uti~, misc, nowsoft, planner, pubs. Binary radio button selected.]

binary transfer mode selected

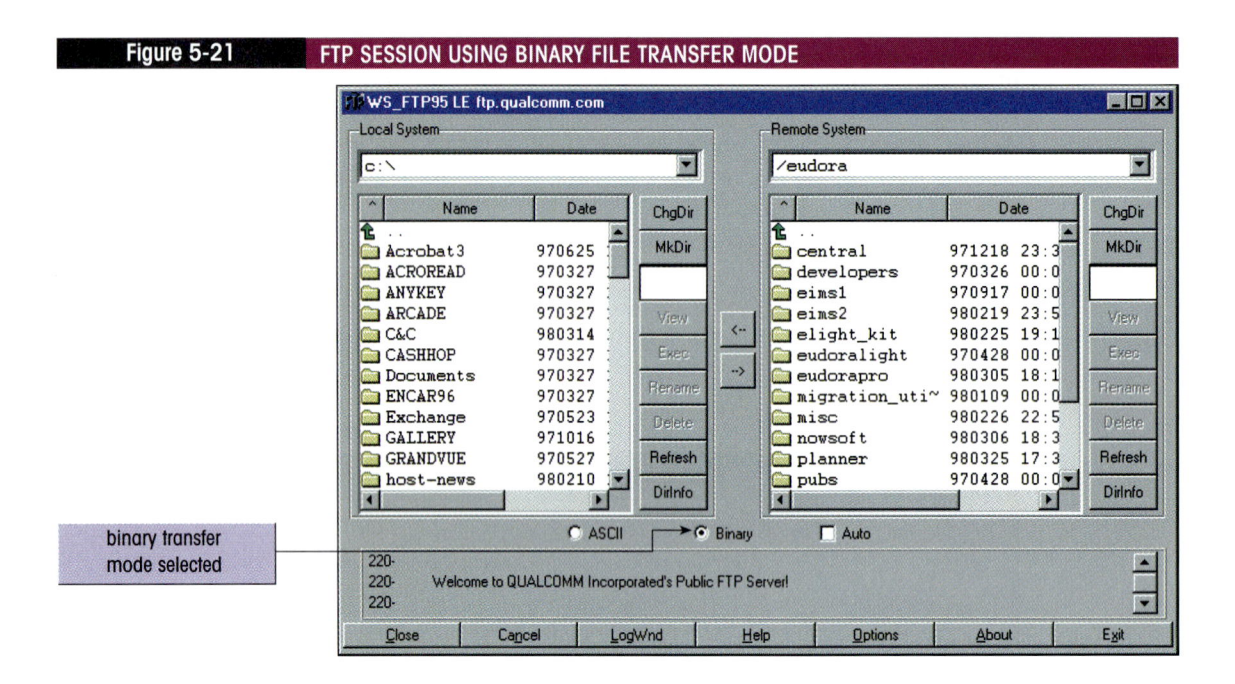

File Types and Extensions

The decision to transfer a file using binary or ASCII mode is largely determined by noting a file's type—much like Windows programs do. Programs such as Excel, Word, or Internet Explorer determine a file's type by its file extension. A **file extension**, or simply an **extension**, is the last three characters following the period in the filename. You can download files with a file extension of .txt in ASCII mode. For other file types, you should use binary FTP mode. It is helpful to understand the relationship between a file's extension and programs that manipulate that file type. That way, you can determine a file's general use before you download it.

File extensions are added automatically by the program that created the file based on a widely agreed-upon convention for associating files with programs. Filenames without periods (called "dots") do not have file extensions. Your PC operating system (Windows, for example) keeps track of most file extension associations and maintains a list of file extensions and programs that can open files with those extensions. Each computer that you use maintains different information about the file types stored on that computer. You can use Windows Explorer to learn about the file associations for your computer.

To view Windows file extension associations:

1. Click the **Start** button on the taskbar, point to **Programs**, and then click **Windows Explorer** to start the program.

2. Click **View** on the menu bar, and then click **Folder Options** (or **Options**) to open that dialog box.

3. Click the **File Types** tab to see your computer's file types and the programs it uses to open those files. This list is known as the **registered file types**. Figure 5-22 shows the registered file types for one user's computer; your list probably will be different. The file types are registered each time you install a new software program, so your list of registered file types depends on what programs are installed on your computer.

Figure 5-22 VIEWING YOUR COMPUTER'S REGISTERED FILE TYPES

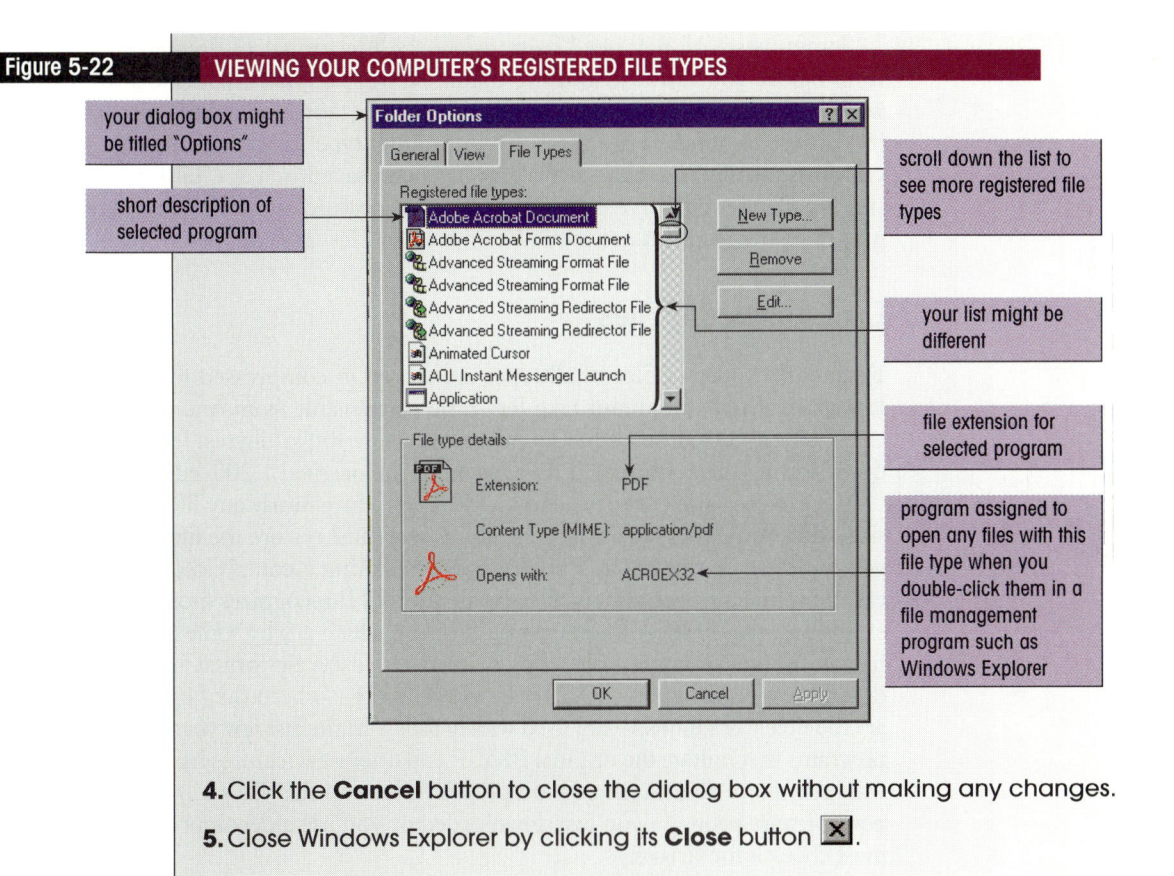

- your dialog box might be titled "Options"
- short description of selected program
- scroll down the list to see more registered file types
- your list might be different
- file extension for selected program
- program assigned to open any files with this file type when you double-click them in a file management program such as Windows Explorer

4. Click the **Cancel** button to close the dialog box without making any changes.
5. Close Windows Explorer by clicking its **Close** button ☒.

Figure 5-23 shows several filenames with common file extensions, transfer modes, and programs that open them. Don't worry about remembering all of the different file extensions. You will encounter only a small number of the listed extensions repeatedly. Most often, you will see files on the Internet with extensions of .doc, .exe, .html, .txt, or .zip. At first, the .doc extension might be confusing because on most computers, any file with the .doc extension indicates a Microsoft Word document. This is not the case on the Internet. Some Internet files with the .doc extension are plain-text files, where the .doc extension is short for "documentation."

Figure 5-23 COMMON INTERNET FILE EXTENSIONS, TRANSFER MODES, AND ASSOCIATED PROGRAMS

FILENAME AND EXTENSION	EXTENSION	TRANSFER MODE	TYPE OF FILE
Picture.bmp	.bmp	Binary	Microsoft Paint
Readme.doc	.doc	ASCII	Plain-text document
Spinner.exe	.exe	Binary	Program
Image.gif	.gif	Binary	Image
Index.html	.html	ASCII	Web page
Employee.mdb	.mdb	Binary	Access database
Help.pdf	.pdf	Binary	Acrobat portable document
Marketing.ppt	.ppt	Binary	PowerPoint slides
Sample.txt	.txt	ASCII	Notepad text file
Profit.xls	.xls	Binary	Excel workbook
File.zip	.zip	Binary	Compressed file

Sometimes, you will need to translate the file format of downloaded files into another form before you can read and use them. To translate files, you use a **file utility program**, which is a computer program that transforms the downloaded file into a form that is usable on your computer. The most common file type that you find on the Internet is a **compressed file**, which is a file that has been saved in a special format that makes its file size smaller to conserve space and shorten download time. There are many file utility programs that you can use to read compressed files, as described next.

Decompressing Files

Frequently, Internet files of all types are stored in compressed form. Compressed files use less space when stored and take less time to transmit from one computer to another. For example, a 1,200-kilobyte file might compress to 400 kilobytes. Imagine the time savings of downloading the compressed file instead of the original 1,200-kilobyte file.

You can use a **file compression** program to reduce nearly any file to a fraction of its original size. After you download a compressed file, you must restore the file to its original form before you can open or execute it. The process of restoring a compressed file to its original form is called **file decompression**, or **file expansion**. FTP recognizes most compressed files by their extensions; the most common extension is .zip, which is why some people refer to compressed files as **zip files** or **zipped files**. Phil Katz invented the zip format and his file compression and decompression programs, PKZIP and PKUNZIP—where the "PK" program name prefixes are the inventor's initials—are used widely today. In the last few years, many other compression programs that imitate the original PKZIP and offer new features have flooded the market. (You will learn more about compression programs later in this tutorial.) But before you install that new software program you just downloaded or you use a decompressed spreadsheet, first you must check it for viruses.

Checking Files for Viruses

For anyone using the Internet, computer viruses pose a real and potentially costly threat. Computer viruses made their debut shortly after 1985 and have evolved from a nuisance to a hazard for your computer. Computer **viruses** are programs that "infect" your computer and cause harm to your disk or programs. People create viruses by coding programs that attach themselves invisibly to other programs you have on your computer. Some viruses simply display an annoying or silly message on your screen and then go away, whereas others can cause real harm by reformatting your hard drive or changing all of your file extensions. You have to know how to detect and eradicate virus programs if you plan to download anything—including data, programs, or e-mail attachments from either reputable or questionable sources—from the Internet.

Virus detection software regularly scans the files on your disk looking for any infected files. It recognizes infected files by a signature that known viruses carry. A **virus signature** is a sequence (string) of characters that is always present in a particular virus program. A virus detection program can scan a single file, folder, or your entire hard drive looking for infected files. When the virus detection software spots a virus signature, it warns you. You can either erase the file containing the virus or ask the virus detection program to remove the virus. **Virus cleaning software** physically removes the virus from files, rendering the infected program "healthy" again.

Uploading Files

Periodically, you might want to upload one or more of your files to another host computer, either to share it with the world or to provide a private copy to an individual. This process of uploading a file is the reverse of downloading one. First, you should check the file(s) for viruses. If your file is large, or if you want to combine several files into one file, then you should compress the file(s) before uploading them to save time in transit and space on the destination computer. With full-privilege access to another computer, you can send the file to a particular folder on another machine. Without full-privilege access, you are restricted to uploading a file to a publicly accessible directory on a remote host.

The job of uploading files falls to either an FTP client program or a command-line FTP program. Though they do a good job uploading files, Web browsers are awkward, at best, when it comes to uploading files. You also can upload files by sending them as e-mail attachments. That may work, but if you send a large file, the recipient might not be able to receive it because many e-mail systems will not transfer files over one or two megabytes, and sometimes a single attachment can easily exceed that limit. If you can choose between using an FTP client program or a command-line FTP program, select the FTP client program because it is intuitive and much easier to use. If you must use a command-line FTP program, then you will need to learn commands to transfer files and navigate FTP folders. You will use both types of programs in this tutorial.

REFERENCE WINDOW	RW

Uploading a file using an FTP client program
- Log on to the remote computer by supplying its Internet address, your user name or *anonymous*, and your password (your full e-mail address if using anonymous FTP).
- Navigate to the folder into which you want to upload the file.
- Click the filename of the local PC file on your computer to upload.
- Select the appropriate transmission mode.
- Click the button or execute the command that sends the file from your PC to the remote computer.
- End the FTP session by logging off and disconnecting from the remote host site.

Compressing and Uploading Files

You can compress files that you upload to another computer to save time and file space. To compress files, you need a compression program. You can download compression programs from the Internet—many programs are free or ask you to send the developer a small licensing fee. Fortunately, nearly all compression programs available on the Internet allow you to try them before you make a purchase decision. In addition to PC compression programs, larger UNIX-based machines provide a built-in compression program that you can run by typing the *compress* command at the UNIX prompt. You can choose to compress files on your PC and then upload them or you can upload them to a UNIX machine and compress them there. The Additional Information section of the Student Online Companion contains links to FTP client program Web sites so you can learn about and download these programs.

You can upload a file with anonymous FTP or full-privilege FTP. With anonymous FTP, most sites to which you are uploading files restrict where you can place files. Sometimes a site also restricts maximum file sizes and the length of time the uploaded files can stay on the site. You already might be familiar with FTP as a means of submitting homework assignments to your instructors. Students and other users frequently use anonymous FTP to upload group projects to university or other publicly accessible sites so each member of the group can access the project files. Most files must be placed in the public directory, and they often have a maximum life span of a few days or weeks. The site's manager determines how long files can remain in the public directory. Usually, the file-deletion schedule and other policy statements stored are in the readme or readme.txt file in the public directory. If you find a file by that name or one like it, be sure to read it carefully.

Freeware, Shareware, and Limited-Use Software

Internet surfers often are pleasantly surprised to discover that many Internet programs are available for downloading at little or no cost. The Internet provides a perfect incubator for programmers who want to test their software in the "real world" or who simply want to demonstrate their programming prowess by providing limited editions of their work for free. When you freely share software, the developer makes the software available for free and requests that any users provide the developer with usage feedback. Later, a new, better version of the software becomes available at little or no cost. Anyone who has used the software and likes it usually is willing to pay a small amount to upgrade to the latest version. Software that is available to anyone for no cost and with no restrictions attached to its user is called **freeware**. Anyone who uses freeware does so with the implicit or explicit knowledge that the software might contain errors, called **bugs**, that could cause the program to halt or misbehave or even to do some real damage to the user's computer. The main risk associated with using freeware is that it is sometimes not well-tested and as a result, might contain a lot of bugs. The software's developer rarely is liable for any damage that the freeware program might cause. On the other hand, a lot of good-quality commercial software started as freeware. Before you use freeware, it is best to read reviews about it to see what kinds of successes and problems its users report. Use a Web search engine to locate newsgroups, discussion groups, or magazine reviews before you download, install, and use the software. Of course, always use a good virus program to scan and clean any viruses from all downloaded software.

Shareware is similar to freeware, but it is not entirely free and usually is available only for a short evaluation period. After that evaluation period expires—usually either a specified number of days or a given number of uses of the software—it stops functioning. Shareware users are expected to stop using the shareware after an initial trial period and uninstall it from their computers. Otherwise, anyone who likes the program and wants to continue using it can purchase a license. The three most popular ways to turn shareware users into paying customers is to build a counter into the program, insert an internal date checker, or use a "nag" screen to remind the user to submit payment to the developer. A counter keeps track of the number of times you have used a program. After you have reached a usage limit, the software is disabled. The time-expiration technique causes the shareware to stop working after a specific time period has elapsed, such as 30 days, from the time that you installed the shareware program. Many shareware developers use a "nag" screen that appears each time you start the program to discourage users who do not purchase a license to stop using the shareware, although the program might continue to work. The screen usually displays a message with the developer's name and Web address and asks you to abide by the licensing agreement and submit payment for the shareware version of the product. You usually click an OK button to move past the nag screen to use the program.

Shareware usually is slightly more reliable than freeware because the shareware developer sometimes is willing to accept responsibility for the operation of the program. Shareware developers usually have an established way for users to report any bugs and receive free or low-cost software upgrades and bug fixes.

Clever developers with good software products sometimes distribute restricted versions of their software for free. A restricted version of a shareware program is called a **limited edition** (or **LE**), and it provides most of the functionality of the full version that is for sale. However, LE software omits one or more useful features of the complete version. You might download an LE version and use it for free. If you really like the LE, then you are likely to want the full version of the same software. Both the e-mail program Eudora Light and the FTP client program WS_FTP LE are examples of free, limited edition programs. WS_FTP LE is the limited edition of the product called WS_FTP. The limited edition performs all the standard FTP tasks but omits some of the advanced features that make the full product especially attractive. Because the complete versions of limited edition software are inexpensive, most users of the limited edition are happy to purchase the upgraded, comprehensive version so they can use its additional capabilities.

Quick Check

1. True or False: Only an FTP client program can download files from the Internet.
2. You can connect to a remote FTP server by logging on to it first. If you do not have an account on the FTP server, you can log on as a guest, which is called _____ FTP.
3. To transfer an Excel workbook to another computer using FTP, you must make sure the transfer mode is set to _____ before you transfer the file so that the file will transfer correctly.
4. The overall structure in which directories and folders are organized is like an upside-down tree called a(n) _____ structure.
5. Suppose you want to go to an FTP server whose domain name is ftp.goodsoftware.com so you can download a file. What is the complete URL that you would enter in your Web browser's address field to go to that FTP site?
6. After you download software, it is always advisable to check it for a(n) _____ to make sure that your use of the program will not damage your computer.
7. Special programs that greatly reduce a file's size and its transmission time on the Internet are called _____ programs.
8. True or False: All software that you can download from the Internet and use is free.

In Session 5.3, you will use your knowledge of FTP to download the files that the members of Nancy's team need to have on their notebook computers.

SESSION 5.3

In this session you will learn how to use an FTP client program and a Web browser to download programs from the Internet. You will visit several sites containing links to several freeware, shareware, and limited edition programs. Also, you will download some useful utility programs.

Locating Software Download Sites

Nancy wants you to locate software tools and information from the Internet and install it on the computers used by the ground-station installation team. Nancy gave you a list of productivity aids and useful software tools to locate and download. Your first objective is to make sure that the software is reliable. Cost is not a high-priority issue, although it is always nice to save money when you can. Perhaps equally important is how various software tools stack up against each other, so you hope to find some sort of ratings system that will guide you in making good decisions about which of several software product alternatives to choose. So far, your software list includes a Web browser, an FTP client program, a program to read special documents in a portable document format, a compression/decompression program, an e-mail client, and an antivirus program. You are sure to locate other useful programs as you conduct your research.

A good way to locate software on the Internet is to use one or more Internet search engines. If you are searching for FTP client programs, you can look for reviews or comparisons of the software by users or vendors. For example, several popular PC magazines feature articles comparing Internet utility programs, where they often designate one or more programs in a class as the "best of the class" or a "best buy." Of course, the criteria they use to judge which program is best might be different from your criteria. However, it never hurts to review the ratings when you can. You decide to use a search engine to find information about FTP client programs.

To use a search engine to locate software on the Internet:

1. Start your Web browser, and then go to the Student Online Companion page by entering the URL **http://www.course.com/NewPerspectives/Internet** in the appropriate location in your Web browser. Click the hyperlink for your book, click the **Tutorial 5** link, and then click the **Session 5.3** link. Click the **HotBot** link and wait while the browser loads the HotBot home page.

2. Type **FTP client** in the Search the Web text box, and then click the **SEARCH** button to start the search. Figure 5-24 shows the search results, which located over 455,000 matches. (Your search list might look different.)

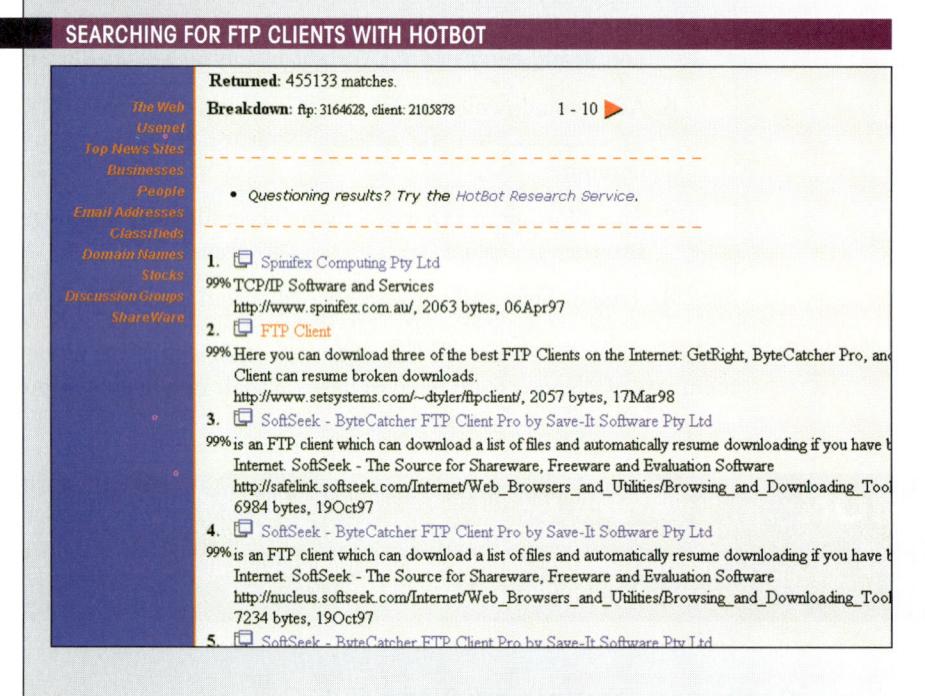

Figure 5-24   **SEARCHING FOR FTP CLIENTS WITH HOTBOT**

Returned: 455133 matches.
Breakdown: ftp: 3164628, client: 2105878   1 - 10

The Web
Usenet
Top News Sites
Businesses
People
Email Addresses
Classifieds
Domain Names
Stocks
Discussion Groups
ShareWare

• Questioning results? Try the HotBot Research Service.

1. Spinifex Computing Pty Ltd
   99% TCP/IP Software and Services
   http://www.spinifex.com.au/, 2063 bytes, 06Apr97
2. FTP Client
   99% Here you can download three of the best FTP Clients on the Internet: GetRight, ByteCatcher Pro, and
   Client can resume broken downloads.
   http://www.setsystems.com/~dtyler/ftpclient/, 2057 bytes, 17Mar98
3. SoftSeek - ByteCatcher FTP Client Pro by Save-It Software Pty Ltd
   99% is an FTP client which can download a list of files and automatically resume downloading if you have b
   Internet. SoftSeek - The Source for Shareware, Freeware and Evaluation Software
   http://safelink.softseek.com/Internet/Web_Browsers_and_Utilities/Browsing_and_Downloading_Tool
   6984 bytes, 19Oct97
4. SoftSeek - ByteCatcher FTP Client Pro by Save-It Software Pty Ltd
   99% is an FTP client which can download a list of files and automatically resume downloading if you have b
   Internet. SoftSeek - The Source for Shareware, Freeware and Evaluation Software
   http://nucleus.softseek.com/Internet/Web_Browsers_and_Utilities/Browsing_and_Downloading_Tool
   7234 bytes, 19Oct97
5. SoftSeek - ByteCatcher FTP Client Pro by Save-It Software Pty Ltd

3. Click the first few links on the results page to learn more about FTP clients.

When you explore some of the links returned by HotBot, you will find that some are relevant and others are not. PC magazines frequently review software using their specially designed software testing laboratories and conduct product comparisons and report the

TUTORIAL 5 EVALUATING AND DOWNLOADING WEB RESOURCES WEB 5.35

results. They should not have a vested interest in the outcome, but you should always view the results with a critical eye to identify any biases.

You also can try searching for software download sites using the search phrase "software download." The search engine will return a list of sites that contain links to software that you can download from the Web. You will visit several of the best download sites in the next section as you conduct your research.

Visiting and Using Popular Download Sites

Several Web sites provide links to freeware and shareware programs; some of these same sites also allow you to download programs directly. Continuing with Nancy's request for you to use the Internet to identify, locate, and download mission critical software, you decide to visit some Web sites that specialize in freeware and shareware. In addition, you will also browse through Microsoft's Web site and a few other vendors' sites. You begin by examining a well-known site, **DOWNLOAD.COM**, which contains many freeware and shareware programs in many different categories.

To browse the DOWNLOAD.COM Web site:

1. Return to the Student Online Companion Web page for Session 5.3, and then click the **DOWNLOAD.COM** hyperlink and wait while your Web browser loads the Web page.

2. Type **ftp client** in the Quick Search text box, as shown in Figure 5-25. Notice that you could select a category in which to search, such as Games, Home & Personal, or Internet. Each category contains subcategories so you can narrow your search.

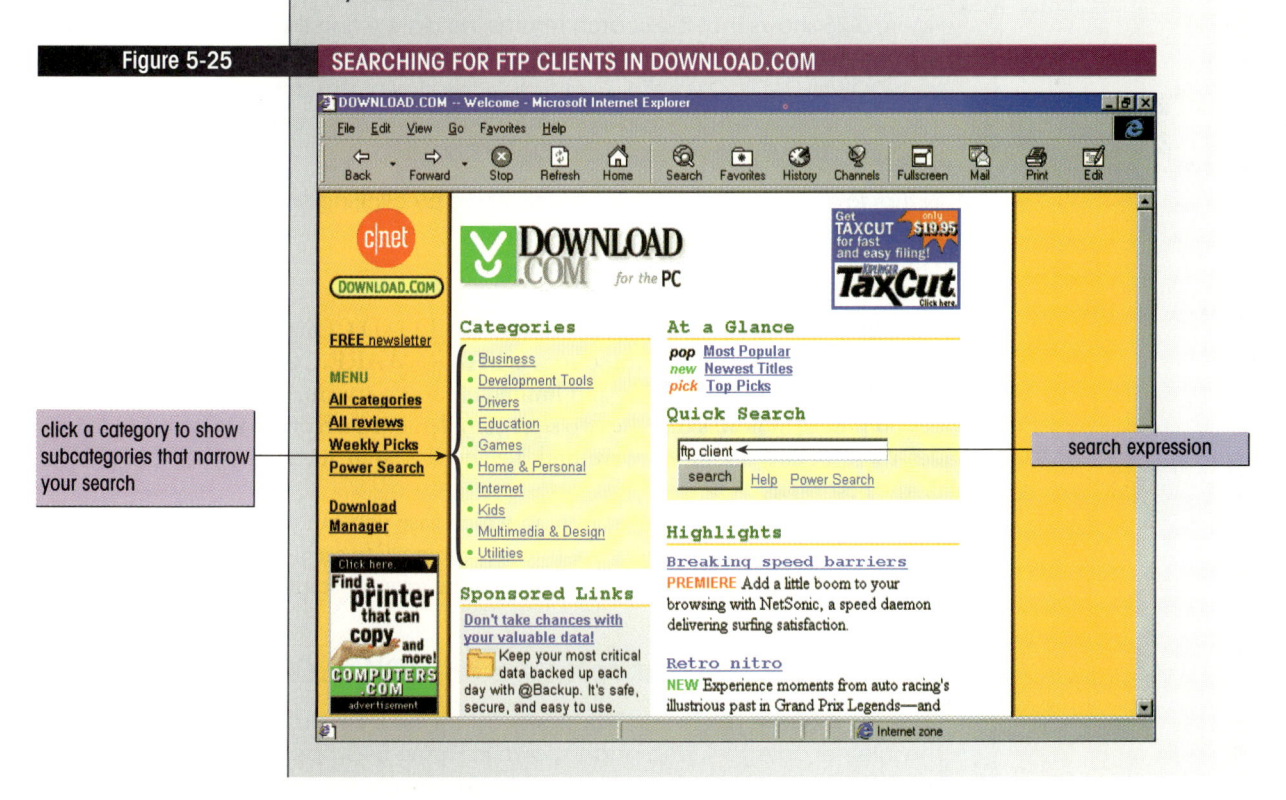

Figure 5-25 SEARCHING FOR FTP CLIENTS IN DOWNLOAD.COM

3. Click the **search** button to search for FTP client programs. Figure 5-26 shows the search results and the different FTP clients that are available for download from DOWNLOAD.COM. (Your list might be different.)

Figure 5-26 FTP CLIENTS FOUND IN DOWNLOAD.COM

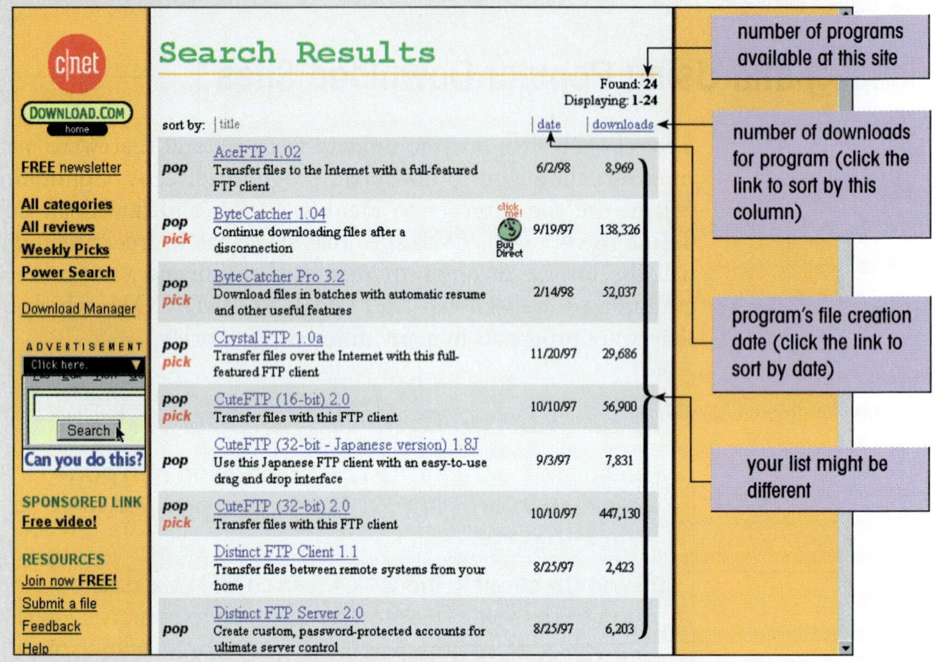

[Screenshot of DOWNLOAD.COM search results page showing a list of FTP client programs including AceFTP 1.02, ByteCatcher 1.04, ByteCatcher Pro 3.2, Crystal FTP 1.0a, CuteFTP (16-bit) 2.0, CuteFTP (32-bit - Japanese version) 1.8J, CuteFTP (32-bit) 2.0, Distinct FTP Client 1.1, and Distinct FTP Server 2.0, with their descriptions, dates, and download counts. Callouts point to: number of programs available at this site; number of downloads for program (click the link to sort by this column); program's file creation date (click the link to sort by date); your list might be different.]

Figure 5-26 shows that the search returns the date when the files were uploaded to the site and the current number of times each file has been downloaded from DOWNLOAD.COM's site. Sometimes, the download count is a good resource for discovering popular and useful programs because popular programs usually have larger download counts.

4. Return to the DOWNLOAD.COM home page by clicking your browser's **Back** button.

You might notice that in the left frame of DOWNLOAD.COM, there is a list of other sites that might be of interest. One of these sites is **SHAREWARE.COM**, which provides search capabilities for freeware, shareware, and limited edition software. C/NET, the company that provides both sites, indicates that the two sites complement each other. DOWNLOAD.COM provides more details about software and advanced search techniques, so that site might provide the best value.

You might need to narrow your search, in which case you can use DOWNLOAD.COM's categories list. Next, you will explore the Internet category to see if you can find any additional Internet utility programs that might be useful for the ground-station installation team.

To browse for Internet software on DOWNLOAD.COM:

1. Click the **Internet** link in the Categories list on the DOWNLOAD.COM home page. The Internet category Web page shown in Figure 5-27 opens and displays a list of Internet software by subcategory. Clicking any of the subcategory links opens a new page that lists related software.

TUTORIAL 5 EVALUATING AND DOWNLOADING WEB RESOURCES WEB 5.37

Figure 5-27 INTERNET SOFTWARE LISTED BY SUBCATEGORIES

links to Internet software subcategories

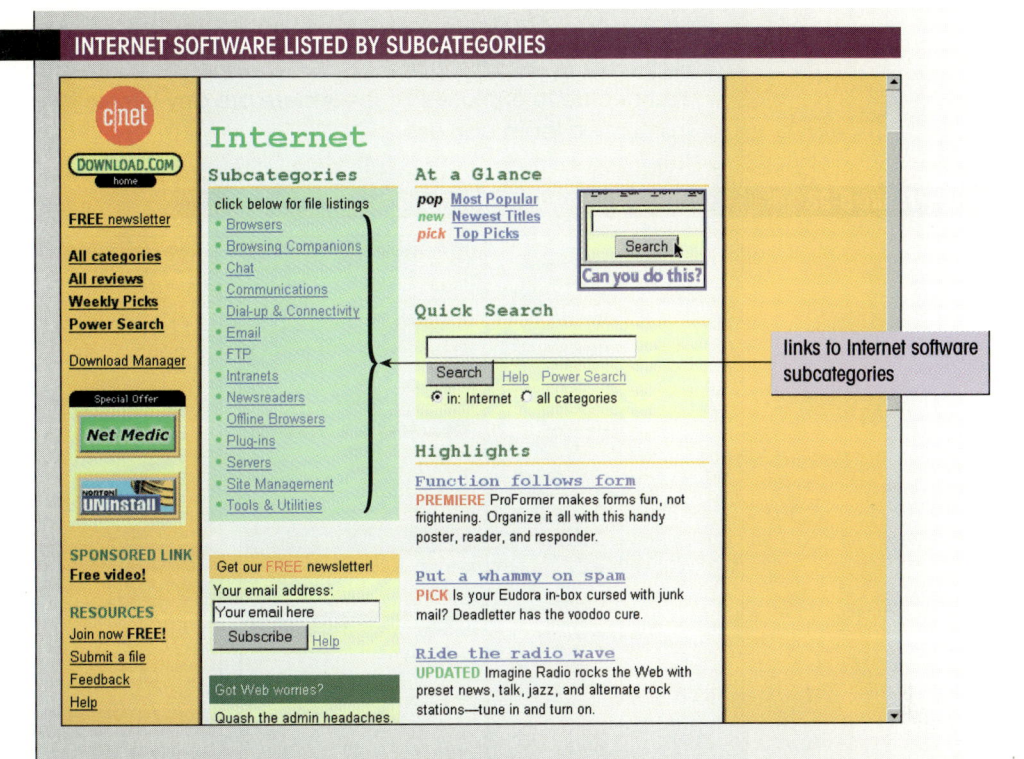

2. Click the **Tools & Utilities** link in the Subcategories list to open a page of Internet software tools and utility programs. (You may need to scroll down the page to find this list.) See if you can find any programs that the ground-station installation team can use, and then explore the links to those sites, but do not download any programs yet.

3. Click your browser's **Back** button twice to return to the DOWNLOAD.COM home page.

TUCOWS (The Ultimate Collection Of Winsock Software) is another popular site that provides quick access to free, inexpensive, and full-cost software. TUCOWS lists its software products by type. You decide to search the TUCOWS site to see if you can find software that would help the installation team.

To browse the TUCOWS Web site:

1. Return to the Student Online Companion Web page for Session 5.3, and then click the **TUCOWS** hyperlink and wait while your Web browser loads the Web page. TUCOWS is a busy site with worldwide servers, so the first thing you need to do is click the link for the server closest to you.

2. Click the continent or country link corresponding closest to your location. For example, U.S. students should click the **United States** link to open a list of states.

3. Click the link that corresponds to your region or state to open the Welcome to TUCOWS page. Notice that you can search for software for different operating systems: Win 95/98, Win NT, Win 3.x, or Macintosh. You will search for Windows 95/98 software because that is what the installation team will use.

TROUBLE? You might see more than one link for your state or region. You can click any entry to open the TUCOWS main page. If you cannot open a link, try another state or region until you succeed.

4. Click the **Win 95/98** link to open the TUCOWS main download page shown in Figure 5-28. Similar to DOWNLOAD.COM, there is a category for Internet tools. You decide to explore it to see if there are any interesting programs that the installation team can use.

Figure 5-28 | TUCOWS SOFTWARE CATEGORIES

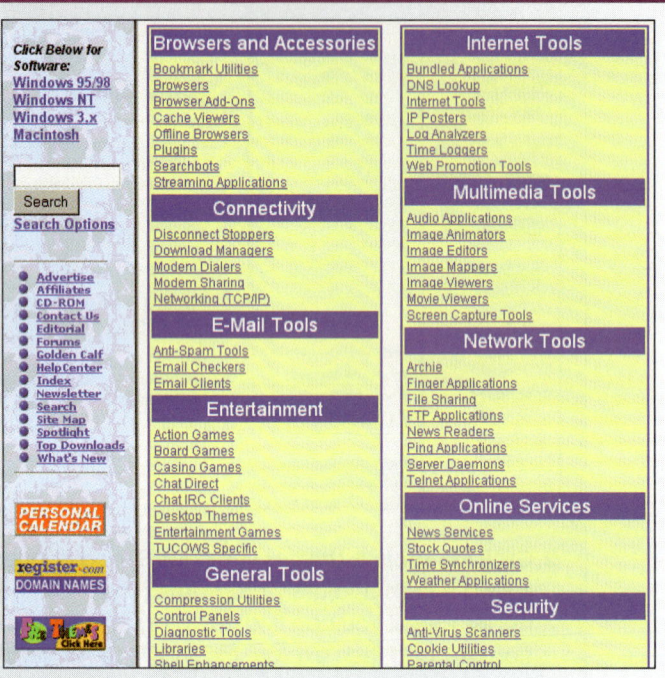

Click Below for Software:	Browsers and Accessories	Internet Tools
Windows 95/98 Windows NT Windows 3.x Macintosh	Bookmark Utilities Browsers Browser Add-Ons Cache Viewers Offline Browsers Plugins Searchbots Streaming Applications	Bundled Applications DNS Lookup Internet Tools IP Posters Log Analyzers Time Loggers Web Promotion Tools
Search Search Options	Connectivity	Multimedia Tools
	Disconnect Stoppers Download Managers Modem Dialers Modem Sharing Networking (TCP/IP)	Audio Applications Image Animators Image Editors Image Mappers Image Viewers Movie Viewers Screen Capture Tools
Advertise Affiliates CD-ROM Contact Us Editorial Forums Golden Calf Help Center Index Newsletter Search Site Map Spotlight Top Downloads What's New	E-Mail Tools	Network Tools
	Anti-Spam Tools Email Checkers Email Clients	Archie Finger Applications File Sharing FTP Applications News Readers Ping Applications Server Daemons Telnet Applications
	Entertainment	
	Action Games Board Games Casino Games Chat Direct Chat IRC Clients Desktop Themes Entertainment Games TUCOWS Specific	
		Online Services
		News Services Stock Quotes Time Synchronizers Weather Applications
PERSONAL CALENDAR register.com DOMAIN NAMES	General Tools	Security
	Compression Utilities Control Panels Diagnostic Tools Libraries Shell Enhancements	Anti-Virus Scanners Cookie Utilities Parental Control

5. Click the **Internet Tools** link in the Internet Tools category. A page opens listing various Internet programs. Examine the page by scrolling up and down the list. Each file contains a description, cost, file size, and other important information that you can use to determine which programs might be valuable for the team.

You realize that most members of the DigiComm team are equipped with at least one Microsoft Office program, and you want to see if there are any enhancements or updates to the Internet Explorer program. You decide to visit the Microsoft site and investigate its free software offerings.

To locate Microsoft Internet Explorer files on Microsoft's Web site:

1. Return to the Student Online Companion Web page for Session 5.3, and then click the **Microsoft Web site** hyperlink and wait while your Web browser loads the Web page shown in Figure 5-29. Notice that the links are organized into categories.

TUTORIAL 5   EVALUATING AND DOWNLOADING WEB RESOURCES   **WEB** 5.39

Figure 5-29   **MICROSOFT FREE DOWNLOADS WEB PAGE**

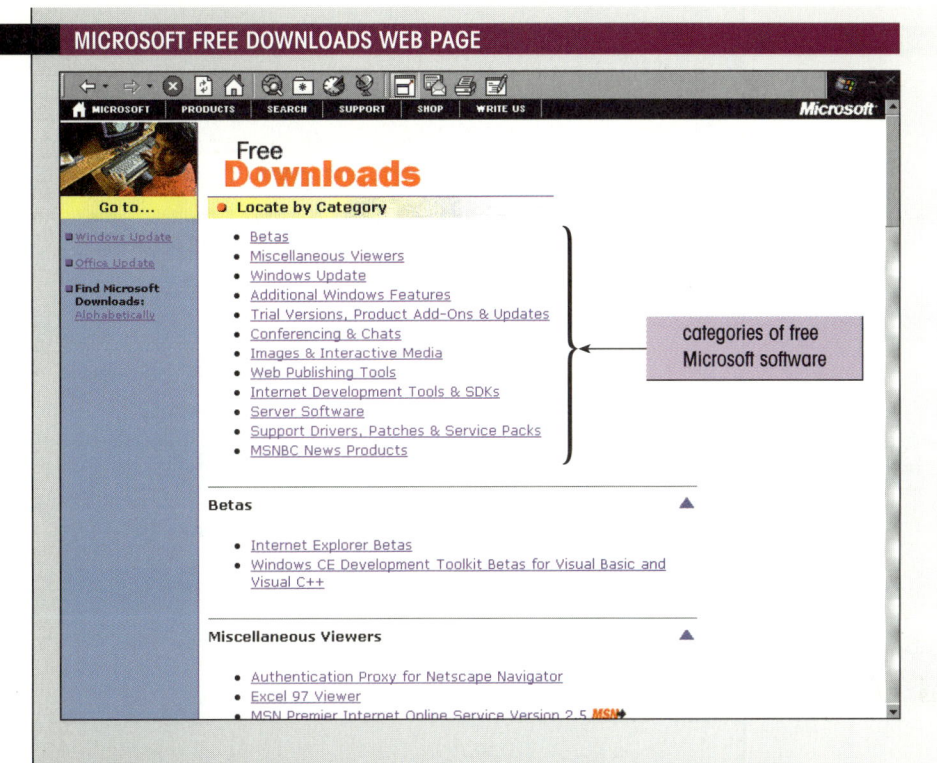

[Screenshot of Microsoft Free Downloads web page showing categories of free Microsoft software, including Betas, Miscellaneous Viewers, Windows Update, Additional Windows Features, Trial Versions, Product Add-Ons & Updates, Conferencing & Chats, Images & Interactive Media, Web Publishing Tools, Internet Development Tools & SDKs, Server Software, Support Drivers, Patches & Service Packs, and MSNBC News Products.]

2. Click the **Windows Update** category link. The page scrolls down to that category listing.

3. Click the **Internet Explorer** link to open the Internet Explorer Products Download page with Internet Explorer plug-ins and enhancements. You can download any of these files for free. See if you can find anything that might help the team, but do not download any programs yet.

Nancy just told you about another software download site that is maintained by a magazine-publishing company, ZDNet. The magazine publisher runs a software-testing laboratory, where it tests some of the freeware and shareware programs it reviews. ZDNet publishes ratings based on tests and evaluations of users who e-mail their impressions to the publisher. You decide to check the site to see if you can locate antivirus programs for the installation team.

To search the ZDNet Software Library Web site for antivirus software:

1. Return to the Student Online Companion Web page for Session 5.3, and then click the **ZDNet Software Library** hyperlink and wait while your Web browser loads the Web page.

2. Locate the search text box near the top of the page, type **antivirus** in the text box, and then click the **SEARCH** button to search for antivirus programs. Your search results are arranged in alphabetical order by program name, as shown in Figure 5-30. Your results might be different from those shown in Figure 5-30, but you should find many antivirus programs in the list.

INTERNET   WEB 5.40   TUTORIAL 5   EVALUATING AND DOWNLOADING WEB RESOURCES

Figure 5-30   ZDNET ANTIVIRUS PROGRAM SEARCH RESULTS

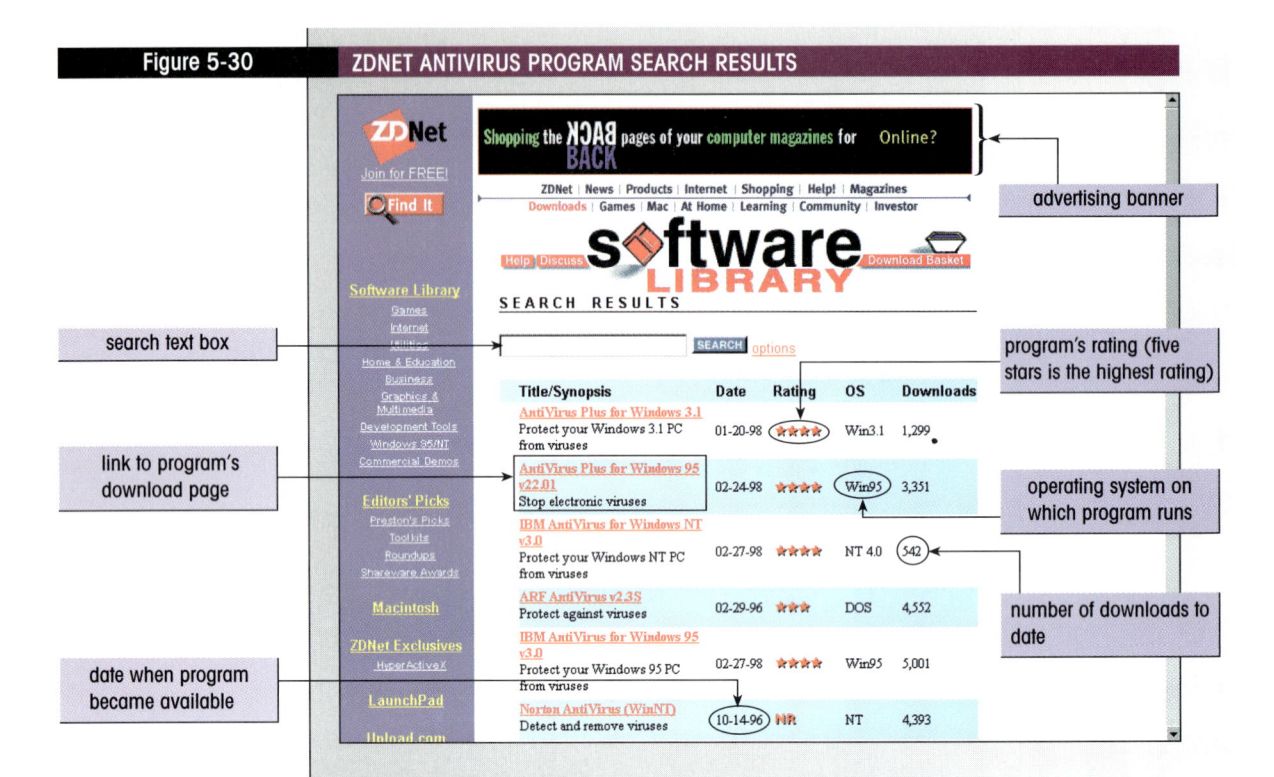

Callouts:
- advertising banner
- search text box
- program's rating (five stars is the highest rating)
- link to program's download page
- operating system on which program runs
- number of downloads to date
- date when program became available

TROUBLE? If the search results pages do not list any files, type "virus" or "antivirus" (without the quotation marks) in the search text box shown in Figure 5-30, and then click the SEARCH button again. You might need to search several times using different search expressions to find the antivirus software.

3. Click the hyperlink for the program named **Norton AntiVirus (Win 95) v4.0** to open the page shown in Figure 5-31 that supplies more information about the program, including a detailed description and its compressed file size.

Figure 5-31   PRODUCT PAGE FOR NORTON ANTIVIRUS PROGRAM

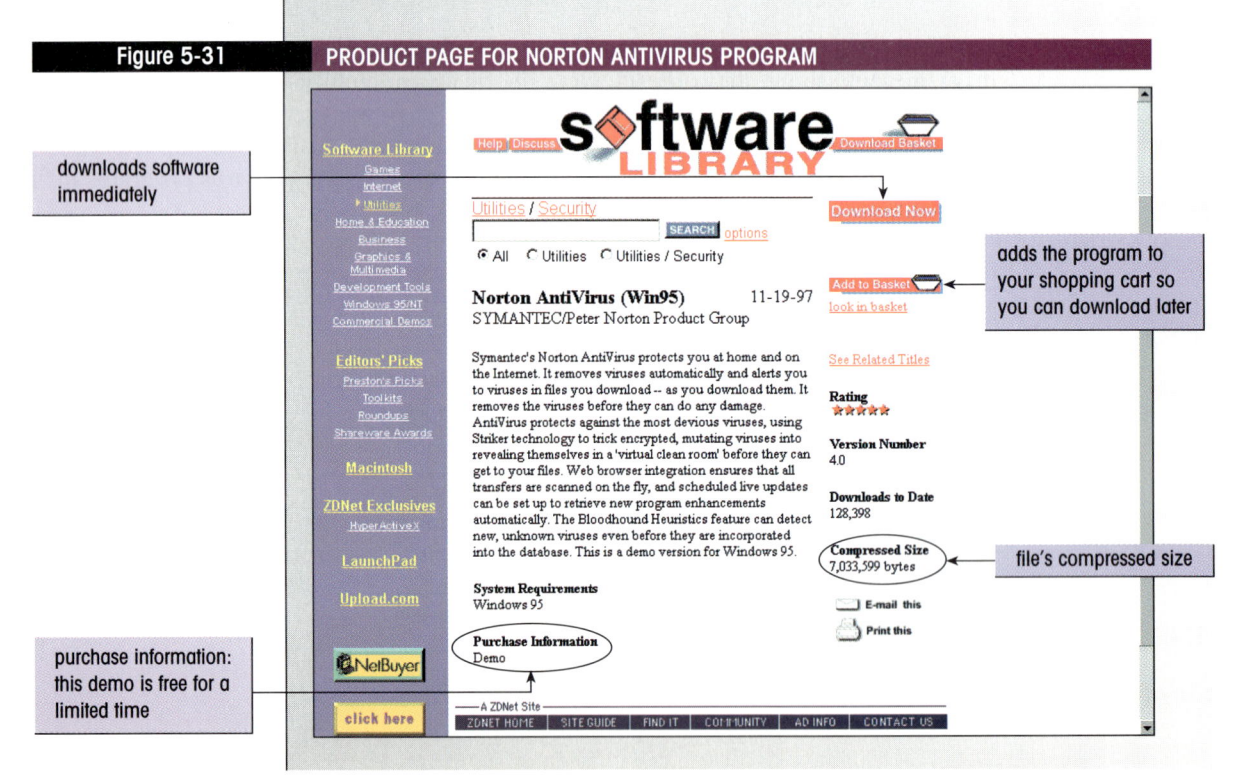

Callouts:
- downloads software immediately
- adds the program to your shopping cart so you can download later
- file's compressed size
- purchase information: this demo is free for a limited time

> You can use this page to download the program by clicking the Download Now button. Or, you can click the Add to Basket button to place the program in your virtual shopping cart so you can continue selecting programs to download at one time.

You are satisfied that you have several good software download sites from which to locate software tools for DigiComm's installation team. Now, you are ready to locate and download selected software. You decided to use a Web browser to download your software, including an FTP client program for future use.

Downloading Programs

You want to locate and download five programs for the DigiComm team members so they can perform various tasks on the Internet quickly and smoothly. The team requires the following programs:

- FTP client program
- Program to read portable document format (PDF) files
- File compression/decompression program
- E-mail client program
- Antivirus program

After you download the programs, you will test them to make sure that they work correctly and will satisfy the team's requirements. (*Note:* Do not install the downloaded programs unless your instructor directs you to.)

Downloading an FTP Client

One of the most important software tools that you want to provide the DigiComm team is a user-friendly, multi-featured FTP client program. You conducted your research on FTP client programs by visiting sites that review software searching and reviewed articles about FTP programs. You conclude from your studies that the WS_FTP Limited Edition FTP client is the best choice for the team, so you will download it next.

> ### To download a limited edition FTP client program:
>
> 1. Return to the Student Online Companion Web page for Session 5.3, and then click the **Ipswitch, Inc.** hyperlink and wait while your Web browser loads the Web page. The Ipswitch home page opens.
>
> 2. Locate and click the **Downloads** link on the navigation bar that appears below the company's logo to open the Evaluation Software page.
>
> 3. Scroll down the page, and locate the WS_FTP Limited Edition 4.6 link shown in Figure 5-32. Notice that the description says that qualified noncommercial users (such as students and professors) can use this program for free; otherwise, you must download another version of the program. You are granted a license to evaluate the program for 15 days, so you can download this program for DigiComm without violating any restrictions.

INTERNET   WEB 5.42   TUTORIAL 5 EVALUATING AND DOWNLOADING WEB RESOURCES

Figure 5-32   **IPSWITCH EVALUATION SOFTWARE PAGE**

Evaluation Software Available for Download

Product	Description
IMail Server 4.0	The latest version of our popular Windows NT based POP3, SMTP, and IMAP4 Mail Server. *NEW! Beeper/Pager and Web Messaging Options now available for evaluation download!* (2.8 MB)
WS_FTP Pro 5.0	The most advanced WS_FTP file transfer client for Windows 3.x, 95, and NT, now with optional explorer interface, and features like drag & drop, auto re-get and firewall usage. (1.2 MB 32bit, 0.4MB 16bit)
WS_FTP Pro Developers Kit 4.5	The WS_FTP Pro Developers Kit allows you to add the ability to FTP to any of your C/C++/Visual Basic applications. For experienced programmers only.
WS_FTP Limited Edition 4.6	Original WS_FTP file transfer client for Windows 3.x, 95, NT. Free *with no expiration* to qualified non-commercial users - others **must** download WS_FTP Pro. (0.6 MB)
WS_Ping ProPack 2.0	WS_Ping ProPack is the ultimate network tool. It provides Ping, Traceroute, DNS

WS_FTP Limited Edition 4.6 link ← circled

description → (points to right column)

4. Click the **WS_FTP Limited Edition 4.6** link to open the WS_FTP® Limited Edition Registration & Download page.

5. Type your first name, last name, and e-mail address in the appropriate text boxes. Use the drop-down list arrows to select **Educational** as your organization type, and **Single User (1 to 10 users)** as the number of users in your organization. (You should be aware that as a student, you will use the Educational option. However, if you were acting as a representative of DigiComm, you would use the Commercial option.) Figure 5-33 shows a completed registration form.

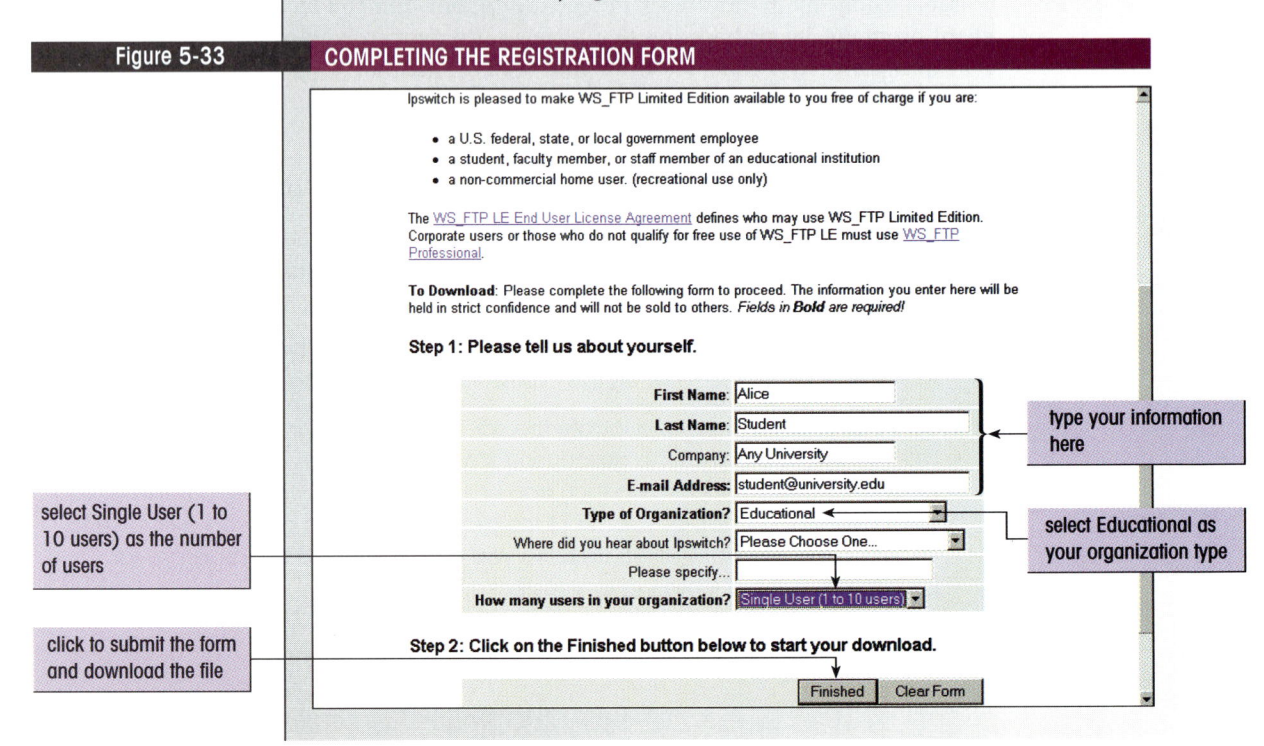

Figure 5-33   **COMPLETING THE REGISTRATION FORM**

Ipswitch is pleased to make WS_FTP Limited Edition available to you free of charge if you are:

- a U.S. federal, state, or local government employee
- a student, faculty member, or staff member of an educational institution
- a non-commercial home user. (recreational use only)

The WS_FTP LE End User License Agreement defines who may use WS_FTP Limited Edition. Corporate users or those who do not qualify for free use of WS_FTP LE must use WS_FTP Professional.

To Download: Please complete the following form to proceed. The information you enter here will be held in strict confidence and will not be sold to others. *Fields in* **Bold** *are required!*

Step 1: Please tell us about yourself.

First Name:	Alice
Last Name:	Student
Company:	Any University
E-mail Address:	student@university.edu
Type of Organization?	Educational
Where did you hear about Ipswitch?	Please Choose One...
Please specify...	
How many users in your organization?	Single User (1 to 10 users)

type your information here

select Educational as your organization type

select Single User (1 to 10 users) as the number of users

click to submit the form and download the file

Step 2: Click on the Finished button below to start your download.

[Finished]   [Clear Form]

TUTORIAL 5 EVALUATING AND DOWNLOADING WEB RESOURCES   WEB 5.43

6. Click the **Finished** button to submit your registration form, and start the download process. A page opens displaying mirror sites from which you can choose.

   TROUBLE? If you receive a message that the Web is busy and that you should try again later, you can bookmark or create a favorite for the Web page, read the remainder of the steps in this series, and then try re-submitting your registration.

   TROUBLE? After registering with the site, you might receive e-mail messages from Ipswitch to inform you of forthcoming products and new versions of existing products. If you do not want to receive these e-mail messages, you can reply to a message that you receive with the word *DELETE* in the Subject line of your reply.

7. Click a link corresponding to the download site that is closest to your current location. Click **Win95/NT** if you have Windows 95 or higher, or click **Win3x** if your operating system is Windows 3.1. If you are using Internet Explorer, then a dialog box opens and asks you to click an option button to either open the application or save it to disk. If this happens, click the option button to save the file to disk, and then click the **OK** button to open the Save As dialog box. If you are using Navigator, the Save As dialog box opens.

8. Make sure your Student Disk is in the appropriate drive, click the **Save in** list arrow, click **3½ Floppy (A:)** (or whichever drive contains your Student Disk), and then double-click the **Tutorial.05** folder to open it. You will accept the default filename of ws_ftple.exe. See Figure 5-34.

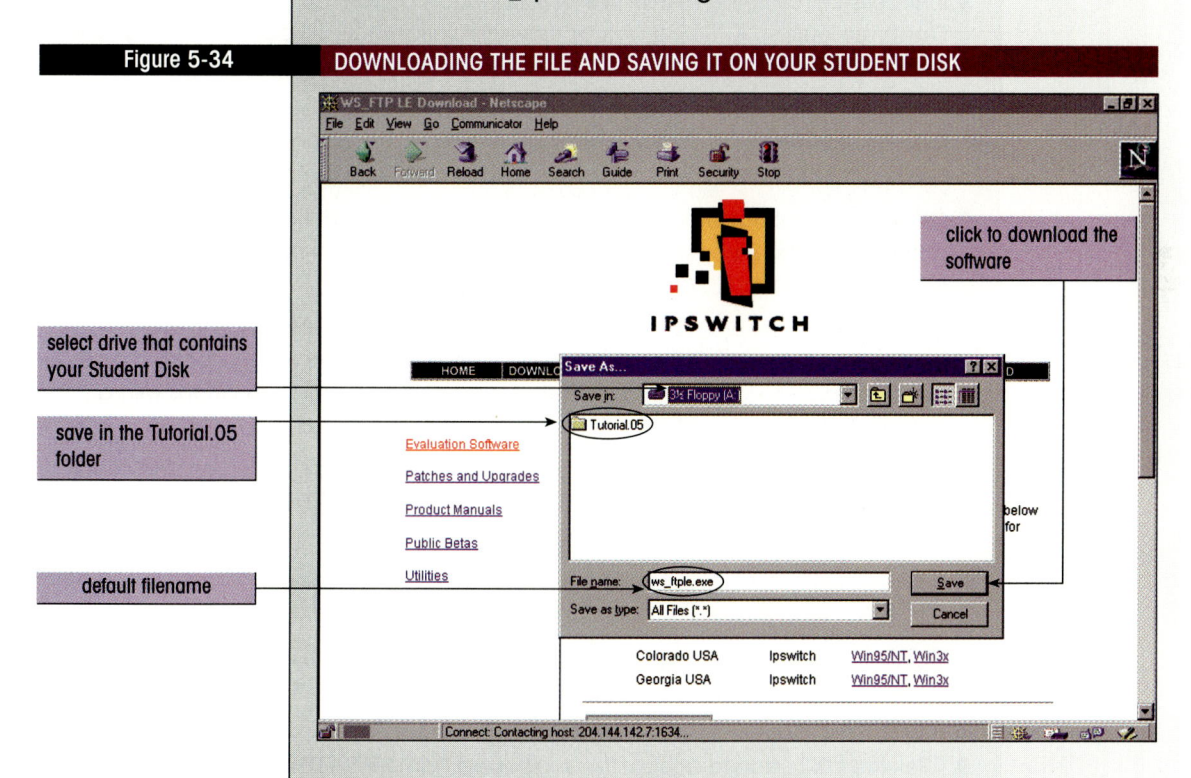

Figure 5-34   DOWNLOADING THE FILE AND SAVING IT ON YOUR STUDENT DISK

- select drive that contains your Student Disk
- save in the Tutorial.05 folder
- default filename
- click to download the software

9. Click the **Save** button to download the file to your disk. When the file is completely transferred, a Download Complete dialog box might open; if it does, click the **OK** button. Now, the compressed file that contains the FTP client program files is saved on your Student Disk.

10. Close your Web browser, and close up your dial-up connection, if necessary.

After you download a file, you must install it on your computer to use it. You can use Windows Explorer to check the Tutorial.05 folder on your Student Disk to make sure that it contains the ws_ftple.exe file. The limited edition lacks only a few features of the full, professional version, which is *not* free.

Note: If your instructor or lab manager tells you that you are allowed to install and use the program, complete the next set of steps to install the software. Otherwise, read the steps so you know how to install the software, but do *not* complete the steps at the computer.

To install WS_FTP LE on your computer:

1. Make sure that your Student Disk is in the appropriate drive, click the **Start** button on the taskbar, click **Run**, and then type **A:\Tutorial.05\ws_ftple.exe** in the Open text box in the Run dialog box. If your Student Disk is not in drive A, then substitute your drive letter in the Open text box.

2. Click the **OK** button to start the installation process. A dialog box opens and displays two options.

   TROUBLE? The installation steps that you encounter might be different from the ones in the following steps. If your on-screen instructions are different, answer the questions in each dialog box, and click the appropriate option buttons and check boxes to continue, or seek your instructor's help. The questions help Ipswitch serve their customers better, but your answers will not affect the installation process.

3. If necessary, click the **Install WS_FTP LE** option button, and then click the **Continue** button. A dialog box opens with option buttons corresponding to several types of users.

4. Click the option button whose label begins **A student, faculty member**, and then click the **Next** button to continue. A dialog box opens with several check boxes, which indicate where and how you might use the program.

5. Click the **At School** box from the Location column and the **For academic work** check box in the Purpose column, Click the **Next** button to continue. The End User License Agreement dialog box opens.

6. Read the End User License Agreement, and click the **Accept** button to indicate that you accept the terms of the agreement. (If you click the Do Not Accept button, then the installation process stops.) A WS_FTP LE Installation dialog box opens with a default destination directory.

7. Click the **OK** button to accept the default directory in which the program files will be stored. (The default directory is C:\Program Files\WS_FTP.) The Preferred Destination for File Transfers dialog box opens.

8. Click the **OK** button to accept the suggested default location for downloaded files (the same directory as the program files).

   TROUBLE? If a dialog box opens indicating that you have an "ini" file that will be erased, click the No button so the installing program does not destroy an important file.

9. Click the **OK** button to accept the suggested name WS_FTP for the Program Manager group name. (The Program Manager group name is the name of the folder whose name appears in the Start menu Programs list.) A Congratulations dialog box opens.

10. Click the **OK** button in the Congratulations dialog box to complete the installation process. The WS_FTP group remains open. You might want to create a desktop shortcut to the program by dragging the WS_FTP LE icon from the program group to the desktop.

After you are finished installing the program, most programs include a "Readme" file to explain how to use the program, or you can use the program's Help files for program instructions.

Downloading Acrobat Reader

The DigiComm Company provides many of its user and training manuals in a special form called Portable Document Format. **Portable Document Format** (**PDF**), developed by Adobe Corporation, provides a convenient, self-contained package for delivering and displaying documents containing text, graphics, charts, and other objects. PDF files and ZIP files are both special formats for storing files, but they are not related. PDF files simply provide a universal and convenient way to represent documents, whereas ZIP files condense files so they occupy much less space. You cannot view compressed files until you decompress them.

When you download a PDF file, you do not need to use the same program as the file's creator to display and print the document; you use the **Adobe Acrobat Reader** program to display, zoom, browse, and print PDF documents. For example, if you download a PDF file that was created in Microsoft Word, then you can use Adobe Acrobat Reader to access the files, even if you don't have the Word program installed on your computer. Most Web browsers contain the Acrobat Reader program so you can use your Web browser to read PDF documents without downloading them first, or you can download the Acrobat Reader program separately to read files that you already downloaded.

Many Web documents are available in PDF format, so you are sure that the Acrobat Reader will be a valuable addition to the DigiComm team's software tools. Acrobat Reader is a relatively small program, and it is free and simple to install. You will use DOWNLOAD.COM's site to search for and download the Acrobat Reader.

Note: You cannot download the Acrobat Reader program to your Student Disk because its file size (approximately four megabytes) exceeds your Student Disk's storage capacity. Your instructor might ask you to download the program to your hard drive or to simply read the following steps without actually downloading the file.

To download the Acrobat Reader from DOWNLOAD.COM:

1. Start your Web browser, return to the Student Online Companion Web page for Session 5.3, and then click the **DOWNLOAD.COM** hyperlink and wait while your Web browser loads the Web page.

2. Type **Acrobat reader** in the Quick Search text box on the DOWNLOAD.COM home page, and then click the **Search** button. Your search results page should look similar to Figure 5-35.

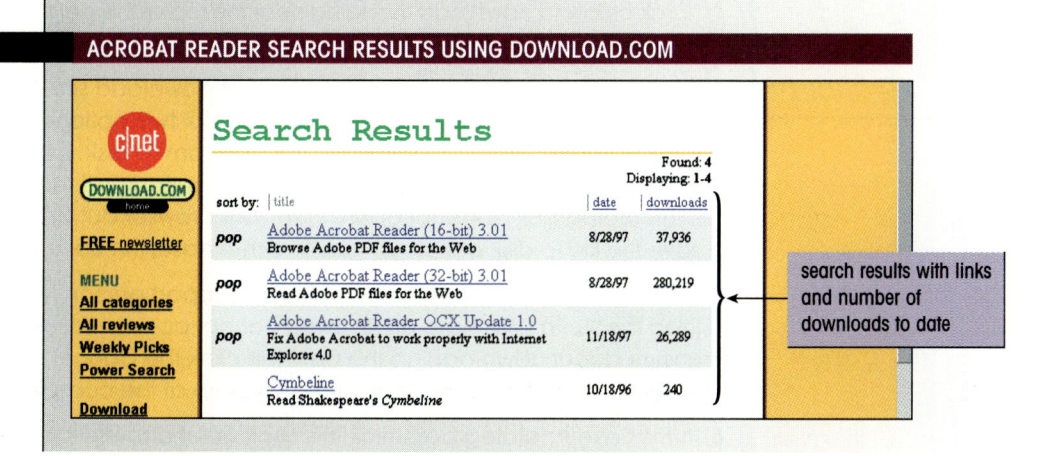

Figure 5-35 | ACROBAT READER SEARCH RESULTS USING DOWNLOAD.COM

Notice that the right column of the search results page shows the number of downloads that have occurred to date—a larger number generally indicates that the software is popular and reliable, whereas a smaller number indicates that the software might be unstable or relatively new.

3. Click the **Adobe Acrobat Reader (32-bit) 3.01** link (or the version for the latest version of Windows) to open the program's description page where you download the software. See Figure 5-36.

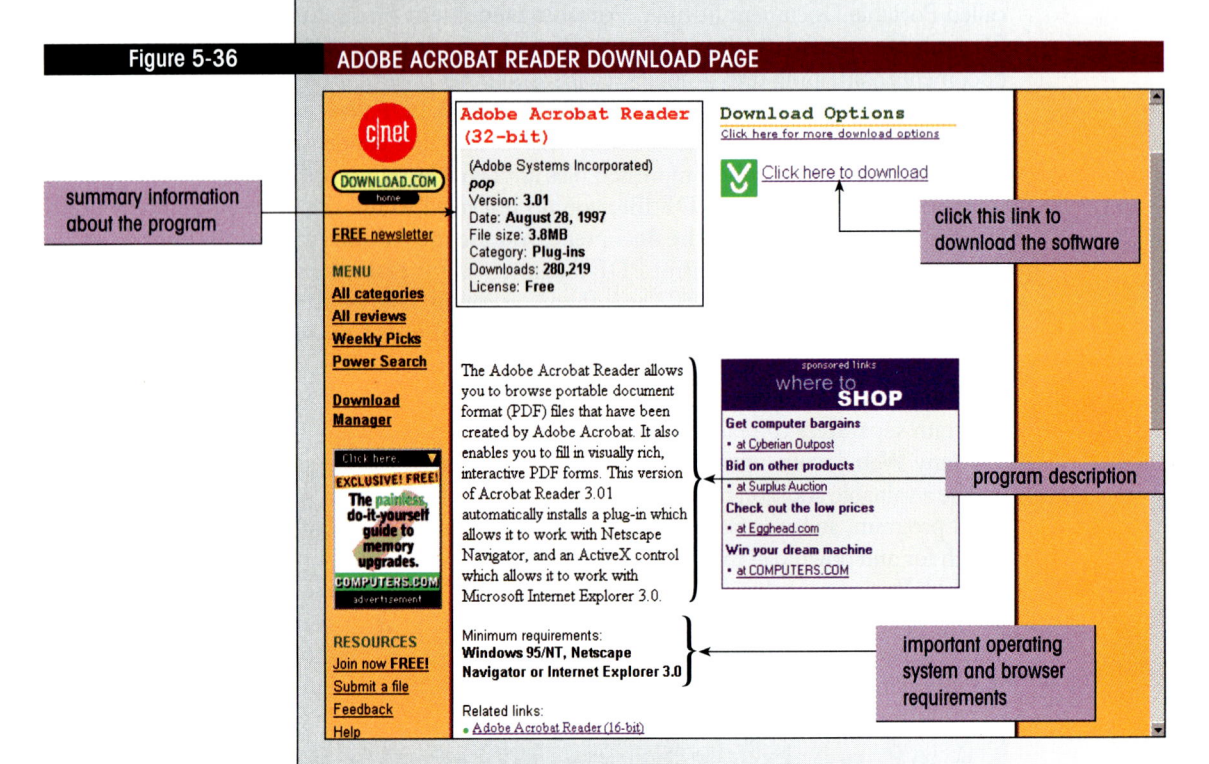

Figure 5-36   ADOBE ACROBAT READER DOWNLOAD PAGE

TROUBLE? Software vendors update and improve their programs regularly, so your Acrobat Reader program version number might be different. If the version number is larger than the one shown in Figure 5-36, then download that program because it will be more current.

4. Read the program summary and requirements, and then click the **Click here to download** link to open the Download page. You have a choice of locations from which you can download the software; these sites are identified with links below the "Click below to download" heading near the top of the page. Each download location has a reliability rating, with three dots indicating the most reliable location.

5. Click the **ftp.adobe.com** link to select that download site. Depending on your browser, a dialog box might open with one of two options: to run this program from its current location or to save this program to disk. If this dialog box opens, click the **Save this program to disk** option button and then click the **OK** button. If this dialog box does not open, then your browser automatically will choose to save the file to disk option for you. In either case, the Save As dialog box opens.

TROUBLE? Ask your instructor or technical support person to see if you can download the file to your hard drive. If you cannot download the file, or if you are unsure about downloading the file, then click the Cancel button now and read the rest of the steps without completing them at the computer.

6. In the Save As dialog box, click the **Look in** list arrow, click the drive and folder in which to save the file, and then click the **Save** button to start downloading

the file. Figure 5-37 shows the dialog box that displays while Internet Explorer downloads the file. (Navigator displays a different dialog box.)

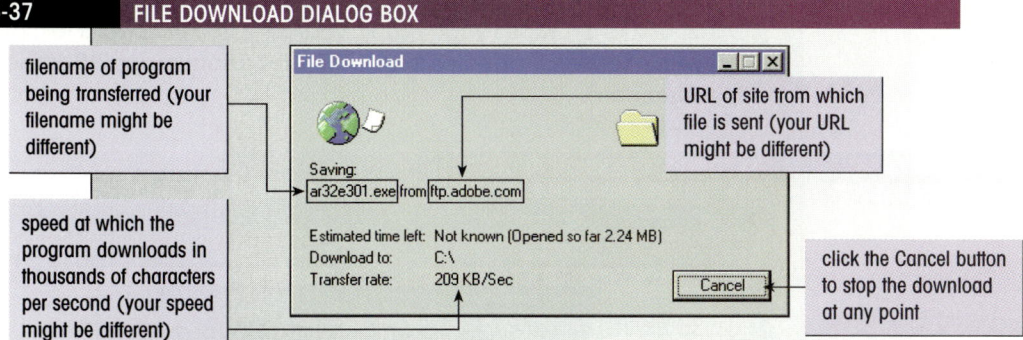

Figure 5-37 FILE DOWNLOAD DIALOG BOX

- filename of program being transferred (your filename might be different)
- URL of site from which file is sent (your URL might be different)
- speed at which the program downloads in thousands of characters per second (your speed might be different)
- click the Cancel button to stop the download at any point

File Download
Saving:
ar32e301.exe from ftp.adobe.com
Estimated time left: Not known (Opened so far 2.24 MB)
Download to: C:\
Transfer rate: 209 KB/Sec
Cancel

7. If you are using Internet Explorer, when the file is completely transferred, a Download Complete dialog box opens. Click the **OK** button to continue.

8. Close your Web browser, and your dial-up connection, if necessary.

Now the downloaded Acrobat Reader file is saved on your hard drive. You can install the program by double-clicking its filename in Windows Explorer and then following the steps. After installing the Acrobat Reader program, you can delete the downloaded executable file from your computer.

Downloading with an FTP Client

Nancy also wants you to train DigiComm staff members to download files using a Web browser and an FTP client, so you decide to use the WS_FTP Limited Edition FTP client that you downloaded to download the next program on Nancy's list.

Many file compression programs available on the Internet are reliable and easy to use. One popular program is *WinZip*, which is available for free during your evaluation. WinZip has been downloaded over five million times and has received a number of awards from computing magazines and other sources.

Note: In the following steps, you will use the WS_FTP Limited Edition FTP client program to download the WinZip program. If you do not have an FTP client or cannot install one on your school's computer, then read the steps without completing them at the computer.

In the first set of steps, you will establish the FTP server address and user login information that you will save in a list of profiles that operates much like an e-mail program's address book. When you want to return to an FTP site, you can select the saved FTP profile information and click the OK button to connect.

To establish and save an FTP session profile:

1. Click the **Start** button on the taskbar, point to **Programs**, point to **Ws_ftp**, and then click **WS_FTP 95 LE** to start the WS_FTP program. The Session Properties dialog box opens.

   TROUBLE? If you do not see Ws_ftp on the Programs menu, then make sure that you downloaded and installed the WS_FTP Limited Edition program. Ask your instructor or technical support person for help, if necessary.

2. Click the **New** button in the Session Properties dialog box to create a new user profile.

3. Type **Winzip** in the Profile Name text box (the name serves only as a way to identify this profile), and then press the **Tab** key to move to the Host Name/Address text box.

4. Type **ftp.winzip.com** in the Host Name/Address text box.

5. Click the **Anonymous** check box to place a check mark in it—this simplifies data entry because the system automatically places "anonymous" in the User ID text box and places your e-mail address in the Password text box. Figure 5-38 shows the Session Properties to establish an anonymous FTP session with the site ftp.winzip.com.

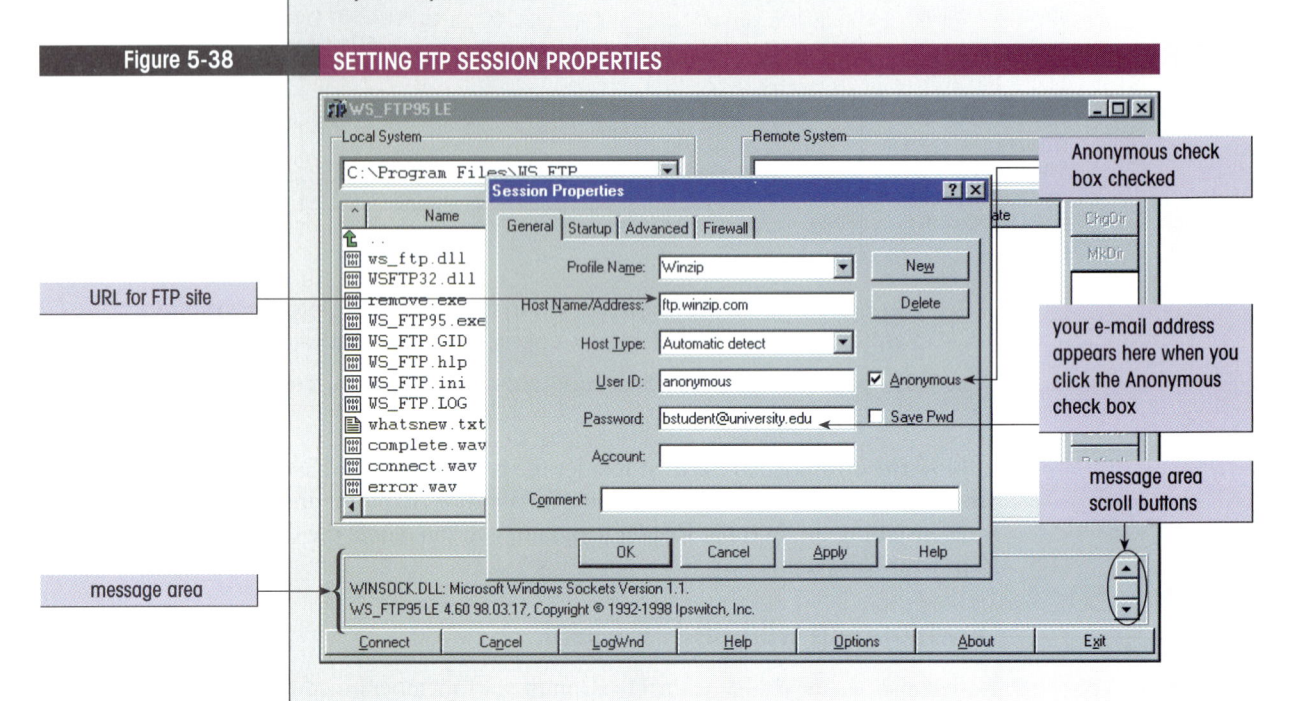

Figure 5-38   SETTING FTP SESSION PROPERTIES

6. Click the **Apply** button to save the Winzip session properties. (Clicking the Apply button will not start the FTP process; it only saves the session properties.)

Now you can revisit the WinZip FTP site easily the next time by clicking the Profile Name list arrow in the Session Properties dialog box and then clicking Winzip. With the URL and user information entered, you are ready to log on to the FTP site anonymously and download the WinZip program.

Note: If you cannot use an FTP client program, then read the following steps without actually completing them at the computer.

To log on anonymously and download a file:

1. Click the **OK** button to log on to the WinZip FTP site anonymously. The main WS_FTP95 LE window opens. Several messages scroll in the message area at the bottom of the WS_FTP window. You can use the up and down arrows to scroll the message area to review all messages passed between your client and the FTP server.

2. If necessary, click the **Maximize** button to maximize the program window.

3. Click the **ChgDir** button in the left panel to open the Input dialog box.

4. Make sure that your Student Disk is in the appropriate drive, type **A:\Tutorial.05** in the text box (see Figure 5-39), and then click the **OK** button. The left panel changes and displays the files in the Tutorial.05 folder on your Student Disk. The left panel

represents your PC, and the right panel represents the FTP site. By changing the left panel to your Student Disk, any files you download will be saved on that drive.

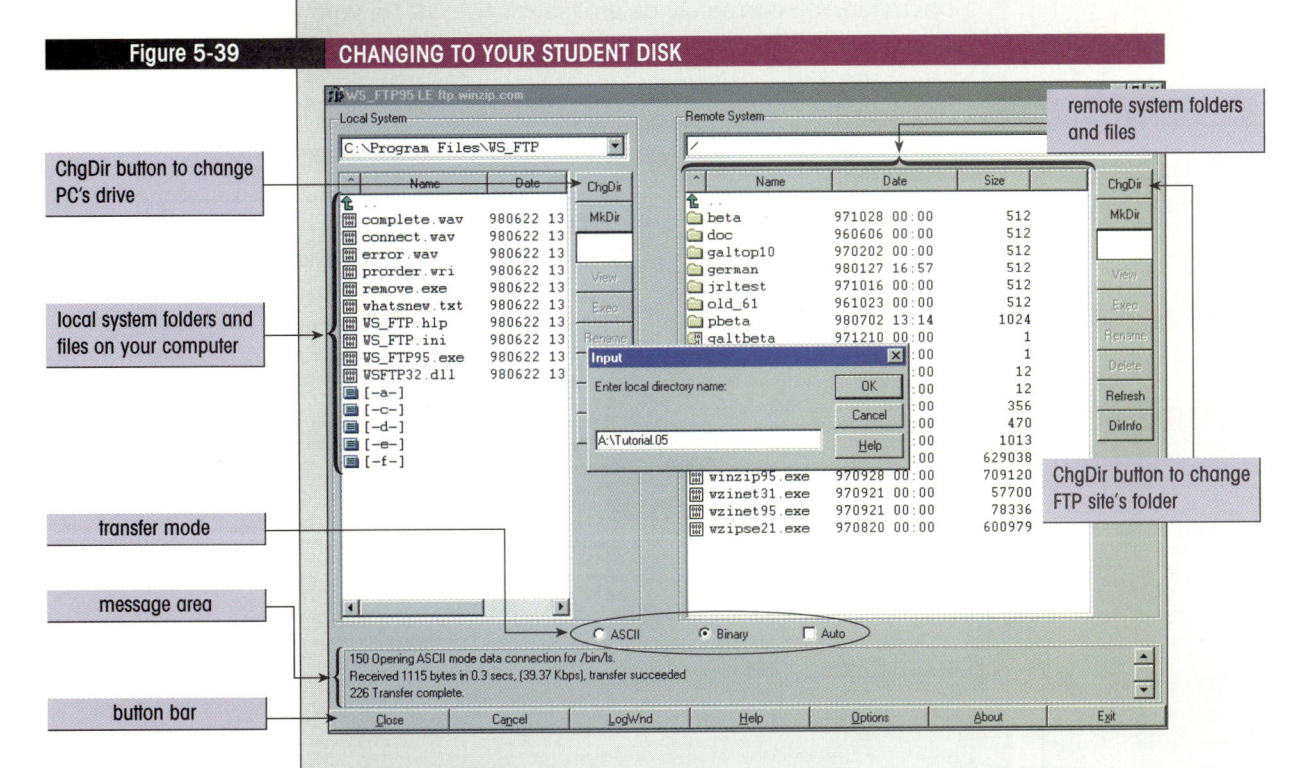

Figure 5-39   CHANGING TO YOUR STUDENT DISK

Callouts:
- ChgDir button to change PC's drive
- local system folders and files on your computer
- transfer mode
- message area
- button bar
- remote system folders and files
- ChgDir button to change FTP site's folder

TROUBLE? If you cannot establish a connection with the WinZip FTP server, then click the Close button on the button bar. Click the Connect button on the button bar to open the Session Properties dialog box, click the Profile Name list arrow, and then click Winzip. Make sure you entered ftp.winzip.com in the Host Name/Address text box. Click the OK button to connect, and then follow the steps.

TROUBLE? If you tried more than once to connect to the WinZip site without success, the site might be busy. When the number of anonymous logins exceeds a large number, the WinZip site rejects all subsequent anonymous FTP sessions. Try again later, or just read the steps so you understand how to use an FTP client to download files.

The file you want to download appears in the right panel in the remote system's listing of folders and files.

5. If necessary, click the **Binary** transfer mode option button to ensure that the program file is transferred correctly.

6. Examine the right panel, which contains the remote site's listing of files and folders. Locate and then click the **winzip95.exe** filename to select it.

7. Click the **left** pointing arrow located in the median strip between the left and right panels. Clicking this arrow begins the transfer process to download the selected file in the left pane to the selected folder in the right pane. A Transfer Status dialog box opens and displays download progress information, including a standard rain gauge and percent indicators (see Figure 5-40). When the Transfer Status dialog box closes, the file transfer is complete and the winzip95.exe program is saved on your Student Disk.

INTERNET   WEB 5.50   TUTORIAL 5 EVALUATING AND DOWNLOADING WEB RESOURCES

TROUBLE? WS_FTP might place a file called WS_FTP.LOG on your disk in addition to the file you download. The log file merely indicates the status of the download operation. You can safely delete the WS_FTP.LOG file from your disk. (Do *not*, of course, delete the winzip95.exe program file from your disk.)

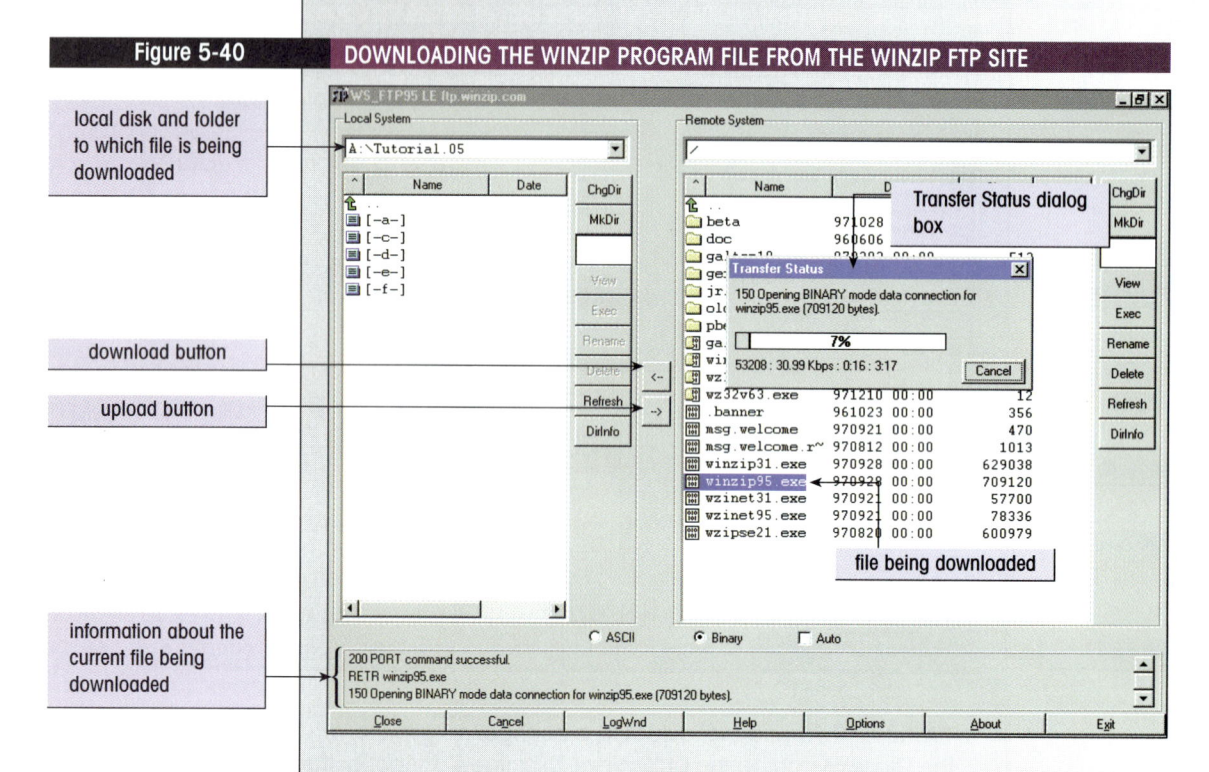

| Figure 5-40 | DOWNLOADING THE WINZIP PROGRAM FILE FROM THE WINZIP FTP SITE |

- local disk and folder to which file is being downloaded
- download button
- upload button
- Transfer Status dialog box
- file being downloaded
- information about the current file being downloaded

8. Click the **Exit** button on the button bar to log off the WinZip FTP site and close the WS_FTP program.

The time it takes to transfer the program file varies with the type of connection you have and your modem's speed. If you are on a local area network (LAN) with a T1 Internet connection, then the transfer time is a few seconds. If you are using a modem and a dial-up network connection, then the transfer time could take several minutes. Another factor in the download time is the amount of traffic at the FTP site. Many simultaneous users (more than 4,000 for example) can affect the download process directly. If you encounter problems while downloading a file, then stop the process by clicking the Cancel button and try again later.

You've accomplished a lot this session. Now that you have the WinZip software on your computer, you can evaluate it for use by the team members. The version you downloaded is called an evaluation version, which means that you can use it to evaluate the software at no charge. Each time you load the software, though, it displays an opening screen to remind you that you are using an evaluation copy that is not yet registered. Typically, opening screens such as WinZip's evaluation reminder require you to acknowledge the screen by clicking a button. If you continue using the software or need the full-capacity version, you will have to pay a small licensing fee to the developer. If you are allowed to install the WinZip program, open Windows Explorer, change to the Tutorial.05 folder on your Student Disk, double-click the winzip95.exe file, and then follow the on-screen instructions. (Ask your instructor or technical support person first before installing the program.)

Downloading with Command-Line FTP

In this tutorial, you have downloaded files using a Web browser and an FTP client program. The third option of transferring files is to use **command-line FTP**, where you execute a series of one-line commands to connect to an FTP site, navigate to a folder at the FTP site, and download a file. You type commands at the command prompt instead of clicking buttons in a Windows program. For example, you might log on to your school's host computer using your user name and password, and then initiate an FTP session from your computer to a remote site on the Internet. You should know how to execute a few simple FTP commands so that you can use command-line FTP if you do not have access to a Windows-based program. Command-line FTP is especially helpful if you have dial-up access to your school's computer and cannot run an FTP client from your home computer. Similarly, if you are traveling and want to transfer files between your notebook computer and your school's or employer's computer, then you usually must use command-line FTP to transfer the files.

By definition, the ground-station installation team is mobile, so it is important for the team members to know how to use command-line FTP. You realize that Nancy does not require the DigiComm staff to use command-line FTP, but you can teach them how to use it in case they need it while traveling on business.

When using command-line FTP, first you start your command-line FTP program either by invoking the Windows built-in version or by logging on to a UNIX computer that has command-line FTP and is executing that version. Then you can execute a series of commands. The first command you execute is to connect to a remote server. Next, you locate the folder containing the file you want to download using a simple command to open successive folders. Finally, you issue the one-line command that downloads the file from the remote host to your computer or the local UNIX computer on which you have an account and a connection. Most of the files that the DigiComm staff will transfer from and to DigiComm's main computer run the UNIX operating system, which has FTP available. DigiComm staff members can log on to that computer with their own accounts, and then they can transfer files using command-line FTP when necessary.

In order to use command-line FTP, you must either have a command-line FTP program installed on your PC or you must have access to a host computer that has a command-line FTP program. In the following steps, you will use the Windows built-in FTP program to access a remote host. As you work, remember that if you use FTP on a UNIX computer, all commands are case-sensitive; that is, typing "FTP" is not the same as typing its lowercase equivalent, "ftp." Figure 5-41 shows some common FTP command-line program commands that FTP client programs issue automatically.

Figure 5-41	COMMON FTP COMMANDS
COMMAND	DESCRIPTION
binary	Sets the transfer mode to binary
cd *directory*	Changes the remote directory to *directory*
close	Disconnects from the current remote computer
get *filename*	Downloads *filename* from the remote computer
help	Obtains help on various FTP topics
lcd *directory*	Changes the current local directory to *directory*
ls or dir	Displays the current folder's filenames and directory names
open *remote*	Connects to a remote FTP server on *remote*
put *filename*	Uploads *filename* to a remote computer
quit	Exits the FTP program and logs off a remote server

> **REFERENCE WINDOW**
>
> **Downloading a file using command-line FTP**
> - Start your FTP program, and then type open *<ftp-address>* where *ftp-address* is the address of the remote FTP server.
> - Log on using "anonymous" as the user name and your e-mail address as the password.
> - Navigate to the program you want to download. Type the *cd* and *dir* commands at the command prompt to change directories and list directory contents, respectively.
> - Set the transfer mode to binary by typing the *binary* command at the command prompt, and then press the Enter key.
> - Download the file by typing the *get* command at the command prompt with the filename you want to download, and then press the Enter key.
> - When the download is complete, disconnect from the remote site by typing the *quit* command, and then press the Enter key.

Three members of the DigiComm installation team prefer to use a different compression program than the one that you downloaded—they are using PKZIP. You could use the FTP command-line program on your company's computer to download the PKZIP file, but you prefer to use your Windows built-in FTP program which is in the Windows directory on your PC's hard drive. The first steps show you how to connect to a remote FTP server.

To connect to a remote FTP server using Windows FTP program:

1. Click the **Start** button on the taskbar, click **Run**, type **C:\Windows\ftp** in the Open text box in the Run dialog box, and then click the **OK** button. The Windows-supplied command-line FTP program opens and executes.

   TROUBLE? If your Windows installation is located on another hard drive, then type that drive letter in place of "C" in the command. If your Windows installation is located in a folder with another name, then type that folder name in place of "Windows" in the command. If the FTP window does not open after clicking the OK button, ask your instructor or technical support person for help.

2. If necessary, click the **Maximize** button to maximize the ftp program window.

3. Type **open ftp.pkware.com** at the ftp> prompt, and then press the **Enter** key to execute the FTP command that establishes a connection to the remote server.

   TROUBLE? If you get an error message that says "ftp.pkware.com Unknown host.", then you need to make a dial-up networking connection to your server before typing the open command. Ask your instructor or technical support person for help.

   TROUBLE? If nothing happens after you press the Enter key, the remote FTP site might be shut down for routine maintenance, or too many users might be attempting to access the site at once. If you cannot connect now, try again later.

4. When the FTP session establishes a connection with the remote FTP site, the remote site responds with a request for you to log on. Type **anonymous** at the User prompt, and then press the **Enter** key to send your user name to the site. When the remote site displays a Password prompt, type your full e-mail address (nothing displays in the password line as you type, so do not be concerned), and then press the **Enter** key. When the remote site accepts your user name and password, the system prompt, ftp>, reappears. See Figure 5-42.

TUTORIAL 5 EVALUATING AND DOWNLOADING WEB RESOURCES   WEB 5.53   INTERNET

Figure 5-42 **COMMAND-LINE FTP CONNECTED TO A REMOTE FTP SERVER**

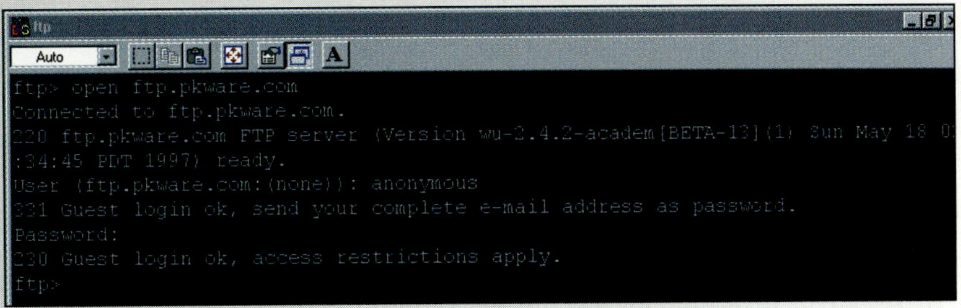

```
ftp> open ftp.pkware.com
Connected to ftp.pkware.com.
220 ftp.pkware.com FTP server (Version wu-2.4.2-academ[BETA-13](1) Sun May 18 0
:34:45 PDT 1997) ready.
User (ftp.pkware.com:(none)): anonymous
331 Guest login ok, send your complete e-mail address as password.
Password:
230 Guest login ok, access restrictions apply.
ftp>
```

Now that you have established a connection between your command-line FTP program and the remote server, you can search for the file you want to download. First, you will list the files at the remote site's root directory. Then, you can determine where the file you need is located. If it is in the root directory, check the spelling of the filename, set the transfer mode to binary, and then send the command to begin sending the file to your PC.

Note: If you cannot use your computer to download the PKZIP program file, then read the following steps without completing them at the computer.

To locate and download a file using a command-line FTP program:

1. Type **dir** at the ftp> prompt, and then press the **Enter** key to display the file listing for the root directory. The file you need is named pk260w32.exe.

2. Type **binary**, and then press the **Enter** key to set the transmission mode to binary (the site will respond with the message "Type set to I."). Always specify binary transmission mode when you send programs or data because only Web pages and e-mail attachments can be sent using ASCII transmission mode.

   TROUBLE? The program that you will download is over 750K. If your Student Disk does not have enough free space available, then use a new disk for these steps. Create a Tutorial.05 folder on the new disk, and write "Student Disk 2: Tutorial 5" on the disk's label.

3. Make sure that your Student Disk is in the appropriate drive, and then type **lcd A:\Tutorial.05** and press the **Enter** key. The site responds to let you know that the local directory is now A:\Tutorial.05, which means that all downloaded files will be saved in the Tutorial.05 folder on your Student Disk.

4. Type **get pk260w32.exe** (make sure to type the space between the word *get* and the filename) at the command prompt, and then press the **Enter** key. Immediately, the site starts downloading the file to your Student Disk (see Figure 5-43). When the file transfer is complete, a message indicates the total number of characters transferred and the transfer rate. Both the time and transfer rate will vary with your Internet connection speed and current Internet traffic.

Figure 5-43 DOWNLOADING THE PKZIP PROGRAM

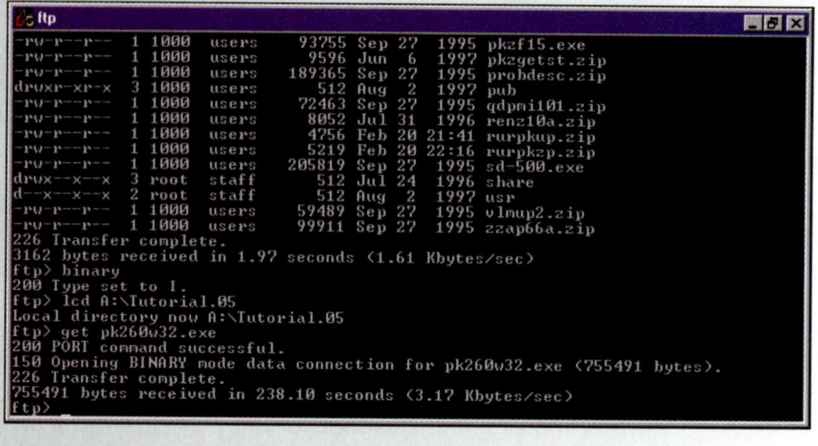

```
ftp
-rw-r--r--   1 1000     users       93755 Sep 27  1995 pkzf15.exe
-rw-r--r--   1 1000     users        9596 Jun  6  1997 pkzgetst.zip
-rw-r--r--   1 1000     users      189365 Sep 27  1995 probdesc.zip
drwxr-xr-x   3 1000     users         512 Aug  2  1997 pub
-rw-r--r--   1 1000     users       72463 Sep 27  1995 qdpmi101.zip
-rw-r--r--   1 1000     users        8052 Jul 31  1996 renz10a.zip
-rw-r--r--   1 1000     users        4756 Feb 20 21:41 rwpkwp.zip
-rw-r--r--   1 1000     users        5219 Feb 20 22:16 rwpkzp.zip
-rw-r--r--   1 1000     users      205819 Sep 27  1995 sd-500.exe
drwx--x--x   3 root     staff         512 Jul 24  1996 share
d--x--x--x   2 root     staff         512 Aug  2  1997 usr
-rw-r--r--   1 1000     users       59489 Sep 27  1995 vlmup2.zip
-rw-r--r--   1 1000     users       99911 Sep 27  1995 zzap66a.zip
226 Transfer complete.
3162 bytes received in 1.97 seconds (1.61 Kbytes/sec)
ftp> binary
200 Type set to I.
ftp> lcd A:\Tutorial.05
Local directory now A:\Tutorial.05
ftp> get pk260w32.exe
200 PORT command successful.
150 Opening BINARY mode data connection for pk260w32.exe (755491 bytes).
226 Transfer complete.
755491 bytes received in 238.10 seconds (3.17 Kbytes/sec)
ftp>
```

5. Type **quit** and then press the **Enter** Key at the command prompt to disconnect from the remote site, and close the FTP command-line session. If you are using a dial-up connection, close it now. (Your instructor will inform you of how to close a dial-up connection, if necessary. However, if you are using your school's computer lab, it is likely that you are not using a dial-up connection.)

Nancy is pleased with the programs that you found for the ground-station installation team. After testing the programs to make sure that they will serve the team's needs and fulfilling any licensing agreements, you can install them on the team's computers.

Quick Check

1. List an advantage of using a download site such as TUCOWS or DOWNLOAD.COM when you want to download a variety of programs.

2. What is the name of the special document format for storing documents on the Web so users can print them without needing the program that originally created the document?

3. Describe several factors that could cause a download to progress slowly.

4. What is the general name for a program that reduces the size of one or more files and can save multiple files using a single filename?

5. What is a file extension and what purpose does it serve? That is, are file extensions simply randomly assigned, three-character names, or do they actually have a purpose?

6. List two advantages of using an FTP client over a Web browser for transferring files between two computers connected to the Internet.

You successfully downloaded many programs from the Internet. Now, you are ready to install and configure the material on the installation team members' computers.

TUTORIAL 5 EVALUATING AND DOWNLOADING WEB RESOURCES   WEB 5.55

TUTORIAL ASSIGNMENTS

DigiComm purchased 25 notebook computers for members of the installation team and its supervisory staff. More than six months have passed since you first started investigating FTP programs and using FTP to download programs and data. You used your personal notebook computer to test the programs, and Nancy has been pleased with your work. You have installed the WS_FTP Limited Edition FTP program and have used it to transfer files on the Internet. In addition, you have downloaded and installed two compression programs—WinZip and PKZIP. Both programs work flawlessly and you are ready to install a standard set of programs on the DigiComm team members' computers. Nancy notices that your suite of programs includes both Navigator and Internet Explorer and their associated e-mail programs. However, seven members of the installation team like to use Eudora Light, an e-mail program from Qualcomm, at work and at home. Nancy has asked you to locate Eudora Light and download it; you will install it later. You will use an FTP client program to download Eudora Light to your PC. Your research reveals that Eudora Light is the free version that you can use without restriction. If it turns out that other members of the installation team like the program, then you can approach Nancy about purchasing 25 licenses to the more powerful, commercial version, Eudora Pro. The file size of the Eudora Light program is nearly five megabytes. You decide to read the user's manual before you download the file to see if you can expect any problems with other programs that you might install on the team members' computer. Fortunately, you can download, and then review and print, a user manual for Eudora Light in PDF. First, you will download the manual so you can review its requirements, and then you will download the program.

Do the following:

1. Place your Student Disk in the appropriate drive.
2. Start the WS_FTP Limited Edition FTP client program on your computer. (*Note:* The Tutorial Assignments are written for the WS_FTP Limited Edition FTP client program. However, you can use any FTP client to complete the steps by using equivalent steps in your FTP client.)
3. Create a new session profile named Eudora. The host name or address is ftp.qualcomm.com. You will log on using an anonymous login and your full e-mail address as the password.
4. Connect and log on to the Qualcomm FTP server. (*Hint*: You might need to make a dial-up connection before connecting to the Qualcomm server.)
5. Change the remote directory to /eudora/eudoralight/windows/english.
6. Change the local PC directory to the Tutorial.05 folder on your Student Disk.
7. Select the file named eul3man1.pdf on the remote server, and then download that file to the Tutorial.05 folder on your Student Disk. This file contains the Eudora Light user's manual in PDF format.
8. After the download is complete, disconnect from the remote server, close your FTP client, and then close your dial-up connection, if necessary.
9. If necessary, install the Adobe Acrobat Reader program saved in the Tutorial.05 folder on your Student Disk. (*Note:* Check with your instructor or technical support person before installing any program on your computer's hard drive.)
10. Open Windows Explorer, open the Tutorial.05 folder on your Student Disk, and then double-click the eul3man1.pdf file that you just downloaded. Acrobat Reader will open the Eudora user's manual on your screen.

Explore
11. Locate the pages that describe "Using a Signature" found somewhere in the first 50 pages. The description of signature files may span more than one page. Print up to two pages describing signature files. (*Hint:* Use the Acrobat Reader's Help system to learn more about using the Reader program to read Eudora's program documentation.)

CASE PROBLEMS

1. Arnaud for Senate Campaign You work for the campaign team of Jessica Arnaud, who is running for a seat in the state senate. One issue that promises to play a prominent role in the upcoming election campaign is her opponent's position on privatization of the state prison system. It is important for Jessica to establish a clear position on the issue early in the campaign, and she has asked you to prepare a briefing document for her to consider. Jessica tells you that she has no particular preference on the issue and that she wants you to obtain a balanced set of arguments for each side. Once the campaign takes a position, however, she will need to defend it. Therefore, Jessica wants to have an idea of the quality of the information you gather. You decide to do part of your research on the Web.

Do the following:

1. Start your Web browser, go to the Student Online Companion (http://www.course.com/NewPerspectives/Internet), click the link for your book, click the Tutorial 5 link, and then click the Case Problems link in the left frame.
2. Click the AltaVista hyperlink to open that search engine.
3. Type the words "privatization prisons" (without the quotation marks) in the search text box, and then click the Search button.
4. Examine your list of search results for authoritative sites that include positions on the issue. You might need to follow a number of results page hyperlinks to find suitable Web pages. In general, you should avoid current news items that appear in the results list.
5. Find one Web page that states a clear position in favor of privatization and another that states a clear position against privatization. Print a copy of each.
6. For each page, prepare a three-paragraph report that evaluates the quality of the page on each of the three criteria: author identity and objectivity, content, and form and appearance.
7. When you are finished, close your Web browser and close your dial-up connection, if necessary.

2. Internet Adventures Internet Adventures is a one-person consulting company providing a variety of consulting services to small- and medium-sized companies. Hannah Leonard, owner of Internet Adventures, charges an hourly rate to help companies find and download information on the Internet. She is working for a large CPA firm that wants her to create bookmarks and favorites to Web sites that interest tax preparers. Some members of the tax-preparation team use Internet Explorer, and others use Navigator. When team members find interesting Web sites, they use their browsers to create either a Navigator bookmark or an Internet Explorer favorite to the location. The team members don't always have time to bookmark the site in the other browser, so they end up losing some of the URLs to important sites. Hannah remembers reading a review about several shareware products that might be able to maintain a library of common bookmarks that Internet Explorer and Navigator can share.

Do the following:

1. Start your Web browser, and then go to the Student Online Companion page by entering the URL http://www.course.com/NewPerspectives/Internet in the appropriate location in your Web browser. Click the hyperlink for your book, click the Tutorial 5 link, and then click the Case Problems link. Click the TUCOWS link and wait while the browser loads the page. Use the links to connect to a server in a region or state that is the closest to your location.
2. Click the Win95/98 link to open the page of Windows Internet programs.
3. Locate the Browsers and Accessories category, and then click the Bookmark Utilities link.
4. On the Bookmark Utilities page, scroll the list and locate Bookmark Converter. If you cannot find that bookmark program in the list, then scroll down the list looking for a

bookmark program whose description indicates it can convert bookmarks between Internet Explorer and Navigator.
5. Download the Bookmark Converter program and save it on the Tutorial.05 folder on your Student Disk.
6. Close your Web browser and close your dial-up connection, if neccessary.

3. Baseline High School Computer Laboratory   Marco Lozario is director of computing at Baseline High School. He and his staff of three people ensure that the school's computer lab of 45 Windows-based computers function properly. Last week, a virus infected every computer in the lab, and Marco had to close the lab to prevent the virus from spreading to students' disks and other computers. Each lab computer has McAfee Virus Scan software installed on it, but the installed version does not recognize and cannot eradicate the new virus pattern. Help Marco download the latest virus data file from McAfee.

Do the following:

1. Start your FTP client program.
2. Create a new session profile using the profile name McAfee and the host address ftp.mcafee.com. You will connect as an anonymous user, and use your full e-mail address as your password.
3. Connect to McAfee's FTP site.
4. Change the remote computer's directory to /pub/antivirus/datfiles/3.x so that you can see the antivirus data files on the remote system's list of files.
5. Change your PC's directory to the Tutorial.05 folder on your Student Disk.
6. Select the file whose name begins with dat and ends with the file extension zip. (There may be several files, but you are interested only in the compressed antivirus file.) Download the file, and save it in the Tutorial.05 folder on your Student Disk.
7. After the data file transfers successfully to your disk, log off the McAfee site and close the FTP client program.

Explore
8. The WS_FTP Limited Edition FTP client program creates a log file showing the date and time you downloaded the software. If you used WS_FTP Limited Edition, then locate the log file (it is called Ws_ftp.log) and open it with Word or WordPad.
9. Print the log file to show that you downloaded the antivirus data file. Be sure to add your name and any other identifying information your instructor requests to the document before you print it.

4. Internet Marketing Pros   Eddie Ponzi owns Internet Marketing Pros, an Internet marketing and advertising agency that helps businesses create a Web presence to attract customers. The U. S. Census Bureau maintains records about retail sales and inventory information at its Web and FTP sites. Eddie wants to download some historic sales information from 1996 so he can compare it to the data for the current year. Use a command-line FTP program to download a retail sales worksheet in Lotus 1-2-3 format and an accompanying FAQ (frequently asked questions) file to print for your instructor.

Do the following:

1. Click the Start button on the taskbar, click Run, type C:\Windows\ftp in the Open text box of the Run dialog box, and then click the OK button to start the Windows-supplied FTP program.
2. Click the FTP window Maximize button to enlarge the window. (It might not maximize to fill your entire screen, however.)
3. To the right of the "ftp>" prompt, type open ftp.census.gov and press the Enter key to execute the command, which opens the U.S. Census Bureau FTP site.
4. Type anonymous, and then press the Enter key at the User prompt.
5. Type your full e-mail address as your password, and then press the Enter key.
6. Type cd pub/svsd/retlmon/download, and then press the Enter key to change the remote directory.

7. Place your Student Disk in the appropriate disk drive.
8. Type lcd A:\Tutorial.05, and press the Enter key to change your local computer's current directory to the Tutorial.05 folder on your Student Disk.
9. Type binary, and then press the Enter key to establish binary transfer mode.
10. Type get 95reldte.txt, and press the Enter key to download a file to the Tutorial.05 folder on your Student Disk.
11. Type get area96.wk1 (the last character in the second name is the digit one), and then press the Enter key to download the file and save it in the Tutorial.05 folder on your Student Disk.
12. Type quit to log off of the Census Bureau FTP server. If necessary, close your dial-up connection.
13. Open the 95reldte.txt file that you downloaded in WordPad or any other word processor, and then type your name at the top of page. Save your changes.
14. Print the page, and then close WordPad.

Quick Check Answers

Session 5.1
1. Author identity and credentials help establish the credibility of Web page content.
2. Their employment or other professional affiliations
3. True
4. Timeliness, inclusion of relevant topics, depth of treatment
5. By adding online resources to their collections and by making their collections accessible to remote users and other libraries.
6. False
7. Available 24 hours a day, seven days a week; can be easier and faster to search.
8. To increase recognition of their brand name among all news information consumers and to provide a sample of their services to potential customers.
9. NewsTracker offers broader coverage; NewsHub offers more timely coverage.
10. False

Session 5.2
1. False
2. anonymous
3. binary
4. hierarchical
5. ftp://ftp.goodsoftware.com
6. virus
7. compression
8. False

Session 5.3
1. Visiting a "download supermarket" provides you much more choice. You can select from dozens of compression programs, for example.
2. Portable Document Format (PDF)
3. Lots of Internet traffic on the site, several people downloading the same program as you or delays along the Internet at one or more hosts.
4. compression program
5. A file extension can be associated with a program that opens the file. For example, a secondary name of .xls means that the file is an Excel workbook file.
6. File transfers are faster with an FTP client; with a browser, you cannot upload files to a site requiring a password and user name—an account. Only anonymous FTP is handled by a browser.

GLOSSARY/INDEX

A

acceptable use policies (AUPs), WEB 1.18, WEB 1.19
The policy of a school or employer that specifies the conditions under which its students and/or employees can use their Internet connections.

Acrobat Reader A program developed by Adobe, Inc. that displays or prints documents stored in the proprietary PDF format.

Address Bar
entering URLs in, WEB 3.42–44
Element of the Internet Explorer browser window into which you can enter the URL of a Web page that you would like to open.

address books, WEB 2.11
adding e-mail addresses to
in Netscape Messenger, WEB 2.27–29
in Outlook Express, WEB 2.46–47
multi-address entries in, WEB 2.11
in Netscape Navigator, WEB 2.29–31
in Outlook Express, WEB 2.48–49
The collection of e-mail addresses maintained by an e-mail program and stored in some convenient way. Often, nicknames can be assigned to address book entries so they are easy to recall and insert into e-mail message headers.

addressing
domain name, WEB 3.6–7
IP (Internet Protocol), WEB 3.5–6

Adobe Acrobat Reader
downloading, WEB 5.45–47

ADSL, WEB 1.16

Advanced Research Projects Agency (ARPA or DARPA), WEB 1.5–6
The U.S. Department of Defense agency that sponsored the early research and development of technologies and systems that later became the Internet.

advanced searches, WEB 4.20–27
using AltaVista, WEB 4.20–23
using Excite, WEB 4.25–26
using HotBot, WEB 4.23–25
using Northern Light, WEB 4.26–27

AltaVista A Web search engine.

AltaVista search engine, WEB 4.5–6, WEB 4.7, WEB 4.9, WEB 4.14
advanced searches in, WEB 4.20–23
date-range searches, WEB 5.10–11
news and current information resources, WEB 5.10–11

American Psychological Association (APA), WEB 5.8–9

anchor tags, WEB 3.3
An HTML tag that links multiple HTML documents to each other. The connection between two HTML documents is called a hypertext link, a hyperlink, or, simply, a link.

AND NOT operator, WEB 4.18

AND operator, WEB 4.18–19

Andreessen, Marc, WEB 1.13

anonymous FTP, WEB 5.19–20
uploading files, WEB 5.31–32
The time period between when you log on to another computer anonymously and when you log off. During that time, FTP transfers files to and from another computer connected to the Internet.

anonymous login Logging on to one of the many publicly accessible remote computers by specifying the username *anonymous* and your e-mail address as the password.

antivirus software, WEB 5.30
searching for, WEB 5.39–41

appearance, of Web pages
evaluating, WEB 5.3–6

Argus Clearinghouse, WEB 4.15–17
A Web bibliography site that reviews and provides hyperlinks and guides to various subjects.

ARPA, WEB 1.6

ARPANET
defined, WEB 1.6
e-mail messages over, WEB 1.7
history, WEB 1.9
The experimental WAN that DARPA established in 1969 to connect universities and research institutions so they could share computer resources.

ASCII text
file transfer, WEB 5.27
Text that contains symbols typed from the keyboard that does not contain any nonprintable, binary codes.

ASCII mode A file transfer setting in which all data being transferred consist of printable characters. Thus, no special treatment of the transferred data is needed to preserve nonprintable characters.

asterisk (*) wildcard character, WEB 4.20

Asymmetric Digital Subscriber Line (ADSL), WEB 1.16
A new type of digital subscriber line (DSL) that offers transmission speeds ranging from 16 to 640 Kbps from the user to the telephone company and from 1.5 to 9 Mbps from the telephone company to the user.

Asynchronous Transfer Mode (ATM)
bandwidth, WEB 1.17
defined, WEB 1.16
A high-bandwidth (622 Mbps) data transmission connection used as part of the Internet backbone.

attachments, to e-mail messages, WEB 2.5
sending, in Netscape Messenger, WEB 2.18–19
viewing, in Netscape Messenger, WEB 2.21
A file encoded so that it can be carried over the Internet safely when affixed to an e-mail message.

AUPs (acceptable use policies), WEB 1.18, WEB 1.19

authors, of Web sites
determining identity of, WEB 5.2–3
determining qualifications of, WEB 5.3

Auto Hide feature
in Internet Explorer, WEB 3.41–42

B

Back button, WEB 3.12, WEB 3.26

bandwidth, WEB 1.16–17
defined, WEB 1.16
for Internet connection types, WEB 1.17
measurement of, WEB 1.16
The amount of data that can travel through a communications circuit in one second.

Bcc line (blind carbon copy), WEB 2.4

Because It's Time Network (BITNET), WEB 1.7
A network of IBM mainframe computers at universities founded by the City University of New York.

Berners-Lee, Tim, WEB 1.12

binary A two-digit numbering system consisting of zero and one. Keyboard characters are formed from binary numbers; there are several binary numbers that have no corresponding printable or readable character.

binary mode A file transfer setting in which all of the characters, whether they can be displayed or not, are preserved during the file transfer process. Graphics files, word-processed documents, and spreadsheets are examples of files that must be transferred in binary mode.

binary mode file transfer, WEB 5.27–28

BITNET, WEB 1.7

bits per second (bps), WEB 1.16
The basic increment in which bandwidth is measured.

blind carbon copy (Bcc) line, WEB 2.4
A copy of an e-mail message sent to a primary recipient without the Bcc recipient's address appearing in the message. The message's original recipient is unaware that others received the message.

.bmp file extension, WEB 5.29

bookmark A feature of Navigator that allows you to save the URL of a specific page so you can return to it.

bookmark folders
creating, WEB 3.22–23
saving bookmarks in, WEB 3.23–24

bookmarks. *See also* **Favorites**
creating, WEB 3.20–24
defined, WEB 3.12
using, WEB 3.13

Bookmarks button, WEB 3.20–24

Bookmarks window
examining bookmark hierarchy in, WEB 3.21

Boolean algebra, WEB 4.18
A branch of mathematics and logic in which all values are reduced to one of two values—in most practical applications of Boolean algebra, these two values are *true* and *false*.

Boolean logic, WEB 4.18–20

Boolean operators, WEB 4.18–19
In Boolean algebra, operators that specify the logical relationship between the elements they join. Also known as logical operators.

bots, WEB 4.5
A program used by Web search engines that automatically searches the Web to find new Web sites and updates information about old Web sites that already are in the search engine's database. Also known as a spider or Web robot.

bps (bits per second), WEB 1.16

bugs
in freeware, WEB 5.32
Errors found in software that can cause a program to halt, misbehave, or damage the user's computer.

Bush, Vannevar, WEB 1.12

C

cable modems, WEB 1.19
Converts a computer's digital signals into radio-frequency analog signals that are similar to television transmission signals. The converted signals travel to and from the user's cable company, which maintains a connection to the Internet.

cables, WEB 1.4

C

cable television
    Internet connections through, WEB 1.16–17

cache folder
    in Web browsers, WEB 3.12
    The folder in which a Web browser stores copies of Web pages that you have visited recently. By loading the Web page from the cache folder instead of the Web server, the browser can increase the speed at which it displays pages.

Calliau, Robert, WEB 1.12

carbon copy (Cc) line, WEB 2.4
    A copy of an e-mail message sent to other people in addition to the primary recipient.

Cerf, Vincent, WEB 1.6

CERN, WEB 1.12

circuit switching, WEB 1.5–6
    A centrally controlled, single-connection method for sending information over a network.

citation, of Web research resources, WEB 5.8–9

Clark, James, WEB 1.13

clearinghouses, WEB 4.15
    A Web site that contains a list of hyperlinks to other Web pages that contain information about a particular topic or group of topics and often includes summaries or reviews of the Web pages listed. Also known as a guide, resource list, virtual library, or Web bibliography.

client computer A computer that is connected to another, usually more powerful, computer called a server. The client computer can use the server computer's resources, such as printers, files, or programs. This way of connecting computers is called a client/server network.

clients, WEB 1.3

client/server FTP, WEB 5.18–19

client/server networks, WEB 1.3
    A way of connecting multiple computers, called client computers, to a main computer, called a server computer. This connection method allows the client computers to share the server computer's resources, such as printers, files, and programs.

C/NET, WEB 5.36

coaxial cable, WEB 1.4
    An insulated copper wire that is encased in a metal shield and then enclosed in plastic insulation. The signal-carrying wire is completely shielded so it resists electrical interference much better than twisted-pair cable does. Coaxial cable also carries signals about 20 times faster than twisted-pair cable, but it is considerably more expensive.

command-line FTP
    defined, WEB 5.17–18
    downloading files with, WEB 5.53–54
    downloading with, WEB 5.51–54
    An FTP interface in which you enter a series of one-line commands to connect to an FTP site.

command-line interface
    A method of entering commands to a program in which you enter a command and press the Enter key; the receiving computer then acts on the command.

commercial e-mail services, WEB 1.8–9

Compose Message button
    in Outlook Express, WEB 2.36

Composition window
    in Netscape Messenger, WEB 2.12–14
    The Netscape Messenger window in which you create e-mail messages.

compressed files, WEB 5.30
    A file that is saved in a special format that makes its file size smaller to conserve space and shorten download time.

compressing files, WEB 5.31–32

CompuServe, WEB 1.9

Computer Science Network (CSNET), WEB 1.6–7
    An internet funded by the NSF for educational and research institutions that did not have access to the ARPANET.

connections to the Internet, WEB 1.15–21
    bandwidth, WEB 1.16–17
    service providers, WEB 1.15
    through cable television companies, WEB 1.16–17, WEB 1.19–20
    through employers, WEB 1.18–19
    through Internet service providers (ISPs), WEB 1.19
    through schools, WEB 1.17–18
    via satellite, WEB 1.17, WEB 1.20

contact information
    on Web sites, WEB 5.2

content, of Web pages
    evaluating, WEB 5.3

cookie A small file that a Web server can write to the disk drive of a Web client computer running Web browser software.

copies, of e-mail messages, WEB 2.4

copyright The legal right of the author or other owner of an original work to control the reproduction, distribution, and sale of that work.

copyright law, WEB 3.14, WEB 5.16

country domain names, WEB 3.7

current events
    Web research resources, WEB 5.9–16

D

date-range restriction searches, WEB 5.10–13

decompressing files, WEB 5.30
    The process of restoring a compressed file to its original form.

Deleted Items folder
    in Outlook Express, WEB 2.44–45

deleting
    e-mail messages, WEB 2.10
        in Netscape Messenger, WEB 2.26–27
        in Outlook Express, WEB 2.44–46
    mail folders
        in Netscape Messenger, WEB 2.26–27
        in Outlook Express, WEB 2.46

demodulation, WEB 1.18
    The process of converting an analog signal to a digital signal.

Digital Subscriber Line, WEB 1.16

Digital Subscriber Loop (DSL), WEB 1.16
    A protocol used by some telephone companies that allows higher bandwidth data transmissions than standard telephone service does.

directories, WEB 3.12, WEB 4.4, WEB 4.5–12
    defined, WEB 4.8
    hybrid search engine directories, WEB 4.9

distribution lists, WEB 2.11
    creating in Outlook Express, WEB 2.48–49
    A single address book nickname that refers to a collection of two or more e-mail addresses. Also known as a group mailing list.

DNS (domain name server) software, WEB 3.6
    A program on an Internet host computer that coordinates the IP addresses and domain names for all of the computers attached to it.

.doc file extension, WEB 5.29

Dogpile, WEB 4.13–14
    A Web meta-search engine.

domain names, WEB 3.6–7
    country, WEB 3.7
    defined, WEB 3.6
    top-level, WEB 3.6–7
    Web site evaluation and, WEB 5.3
    A unique name that is associated with a specific IP address by a program that runs on an Internet host computer.

domain name servers, WEB 3.6
    The Internet host computer that runs DNS software to coordinate the IP addresses and domain names for every computer attached to it.

double quotation marks
    in search expressions, WEB 4.19

download The process of getting a file or data from a computer connected to the Internet and saving the file or data on your PC.

DOWNLOAD.COM, WEB 5.35–36
    downloading files from, WEB 5.45–47

downloading files, WEB 5.41–54
    Adobe Acrobat Reader, WEB 5.45–47
    in binary mode, WEB 5.27–28
    with command-line FTP, WEB 5.51–54
    defined, WEB 5.16
    FTP clients, WEB 5.41–45
    with FTP clients, WEB 5.47–51
    from FTP sites, WEB 5.26–30
    WinZip, WEB 5.47–51

Down scroll arrow, WEB 3.11

DSL, WEB 1.16

dumb terminals, WEB 2.8
    An otherwise "smart" computer that passes all your keystrokes to another computer to which you are connected and does not attempt to do anything else.

E

educational institutions
    Internet connections through, WEB 1.17–18

.edu domain names, WEB 5.3

electronic mail. *See* **e-mail**

electronic publishing, WEB 5.9

e-mail
    defined, WEB 1.2, WEB 2.2
    history of, WEB 1.7
    mail client software, WEB 2.2
    protocols, WEB 2.2
    Web-based, WEB 2.8
    The transmission of messages over communications networks, such as the Internet.

e-mail addresses
    adding to address books, WEB 2.11
        in Netscape Messenger, WEB 2.27–29
        in Outlook Express, WEB 2.46–47
    in Cc and Bcc lines of e-mail messages, WEB 2.4
    distribution lists, WEB 2.11
    host names, WEB 2.7
    in From line of e-mail messages, WEB 2.4
    in To line of e-mail messages, WEB 2.4
    user names, WEB 2.6–7

e-mail clients, WEB 2.7–11. *See also* **Microsoft Outlook Express; Netscape Messenger**
    free, WEB 2.8–9
    setting up, WEB 2.9
    shareware, WEB 2.8
    using, WEB 2.9–10

e-mail messages
    attachments, WEB 2.5
    Bcc line, WEB 2.4
    Cc line, WEB 2.4

components of, WEB 2.3–6
defined, WEB 2.6
deleting, WEB 2.10
    in Netscape Messenger, WEB 2.26–27
    in Outlook Express, WEB 2.44–46
filing
    in Netscape Messenger, WEB 2.24–25
    in Outlook Express, WEB 2.43–44
filing, with filters, WEB 2.10
forwarding, WEB 2.10
    in Netscape Messenger, WEB 2.23–24
    in Outlook Express, WEB 2.42
guidelines for writing, WEB 2.9
From line, WEB 2.4
To line, WEB 2.3–4
message body, WEB 2.3, WEB 2.5
message header, WEB 2.3
opening
    in Netscape Messenger, WEB 2.21
    in Outlook Express, WEB 2.39–40
printing, WEB 2.9
    in Netscape Messenger, WEB 2.25
    in Outlook Express, WEB 2.44
queued
    in Outlook Express, WEB 2.36
queuing, WEB 2.9
quoted, WEB 2.10
receiving, WEB 2.9
    in Netscape Messenger, WEB 2.19–20
    in Outlook Express, WEB 2.38–39
replying to, WEB 2.10
    in Netscape Messenger, WEB 2.22–23
    in Outlook Express, WEB 2.40–41
saving
    in Netscape Messenger, WEB 2.21
    in Outlook Express, WEB 2.39–40
sending
    with attachments, in Netscape
        Messenger, WEB 2.18–19
    copies of, WEB 2.4
    in Netscape Messenger, WEB 2.17–19
    in Outlook Express, WEB 2.35–38
signature files, WEB 2.5–6
Subject line, WEB 2.4
transferring between folders
    in Outlook Express, WEB 2.44

e-mail services, commercial, WEB 1.8–9
encryption, WEB 3.31, WEB 3.53–54
    A way of scrambling and encoding data transmissions that reduces the risk that a person who intercepted the Web page as it traveled across the Internet would be able to decode and read the transmission's contents.
error messages
    for nonworking hyperlinks, WEB 3.5
Ethernet networks, WEB 1.16
Eudora Light, WEB 5.33
Excite
    advanced searches in, WEB 4.25–26
    news and current information resources,
        WEB 5.9–10
    NewsTracker, WEB 5.14–16
ExciteMail, WEB 2.8
.exe file extension, WEB 5.29
expansion, file The process of restoring a file to its original, uncompressed form.
exploratory questions, WEB 4.2–3
    An open-ended question that can be difficult to phrase; also it is difficult to determine when you find a good answer.
exploratory searches
    using Argus Clearinghouse, WEB 4.15–17
extensions, WEB 5.28–29
e-zines, WEB 5.9
    A Web-based electronic magazine.

F

Fast Ethernet, WEB 1.16
Favorites, WEB 3.44–47. *See also* **bookmarks**
    creating new folders, WEB 3.45–46
    defined, WEB 3.12
    organizing, WEB 3.46–47
    using, WEB 3.13
    A feature of Internet Explorer that allows you to save the URL of a specific page so you can return to it.
Favorites button, WEB 3.44
Federal Networking Council (FNC), WEB 1.9
fiber-optic cable, WEB 1.4
    A type of cable that transmits information by pulsing beams of light through very thin strands of glass. Fiber-optic cable transmits signals much faster than coaxial cable does and, because it does not use electricity, is immune to electrical interference. Fiber-optic cable is lighter and more durable than coaxial cable is, but it is harder to work with and much more expensive.
file compression The process of reducing the size of one or more files and saving them in a special storage format.
file compression programs, WEB 5.30
    UNIX built-in, WEB 5.31
file extensions
    defined, WEB 5.28
    file types and, WEB 5.28–29
    in Windows, viewing, WEB 5.28–29
    The last three characters following the period in a filename.
file transfer modes, FTP, WEB 5.27–28
    Transferring a file so its special, nonprintable codes are preserved during the transfer by using a binary transfer mode. If the file consists entirely of plain text—with no special, unprintable characters—then an ASCII file transfer mode is appropriate.
File Transfer Protocol (FTP). *See* **FTP**
    The part of the TCP/IP protocol set that includes rules for formatting, ordering, and error-checking files sent across a network.
file utility programs, WEB 5.30
    A computer program that transforms the downloaded file into a form that is usable on your computer.
filter (e-mail) An automatic method of filing incoming mail into one or several mailboxes or folders based on characters found in the message header or message body.
filing e-mail messages, WEB 2.10
    in Netscape Messenger, WEB 2.24–25
    in Outlook Express, WEB 2.43–44
filters
    for filing e-mail messages, WEB 2.10
floating toolbar component
    in Netscape Navigator, WEB 3.16
floppy disks
    saving bookmark files to, WEB 3.23–24
    saving Web pages to, WEB 3.33–38,
        WEB 3.55–59
FNC (Federal Networking Council), WEB 1.9
folders
    creating in Outlook Express, WEB 2.43–44
    deleting in Outlook Express, WEB 2.46
Folder list
    A list of e-mail folders for receiving, saving, and deleting mail messages.

form, of Web pages
    evaluating, WEB 5.3–6
formal signatures
    for e-mail messages, WEB 2.5
    An e-mail signature that typically contains the sender's name, title, company name, company address, telephone and fax numbers, and e-mail address.
Forward button, WEB 3.12, WEB 3.26
forwarding e-mail messages, WEB 2.10
    in Netscape Messenger, WEB 2.23–24
    in Outlook Express, WEB 2.42
    The process of sending a copy of an e-mail message to another recipient whom you specify without the original sender's knowledge.
forward slash (/), WEB 3.8
    in FTP sites, WEB 5.26
freeware, WEB 5.32
    Software that is available to anyone for no cost and with no restrictions attached to its user.
From line, WEB 2.4
From line (e-mail) Contains the e-mail address of a message's sender.
FTP, WEB 3.8, WEB 5.16–33
    anonymous sessions, WEB 5.19–20
    commands, WEB 5.51–52
    defined, WEB 1.7, WEB 5.16
    file transfer modes, WEB 5.27–28
    full-privilege, WEB 5.20–21
    uploading files, WEB 5.31–33
ftp://, WEB 5.20
FTP client A Windows program residing on your PC that facilitates transferring files between your PC and a computer connected to the Internet.
FTP client programs, WEB 5.21–22
    command-line interface, WEB 5.17–18,
        WEB 5.21
    defined, WEB 5.17
    downloading, WEB 5.41–45
    downloading files with, WEB 5.47–51
    using, WEB 5.23–26
    Windows-based (GUI), WEB 5.17–18,
        WEB 5.21–22
FTP servers, WEB 5.18–19, WEB 5.19–23
    A program that receives file transfer requests from your FTP client program and then acts on those commands.
FTP sites
    determining location in, WEB 5.25–26
    hierarchy of, WEB 5.23
    opening, using a Web browser, WEB 5.24–25
    public (pub) directories, WEB 5.26
    root directory in, WEB 5.23, WEB 5.25–26
full-privilege FTP, WEB 5.20–21
    Logging on to a computer on which you have an account, including a user name and password, and using it to send and receive files.
Fullscreen button
    in Internet Explorer, WEB 3.41–42
full text indexing, WEB 4.8
    A method that some search engines use for creating their databases in which the entire content of included Web pages is stored in the database.

G

Gbps (gigibits per second), WEB 1.16
.gif file extension, WEB 5.29
gigibits per second (Gbps), WEB 1.16
    A measure of bandwidth; 1,073,741,824 bits per second (bps).

Go command
in Netscape Navigator, WEB 3.26
.gov domain names, WEB 5.3
graphical transfer process indicator
in Internet Explorer, WEB 3.40
Element of the Internet Explorer status bar that indicates how much of a Web page has loaded from the Web server.
graphical user interface (GUI), WEB 1.13, WEB 3.9–11
A way of presenting program output to users that uses pictures, icons, and other graphical elements instead of just displaying text.
graphic images
as hyperlinks, WEB 3.4
public domain files, WEB 5.16
saving from Web pages, WEB 3.13
saving to disk, WEB 3.36–37, WEB 3.58–59
group address entries
creating in Outlook Express, WEB 2.48–49
group mailing lists, WEB 2.11
See distribution list.
grouping operators, WEB 4.19
Operators that clarify the grouping within complex search expressions; usually indicated by parentheses or double quotation marks. Also known as inclusion operators or precedence operators.
GUI. *See* **graphical user interface (GUI)**
Guide *See* **clearinghouse**
Guide button
in Netscape Navigator, WEB 3.28
guides, WEB 4.15
GUI programs
FTP, WEB 5.17–18, WEB 5.21–22

H

Help
in Internet Explorer, WEB 3.54–55
in Netscape Navigator, WEB 3.32–33
hierarchical structure
of bookmarks window, WEB 3.21
of FTP sites, WEB 5.23
The organized, inverted tree containing folders and files on a computer.
History button
in Internet Explorer, WEB 3.49
history list, WEB 3.12–13
viewing, WEB 3.26–27
viewing in Internet Explorer, WEB 3.49–50
A file in which the Web browser stores the location of each page you visit as you navigate hyperlinks from one Web page to another.
hits, WEB 4.5
A Web page that is indexed in a search engine's database and contains text that matches the search expression entered into the search engine. Search engines provide hyperlinks to hits on results pages.
Home button
in Netscape Navigator, WEB 3.27
in Web browsers, WEB 3.11
home directory
of FTP sites, WEB 5.23
See root directory.
home pages
default
in Internet Explorer, WEB 3.51
in Netscape Navigator, WEB 3.27–28
defined, WEB 3.5

displaying in Netscape Navigator, WEB 3.27
modifying, in Internet Explorer, WEB 3.51
returning to, in Internet Explorer, WEB 3.50–51
use of term, WEB 3.5
The main page that all of the pages on a particular Web site are organized around and to which they link back; or the first page that opens when a particular Web browser program is started; or the page that a particular Web browser program loads the first time it is run. This page usually is stored at the Web site of the firm or other organization that created the Web browser software. Home pages under the second and third definitions also are called start pages.
host names, WEB 2.6–7
A user-friendly name that uniquely identifies a computer connected to the Internet. You can use it in place of an IP address.
host name suffix, WEB 2.7
HotBot A Web search engine.
HotBot search engine, WEB 4.6–7
advanced searches in, WEB 4.23–25
date-range searches, WEB 5.10–11
last-modified date searches, WEB 5.12–13
news and current information resources, WEB 5.10–11
searching for software with, WEB 5.34–35
SuperSearch page, WEB 5.10–11
A Web site that combines the functions of a Web search engine and a Web directory.
HotMail, WEB 2.8
HTML, WEB 1.12, WEB 3.3
HTML documents, WEB 1.13
.html file extension, WEB 5.29
http://, WEB 3.8
hybrid search engine directories, WEB 4.9
A Web site that combines the function of a Web search engine and a Web directory.
hyperlink navigation
with the mouse, in Internet Explorer, WEB 3.47–39
with the mouse, in Netscape Navigator, WEB 3.24–28
hyperlinks
defined, WEB 1.12, WEB 3.3
following, WEB 3.25–26, WEB 3.48–49
graphic images as, WEB 3.4
locating on a page, WEB 3.4
nonworking, error messages for, WEB 3.5
uses of, WEB 3.3–4
A connection between two HTML pages. Also known as a link or a hypertext link.
hypermedia links, WEB 3.4
A connection between an HTML document and a multimedia file, such as a graphics image file (GIF), sound clip file, or video file.
hypertext
defined, WEB 1.12
origins of, WEB 1.12
A page-linking system described by Ted Nelson in the 1960s in which text on one page links to text on other pages.
hypertext links. *See* **hyperlinks**
Hypertext Markup Language. *See* **HTML**
A language that includes a set of codes (or tags) attached to text that describes the relationships among text elements.
hypertext servers, WEB 1.12
A computer that stores HTML documents and lets other computers connect to it and read those documents.
hypertext transfer protocol (HTTP), WEB 3.8

I

IETF (Internet Engineering Task Force), WEB 1.9
images. *See* **graphic images**
IMAP, WEB 2.2
A protocol for retrieving e-mail messages from a mail server.
Inbox
in Netscape Messenger, WEB 2.13
inclusion operators, WEB 4.19
See grouping operators.
index.html The default name for the HTML document that serves as a Web site's home or main page.
index.html filename, WEB 3.8
indexing, full text, WEB 4.8
informal signatures
for e-mail messages, WEB 2.5–2.6
An e-mail signature that sometimes contains graphics or quotations that express a more casual style found in correspondence between friends and acquaintances.
Integrated Services Digital Network (ISDN), WEB 1.16
A type of DSL that allows data transmission at bandwidths of up to 128 Kbps.
Interconnected Network A general term for *any* network of networks. Also known as an internet (lowercase *i*).
internet (lowercase *i*) See interconnected network.
Internet. *See also* **World Wide Web**
commercial use of, WEB 1.8–9
communication tools available on, WEB 1.2
connection options, WEB 1.15–21
defined, WEB 1.2, WEB 1.5
Federal Networking Council's definition of, WEB 1.9
first use of term, WEB 1.6
growth of, WEB 1.9–12
history of, WEB 1.5–9
information resources available on, WEB 1.2
privatization of, WEB 1.9–10
structure of, WEB 1.11–12
A specific worldwide collection of interconnected networks whose owners have voluntarily agreed to share resources and network connections with each other.
Internet 2, WEB 1.16
A network being developed by a group of universities and the NSF that will have backbone bandwidths that exceed 1 Gbps.
internet (interconnected network), WEB 1.5
A general term for *any* network of networks. Also known as an internet (lowercase *i*).
Internet access providers (IAPs), WEB 1.15
Firms that purchase Internet access from network access points and sell it to businesses, individuals, and smaller IAPs. Also known as an Internet service provider (ISP).
Internet Engineering Task Force (IETF), WEB 1.9
A self-organized group that makes technical contributions to the Internet and related technologies. It is the main body that develops new Internet standards.
Internet Explorer. *See* **Microsoft Internet Explorer**
Internet Explorer icon button, WEB 3.50
Internet Message Access Protocol. *See* **IMAP**
Internet Protocol (IP), WEB 1.6
A part of the TCP/IP set of rules for sending data over a network.

Internet Protocol (IP) addressing, WEB 2.6, WEB 3.5–6
A series of four numbers separated by periods that uniquely identifies each computer connected to the Internet.

Internet Public Library, WEB 5.13–14

Internet Security Properties dialog box
in Internet Explorer, WEB 3.40

Internet service providers (ISPs), WEB 1.15
advantages and disadvantages of, WEB 1.19
connecting to the Internet through, WEB 1.19
See Internet access providers (IAPs).

Internet Worm, WEB 1.9
A program launched by Robert Morris in 1988 that used weaknesses in e-mail programs and operating systems to distribute itself to some of the computers that were then connected to the Internet. The program created multiple copies of itself on the computers it infected, which then consumed the processing power of the infected computers and prevented them from running other programs.

intranet A LAN or WAN that uses the TCP/IP protocol but does not connect to sites outside the host firm or organization.

intranets, WEB 1.8–9

IP addresses. See **Internet Protocol (IP) addressing**
See Internet Protocol (IP) address.

ISDN services, WEB 1.16

ISPs. See **Internet service providers (ISPs)**

J

Janet (Joint Academic Network) Web 1.8

Joint Academic Network (Janet), WEB 1.8
An internet established by U.K. universities.

Juno, WEB 2.8

K

Kbps (kilobits per second), WEB 1.16

kilobits per second (Kbps), WEB 1.16
A measure of bandwidth; 1,024 bps.

kilobytes, WEB 2.5
A unit of measure that is approximately 1,000 characters.

L

LANs. See **local area networks (LANs)**

last-modified date searches, WEB 5.11–13

library resources, WEB 5.6–8

LibrarySpot Web site, WEB 5.6–7

limited edition (LE) software, WEB 5.32–33
A restricted version of a shareware program that provides most of the functionality of the full version that is for sale. LE software omits one or more useful features of the complete version.

line-splitters, WEB 1.19
A device that divides combined signals from a cable television company into their television and data components.

links. See **hyperlinks**

LISTSERV, WEB 1.7
Software for running mailing lists on IBM mainframe computers.

local area networks (LANs)
connecting computers to, WEB 1.4–5
defined, WEB 1.3
wireless, WEB 1.5
Any of several ways of connecting computers to each other when the computers are located close to each other (no more than a few thousand feet apart).

Location field
entering URLs in, WEB 3.18–20
The Navigator control into which you can enter the URL of a Web page that you would like to open.

location operators, WEB 4.20
A Web search engine operator that lets you search for terms that appear close to each other in the text of a Web page; the most common is the NEAR operator. Also known as a proximity operator.

Location toolbar
hiding and showing in Netscape Navigator, WEB 3.18
The Navigator toolbar that contains the Location field, the page proxy icon, and the Bookmarks button.

logical operators, WEB 4.18–19
See Boolean operators.

M

mail client software, WEB 2.2
An e-mail program that requests mail delivery from a mail server to your PC.

mail folders
creating, in Netscape Messenger, WEB 2.24
deleting, in Netscape Messenger, WEB 2.27
transferring mail to, in Netscape Messenger, WEB 2.25

mailing lists
creating in Netscape Messenger, WEB 2.29–31
defined, WEB 1.7, WEB 2.4
group, WEB 2.11
modifying in Netscape Messenger, WEB 2.31
An e-mail address that takes any message it receives and forwards it to any user who has subscribed to the list.

mail servers, WEB 2.2
A hardware and software system that determines from the recipient's address one of several electronic routes to send your message over the Internet.

mainframe computers, WEB 1.4
A computer that is larger and more expensive than either a minicomputer or a PC. Businesses and other organizations use mainframe computers to process large volumes of work at high speeds.

Maximize button, WEB 3.15
in Internet Explorer, WEB 3.39

Mbps (megabits per second), WEB 1.16

MCI Mail, WEB 1.9

.mdb file extension, WEB 5.29

megabits per second (Mbps), WEB 1.16
A measure of bandwidth; 1,048,576 bps.

Memex, WEB 1.12
A memory extension device envisioned by Vannevar Bush in 1945 that stored all of a person's books, records, letters, and research results on microfilm. The idea included mechanical aids to help users consult their collected knowledge quickly and flexibly.

menu bar
in Internet Explorer, WEB 3.41
in Web browsers, WEB 3.11

menu commands
in Netscape Navigator, WEB 3.16–18

message body (e-mail) The content of an e-mail message.

message body, WEB 2.3, WEB 2.5

Message Center window
in Netscape Messenger, WEB 2.12–13

message content panel
in Netscape Messenger, WEB 2.13

message header (e-mail) The part of an e-mail message containing information about the message's sender, receiver, and subject.

message headers, WEB 2.3

message header summaries
in Netscape Messenger, WEB 2.13
Subject lines from the e-mail messages in a mail folder that are displayed in a list.

Message List window
in Netscape Messenger, WEB 2.12–13

Message window
in Netscape Messenger, WEB 2.12–14

Messenger. See **Netscape Messenger**

meta-search engines, WEB 4.4, WEB 4.13–14

META tags, WEB 4.7–8
An HTML element that a Web page creator places in a Web page header to inform Web robots about the page's content.

meta-search engine
A tool that accepts a search expression and transmits it to several search engines that run the search expression against their databases of Web page information and return results that the meta-search engine consolidates and reports.

Microsoft, WEB 1.13
Web site, finding Internet Explorer files on, WEB 5.38–39

Microsoft Internet Explorer, WEB 1.13. See also **Web browsers**
elements of, WEB 3.9–11
entering URLs in Address Bar, WEB 3.42–44
Favorites feature, WEB 3.44–47
Help facility, WEB 3.54–55
hiding and showing toolbars in, WEB 3.41–42
history list, WEB 3.49–50
hyperlink navigation with the mouse, WEB 3.47–51
locating on the Microsoft Web site, WEB 5.38–39
menu bar, WEB 3.41
printing Web pages in, WEB 3.52–53
refreshing a Web page in, WEB 3.50
returning to start page in, WEB 3.50–51
saving Web pages in, WEB 3.55–59
security features, WEB 3.53–54
starting, WEB 3.38–40
status bar, WEB 3.40
toolbar buttons, WEB 3.40
A popular Web browser program. Also known as Internet Explorer.

Microsoft Outlook Express, WEB 2.32–49
address books, WEB 2.46–49
configuring for e-mail, WEB 2.33–35
Deleted Items folder in, WEB 2.32
deleting messages, WEB 2.44–46
features, WEB 2.32

filing messages, WEB 2.43–44
Folder list in, WEB 2.32
forwarding messages, WEB 2.42
Inbox folder in, WEB 2.32
Internet Connection Wizard, WEB 2.34
opening and saving attached files in, WEB 2.39–40
receiving messages in, WEB 2.38–39
replying to messages, WEB 2.40–41
sending messages in, WEB 2.35–38
Sent Items folder in, WEB 2.32

An e-mail client program that works with Internet Explorer Web browser software. Also known as Outlook Express.

MILNET (Military Network), WEB 1.8
The part of ARPANET, created in 1984, reserved for military uses that required high levels of security.

MIME, WEB 2.2
A protocol specifying how to encode non-text data, such as graphics and sound, so you can send them over the Internet.

minicomputers, WEB 1.4
A computer that is larger and more expensive than a PC. Businesses and other organizations use minicomputers to process large volumes of work at high speeds.

modems
cable, WEB 1.19
defined, WEB 1.18

A device that converts a computer's digital signal to an analog signal (modulation) so it can travel through a telephone line and also converts analog signals arriving through a telephone line to digital signals that the computer can use (demodulation).

Modern Language Association (MLA), WEB 5.8–9

modulation, WEB 1.18
The process of converting a digital signal to an analog signal.

modulator-demodulators. *See* **modems**

Morris, Robert, WEB 1.9

Mosaic, WEB 1.13
The first program with a GUI that could read HTML and use HTML documents' hyperlinks to navigate from page to page on computers anywhere on the Internet. Mosaic was the first Web browser that became widely available for PCs.

mouse
hyperlink navigation with, WEB 3.24–28, WEB 3.47–39

MUDs, WEB 1.7
Any of a series of interactive online adventure games that allows users to assume characters and, in some cases, construct elements of the game. Also known as multi-user dungeon, multiuser domain, or multi-user dimension.

multi-address entries, WEB 2.11
in Netscape Navigator, WEB 2.29–31
in Outlook Express, WEB 2.48–49

Multipurpose Internet Mail Extensions. *See* **MIME**

multiuser dimensions. *See* **MUDs**

multiuser domains. *See* **MUDs**

multiuser dungeons. *See* **MUDs**

N

"nag" screens
in shareware, WEB 5.32

named FTP, WEB 5.20–21
Logging on to a computer on which you have an account, including a username and password, and using it to send and receive files.

NAPs, WEB 1.15
Internet connections, WEB 1.16

National Science Foundation (NSF), WEB 1.6
privatization of Internet and, WEB 1.10
The 1984 addition to CSNET.

National Science Foundation Network. *See* **NSFNet**

Navigation toolbar The Navigator toolbar that contains buttons for commonly used Web browsing commands.

Nelson, Ted, WEB 1.12

Netscape Communications, WEB 1.13
The suite of programs developed by Netscape Communications Corporation that includes the Navigator Web browser and the Messenger e-mail program.

Netscape Communicator Suite, WEB 2.12
Help in, WEB 3.32–33

Netscape Message Center window
Contains a list of the current user's mailboxes, mail folders, and discussion groups.

Netscape Messenger, WEB 2.12–31
address books, WEB 2.27–31
Composition window, WEB 2.12–14
configuring e-mail in, WEB 2.14–17
defined, WEB 2.12
deleting e-mail messages, WEB 2.26–27
filing e-mail messages, WEB 2.24–26
forwarding e-mail messages, WEB 2.23–24
Message Center window, WEB 2.12–13
Message List window, WEB 2.12–13
Message window, WEB 2.12–14
Preferences window, WEB 2.15
receiving and reading messages, WEB 2.19–21
replying to e-mail messages, WEB 2.22–23
sending messages, WEB 2.17–19
windows, WEB 2.12–14

The e-mail client program that is an integral part of the Netscape Communicator suite. Also known as Messenger.

Netscape Navigator, WEB 1.13
changing default home page, WEB 3.26–27
creating bookmarks in, WEB 3.20–24
elements of, WEB 3.9–11
floating toolbar component, WEB 3.16
Guide button in, WEB 3.28
Help in, WEB 3.32–33
hiding and showing the toolbar, WEB 3.17–18
history list, WEB 3.26–27
hyperlink navigation in, WEB 3.24–28
Location toolbar elements, WEB 3.18–24
menu commands, WEB 3.16–18
print options in, WEB 3.29–31
saving Web pages in, WEB 3.33–38
security features, WEB 3.31–32
starting, WEB 3.15–16
toolbar buttons, WEB 3.16–18
A popular Web browser program. Also known as Navigator.

network access points. *See* **NAPs**

network backbone, WEB 1.8
The long-distance lines and supporting technology that transport large amounts of data between major network nodes.

Network Control Protocol (NCP), WEB 1.6
A set of rules for formatting, ordering, and error checking data used by the ARPANET and other early forerunners of the Internet.

network interface cards (NICs), WEB 1.3
A card or other device that is used to connect a computer to a network of other computers.

network operating system Software that runs on a server computer that allows other computers, called client computers, to be connected to it and share its resources, such as printers, files, or programs.

networks, WEB 1.3–5
circuit switching, WEB 1.5–6
connecting to, WEB 1.4–5, WEB 1.15
interconnecting, WEB 1.8–9
packet switching, WEB 1.5–6
wireless, WEB 1.5

New Card button
in Netscape Messenger address book, WEB 2.27

New Contact button
in Outlook Express, WEB 2.46

New Message button
in Netscape Messenger, WEB 2.13

news
Web research resources, WEB 5.9–16

newsgroups
defined, WEB 1.7
mail from, in Netscape Messenger, WEB 2.13
The topic areas in Usenet (the User's News Network).

NewsHub, WEB 5.14–15
A Web search engine that indexes current news.

NewsTracker, WEB 5.14–16
A Web search engine that indexes current news.

nicknames
in address books, WEB 2.11
as e-mail addresses, WEB 2.7

Northern Light
advanced searches in, WEB 4.26–27
A Web search engine.

Norton AntiVirus, WEB 5.41

NOT operator, WEB 4.18–19

NSFNet
defined, WEB 1.8
privatization of the Internet and, WEB 1.10, WEB 1.11

O

objectivity
of Web sites, determining, WEB 5.2–3

open architecture, WEB 1.6–7
An approach that allows each network in an internet to continue using its own protocols and data transmission methods for moving data internally.

.org domain names, WEB 5.3

OR operator, WEB 4.18–19

Outbox The e-mail folder that holds messages waiting to be sent.

Outlook Express. *See* **Microsoft Outlook Express**

P

packet switching, WEB 1.5–6
A method for sending information over a network in which files and messages are broken down into packets that are labeled electronically with codes for their origins and destinations. The packets are sent through the network, each possibly by a different path. The packets are reassembled at their destination.

Page proxy icon
in Netscape Navigator, WEB 3.20

Page Setup dialog box
in Internet Explorer, WEB 3.52–53
in Netscape Navigator, WEB 3.30–31

Paste button
in Netscape Navigator, WEB 3.35–36

.pdf file extension, WEB 5.29

personal computers (PCs)
as servers, WEB 1.3–4

Pine, WEB 2.8

PKUNZIP, WEB 5.30

PKZIP, WEB 5.30

plain old telephone service (POTS)
The standard telephone service provided by telephone companies to business and individual customers for voice communications. This service allows users to transmit data by using a modem at a bandwidth of between 28.8 and 56 Kbps.

point-to-point protocol (PPP), WEB 1.18
A set of rules for transmitting data that makes a PC's modem connection appear to be a TCP/IP connection.

POP, (Post Office protocol) WEB 2.2, WEB 2.9
One of the Internet-defined procedures that handles incoming e-mail messages. POP is a standard, extensively used protocol that is part of the Internet suite of recognized protocols.

Portable Document Format (PDF), WEB 5.45
A specific file format, developed by Adobe Corporation, that provides a convenient, self-contained package for delivering and displaying documents containing text, graphics, charts, and other objects.

Post Office Protocol. *See* **POP**

POTS (plain old telephone service), WEB 1.16

PPP connections, WEB 1.18

precedence operators, WEB 4.19
See grouping operators.

Preferences window
in Netscape Messenger, WEB 2.15

Print button
in Web browsers, WEB 3.13

printing
e-mail messages, WEB 2.9
in Netscape Messenger, WEB 2.25
in Outlook Express, WEB 2.44
Web pages, WEB 3.13, WEB 3.29–31, WEB 3.52–53

Project Bartley, WEB 5.8

Project Gutenberg, WEB 5.8

protocols
defined, WEB 1.6

for e-mail, WEB 2.2
A collection of rules for formatting, ordering, and error-checking data sent across a network.

proximity operators, WEB 4.20
See location operator.

public (pub) directories
in FTP sites, WEB 5.26
uploading files to, WEB 5.26

public domain files, WEB 5.16
Copyrighted works or works that are eligible for copyright protection whose copyrights have expired or been relinquished voluntarily by the copyright owner. You are free to copy text, images, and other items in the public domain without obtaining permission.

Q

queued e-mail messages, WEB 2.9
in Outlook Express, WEB 2.36
E-mail messages that are held temporarily by the client before processing.

queries, WEB 4.5
The word or phrase that you enter into a Web search engine; it also might include instructions that tell the search engine how to conduct its search. Also known as a search expression.

queued E-mail messages that are held temporarily by the client before processing

quotation marks, double
in search expressions, WEB 4.19

quoted e-mail messages, WEB 2.10

quoted message (e-mail) That portion of the body of a sender's original message that you include in your reply to the sender. Usually, you add your comments to the message.

R

receiving e-mail messages, WEB 2.9
in Netscape Messenger, WEB 2.19–20
in Outlook Express, WEB 2.38–39

Refresh button, WEB 3.12
in Internet Explorer, WEB 3.50

Reload button, WEB 3.12
in Netscape Navigator, WEB 3.27

reloading Web pages, WEB 3.27

reply (e-mail) A response to an e-mail message you receive.

replying to e-mail messages, WEB 2.10
in Netscape Messenger, WEB 2.22–23
in Outlook Express, WEB 2.40–41

resource lists, WEB 4.15
See clearinghouse.

results pages, WEB 4.5
A Web page generated by a Web search engine that contains hyperlinks to the Web pages that contain matches to the search expression entered into the search engine.

root directory, of FTP sites, WEB 5.23–26
The top level of a disk's directory. Beneath the root directory are several "branches" corresponding to other directories. Also known as a home directory or a top-level directory.

routers, WEB 1.6
A computer on a packet-switching internet that accepts packets from other networks and determines the best way to move each packet forward to its destination.

routing algorithms, WEB 1.6
The program on a router computer in a packet-switching internet that determines the best path on which to send packets.

S

satellite Internet connections, WEB 1.17, WEB 1.19

Save Image As command, WEB 3.37

Save Picture As command, WEB 3.59

saving e-mail messages
in Netscape Navigator, WEB 2.21
in Outlook Express, WEB 2.39–40

saving Web pages
in Netscape Navigator, WEB 3.33–38
in Web browsers, WEB 3.13

scroll bar
in Web browsers, WEB 3.10

search engines, WEB 4.4
date-range restriction searches, WEB 5.10–13
defined, WEB 4.5
finding news and current information resources, WEB 5.9–16
finding software download sites with, WEB 5.34
hybrid search engine directories, WEB 4.9
meta-search engines, WEB 4.13–14
META tags and, WEB 4.7–8
using, WEB 4.5–8

search expressions, WEB 4.5
See query.

search filters, WEB 4.20
Web search engine feature that allows you to eliminate Web pages from a search based on attributes such as language, date, domain, host, or page component (hyperlink, image tag, title tag).

search questions
exploratory, WEB 4.2–3
specific, WEB 4.2–3

search strategies, WEB 4.4

search tools
advanced searches, WEB 4.20–27
directories, WEB 4.4, WEB 4.5–12
meta-search engines, WEB 4.4, WEB 4.13–14
search engines, WEB 4.4, WEB 4.5–8
types of, WEB 4.4
using Boolean logic in, WEB 4.18–20
Web resources, WEB 4.4, WEB 4.14–17

security
in Internet Explorer, WEB 3.40, WEB 3.53–54
in Netscape Navigator, WEB 3.31–32

Security zone Classification levels of Web page security risk in Internet Explorer.

sending e-mail messages
with attachments, in Netscape Messenger, WEB 2.18–19
copies, WEB 2.4
in Netscape Messenger, WEB 2.17–19
in Outlook Express, WEB 2.35–38

Sent Items folder A folder that contains copies of your sent e-mail messages.

serial line Internet protocol (SLIP), WEB 1.18
A set of rules for transmitting data that makes a PC's modem connection appear to be a TCP/IP connection.

server computer A computer that accepts requests from other computers, called clients, that are connected to it and shares some or all of its resources, such as printers, files, or programs, with those client computers. This way of connecting computers is called a client/server network.

servers, WEB 1.3

SGML, WEB 1.12

shareware, WEB 5.32
  e-mail programs, WEB 2.8
  Free or inexpensive software that you can try before you purchase it.

SHAREWARE.COM, WEB 5.36–37

signature (e-mail) One or more lines in an e-mail message that identify more detailed information about the sender (such as his or her name, address, and phone number).

signature files, WEB 2.5–6
  A file, which is appended automatically to your outgoing e-mail messages, that contains your contact information.

Simple Mail Transfer Protocol. *See* **SMTP**

SLIP connections, WEB 1.18

SMTP (Simple Mail Transfer Protocol), WEB 2.2, WEB 2.9
  One of the Internet-defined procedures that determines which path your message takes on the Internet.

software download sites
  browsing, WEB 5.35–41
  downloading programs from, WEB 5.41–54
  locating, WEB 5.33–35

specific questions, WEB 4.2–3
  A question that you can phrase easily and one for which you will recognize the answer when you find it.

spiders, WEB 4.5
  See bot.

Standard Generalized Markup Language (SGML), WEB 1.12
  The document description language on which HTML is based. Organizations have used SGML for many years to manage large document-filing systems.

start pages
  defined, WEB 3.5
  displaying in Netscape Navigator, WEB 3.27
  returning to, in Internet Explorer, WEB 3.50–51
  The page that opens when a particular Web browser program is started or the page that a particular Web browser program loads the first time it is run. Usually, this page is stored at the Web site of the firm or other organization that created the Web browser software. See also home page.

status bar
  in Internet Explorer, WEB 3.40
  in Web browsers, WEB 3.10–11

Stop button, WEB 3.12–13

Subject line, WEB 2.4
  A brief summary of a message's content.

T

tags, WEB 1.12, WEB 3.3

T1 connections, WEB 1.16, WEB 1.17
  A high-bandwidth (1.544 Mbps) data transmission connection used as part of the Internet backbone and by large firms and ISPs as a connection to the Internet.

T3 connections, WEB 1.16, WEB 1.17
  A high-bandwidth (44.736 Mbps) data transmission connection used as part of the Internet backbone and by large firms and ISPs as a connection to the Internet.

TCP/IP
  addresses available under, WEB 1.11
  defined, WEB 1.6
  growth of Internet and, WEB 1.7

telephone service
  Internet connections and, WEB 1.16, WEB 1.17

Telnet, WEB 1.7
  protocol, WEB 3.8
  sessions, WEB 5.27
  The part of the TCP/IP protocol set that lets users log on to their computer accounts from remote sites.

Telnet session The period during which you establish a connection on the Internet with another computer and log on to it with a user name and password. Telnet is one of the several protocols that the Internet supports.

Temporary Internet Files
  in Internet Explorer, WEB 3.50
  The name of the folder (in the Windows folder) in which Internet Explorer stores copies of Web pages you have viewed recently.

text, Web page
  copying and saving, WEB 3.35–36, WEB 3.56–58

text resources
  on the Web, WEB 5.8

Thomas Web site, WEB 5.8

title bar
  in Web browsers, WEB 3.10

toggle A type of control in a program that works like a push button on a television set; you press the button once to turn on the television and press it a second time to turn it off.

toggle commands, WEB 3.17, WEB 3.42

To line, WEB 2.3–4
  Part of a message header that contains an e-mail message recipient's full e-mail address.

Tomlinson, Ray, WEB 1.7

toolbar buttons
  in Internet Explorer, WEB 3.40
  in Netscape Navigator, WEB 3.16–18

toolbars
  hiding and showing in Internet Explorer, WEB 3.41–42
  hiding and showing in Netscape Navigator, WEB 3.17–18

top-level directory
  of FTP sites, WEB 5.23
  See root directory.

top-level domains, WEB 3.6–7
  proposed, WEB 3.7
  The last part of a domain name, which is the unique name that is associated with a specific IP address by a program that runs on an Internet host computer.

transfer progress report
  in Internet Explorer, WEB 3.40

transfer progress report panel A section of the status bar in Internet Explorer that presents status messages, such as the URL of a page while it is loading, the text "Done" after a page has loaded, or the URL of any hyperlink on the page when you move the pointer over it.

transfer protocols, WEB 3.8
  The set of rules that computers use to move files from one computer to another on an internet. The most common transfer protocol used on the Internet is HTTP.

Transmission Control Protocol, WEB 1.6
  A part of the TCP/IP set of rules for sending data over a network.

Transmission Control Protocol/Internet Protocol. *See* **TCP/IP**
  A combined set of rules for data transmission. TCP includes rules that computers on a network use to establish and break connections; IP includes rules for routing of individual data packets.

TUCOWS Web site, WEB 5.37–38

twisted-pair cable, WEB 1.4
  The type of cable that telephone companies have used for years to wire residences and businesses, twisted-pair cable has two or more insulated copper wires that are twisted around each other and enclosed in another layer of plastic insulation.

.txt file extension, WEB 5.29

U

Uniform Resource Locators (URLs). *See* **URLs**
  The four-part addressing scheme for an HTML document that tells Web browser software which transfer protocol to use when transporting the document, the domain name of the computer on which the document resides, the pathname of the folder or directory on the computer in which the document resides, and the document's filename.

UNIX-based machines
  built-in compression programs, WEB 5.31
  command-line FTP, WEB 5.51

upload The process of sending a file from a PC to another, usually larger, computer connected to the Internet.

uploading files, WEB 5.31–33
  defined, WEB 5.16
  to public directories, WEB 5.26
  Web pages, WEB 5.21

Up scroll arrow, WEB 3.11

URLs
  components of, WEB 3.8–9
  defined, WEB 3.8
  entering in Internet Explorer Address Bar, WEB 3.42–44
  entering in location field, WEB 3.18–20
  moving and disappearing, WEB 5.9
  typesetting problems for citations, WEB 5.9

Usenet, WEB 1.7
  A network that allows anyone who connects to the network to read and post articles on a variety of subjects.

user names
  defined, WEB 2.6
  selection of, WEB 2.7
  The character string that identifies a person to a particular computer system or family of systems.

User's News Network. See Usenet

V

virtual libraries, WEB 4.15
  See clearinghouse.

virus cleaning software, WEB 5.30, WEB 5.39–41
  A program that removes viruses from files physically, restoring the infected program or files to its pre-virus condition.

virus detection software, WEB 5.30, WEB 5.39–41
A program that regularly scans disk files looking for infected files by recognizing signatures that known viruses carry.

viruses, WEB 5.30
Programs that "infect" your computer and harm your disk or programs.

virus signature, WEB 5.30
A sequence of characters that is always present in a particular virus program.

VPOP Technologies
NewsHub, WEB 5.14–15

W

WANs. *See* **wide area networks (WANs)**

Web-based e-mail, WEB 2.8

Web bibliographies, WEB 4.15
See clearinghouse.

Web browsers, WEB 3.2–5. *See also* **Microsoft Internet Explorer; Netscape Navigator**
connecting to FTP sites with, WEB 5.20
defined, WEB 1.12, WEB 3.2
development of, WEB 1.13
display of HTML documents by, WEB 1.13
elements of, WEB 3.9–11
history list, WEB 3.12–13
Home button, WEB 3.11
menu bar, WEB 3.11
opening FTP sites with, WEB 5.24–25
scroll bars, WEB 3.10
status bar, WEB 3.10–11
title bar, WEB 3.10
uploading files with, WEB 5.31
Software that lets users read (or browse) HTML documents and move from one HTML document to another through the text formatted with hypertext link tags in each file. HTML documents can be on the user's computer or on another computer that is part of the WWW.

Web clients, WEB 3.2
A computer that is connected to the Web and runs software called a Web browser that enables its user to read HTML documents on other computers, called Web servers, that are also connected to the Web.

Web directories. *See* **directories**
A Web site that contains a list of Web page categories, such as education or recreation. The hyperlinks on a Web directory page lead to other pages that contain lists of subcategories that lead to other category lists and Web pages that relate to the category topics.

webmasters, WEB 3.14

Web page area, WEB 3.11
The portion of a Web browser window that displays the contents of the HTML document or other file as a Web page.

Web page design, WEB 5.3–6

Web page directories. *See* **directories**

Web page guides, WEB 3.12

Web pages. *See also* **Web sites**
copying and saving text from, WEB 3.35–36
copyright law and, WEB 3.14
defined, WEB 3.3
number of, WEB 4.4
printing, WEB 3.13, WEB 3.29–31, WEB 3.52–53
refreshing, WEB 3.50
reloading, WEB 3.27
returning to, WEB 3.13
saving, WEB 3.13, WEB 3.33–38, WEB 3.55–59
security issues, WEB 3.53–54
stopping transfer of, WEB 3.12–13
uploading, WEB 5.21

Web research resources, WEB 4.4, WEB 4.14–17
citing, WEB 5.8–9
copyright issues, WEB 5.16
current news and information, WEB 5.9–16
determining objectivity of, WEB 5.2–3
electronic publishing, WEB 5.9
evaluating content of, WEB 5.3
evaluating form and appearance of, WEB 5.3–6
evaluating the quality of, WEB 5.2–6
identifying author of, WEB 5.2–3
library resources, WEB 5.6–8
news and current information, WEB 5.9–16
text resources, WEB 5.8

Web robots, WEB 4.5
See bot.

Web search engines, WEB 3.12
A Web site that allows you to conduct searches of the Web to find specific words or expressions. The result of a search engine's search is a Web page that contains hyperlinks to Web pages that contain text or expressions that match those you entered.

Web servers, WEB 3.2
A computer that is connected to the Web and contains HTML documents that it makes available to other computers connected to the Web.

Web Site
A collection of linked Web pages that has a common theme or focus.

Web sites. *See also* **Web pages**
contact information on, WEB 5.2
defined, WEB 3.5
evaluating the quality of information on, WEB 5.2–6
growth of, WEB 1.13–14
Computers that are connected to the Internet and that store HTML documents. All Web sites taken together make up the Web.

webmaster
The title often used for the person who is responsible for maintaining a Web page or Web site.

wide area networks (WANs), WEB 1.5
Any of several ways of connecting individual computers or networks to each other over distances greater than those included in LANs.

wildcard characters, WEB 4.20
The character, usually the asterisk (*), that you can use to indicate that part of the term or terms entered into a Web search engine has been omitted.

WinZip, downloading, WEB 5.47–51

wireless networks, WEB 1.5
A way of connecting computers to each other that does not use cable. Instead, a wireless network uses wireless transmitters and receivers that plug into network interface cards (NICs).

workplace, Internet connections through, WEB 1.18

World Wide Web
commercial use of, WEB 1.13
defined, WEB 1.2
history of, WEB 1.12–14
A worldwide system of hyperlinked HTML documents on the Internet.

WS_FTP LE, WEB 5.33
downloading, WEB 5.41–43
installing, WEB 5.44–45
using, WEB 5.48

WS_FTP95 LE, WEB 5.17, WEB 5.22

X

Xanadu, WEB 1.12
A global system for online hypertext publishing and commerce outlined by Ted Nelson in his book *Literary Machines*.

.xls file extension, WEB 5.29

Y

Yahoo!, WEB 4.8–12
data-range restriction searches, WEB 5.11–12
news and current information resources, WEB 5.9
A Web directory.

Yahoo!Mail, WEB 2.8

Z

ZDNet Software Library, WEB 5.39–41

.zip file extension, WEB 5.29

zip files
decompressing, WEB 5.30
A widespread file format for storing compressed files. Phil Katz invented the zip file format and his file-compression and -decompression programs, PKZIP and PKUNZIP.

TASK REFERENCE

NETSCAPE NAVIGATOR

TASK	PAGE #	RECOMMENDED METHOD	WHERE USED
Address book entry, create	WEB 2.27	Click Communicator, click Address Book, click [New Card]	Messenger
Address book group, create	WEB 2.30	Click Communicator, click Address Book, click [New List]	Messenger
Attached file, open in Message List window	WEB 2.21	Click File, click Open Attachments, click attachment name, click Open it	Messenger
Attached file, save in Netscape Message window	WEB 2.21	Right-click attachment icon, click Save Attachment As, type filename, click Save	Messenger
Bookmark folder, create	WEB 3.22	See Reference Window "Creating a Bookmark folder"	Navigator
Bookmark, create	WEB 3.23	Click [Bookmarks], click Add Bookmark	Navigator
Bookmark, create in a specific folder	WEB 3.23	See Reference Window "Creating a bookmark in a bookmark folder"	Navigator
Bookmarks file, save to floppy disk	WEB 3.23	See Reference Window "Saving a bookmark to a floppy disk"	Navigator
Bookmarks window, open	WEB 3.22	Click [Bookmarks], click Edit Bookmarks	Navigator
E-mail name, set up	WEB 2.16	Click Edit, click Preferences, click Identity, type your first and last names, type your full e-mail address, click OK	Messenger
File, attach in Message Composition window	WEB 2.21	Click [Attach], click File, type filename to attach	Messenger
Font size of a Web page, change	WEB 3.31	Click Edit, click Preferences, click the Fonts category, type desired Font size in Size text boxes, click OK	Navigator
FTP, anonymous login	WEB 5.53	Type anonymous, press Enter	FTP
FTP, download file	WEB 5.54	Type get followed by filename, press Enter	FTP
FTP, end session	WEB 5.54	Type quit, press Enter	FTP
FTP, list files and folders	WEB 5.53	Type dir, press Enter	FTP
FTP, open a connection	WEB 5.53	Type open followed by connection URL, press Enter	FTP
FTP, use Windows built-in	WEB 5.52	Click Start, click Run, type c:\windows\ftp, click OK	FTP
Help, get	WEB 3.32	See Reference Window "Getting Help in Netscape Navigator"	Navigator
History list, open	WEB 3.26	Click Communicator, click History	Navigator
Home page, change default	WEB 3.27	See Reference Window "Changing the default home page"	Navigator
Home page, return to	WEB 3.27	Click [Home]	Navigator
Mail folder, create	WEB 2.24	Click File, click New Folder	Messenger

TASK REFERENCE

TASK	PAGE #	RECOMMENDED METHOD	WHERE USED
Mail folder, delete	WEB 2.27	Click Communicator, click Message Center, right-click folder, click Delete Folder	Messenger
Mail preferences, set servers	WEB 2.15	Click Edit, click Preferences, click Mail & Groups category, click Mail Server, type SMTP and POP server names, click OK	Messenger
Mail, compose	WEB 2.15	Click [Compose Message]	Messenger
Mail, copy to another folder in Message List window	WEB 2.25	Click Message, point to Copy Message, click destination folder	Messenger
Mail, delete	WEB 2.26	Right-click the message summary, click Delete Message	Messenger
Mail, delete permanently	WEB 2.27	Click File, click Empty Trash Folder	Messenger
Mail, forward from Message List window	WEB 2.23	Click [Forward]	Messenger
Mail, move to another folder in Message List window	WEB 2.25	Click [File], click destination folder	Messenger
Mail, print message	WEB 2.25	Right-click the message summary, click Print Message	Messenger
Mail, read in Message List window	WEB 2.20	Click message summary line	Messenger
Mail, receive messages in Message List window	WEB 2.20	Click [Get Msg], type your user name and password, click OK	Messenger
Mail, reply to sender and all recipients in Message List window	WEB 2.22	Click message summary line, click [Reply], click Reply to Sender and All Recipients	Messenger
Mail, reply to sender in Message List window	WEB 2.22	Click message summary line, click [Reply], click Reply to Sender	Messenger
Mail, send from Message Composition window	WEB 2.18	Click [Send]	Messenger
Mail, spell check in Message Composition window	WEB 2.18	Click [Spelling]	Messenger
Messenger, start	WEB 2.15	Click the Start button, point to Programs, point to Netscape Communicator, click Netscape Messenger	
Navigator window, maximize	WEB 3.15	Click [ ]	Navigator, Messenger
Navigator window, minimize		Click [ ]	Navigator, Messenger
Navigator window, restore maximized		Click [ ]	Navigator, Messenger

TASK REFERENCE

TASK	PAGE #	RECOMMENDED METHOD	WHERE USED
Navigator, close	WEB 3.9	Click [X]	Navigator
Navigator, start	WEB 3.15	Click the start button, point to Programs, point to Netscape Communications, click Netscape Navigator	
Page print settings, change	WEB 3.30	Click File, click Page Setup	Navigator
Start page, return to	WEB 3.11	Click [Home]	Navigator
Toolbar, hide	WEB 3.17	Click View, click Hide option for toolbar to hide	Navigator
Toolbar, show	WEB 3.17	Click View, click Show option for toolbar to show	Navigator
URL, enter and go to	WEB 3.18	See Reference Window "Entering a URL in the Location field"	Navigator
Web page graphic, save	WEB 3.37	See Reference Window "Saving an image from a Web page on a floppy disk"	Navigator
Web page in history list, go to previous	WEB 3.17	Click [Forward]	Navigator
Web page in history list, return to previous	WEB 3.25	Click [Back]	Navigator
Web page text, save	WEB 3.25	See Reference Window "Copying text from a Web page to a WordPad document"	Navigator
Web page, print all pages	WEB 3.29	Click [Print]	Navigator
Web page, print one or a few pages	WEB 3.29	See Reference Window "Printing the current Web page"	Navigator
Web page, reload	WEB 3.12	Click [Reload]	Navigator
Web page, save to floppy disk	WEB 3.34	See Reference Window "Saving a Web page to a floppy disk"	Navigator
Web page, stop loading	WEB 3.12	Click [Stop]	Navigator

MICROSOFT INTERNET EXPLORER

TASK	PAGE #	RECOMMENDED METHOD	WHERE USED
Address book entry, create	WEB 2.46	Click [Address Book], click [New Contact]	Outlook Express
Address book group, create	WEB 2.48	Click [Address Book], click [New Group]	Outlook Express
Attached file, open in Message List window	WEB 2.39	Double-click message summary line, double-click message's attachment icon	Outlook Express
Attached file, save	WEB 2.39	Right-click file icon, click Save As, click Save	Outlook Express
Favorite, move to a new folder	WEB 3.46	See Reference Window "Moving an existing favorite into a new folder"	Internet Explorer
Favorites folder, create	WEB 3.46	See Reference Window "Creating a new Favorites folder"	Internet Explorer

TASK REFERENCE

TASK	PAGE #	RECOMMENDED METHOD	WHERE USED
Favorites frame, open	WEB 3.44	Click [Favorites]	Internet Explorer
File, attach in New Message window	WEB 2.37	Click [Attach], locate the file, click Attach	Outlook Express
FTP, anonymous login	WEB 5.53	Type anonymous, press Enter	FTP
FTP, download file	WEB 5.54	Type get followed by filename, press Enter	FTP
FTP, end session	WEB 5.54	Type quit, press Enter	FTP
FTP, list files and folders	WEB 5.53	Type dir, press Enter	FTP
FTP, open a connection	WEB 5.53	Type open followed by connection URL, press Enter	FTP
FTP, use Windows built in	WEB 5.52	Click Start, click Run, type c:\windows\ftp, click OK	FTP
Help, get	WEB 3.54	See Reference Window "Getting Help in Internet Explorer"	Internet Explorer
History list, open	WEB 3.49	Click [History]	Internet Explorer
Home page, change default	WEB 3.51	See Reference Window "Changing the Home toolbar button settings"	Internet Explorer
Home page, return to	WEB 3.50	Click [Home]	Internet Explorer
Internet Explorer window, maximize	WEB 3.39	Click [□]	Internet Explorer, Outlook Express
Internet Explorer window, minimize		Click [_]	Internet Explorer, Outlook Express
Internet Explorer window, restore maximized		Click [⧉]	Internet Explorer, Outlook Express
Internet Explorer, close	WEB 3.39	Click [X]	Internet Explorer
Internet Explorer start	WEB 3.38	Click the Start button, point to programs, point to Internet Explorer, click Internet Explorer	
Mail account, set up	WEB 2.33	Click Tools, click Accounts, click the Add button, click Mail, follow steps in the Internet Connection Wizard	Outlook Express
Mail folder, create	WEB 2.43	Click File, point to Folder, click New Folder	Outlook Express
Mail folder, delete	WEB 2.46	Right-click the folder, click Delete	Outlook Express
Mail, compose	WEB 2.36	Click [New Msg]	Outlook Express
Mail, copy to another folder	WEB 2.44	Open mail folder, click message summary line, click Edit, click Copy To Folder	Outlook Express
Mail, delete	WEB 2.45	Open mail folder, click message summary lines, click [Delete]	Outlook Express
Mail, delete permanently	WEB 2.45	Right-click the Deleted Items folder, click Empty Folder	Outlook Express

TASK REFERENCE

TASK	PAGE #	RECOMMENDED METHOD	WHERE USED
Mail, forward from Inbox window	WEB 2.42	Click	Outlook Express
Mail, move to another folder	WEB 2.44	Open mail folder, click message summary line, click Edit, click Move To Folder	Outlook Express
Mail, print	WEB 2.44	Click	Outlook Express
Mail, read	WEB 2.38	Double-click the message summary	Outlook Express
Mail, reply to all from Inbox window	WEB 2.41	Click	Outlook Express
Mail, reply to author from Inbox window	WEB 2.41	Click	Outlook Express
Mail, send and receive	WEB 2.38	Click	Outlook Express
Mail, send from New Message window	WEB 2.35	Click Send	Outlook Express
Mail, spell check in New Message window	WEB 2.37	Click Tools, click Spelling	Outlook Express
Outlook Express, start	WEB 2.33	Click the Start button, point to Programs, point to Internet Explorer, click Outlook Express	
Page print settings, change	WEB 3.53	Click File, click Page Setup	Internet Explorer
Start page, return to	WEB 3.50	Click	Internet Explorer
Toolbar, hide or show	WEB 3.41	See Reference Window "Hiding and restoring the toolbars"	Internet Explorer
URL, enter and go to	WEB 3.42	See Reference Window "Entering a URL in the Address Bar"	Internet Explorer
Web page graphic, save	WEB 3.58	See Reference Window "Saving an image from a Web page on a floppy disk"	Internet Explorer
Web page in history list, move forward to previous	WEB 3.45	Click	Internet Explorer
Web page in history list, return to previous	WEB 3.44	Click	Internet Explorer
Web page text, save	WEB 3.56	See Reference Window "Copying text from a Web page to a WordPad document"	Internet Explorer
Web page, print all pages	WEB 3.52	Click	Internet Explorer
Web page, print one or a few pages	WEB 3.52	See Reference Window "Printing the current Web page"	Internet Explorer
Web page, reload	WEB 3.50	Click	Internet Explorer
Web page, save to floppy disk	WEB 3.55	See Reference Window "Saving a Web page to a floppy disk"	Internet Explorer
Web page, stop loading	WEB 3.40	Click	Internet Explorer